CW01188717

IN
BED
WITH THE
ROMANS

IN
BED
WITH THE
ROMANS

PAUL CHRYSTAL

AMBERLEY

First published 2015

Amberley Publishing
The Hill, Stroud
Gloucestershire, GL5 4EP

www.amberley-books.com

Copyright © Paul Chrystal, 2015

The right of Paul Chrystal to be identified as the Author of this work has been asserted in accordance with the Copyrights, Designs and Patents Act 1988.

All rights reserved. No part of this book may be reprinted or reproduced or utilised in any form or by any electronic, mechanical or other means, now known or hereafter invented, including photocopying and recording, or in any information storage or retrieval system, without the permission in writing from the Publishers.

British Library Cataloguing in Publication Data.
A catalogue record for this book is available from the British Library.

ISBN 978 1 4456 4344 1 (hardback)
ISBN 978 1 4456 4352 6 (ebook)

Typesetting and Origination by Amberley Publishing.
Printed in the UK.

Contents

Acknowledgements 7

Part One: In Bed with a Roman 9

    Introduction: Whose Bed Is It Anyway? 10

1 Love, and Being a *Matrona* 13
2 Marriage, Divorce and Adultery 36
3 'The Incomplete Woman' and Sexual Medicine 50
4 Birth Control, Aphrodisiacs and Love Potions: the Need (or Not) for Venus 79
5 Buggery, Beasts and Brothels: the Need for *Virtus* 92
6 Sex in the Afternoon: the *domina* and Her Love Slave 127
7 Cross-Dressing, Transsexualism and Same-Sex Marriage 139
8 Bacchanalian Orgies and Vestal Virginity 144
9 Raping the Romans 157
10 The Power of Sex: In Bed with a Soldier 163
11 Gladiator Adulator 168
12 Bad Language: Roman Sexual Vocabulary 174

Part Two: In Bed with the Emperors, and an Empress or Two 181

13 Augustus' Women: Flawless, Faithful and Fornicating 182
14 Capricious Depravity with Tiberius 188
15 'The Whore Augusta', Incest with Caligula and Claudius, and Nero's Necrophilia 191
16 Hadrian and Antinous: A Man Worth Dying For 214
17 Faustina and the Gladiator's Bloodbath; the Vile Corruption of Commodus 219
18 Elagabalus: 'An Unspeakably Disgusting Life' 223
19 Theodora: Slut or Saint? 229

Primary Sources Cited 234
Abbreviations 258
Bibliography 260

Acknowledgements

My thanks to Maria Daniela Donninelli, Soprintendenza speciale per il Colosseo, il Museo Nazionale Romano e l'area archeologica di Roma Servizio di Fotoriproduzione Museo Nazionale Romano in Palazzo Massimo for image 4. Dominique Tisserand, Documentaliste, Musée et Sites Gallo-romains Lyon Fourvière/ Service scientifique for the NAVIGIUM VENERIS. Inv. 1999.5.82 for image 24 © J.-M. Degueule, Gallo-Roman Museum of Lyon. Musée Saint-Raymond, Toulouse © J.-F. Peiré for image 29.

PART ONE

In Bed with a Roman

INTRODUCTION

Whose Bed Is It Anyway?

Some Romans spent a lot of time in bed. Illness or hangover-recovery apart, they were often busy procreating or, in the case of women, procreating and giving birth. Serial childbirth was an expected duty of Roman women, particularly of the *matrona*, just as virility was required of men. Men also spent time in bed fornicating with mistresses, whores or catamites. It was expected of wifely *matronae* to connive at these infelicities – where else was a Roman to go when his wife was indisposed home-spinning, running the house or giving birth to yet another son or daughter? What else do you do when your posting takes you to the edge of empire for years on end? The production of children, especially male children, was the whole point of marriage – unless, of course, you were part of the political elite, in which case you could use your wife, and your daughters, as pawns in your efforts to better yourself and side with the right sort of people.

Sex, then, was something that had to be given and taken, if only for the children. To put it into a kind of Mediterranean context, Rabbi Eleizer, writing in Palestine in AD 80 and quoting from the *Torah,* prescribed the following programme of sexual activity: for students and the unemployed, every day; workers, twice a week; donkey drivers, once a week; camel drivers, once a month; sailors, once every six months. As arbitrary as it is, no Roman (man) would argue with that, except perhaps the odd port-based sailor and a camel driver or two. Two hundred years later, Rabbi Abba Bar Ayvo, founder of the Rabinnic Academy in Sura, Persia, would seem to endorse this when he euphemistically says of someone he knows, 'She eats with him every Friday night.'[1]

This rather flippant introduction raises a number of interesting issues relating to sex and sexuality among the Romans during their hegemony over the Mediterranean world and in central and northern Europe, from the foundation of Rome in 753 BC until the fall of the western empire in the fourth century AD. The famous television adaptations of Robert Graves' *I, Claudius* and *Claudius the God* have left an indelible impression of the early Roman Empire as a seamy, salacious world in which intrigue and sexual licence were ubiquitous at the highest levels of state. By examining contemporary sources, this book gives a less sensational, more reasoned description of the elite world familiar to us from Graves' books and of course the role sex played in broader Roman society from the foundation of Rome to the fifth century AD. It does so in the context of sex in Roman society generally, and through what we know of the lives of the men and women who have come down to us, some as alleged or actual adulterers, sexual predators or deviants but most as everyday, normal Roman men and women. It also attempts to show how far what we learn from Roman historians and other writers was influenced by political chicanery and unconcealed attempts to discredit.

In Bed with the Romans provides a balanced account of sex and sexuality in ancient Rome over twelve hundred or so years, while at the same time, in Part II, providing a lively and explicit account of the sexual exploits of a number of key protagonists at the end of the Republic and in the empire. While permissiveness certainly characterises aspects of the Roman world, there were various checks and balances in place to curb the worst excesses; it was never all sensational depravity, despite the best efforts of some of the emperors and their empresses to make it so. Indeed, one of the responsibilities of the Censors, an important office in Rome, was to look after public morality and to keep the state on the rails by promoting marriage and acting as guardians of public morals.[2] This power earned them reverence and fear in equal measure; they were known as the *castigatores* – the chastisers. Their ultimate weapon against transgressors was the withdrawal of rank and citizenship in recognition of a failure to uphold the *mos maiorum*, the code of behaviour, ethics and character which embodied everything that distinguished the Roman from the barbarian. Living as a single celibate, casual divorce,[3] treating a wife and children badly, spoiling children and allowing them to be naughty with their parents, sumptuous living, neglecting the fields, being cruel to the slaves, and being an actor or engaging in similar disreputable professions – all of these and more attracted the censure of the *censores*, winning the accused a dreaded *nota censoria*, and, to some extent, modulating public and private life.[4]

We cover a wide range of issues relating to sex and sexuality, although it should be remembered that much of what we know is seen through the prism of the male elite; women are, by and large, silent and have minimal contributions to make. Nevertheless, we can obtain a reasonably precise picture of how things were in bed with the Romans. Literary evidence apart, we glean much from archaeology, the visual arts, graffiti and inscriptional evidence.

On a personal note, we meet Clodia, vituperated by Cicero, loved and hated by Catullus; Fulvia, excoriated by Octavian; the mothers, wives, mistresses, siblings and children of the Julio-Claudian emperors; Hadrian and his infatuation with Antinous; and we witness the serial depravity of Elagabalus and the fascinating paradox that is Theodora. The impact of their sexual escapades on legal, social, military and political history is also examined to provide a balanced and considered account of sex and sexuality in the age of the Romans.

Some readers will be familiar with my earlier book, *Women in Ancient Rome* – published by Amberley in 2013 and 2014. As the title suggests, this book covers many aspects of the lives of Roman women with chapters on marriage, women in the public arena, education, women and the occult and women's role in religion. There is also coverage of women's medicine and of sex and sexuality – themes which it shares with *In Bed with the Romans*. Readers, then, should be aware that while these are two very different books, there is, necessarily, some overlap in the content of *In Bed with the Romans* and with *Women in Ancient Rome*, not least for reasons of completeness in both books.

CHAPTER ONE

Love, and Being a *Matrona*

This chapter looks at the concept of love between Roman men and women, the attitudes of Roman men and the Roman state towards women and the role Roman women were expected to play in their relationships with men as daughters, wives and mothers. As already noted, the purpose of a Roman woman in life was to get married and have children – preferably boys, to replenish battlefield and bar. The Roman war machine, and Roman administrations in territories all over the empire (before and after Augustus), demanded an endless supply of recruits if Rome was to maintain its position as *the* superpower in the known world. Furthermore, male offspring could guarantee the survival of the family line and the maintenance of the ever-increasing labour force. The Stoic philosopher Musonius Rufus strengthened the procreation argument when he reasoned, in his first-century-AD *Whether Marriage is an Impediment to Doing Philosophy*, that the whole point of having genitals, and of marrying, was to have children and ensure the survival of the human race.

Augustus encouraged and rewarded a woman's fecundity when he introduced the *ius triorum liberorum* – have three children and lose your guardian. Girls were fine, particularly after puberty; how else were the Romans to get their boys and men? Wives, though, despite being biologically vital, were on a legal par with children and slaves, and they were subordinate to fathers or to husbands. As far back as the laws of Romulus, enacted in the misty, legendary past, the absolute power of the father was inviolable and enshrined within the family unit; his *patria potestas* was pivotal. This was a defining factor in the role of women within the family, although we can only speculate on how far exactly it governed and dictated women's lives on a day to day basis. Men were obliged to demonstrate *virtus* – bravery, virtue, virility, masculinity and manliness; women had to display *pudicitia*, sexual propriety and chastity – between the two, the Romans had the glue which bound the family unit together and the wherewithal to produce children, continue the line and satisfy the demands of being a Roman, '*Romanitas*'.

Our evidence for the lives of men and women is seen through the refracted lens of male writers or in funerary inscriptions, written largely by men. Much of the inscriptional evidence would suggest that, among women, subservience and complicity was the norm. Much of what we read, time and time again, is starkly formulaic, husbands and sons trotting out standard traits and typical domestic virtues; its value as evidence of a woman's actual life may well be compromised as a result. Perhaps the reason is simply because it was cheaper, and quicker, to have the mason etch words from a template which could be selected from his catalogue of stock eulogies?

Fairly typical is 'Here lies Amymone, wife of Marcus, the best and most beautiful, wool spinner, dutiful, modest, careful with money, chaste (*casta*), a 'stay-at-home' girl.[1] The epithets inscribed for Amymone's virtues reflect the ideal, stereotypical Roman wife, the *matrona*. Claudia was much the same: beautiful, loving, mother of two children, clever in conversation, held herself well, looked after the home, and made her wool.[2] Chastity, domesticity, fertility and fidelity, being a one-man woman (*univira*), unobtrusive and low profile – these are some of the key attributes of a good Roman wife and mother.

We see the same on the tombstone of Allia Potestas; perfect in every way, she is first up in the morning and the last to go to bed in the evening, forever weaving, faultless to the end. But here there is a difference: the widower sees fit also to remark on her fine breasts and thighs. The erotic is also found on the grave relief built for Ulpia Epigone; she is depicted half-naked, although the suggestive (to us) image is balanced by the presence of a wool basket – another of the enduring badges of the good Roman *matrona* – and of a small dog, symbolizing fidelity and affection. The widowed author of a Flavian tomb now in the Lady Lever Art Gallery in Port Sunlight has no qualms about mentioning that he took his wife's virginity and still burns with love for her – all this within the small amount of space available to him. The relief above shows them on a couch together in an intimate pose. A woman's sexuality, then, was important in Roman life – one of the key attributes, up there with home-spinning, household management, love and perfection – even to the extent that it was quite normal to extol and celebrate that sexuality after her death, visible for time immemorial.[3]

Nevertheless, inscriptions are, to a greater or lesser extent, clichéd. They describe an ideal, if not the absolute reality, of wifely, feminine virtue; they tell us what men expected from a wife or a mother. They reflect the normal, the everyday, tolerably happy marriage in which husband and wife just rub along together. Some inscriptions, though, are patently not formulaic; they are subjective and personal, probably reflecting aspects of real life, exposing real characteristics, describing real love.

One widower says as much. He lists his wife's virtues in the usual way but then adds a poignant postcript explaining just why he has set up the tombstone. Why did he? To tell people just how much he and his wife were in love.[4] Then there is the eternally grateful freedwoman who describes on her tombstone the (then future) husband who befriended her when she was seven, bought her out of slavery and married her. We can see devotion glowing out of an inscription from Rome set up by Furia Spes, a freedwoman: Furia and her husband were childhood sweethearts; she implores the spirits of the dead to take good care of him until they meet again in the afterlife which, hopefully, will be in the not too distant future. Another tombstone from Rome commemorates Ummidia Ge and Primigenius, buried together after they were crushed to death in a crowd on the Capitol.[5] The first-century-BC inscription of a butcher and his wife gives both sides of the story. Lucius Aurelius Hermia fondly inscribes that his loving and much-loved wife, Aurelia Philematium, was devoted and dutiful. But why take his word for it? She herself tells us that she was chaste, modest, faithful and enjoyed a nice quiet life with Lucius. They had known each other since she was seven – some thirty-three years previously.[6] Not all wives were totally subservient; Naevoleia Tyche set up a tomb to herself, her husband and their slaves outside the Herculaneum Gate in Pompeii. Her name it is at the top, in letters etched larger than her husband's; she did all the work organising the tombstone – so *her* name takes top place. Elsewhere, Pompeius urges passing visitors to go and bathe in the baths of Apollo after reading his tombstone – he only wishes he could do the same, with his wife, just like they used to. Unfortunately, it was not all love and affection. The epitaph left for Julia Maiana at Lugudunum by her brother and son is tragic: her husband murdered her after a marriage that had lasted twenty-eight years.[7]

The *infelix uxor*, the unhappy, grieving widow, can be seen on the tombstone of Julius Classicianus, who died in Britannia in the wake of the Boudiccan rebellion; his widow, Julia Pacata, set up the tombstone. We have a list of women from Seneca who were determined to stay *univira*, a one-man women, on the deaths of their husbands. *Univira* can be qualified by *unicuba* – married one man only, slept with one man only,[8] as is the case with Postumia Matronilla and Veturia, who gave birth to six children in her sixteen-year marriage before she died, aged twenty-seven. Only one child survived her.[9]

Generally, the funerary evidence provides a standard eulogy for a standard Roman woman's life. Many wives and mothers would have been loyal and unobtrusive and would have just got on with looking after the household and bringing up the children. Nevertheless, we have glimpsed flashes of personal emotion left for the world to see, indicators of marriages and families that obviously thrived on mutual love, respect and affection. Any sexual references were quite normal, part and parcel of the Roman marriage, celebrated in death as a virtue.

The social context is important. We have already noted that much of what we read comes filtered through the eyes and attitudes of middle or upper-class Roman men; it also largely focuses on middle and upper-class women in their comfortable households, with their comfortable lifestyles. Although we do, and will, meet prostitutes, slave women and freedwomen, there is comparatively little evidence relating to the servile and poorer classes, busy as they are serving in their shops, working in their businesses, toiling in the fields, raising their families, looking after the house and complying with their husbands and fathers.

Pliny the Younger, in a letter to Marcellinus (5, 16), reveals for us the critical importance of marriage for Roman girls. He mourns the premature death of Minicia Marcella, soon before her thirteenth birthday. What she lacked in years she more than made up for in precocious maturity and all the qualities of a grown woman, a *matrona*. She was a sweet child and demure, kind to her father and respectful to her nurses and teachers; she died with Stoic bravery. Pliny, though, is equally upset by the fact that Minicia, although betrothed, died before she could experience marriage – marriage being the be-all and end-all for girls around that age. The letter neatly describes the situation of girls in middle-class Roman society. Girls married young, at or soon after puberty – marriage and producing babies was the expectation, their goal in life. Minicia, in common with all her sex, went straight from being a little girl to womanhood, with all the stresses and responsibility that brought.

Marriages were studiously pre-arranged by the father, in line with his authority at the head of the family, or by a guardian or some other male relative; girls rarely had a say in whom they married. Catullus prescribes the business-like protocol: marriage not only makes the young girl dear to her husband but also less objectionable to her father; she should not oppose her father's choice – she must obey him and her mother. After all, the girl's virginity is only one-third hers – her parents are responsible for the other two-thirds and they will exercise their right to pass her on to their future son-in-law, along with the dowry.[10]

A Roman wife, was expected to embody all the qualities embodied in a *matrona*: the woman of the family and household. Chastity (*castita*) and fidelity loom large; *pudicitia* (sexual propriety, the opposite, almost, of *stuprum* (permissiveness)), modesty, virtuousness, loyalty, strength of character and courage, *pietas* towards the family, being a one-man woman (*univira*) and devotion to her children. A girl took on these onerous responsibilities the minute she arrived at her husband's house during her wedding ceremony.

Given that sexual virtue was paramount, it gave the *matrona* status and respect in Roman society; her role models were the mythical Helen of Troy and Cornelia, while her day-to day activities were wool-working and looking after the house. On a wider scale, sexual virtue in the home guaranteed social and political stability; if compromised, it unsettled the state and put Rome in peril. The woman who confined her sexual activity to her husband, marriage and home was a respected and honoured in Roman society.

Virginity was never a desirable state once puberty was reached. The assumption was that as soon as a girl married, the marriage would be consummated and children would be born. Even the Vestal Virgins were not required to be virgins forever; once their thirty years of service were up, they were free to marry. However, virginity during the period of Vestal service was non-negotiable. In the outside world, pre-marital sex with a fiancé was punishable, as it was in pregnant women who did not abstain from sex during the festival of Artemis, the virgin goddess.

The epitome of good wifely conduct can be seen in the second-century-BC Turia inscription – the *Laudatio Turiae,* erected in Rome by Turia's husband, Quintus Lucretius Vespillo. She demonstrated *pietas*, was wool-working, looked after the household gods, was modest of dress and elegant and financially generous. Moreover, she showed bravery and shrewdness in the face of her husband's enemy, Lepidus, in 46 BC after his proscription: Turia hid Lucretius in their roof space while convincingly playing the role of the bereft wife, dressing in rags, looking disheveled and grieving over an apparently dead, but very alive, husband.[11]

In the *Agricola*, published in AD 98, Tacitus ascribes matronly, maternal qualities to Agricola's mother, Julia Procilla; she exhibits *rara castitas* and is a paragon of feminine virtue.[12] It was she who imbued Agricola with all the right qualities; it was she who 'in her wisdom, tempered his ardent passion' and diverted him from the emasculating philosophizing going on in Massilia, a city steeped in all things Greek and the effeminacy that meant.

Tacitus believed that 'in the good old days the children of any respectable mother were brought up, not in the room of a hired nurse but on their mother's knee. She was honoured to look after the home and to do right by her children.' He cites the examples of Cornelia, mother of the Gracchi; Aurelia Cotta, Julius Caesar's mother; and the mother of Augustus, Atia Balba Caesonia, as *the* three role-model *matronae* to emulate.[13] Quintilian agrees that it was a mother's duty to ensure their children receive the best possible education, also citing Cornelia as a fine role model.[14]

But it was Cornelia, Lucretia and Verginia who exuded *castitas* and *pudicitia* – they were the three peerless women of virtue. *Pudicitia* is chastity, sexual honour or sexual propriety and is, according to Livy, equivalent to the laudable quality of *virtus* in men.[15] For Lucretia and Verginia the preservation of *pudicitia* was of such importance that it cost them their lives.

Matronly virtues, familial devotion and *pietas* were not, of course, exclusive to the middle and upper classes. These qualities were also exhibited by women of the lower classes. A first century BC inscription for Larcia Horaea gives us one example: she was a confident and faithful freedwoman, respected in her social circle, obedient to her master and mistress, faithful to her husband – virtues which won her her freedom and status as a *matrona* in her own right.[16] As we have seen, another freedwoman, Allia Potestas, has more than her fair share of feminine virtues. And matronly virtues were not just confined to women of Roman birth. Martial describes a Claudia Rufina; she is British, a barbarian, but nevertheless is a Latin at heart and would pass any time for a Roman or a Greek. Like all the best *matronae* she is fertile, *fecunda*, *univira* and looking forward to her children's marriages and, no doubt, grandchildren.[17]

Statius paints a moving picture of wifely devotion, a mother's love for her daughter and a stepfather's pride in his stepdaughter – but also, just as importantly, the anxiety caused by not being able to marry off a daughter. The poet wants to move the family back to Naples from Rome. His wife is Claudia; her loyalty to him has been on a par with that shown by the legendary heroines of Greece and Rome. Her devotion to her daughter is just as great: Claudia's concern is that her daughter is unmarried and that Rome is the best place for her to find a husband; Statius argues that she will find a husband be she in Rome or Naples.[18] It's a warming domestic situation which could occur in any age.

Literature gives us examples of love in marriage. Martial describes with pathos a widow's tragic double grief when Nigrina brought home her dear husband's ashes, holding them close to her heart and complaining that the journey home with them/him was all too brief. When she surrendered the sacred urn to the tomb (and she was jealous of that tomb because it, and not she, now possessed her husband), she could not help feeling that she had been widowed twice over by the husband who had been snatched from her.[19] Quintilian too is distraught at his young wife's death when she was only nineteen, by which time she had given birth to two sons who also predeceased their father. She exhibited every virtue a woman could have; he adds poignantly that her girlish qualities made it seem as if he had lost a daughter as well as a wife.[20]

We have evidence of love for living wives. A touching love letter from Pliny to Calpurnia reveals mutual affection when he writes that she writes that she is missing him terribly and takes comfort only when she holds his books, often placing them where he should be. He tells her, 'I'm glad that you miss me and I'm glad that you are comforted in this way. As for me, I read your letters over and over again, constantly picking them up as if they had just arrived. In doing this I burn with desire all the more.'[21] Elsewhere, he writes, 'I am seized by an amazing longing for you. The reason is, most of all, my love, but also the fact that we are not used to being apart. This is why I spend most of the night haunted by your image; this is why, now and again, my feet take me [the right expression!] of their own accord to your room at the times I used to visit you; this is why, in short, I retreat, morbid and disconsolate, like an excluded lover from an unwelcoming doorway.' Here Pliny is reduced to the state of a pathetic *exclusus amator*.

Seneca, as a philosopher, can list many good reasons why a wise man should never marry; however, Tacitus shatters this professional façade when he tells us how much Seneca really loved his wife.[22] Ovid, in his *Tristia*, composed during his Black Sea exile, describes his loyal and devoted wife: she is the model of a good wife; she would hold first place among the sacred heroines of mythology and would be an equal to the first lady, Livia, wife of Augustus – if one can go so far as to compare the great with the small. Exaggerated, sycophantic and patronising – but it is, nevertheless, moving for all that.[23]

Arria, a shining example and comfort, shows exceptional devotion to her husband when she does everything she possibly can to show Aulus Caecina Paetus that his impending suicide, ordered by Claudius, will not be painful. And this after she has courageously shielded the news of their son's recent death from her husband, to spare him additional grief; whenever Paetus asked how the boy was doing she responded, 'He's had a good rest and is ready to eat something.' Then, when she couldn't hold her grief back any longer, she left the room and burst into tears, succumbing to her anguish. Her grief exhausted, she dried her eyes, composed herself and went back into the room, almost as if she had left her bereavement outside. It was a glorious thing for her when she drew a dagger and plunged it into her breast, pulled it out and offered it to her husband with the immortal, almost divine, words, 'Paetus, it doesn't hurt.' (*Paete, non dolet.*)

> By doing what she did, and saying what she said she looked glory and immortality straight in the eye. On the other hand, it was an even greater thing when, without the reward of immortality and without the reward of glory, she hid her tears and concealed her grief and continued to play the mother, even though she had just lost her son.[24]

Later in the letter we learn of Arria's brave determination to end her own life. 'It's no use,' she said. 'I can die a horrible death but you can't stop me dying.' As she said this she leapt from her chair, smacked her head really hard against the wall opposite and slumped to the ground. When she came round she said, 'I told you that I would find a hard way to die if you denied me the easy way out.' Martial too honours *casta* Arria's bravery; he, perceptively, has her say that her wound doesn't hurt but the one that Paetus is about to inflict on himself, suicide, certainly will hurt her.[25]

Such courage ran in the family. Arria's granddaughter, Fannia, had married Helvidius Priscus, an agitator against Vespasian who had him executed in AD 75. Pliny extols Fannia, doubting very much that the world will see her kind again – the model of a perfect wife with the rare qualities of charm and amiability, and clever enough to appreciate the value of her husband's library, which she spirited away into safekeeping despite official orders to burn his books. Fannia has displayed bravery, purity of mind, purity of body, dignity and self-control. She followed her husband twice into exile and was herself condemned to exile for her troubles; Fannia later died from tuberculosis contracted from a consumptive Vestal Virgin whom she had volunteered to nurse.[26]

Arria and Fannia were not alone. Pliny the Elder describes how a woman joined her husband in suicide by jumping, roped together, into Lake Como after she had diagnosed his uncurable condition (variously thought to be a urogenital cancer, syphilis or urogenital tuberculosis).[27] Porcia, the wife of Brutus the conspirator, plunged a dagger into her thigh to show her husband that she too could endure pain, and was worthy of sharing his troubles.[28] When Brutus was killed in 43 BC she committed suicide by swallowing hot coals, an act which Valerius Maximus describes as her woman's spirit equal to her father's manly death.[29]

Tacitus recounts a number of incidences where women join their husbands in suicide as a mark of their devotion. Paxaea commits suicide with her husband Pomponius Labeo, governor of Moesia, charged by Tiberius in AD 34 of maladministration. Lucius Antistius Vetus was proscribed by Nero for his involvement in the Pisonian conspiracy in AD 65; his mother-in-law, Sextia and daughter, Antistia Pollitta, joined him in opening their veins,[30] but not before Pollitta had remonstrated with Nero when she wailed like a woman but also screamed at him in a most unwomanly rage.[31] Aemilia Lepida takes her life to avoid persecution, Sextia opts to die with her husband, Mamercus Aemilius Scaurus, who is under prosecution,[32] as does Paulina, the wife of Seneca,[33] although she is confounded by Nero and lives a long life, praiseworthy for her abiding memory of her husband.

Suicide is an extension of the *univira* ideal; in an ideal world, not only should a woman marry, and sleep with, only one man but she should also not outlive him. Arria rebukes Vibia, wife of Scribonianus, who lived on after her husband had been murdered in her very arms;[34] she also urges her own daughter to commit suicide should her husband predecease her. Arria exhibited other signs of dedication and devotion, risking her life when Paetus was dragged back to Rome. He was about to board the boat when Arria begged the soldiers to take her too. 'Surely a consul should be allowed a few slaves to serve his meals, dress him and put on his shoes – I am the only one who excels at all these things.' The soldiers did not allow her to board, so she followed behind in a hired fishing boat.[35]

Sulpicia dressed up as a slave to follow her proscribed husband, Lentulus Cruscellio, into exile in Sicily.[36] The wife of Rubellius Plautus accompanied him in exile and two of the wives of the exiled Piso conspirators joined their husbands. Valerius tells how Tertia Aemilia, wife of Scipio Africanus, had full knowledge of her husband's affair with a slave girl but chose to turn a blind eye; on Scipio's death, she freed the girl and even organised her marriage to one of her freedmen.[37] Quintilian tells us about the defiant Cloatilla, who was pardoned by Claudius when she buried her husband in defiance of the law against burying anyone convicted of treason.[38]

Appian adds to the list of brave and devoted acts by women. Following the proscriptions imposed after the assassination of Julius Caesar in 44 BC, the wife of Acilius used her jewellery to bribe and deflect the soldiers who had come to arrest him and escaped with him to Sicily; Apuleius' wife threatened to turn him in if he refused to let her escape with him; Antius' wife concealed him in a blanket to effect their escape; and the wife of Rheginus hid him in a sewer and dressed him as a donkey-driving charcoal seller to make good their escape.[39] Dio Cassius describes a woman who heroically defends another woman's virtue in his record of Pythias, a slave girl who, under interrogation and subjected to torture, stands up for Nero's wife, Octavia, in AD 63. She defiantly spits in the face of her interrogator, the evil Tigellinus, when questioned about Octavia's virtue, exclaiming, 'My mistress's vagina is cleaner than your mouth.'[40]

Sempronia, the Catiline conspirator, was also brave, but her courage was rewarded by condemnation and vilification. Sallust grudgingly admits that she exhibited a boldness worthy of a man; that she was well married with children; she was versed in Latin and Greek, accomplished in the lyre and a good dancer; she was an excellent and convivial conversationalist. In short, her social and artistic skills and abilities were highly commendable. That said, Sallust adds that, marriage and good motherhood apart, she displayed few of the qualities expected of the conventional *matrona*: she was impulsive, louche, passionate, a perjurer, an accessory to murder, a liar and a spendthrift. Sempronia to Sallust was a kind of anti-*matrona*; while undoubtedly brave and gifted she broke the mould and stepped far beyond the traditional boundaries laid down for Roman women.[41] It is significant, however, that Sallust cannot resist praising her motherhood while denigrating her alleged passion and permissiveness.

Tertia Aemilia, in illustrating the tolerance and resignation expected of Roman wives, highlights the double standards prevalent in Roman marriage. A woman was adulterous if she had a liaison with any man, while a man was only an adulterer if his mistress was married, thus leaving the door wide open to him for legitimate extramarital affairs with prostitutes, concubines, slave girls, catamites, men and widows. Plautus says it all when it comes to free love: 'No one stops anyone from going down the public way so long as you do not trespass, as long as you keep off brides, single women, maidens, the youth and free boys, love whatever you want.' Augustine, converted to Christianity in AD 387, explains how his mother never fell out with his father over his sexual indiscretions.[42] We cannot know what women thought of this; most probably they accepted the situation, seeing it as a relief from the often relentless cycle of sexual intercourse, impregnation, childbirth and more sex. However, the very real possibility of a promiscuous man infecting his wife, or indeed his unborn child, with a sexually transmitted infection has gone unremarked in Roman historiography.[43]

Women were relentlessly stereotyped by men. We have seen plenty of evidence in the funerary inscriptions, where it was generally good. To Seneca all women have their vices, *vitia; cosi fan tutte*.[44] In 195 BC, during the proposed repeal of the *Lex Oppia* of 215 BC, demonstrating women evoked distaste and condemnation. The law had restricted the use of luxuries by well-off women in the wake of the calamitous battle of Cannae some twenty years before; the feeling among these women was that the law had served its purpose and had run its course. Livy records the speech given by Marcus Porcius Cato and his embarrassment and disgust at what he saw as indecorous behaviour, ill-befitting Roman women. Cato, generally no friend of women, had famously paraphrased Themistocles when he asserted that 'all men rule their wives; we rule all men; our wives rule us'.[45] He harps back to the days of the ancestors who permitted women no public activity or commercial dealings without the involvement of a guardian, and who safeguarded the power of fathers and husbands. Cato is appalled by this vulgar, populist action.[46] The repeal, nevertheless, was approved, thanks in no small part to the counter-arguments of an enlightened Lucius Valerius.

> For a long time our matrons lived by the highest standards of behaviour without any law, what is the risk when it is repealed,

that they will give in to luxury?...Are we to forbid only women to wear purple? When you, a man, can use purple on your clothes, can you not permit the mother of your family to have a purple cloak, and will you let your horse be more finely saddled than your wife is dressed?

Around the same time Plautus adds to the paranoia and hand wringing when he has Megadorus in the *Aulularia* deliver a rant on female extravagance, with particular reference to those employed in the tailoring and clothing trades.[47] The palaver had not died down some 200 years later, when Valerius Maximus reminded his readers that contemporary men of the period had no conception of the extravagance to which women's indomitable passion for novelty in fashion would lead, or the extremes to which their brazenness would go.[48]

As we have said, women, including *matronae*, like slaves and children, were second-class citizens on the margins of society; they were, theoretically at least, always under the control of a man – be it a father or a husband or a guardian, depending on time of life and circumstances. They had no place in public office and were excluded from the Roman war machine, they were politically invisible because they could not vote, and they had a limited role in state religion; from what survives of Roman literature they are largely silent; their education was often curtailed by early marriage, by household management and by serial childbirth.

Livy gives the standard male attitude when he describes the debate on the repeal of the Oppian Law in 195 BC, that rare example of woman power exerting itself in Roman politics. 'Women cannot hold magistracies, priesthoods, celebrate triumphs, wear badges of office, enjoy gifts, or booty; elegance, finery, and beautiful clothes are women's emblems, this is what they love and are proud of, this is what our ancestors called women's world of adornment.'[49] Cato the Elder tetchily argued that the minute you give women equality, they will take over and be your superiors.

Let them just go shopping, no less. According to Philo of Alexandria, writing soon after Livy, woe betide any woman who acts intemperately, indeed acts anything like a man, even in defence of a husband under attack. He says that if any woman, out of love, should yield to the feelings which overpower her and rush forth to help him, even then let her not be so bold as to behave like a man, exceeding the nature of a woman; but even while aiding him let her still be a woman. It would be a very terrible thing if a woman should expose herself to insult by exposing a life full of shamelessness and liable to great reproaches for her incurable boldness; for shall a woman be abusive in the marketplace and give vent to bad language? And if a man uses foul language, will not she block her ears and run away?

For Philo, things have already gone too far.

> Nowadays, some women have reached such a level of shamelessness that, though they are women, use intemperate language and abuse among a crowd of men, and even strike men and insult them, with hands used to working the loom and spinning than in blows and assaults... but it is shocking if a woman were to be so bold as to grab the balls of one of the men quarrelling... and let the punishment be to chop off of the hand which has touched what it ought not to have touched.[50]

Philo may have come over as unintentionally amusing to his contemporaries, but Plautus, writing plays aimed at making his audience laugh out loud, had earlier said that there was nothing more miserable than a woman. One assumes that this did raise a laugh and, being the well-to-do educated Roman man he was, was referring to woman's psychological mood rather than to her general social situation – although both are probably appropriate, with the latter often accounting for the former.[51] A nostalgic Cicero had already famously pronounced that his ancestors, in their wisdom, wanted 'all women, because of their feebleness of mind, to be in the power of guardians'.[52] In the second century AD not that much had changed when Martial asserted that the *matrona* will never be equal to men unless she remains *inferior marito* – under the thumb of her husband.[53]

But the chauvinism was not confined to the pagans. Origen Adamantius, the theologian, was one of the earliest Christian misogynists. Writing in the early third century, he erased from the 'honest' Tatiana her femininity, describing her as 'manly' – a woman with sound virtues must owe these virtues to masculine characteristics. Tertullian, a third-century convert to Christianity, confirmed in his *On the Apparel of Women* (1, 1, 1–3) women's role as childbearers, lorded over by men, that all women are Eve and share her guilt and that they are the Devil's Door and responsible for the death of Christ, worthy of nothing better than to wear animal pelts. Women are the font of all sexual evil and should nullify any physical attraction they may have which may tempt men (2, 2, 4–6). Long before him, Paul (Saul) of Tarsus, a Jew with Roman citizenship who converted to Christianity on the road to Damascus in the early first century AD, made the following influential statement in *I Timothy* 2, 11–15:

> A woman should learn silently and submissively. I allow no woman to teach or have authority over men. She should remain silent. Adam was created first, then Eve ... she became a sinner. However, woman shall be saved by bearing children, if she behaves modestly, in faith, love and sanctity.

The die was cast, the damage was done – for many, a woman was officially consigned to providing sex for child rearing, 2,000 years before Finley's 'silent women of Rome'. John Chrysostom, the fourth-century-AD Archbishop of Constantinople, looking back on Greeks, Romans and Christians, said it all in his *The Type of Women Who Ought to be Taken as Wives*: 'a woman's role exclusively is to care for children, for her husband, and for her home... God assigned a role to each of the sexes: women look after the home, men take care of public affairs, business and military matters – in other words, everything outside the home'.

Such was the general attitude Roman men had towards women. But it was by no means all bitter misogyny and sexism. Cicero, for one, should have been grateful to his wife and daughter. He relies heavily on the emotional and political support of Terentia during his exile in 58 and 57 BC;[54] his letters, like some of Pliny's to his wife, reflect isolation, homesickness and affection, both for her and for their daughter Tullia. 'Terentia is *the* most faithful and best of wives... light of my life.' Tullia and Terentia both interceded bravely on Cicero's behalf.[55] They also had to deal with his business affairs, the slaves and household as well as the upbringing of their young son; Terentia remained the supportive wife even though their marriage was actually annulled by virtue of his exile. The two women demonstrated ostentatiously by wearing their hair unkempt and donning black mourning clothes, canvassing support from friends and allies for Cicero's return. Plutarch records how Cicero himself says that Terentia was more active in his political life than she ever was in domestic affairs.

Ovid's third and last wife is equally supportive and loyal to Ovid in his exile; nine of his *Tristia* are addressed to her. He describes his first two wives as 'useless', 'faultless but faithless' and in the same poem he expresses his gratitude to the third.[56]

You could spot a *matrona* in the street by her *stola* (or *instita*, the shoulder straps of the *stola*) – a long, ankle length dress – and by her *vittae*, hair bands. These instantly marked out the *matrona* from other women: unmarried girls, women without Roman citizenship, adulteresses, prostitutes and other females of dubious occupations such as dancers, actresses and anyone else working in the entertainment or catering industries. The words *stola*, *instita* and *vittae* themselves became metonyms for respectability and chastity: Ovid uses them when he insincerely dissuades *matronae* from reading his *Ars Amatoria*; Martial mentions the sheer decency (*pudor*) of the *stola*; Valerius Maximus *verecundia stolae*, the modesty of the stola.[57] Modesty, though, was not universal. Seneca in the early empire deplored the modern fashion for translucent silks which, to his mind, indicated permissiveness and revealed too much body – virtual nakedness for all to see when it should have been exclusive to the husband.

What did a (modest) Roman woman wear under her s*tola*, or toga? Roman women more or less followed the Greeks: Martial describes a *cestus*, which is similar to the Greek *zoné* but wider, and Cicero also describes a *strophium* or breast band. There were also the *mamillere* and *fascia*, which were tight bands of cloth that primarily supported the bust rather than the abdomen. A well-known mosaic from AD 400 Piazza Amerina shows several women wearing what appear to be bikinis or briefs (see image 9). For the Romans, underwear was designed to be functional rather than sexy.

Where did the conservative Roman view come from that said that women of old were all paragons of virtue while contemporary women were inceasingly and dangerously permissive? Virtue always has a whiff of nostalgia about it – every successive age harps back to 'the good old days' and modern life is always rubbish. The Romans were no different. For the first 500 years or so of Rome's history there was little or no real history writing. It was only with Quintus Fabius Pictor around 200 BC and the *Origines* of Marcus Porcius Cato the Censor some forty years later that historical events began to be recorded; the detailed and exhaustive work only really began with Livy and Dionysius of Halicarnassus at the end of the republic. In the absence of actual and verifiable facts, then, much of the early history of Rome comprised ideals and stereotypes based on legends and stories, some of which were re-fashioned to fit the historian's agenda, or to reinforce the version of the past he or his patron wanted to promulgate. The *matrona* ideal did not, of course, escape this process of semi-fictionalisation when the later Roman historians, as spokesmen for the official line, embellished the legendary women of the misty past with the qualities they insisted contemporary women should enshrine.

The rape of Lucretia by Sextus Tarquinius, and her subsequent suicide, firmly implicates matronly *pudicitia* and valour in the traditional foundation of Rome. Livy tells how Tarquinius blackmails Lucretia by threatening to put it about that she had been discovered *in flagrante delicto* with a slave, a crime beyond the pale; he threatened to have her and a slave killed, their corpses placed alongside each other in bed, if she does not yield to him.[58] Lucretia cannot live with the shame that such a calumny would bring and succumbs; her body is defiled but, she protests, her mind remains pure.[59] Despite the unconditional forgiveness offered by her father, Lucretius, and of Collatinus, her husband, Lucretia commits suicide – brave, virtuous and now inextricably linked with Rome's proud early beginnings. Livy makes her an unimpeachable exemplar of feminine virtue in a Rome, his Rome now beset by increasing adultery and failing marriages.[60]

The rape is all the more outrageous because Livy prefaces it with a story focussing on Lucretia's virtue. Tarquinius and Collatinus were present at a lively drinking session at the siege of Ardea: the subject of wives, good or otherwise, came up; the outcome was an alcohol-fuelled decision to ride back to Rome and Collatia to establish whose was the most virtuous. On arrival, Tarquinius' wife was found enjoying a sumptuous dinner party, *in convivio luxuque*. Lucretia, however, despite the lateness of the hour, was found to be surrounded by her maids in the hall, working away at the wool by lamplight. This, of course, left no doubt as to who had won the virtue contest.

The legendary death of Verginia in 449 BC had similar repercussions and ramifications. It occurred during the Conflict of the Orders when the actions of Verginius, father of Verginia, provoked a secession of the plebeians. Appius Claudius had his eye on Verginia. His attempts to bribe her and woo her fell flat. Verginia was from a humble, honourable, principled family, and although she was already betrothed to Lucius Icilius, Claudius contrived a plan whereby Marcus Claudius – 'the decemvir's pimp' – claimed that Verginia was his slave and had been illegally adopted by Verginius. On her way to school one day, Marcus Claudius tried to abduct Verginia. A shocked and outraged crowd gathered to help the girl. The distraught father arrived back in Rome and next morning led his daughter into the forum for a trial to decide if Claudius is to get Verginia.; he is in mourning, she is dressed in rags, attended by *matronae*. Appius finds in favour of Claudius. Livy tells us that the supportive women in the crowd were 'more effective with their silent tears than words could be'. Nevertheless, the incident ended tragically when Verginius exercised his right as *paterfamilias*, grabbed a butcher's knife and stabbed his daughter in the heart to liberate her from the shame (*stuprum*) a marriage to Appius Claudius would inevitably bring: *in libertatem vindico*. Verginius cursed Appius; the women angrily and indignantly demanded to know if this be the scant reward they get for raising children and remaining chaste: *pudicitiae praemia*. According to Livy, *muliebris dolor*, 'the grief of women', is so much more powerful, their grief so much deeper due to their lack of restraint. The upshot was that the *decemvirate* was disbanded and the Republic was restored. Another hugely significant event in the history of Rome.

The story, as related by Livy and Dionysius of Halicarnassus,[61] is significant on two levels. First, it reinforces the traditional Roman values of chastity and virtue we saw in Lucretia: the aptly named Verginia became a symbol of Roman *pudicitia*. Second, it gives an example of a father exerting his *patria potestas*, his power as a father over his daughter. As *paterfamilias* Verginius had, under Roman law, an obligation to preserve the integrity of his family, including the chastity of his daughters; when this was compromised he had little choice other than kill his daughter if he wanted to preserve her *pudicitia*.

Pontus Aufidius was another father who had to bury his daughter prematurely due to his own moralistic actions. She had lost her virginity to her tutor, Fannius Saturninus, so Aufidius killed both slave and daughter. The daughter of P. Maenius learnt the hard way the lessons of compromising her purity: she had been kissed (possibly quite innocuously) by a freedman in the household – Maenius slew him as a harsh lesson to his daughter to remain absolutely pure until her wedding night (Valerius Maximus, *Memorable Deeds and Sayings* 6, 1, 4). Chariclea, an Ethiopean princess and priestess of Apollo, is the model of purity; she elopes with the handsome Theagenes but makes him swear not to take her virginity. When they find themselves alone, much kissing and fondling ensues but she resists his increasingly manly urges with a reminder of the oath; he restrains himself – a model of self-control (Heliodorus, *Aethiopica* 5, 4, 4–5).

Cornelia Scipionis Africana (*c.* 180 BC–*c.* 105 BC) brings us into more accountable history. She is the epitome of the ideal Roman *matrona*; she was wife of Tiberius Sempronius Gracchus whom she married around 175 BC and mother of the brothers Gracchi, Tiberius and Gaius – and of Sempronia. She is described as the ideal *matrona* by Plutarch in his *Life of Gaius Gracchus*. She achieved fame and respect down the ages for maintaining her dignity when speaking of the exploits and tragic deaths of her two boys; her company and conversation were much enjoyed by scholars and monarchs in the salons she held in her villa at Misenum – an example of 'how far a noble nature, an honourable ancestry and a virtuous upbringing, can fortify [wo]men against grief'.[62]

There is, though, earlier praise in Plutarch's *Life of Tiberius Gracchus* where he narrates the story of how her husband elected to die in place of her. Two snakes had ominously appeared on the marital bed; alarmed and superstitious, Tiberius took them to a soothsayer, *haruspex*, to divine their meaning. The *haruspex* explained that the female represented Cornelia and the male himself, and that Cornelia would die if the female snake was released first – and vice versa. Tiberius gallantly chose to release the male snake rather than the female – the anonymous author of the *De Viris Illustribus* sees his unenviable decision as a demonstration of his love and respect for Cornelia, *amore Corneliae coniugis*. Tiberius duly died soon after, around 154 BC, leaving his still relatively young widow with their twelve children to raise, nine of whom died in infancy, and an extensive estate to run.[63]

Despite a proposal of marriage from the very eligible (politically at least) Ptolemy VIII (Physkon, his nickname, or 'big belly', says it all physically), Cornelia remained a widow and *univira*, retiring to Misenum in relative comfort. The surviving daughter, Sempronia, married Scipio Africanus the Younger.[64]

Cornelia's reputation was assured even during her lifetime. Plutarch gives us this stinging retort by Gaius Gracchus when his mother was criticised by a political opponent, highlighting the respect in which fertility and chastity were held:

'What,' he said, 'do you abuse Cornelia, she who gave birth to Tiberius [Gracchus]?' 'With what cheek,' demanded Gaius, 'can you compare yourself with Cornelia? Have you had as many children as her? Indeed all Rome knows that she refrained from commerce with men for longer than you, even though you are a man.'

Even by the prodigious standards of the Romans, Cornelia's twelve children in twenty years is some achievement; it becomes even more impressive when her husband's long postings overseas are taken into account. The number may be exaggerated by stillbirths and miscarriages, but, at the same time, it seems more credible if we factor in the likely sets of twins, triplets even, who did not survive. In any event her fertility, one of the badges of the good *matrona*, was never questioned too closely if her iconic status was to be maintained. Pliny the Elder, who brings us the statistic, seems equally amazed by the fact that she produced babies of alternating sex: boy, girl, boy, girl etc, or possibly, six of one followed by six of the other.[65]

Cornelia was destined to become the epitome of the perfect Roman *matrona*, a champion of the *familia*, that glue which held Roman society together. She was a caring mother who ensured the education of her children. She supported them in life and in death; she was sophisticated and urbane herself; she was dignified and modest, erudite yet unobtrusively so; and she was *univira*, a one-man woman, electing not to remarry after her husband's death. This role as a paradigm of matronly behaviour was to grow increasingly significant as Roman society became more and more decadent, with rising adultery, declining numbers of people marrying, falling birthrates among native Italians, and more divorce. Augustus' attempts to curb this moral decay in 18 BC – the *lex Julia de maritandis ordinibus* – were enacted, no doubt, with Cornelia cited as the model every Roman woman should emulate.

In the earlier days of the Republic, spinning and weaving were crucial feminine skills in Roman households at all levels of society; they were recognisable hallmarks of the good mother and wife. Augustus wore homespun clothes and promoted the traditional skill of weaving,[66] boasting that all the women in his household could spin. His wife, Livia, included in her domestic staff five patchers, two supervisors, six women in charge of clothing, one cloak maker, one tailor and two fullers. The Statilii Tauri family had eight spinners, one supervisor of the wool, four patchers, four weavers, two dyers and four fullers.[67] Ovid reminds us that the goddess Pallas Minerva not only teaches children reading and literature but also how to weave and spin.[68] By the mid-first century AD, Columella, the Spanish-born writer on agriculture (*de re Rustica*) and husbandry, complains that homespun clothes were now unfashionable and clothing was usually bought from shops instead, at extortionate prices.[69] Bread-making suffered the same fate when bakeries and bakers shops replaced home-made bread (courtesy of the women of the house) in the second century BC. Indeed, Aelius Aristeides tells us that only in the poorest households did women now do routine housework – slaves did most, if not all, of it.[70] On the catering front, if Trimalchio's Fortunata in Petronius' *Satyricon* is anything to go by, the *materfamilias* was heavily involved, in a managerial capacity, in the preparation and serving of meals.[71]

As important as spinning and weaving was in the Roman family, over time it became increasingly redundant and merely symbolic as Roman society became more and more sophisticated and urbanised. The better off Roman woman would spend much of her time supervising the slaves – ensuring that they performed all the mundane tasks a lower-class housewife might be expected to do. This freed her up to go out – shopping, attending festivals and spectacles, visiting friends, educating their children and going to those dinner parties Cornelius Nepos tells us about.[72]

Columella is also nostalgic for the times when women reputedly did do all the housework, when they provided a sanctuary for stressed husbands returning from work to a home of complete respect and harmony, where even the prettiest wife complemented and complimented her husband's achievements by her own enthusiastic efforts managing the household. Nowadays, he laments, women are obsessed with luxury and laziness, sewing, stitching and darning is no more, and women moan when they have to look after the farm just for a few days.

Later, he lays down a woman's responsibilities in the rural homestead. When the weather prevents work in the fields she should busy herself with wool-work, using all that wool she has prepared earlier. She should check that the slaves are fully occupied; anyone who is ill – or pretending to be – should be taken for treatment (an unproductive slave is no asset); she should never stand still but keep on the move: teaching wool-work, learning wool-work, doing wool-work, checking on the slaves in the kitchen, ensuring that the kitchens, cowsheds and pens are clean; she should periodically clean the sick-room.[73] No rest, then, for the women in Columella's farmhouse.

A further restriction on women's lives were their guardians, *tutores*. Cicero, and later Ulpian writing in the early third century AD, both explain that women need guardians because women are socially and intellectually inferior, and they have no knowledge of legal or commercial matters.[74] Gaius, in his *Institutiones*, confirmed that, on reaching puberty, boys relinquished their guardians, but not girls – the reason being *propter animi levitatem* – they were considered to be what today some would disparagingly call 'airheads'. Even less flatteringly, when a woman was about to marry, a new guardian would be appointed to arrange her dowry only if the existing one was deaf or insane.[75]

From a financial standpoint, the best thing for a woman to be was a *vidua* – a woman without a man. This gave her a status of *sui iuris*, brought about by widowhood or divorce or by taking over the household after the death of parents and before marriage. Even then, though, a guardian was obligatory. *Viduae* were naturally much sought after by bounty hunters. Fertility encroached on family law when the *Leges Iuliae* and the *Lex Papia-Poppaea* allowed freeborn women to be released from guardianship on the birth of their third child (*ius trium liberorum*), freedwomen on the birth of the fourth;[76] one of the benefits of this independence was that women could now make their own wills. Women also won some protection, in theory at least, from rape by their guardians, who could face a sentence of deportation and confiscation of property if convicted.[77]

British women must have seemed very odd to the Roman invaders in 44 BC. Caesar observed that up to ten or twelve men shared one wife, with brothers and fathers even sharing; any offspring was officially fathered by the man who took the woman's viriginity.[78] Dio adds to this when he describes an encounter between Julia Domna, empress of Septimius Severus, and the wife of a Caledonian chieftain. Julia Domna remarks on how the tribal women are somewhat free with their sexual favours; the barbarian replies tartly, 'We satisfy our desires in a better way than you Roman women do. We have sex openly with the best men while you are seduced in secret by the worst.'[79]

Such was the lot and life of Roman girls and women in the domestic setting, or what we can know about it from the surviving evidence. Funerary inscriptions are often impersonal, clichéd and formulaic but some are tinged with personal, real emotion. They idealise and lionise what was expected of the Roman wife and mother but, in some instances, reveal real love between wives and their husbands. A girl or woman was in the power of her father and, after marriage, was expected to take an active but discreet role in running the marital home. As a *matrona* she was expected to be virtuous, strong-willed but not obtrusively so, conversational, modestly dressed, loyal, compliant, and to look after her children, particularly their education. The *univira* was the ideal, wool-working was essential and was highly respected – both were emblems of the good wife. Literature gives examples of genuine affection between spouses. As time went by, richer women acquired a greater degree of domestic authority and influence, delegating mundane and menial tasks to slaves and enjoying an active social life outside the home. They, nevertheless, remained under the control of fathers, husbands and guardians although increasing wealth and independence allowed them to take more of the initiative in public and in family matters. But they were never able to shrug off the traditional suspicion and discrimination vocalised by Roman men when they did exceed their role as *matronae*.

At the other end of the social spectrum was the slave. Both female and male slaves were, to their owners, 'property', pure and simple. It is hardly surprising, then, that slaves were expoited sexually on an ongoing basis. Women, in particular, were especially vulnerable from an early age, providing a safety valve for masters who were tired of their wives or needed to give them a break when pregnant or nursing an infant. Many wives were probably glad of this respite from serial sex and childbirth and connived at the infidelity, as they may have done at their husbands' philandering with freeborn women and *matronae*. Sheer lust was obviously another factor. And it was not just the men who exploited this servile sexual facility. Some women of the household were equally likely to seek a change and used male slaves as an outlet; one modern scholar has described the male slave as 'a form of dildo for the women of the master class'.[80] Slave women were also prey to other male slaves – sexual relations between them was permitted since it was one easy way of providing a ready supply of replacement help in the form of baby slaves.

For many slaves, life got even worse if he or she descended yet further down the social scale into prostitution, with its attendant humiliation, disease and abuses. Brothel keepers were among the most active buyers of *vernae*, women born into slavery. Excavated slave burial tombs in Rome have revealed many more male skeletons than females, suggesting, perhaps, that many women and girls were sold off, although the discrepancies may also be down to exposure of infant girls.

It was not always indescribably horrid though. Many slaves found mutual companionship and affection in marriages of sorts (they were banned from marrying), monogamous relationships called *contubernia*.[81] Funerary inscriptional evidence supports the literary evidence with references to *maritus, uxor* and *coniunx* – words for husband and wife identical to terminology used by freeborns.[82] The arrangements sometimes became so indistinguishable from legal marriages that some jurists, Ulpian and Paul for example, treated them in the same way. Some slaves did very well for themselves, as we shall see, in the bureaucracies of the emperors and 'married' freeborn women; others competed with their masters for women or prostitutes, one slave even killing his master, Pedanius Secundus, in a squabble over a prostitute.[83] The implications for slave and master after the passing of Augustus' moral legislation outlawing non-marital sexual relations, the *lex ulia de adulteriis coercendis*, remain unclear.

CHAPTER TWO

Marriage, Divorce and Adultery

So, the function of a Roman wife was to bear children and keep the home while her husband went about his work, advancing his career, his *cursus honorum,* or perfecting his trade. The very word for marriage, *matrimonium*, is rooted in *mater*, mother; marriage literally meant motherhood. In the early years of the Republic the Roman woman married into a state of *manus*, dependence before the law; she had little chance of initiating divorce, no rights over property and no jurisdiction over her children. If a woman's husband died when she was pregnant, the baby became the property of her late husband's family. A woman was someone else's property throughout her life. She was, first and foremost, dependent daughter, dependent wife and dependable mother.

Girls of the upper classes seem to have married, in general, earlier than their counterparts lower down the social scale: the former wed between their early and late teens while the latter tied the knot in their late teens and early twenties. As menarche usually occurred around the ages of thirteen and fourteen it seems very likely that some marriages were pre-pubescent.[1] Early marriage suited men; with it came social and political respectability, and sexual gratification – a married man could more easily propel himself along his *cursus honorum* and climb the ladder of political, military or forensic success. For the elite, it was important to arrange an appropriate match between a couple who were social equals, *digna condicia*. Romantic love was largely irrelevant, at best a fortunate development in the relationship over time; the production of babies, especially male babies who might become heirs and prolong the line, was the aim.

Arranged marriages were not necessarily the emotionally arid and restrictive contracts they are often made out to be; they probably involved more mutual consent, *concordia*, than we have actual evidence for. They were prudent arrangements designed to protect the family politically, economically and socially. No doubt Roman parents would have argued that the arrangement was intended to be in the daughter's best interests; how many twelve or thirteen-year-olds would have been in a position to make an informed decision about whom to marry?

There were restrictions on marriage including a bar on marriage to convicted adulteresses or those in a dubious profession: actors, dancers, prostitutes. *Incestum* originally prohibited second cousins and nearer relatives from marrying, but over time was relaxed to allow even first cousins to marry. *Incestum* was punishable by death.

The Apostle Paul lays down some of the basics in his *Opinions*, from about AD 150: a couple can get engaged before or after puberty; marriage cannot take place without the consent of the father where he retains *patria potestas*; the insane cannot be married, and subsequent insanity is not grounds for dissolving a valid marriage; a freedman who marries his patroness or her daughter will be sentenced to hard labour in the mines; a man cannot have both a wife and a concubine; marriage is ended either by divorce, death or captivity (by a foreign power) lasting over three years.[2] A woman was not allowed to get engaged to a prepubescent male.[3]

The betrothal was sealed with a kiss and by slipping an iron ring (*anulus pronubus*) onto the third finger of the bride's left hand. According to Aulus Gellius this finger was significant because it is connected by the autonomic nervous system to the heart.[4] A man or woman who got engaged or married without terminating an existing betrothal was guilty of disgraceful behaviour, *infamia*. Under Severus a man could prosecute an unfaithful fiancée for *stuprum* and adultery, although there was still no corresponding obligation for him to be faithful so long as his indiscretion did not involve a married woman or an unmarried Roman citizen.

There were five types of marriage. In *usus* the wife passed from *patria potestas* into her husband's family after one year of uninterrupted cohabitation and the wife became mother of the family, *materfamilias*. In *manus* the wife came under the control (*manus*) of her husband and her property became his; for a woman, marrying into *manus* also meant renouncing her religion and assuming her husband's; she adopted his gods and his ancestors.

Confarreatio, sharing of bread, was a rare religious ceremony largely restricted to patrician families and to those applying to hold various priesthoods for which birth from a *confarreatio* marriage was obligatory. *Coemptio* was a legal procedure in which the husband notionally buys his wife. He paid one 'penny' to the father or guardian and received his bride in return.[5] *Sine manu* afforded the husband no rights over the wife's property.

Marriage itself was in some ways rather nebulous. No ceremony was legally required; the trigger was the intention of both parties to cohabit and form a union together in which they would recognise each other as man and wife, *affectio maritalis*.[6] Once she was over her husband's threshold, the bride assumed the status and responsibilities of a *matrona*. According to Modestinus, marriage was the union of a man and a woman and the sharing of the rest of their lives.[7] Ulpian declared that just having sex does not a marriage make;[8] what does make a marriage is a favourable disposition toward the idea of marriage. A man could get married without actually going to the ceremony – *in absentia* – through a letter of intent or through a messenger slave; the woman had to show up.[9] Ulpian tells the amusing story where Cinna said that if a man married by proxy and then fell into the Tiber on his way home from a dinner party (presumably celebrating his *in absentia* wedding) then the wife must still mourn his death.

Wedding ceremonies may have been optional but they were common.[10] Our evidence for the Roman wedding ceremony is scanty to say the least; however, it is possible to piece together some detail from various sources. Typically, among middle and upper-class families, the bride was specially made up; her hair was done in a traditionally primitive style (*tutulus*); – separated into six locks with headbands (*vittae*) and piled on top in a cone (*meta*); the parting was done using an iron spearhead (*hasta recurva* or *caelibaris*); she wore a wreath of flowers and marjoram (*amaracus*). Her dress (*tunica recta*) – for one-time use – was a plain white tunic fastened with the 'knot of Hercules' (a good luck charm) which had been spun on a vintage loom; her transparent veil (*flammeum*) was highly symbolic, flame-coloured and matched her yellow shoes (*lutei socii*). Yellow was a quintessentially female colour made from saffron, the stamens of the crocus, which was used in treatment of some gynaecolocical disorders such as period pain. Jewels would have been worn by the rich; the bride would be dressed by friends and female relatives. She would surrender her childhood dolls, toys and girl's dress (*toga praetexta*) to the household gods.

The ceremony took place in the house of the bride's father (who paid), where the words of consent were spoken (*Ubi tu Gaius, ego Gaia*) and the matron of honour (*pronuba*) joined the couple's right hands (*dextrarum iunctio*), the defining point of the ceremony. A pig was sacrificed and the *tabulae nuptales*, the marriage contract (where there was one) was presented by the *auspex*, the priest in attendance to take the omens, signed and the first instalment of the dowry handed over. The guests cried out *'feliciter!'* (Good luck!) Then there was the feast (*cena*) paid for by the groom (limited by Augustus to 1,000 sesterces) after which the bride was formally taken from her mother's arms and escorted to the groom's house by three boys whose parents had still to be living: one on the bride's right, one on the left and the third in front carrying a torch. The crowds would chant *Thalassius* as they passed by. Obscene verses (*Fescennine*) were sung and walnuts were thrown to foster fertility. On arrival at the groom's house the torch was thrown away and the bride smeared the doorway with oil fat and sheep's wool, indicative of impending domesticity and fertility. The groom lifted the bride over the threshold to avoid that unlucky stumble – reminiscent of the Sabine women carried away by the Romans. She then touched fire and water and was led to the bedroom by *univirae*. Wedding songs were now sung to encourage the consummation of the marriage. The bedroom was festooned with flowers, greenery and fruit to promote fertility. The bride woke the following morning a *matrona*, and started the day with her first offering to her new household gods, the *penates* and *lares*. The next few days would be spent in partying and more celebration.

Statius' epithalamium (*Silvae* 1, 2) gives more detail. The divinely beautiful Violentilla surpasses all the *matronae* of Latium and is urged by the goddess Venus to make the most of her beauty and renounce her chastity for Stella, her soon-to-be husband. She is financially independent but her mind is richer still. Much of the content of the poem is conventional but the allusion to wealth and intelligence is an interesting indication, perhaps, of what Lucius Arruntius Stella was really looking for in a wife.

Superstition, practicalities and religion played their parts; there were certain days on which marriage ceremonies were avoided because they were deemed unlucky. Kalends, Nones and Ides were out because, as Varro tells us, the days after these were 'black days'; *Mundus Cereris*, the three days of the year (2 August, 5 October, and 8 November) when ghosts were afoot because the doors of

Hades (*mundus*) gaped open; the Lemuralia, the 9, 11 and 13 of May devoted to celebrating the festival of the dead, hence, *they marry ill who marry in May*; 18–21 February for similar reasons; the Parentalia in honour of family ancestors; May and early June because time was better spent farming the land, or because the cleaning of the temple of Vesta by the Vestal Virgins was not completed until the 15 May; 1, 9 and 23 March were to be avoided because the dancing priests of Mars, the Salii, were moving the shields. In short, a wedding should take place on a happy day. One famous anecdote from the end of the second century BC involved Caecilia, who was married to Metellus; she was anxious to find out what the future held for her betrothed niece so she and the niece took up post in a temple and waited... the gods were reticent, until the bored niece asked to sit down next to her aunt. Her aunt innocently, but prophetically, invited her to take her place – and dropped down dead. Niece had literally taken aunt's place; Metellus then married the niece.

Happy day notwithstanding, so long as three main conditions were met then the marriage was permitted and legal. The first was *conubium* – legal right to marry; slaves had no *conubium* and *conubium* did not exist between Roman citizens and foreigners. The second required that the couple had reached marriageable age, or puberty, twelve for girls and fourteen for boys. The third was consent between the man and his wife. Marriage and betrothal (*sponsalia*) were both consensual in Roman law; according to Paul a marriage only exists if all parties are in agreement. According to Ulpian, non-objection on the part of the girl was tantamount to consent; she could only refuse where there were questions regarding the moral integrity of the groom.

Sham weddings were not unknown during the early Empire: Nero 'married' a male lover, Pythagoras, in AD 64 and, according to Suetonius, in between raping a Vestal Virgin and committing incest with his mother, had a young boy, Sporus, castrated before marrying him. Around the same time Sempronius Gracchus married a boy cornet player with a dowry of 400,000 sesterces.[11] Valeria Messalina, while wife of Claudius, astonishingly married a common Roman citizen, much to the surprise and indignation of her husband, the emperor of Rome. Martial describes the wedding between Callistratus and Afro, complete with dowry.

Women and drink did not make a happy mix. Whatever its effect on men, alcohol was seen as a catalyst for sexual infelicities in women. Juvenal probably spoke for many contemporary men when he asked, 'What does love care when she is drunk?'[12] Servius says that in the old days women were forbidden to drink wine, except at a few religious festivals, citing as evidence Egnatius Metennius, who whipped his wife to death for drinking from a pitcher; he literally got away with murder when tried by Romulus.[13] According to Valerius Maximus, women in the old days did not drink because it led to depravity; a drunk woman was only one step removed from a fornicating woman.[14]

Pliny the Elder leaves a number of unfortunate drink-related stories in his chapter on viticulture. He tells how, according to Fabius Pictor, a *matrona* was starved to death by her family because she broke open the box containing the keys to the wine cellar. He explains how Cato asserted the right of male relatives to kiss their women on meeting, not to show affection or courtesy, but to detect whether they had been drinking – social breathalising. Gnaeus Domitius judged that one woman had drunk more than was good for her, and without her husband's knowledge; he fined her a sum equal to the value of her dowry.[15] Alcohol was implicated in the exile of Julia, Augustus' daughter, to Pandateria – not only did she have to put up with lonely isolation but her father decreed that the island would be alcohol-free.

Counselling for alcohol abuse or wife-battering was doubtless unavailable, but there was a form of marriage guidance. The temple of Juno Viriplaca (husband appeaser) on the Palatine Hill offered reconciliation between bickering couples.[16]

Roman girls could be betrothed at twelve and married within the year.[17] An example of a thirteen-year-old wife is an inscription found in Gaul; it remembers Blandinia Martiola who died aged eighteen years, nine months and five days, the wife of Sequanian, a plasterer. We have already met Aurelia Philematium; her marriage when she was seven was precocious even by Roman standards.[18]

Pliny had already been married twice before when, aged forty or so, he wed the much younger Calpurnia Fabata in AD 100. We have witnessed Quintilian's grief at the death of his nineteen-year-old wife, the mother of two deceased sons even then. We have also noted Pliny's concern that the young Minicia died before she could be married off. Faggura, wife of Julianus, was married and a mother by the time she was fourteen years old.[19] Tullia, Cicero's daughter, got engaged when she was twelve, married at sixteen and was widowed when she was twenty-two. Octavia, daughter of the emperor Claudius, married at thirteen while Agrippina, mother of Nero, wed when she was twelve. On the other hand it was not unknown for some elite women to marry later; Julia, Caesar's permissive daughter, was twenty when she married Pompey; Agrippina Maior was about eighteen when she and Germanicus tied the knot in AD 4; and Antonia Minor was twenty or so when she married Drusus.

Harkness shows how inscriptional evidence backs up the early age of female marriage, particularly in the middle and upper class families, who were more likely to be able to afford tombstones. From the 171 inscriptions in the study, sixty-seven (39 per cent) showed women married before they were fifteen and 127 before age nineteen (74 per cent).[20]

A fascinating marriage contract from 13 BC survives from Egypt and, although it probably owes as much to Egyptian practice and legislation as it does to Roman, it is, nevertheless, interesting. Thermion and Apollonius, and Thermion's guardian, agree to share their lives together (*affectio maritalis*) and that Thermion has delivered a dowry, including a pair of gold earrings weighing three quarters and some silver drachmas. He will now feed and clothe her; he will not abuse her verbally or physically, kick her out or marry another woman – if he does any of these things, the dowry goes back. For her part, she will fulfil her obligations, she will not sleep away from the home without his permission, she will not wreck the house or have an affair – if she does, she loses the dowry.[21] Cato the Elder was probably not altogether typical when he famously expelled Manilius from the Senate for kissing his wife in front of their daughter and admitted that *he* only ever kissed his wife during thunderstorms.[22]

Adultery on the part of a woman could be an expensive business if discovered. A husband whose wife had been found guilty might retain one sixth of the dowry; as he would have custody of the children he would also keep one sixth for each child up to a maximum of three children. After Augustus' *Julian* laws, a wife found guilty of adultery was punished by exile and a fine equal to half her dowry. As we have seen, double standards prevailed in the interpretation of culpability in extramarital sex and adultery. An adulterous husband attracted no stigma. An adulterous women did, and much worse, as Cato the Elder tells. If a man discovers his wife in the act he can kill her with impunity; when the boot is on the other foot, she can do absolutely nothing. We should perhaps take with a pinch of salt some of the stories narrated by satirists Horace and Juvenal about cuckolded husbands subjecting their wives' lovers to castration, beatings, being urinated on by the kitchen slaves, anal rape by the husband or his slaves, or anal penetration with a red mullet. Under the *Lex Julia,* women convicted of adultery joined that group of fallen and stigmatised women which included prostitutes, actresses, dancing girls, women with criminal records – collectively, the shameful, *probrosae* – and were forbidden to marry freeborn citizens of Rome. They could not henceforth testify in a court of law, nor could they, while unmarried, inherit. Prostitution was sometimes the only escape. The cuckolded husband had to act quickly and instigate divorce proceedings promptly, otherwise he could be convicted of complicity, as a pimp. A father could kill his daughter's lover, whatever his status, but he had to murder his daughter too. An adulterous man could expect a severe fine and *relegatio* – temporary exile.

The old slavewoman in Plautus' *Mercator* vocalises this hypocrisy, bewailing the legal double standard and declaring that there would be more men living on their own than there are women if they were judged the same in law.[23] To Ovid, the man who worried about his wife's adultery was nothing short of provincial.[24] At the Imperial level, Scribonia was divorced by Augustus because of her intolerance to his affairs; her long-lasting successor, Livia, was much more understanding. Claudius' wandering wives were sensible enough to ensure that his bed was warmed by surrogates when they fled in the night to their paramours. The double standard was not lost on Plutarch, who noted that a husband who bars his wife from the pleasures in which he himself indulges is like a man who surrenders to the enemy and tells his wife to go on fighting.

Accusations of adultery and other sexual improprieties were, of course, popular and effective weapons in the armouries of invidious rival politicians and unsympathetic historians. Julia Avita Mamaea, niece of empress Julia Domna and Septimius Severus, and sister of Julia Soaemias Bassiana (mother of Elagabalus), wielded considerable power in the Severan dynasty. She must be the only elite women of that much-maligned family not accused of adultery by later historians but who was accused of adultery by her own mother, Julia Maesa. In order to promote her son to the succession, Julia Mamaea confirmed her mother's story, admitting that Alexander, like Elagabalus, was born of an adulterous affair with Caracella.[25]

The anonymous *To Herennius on Rhetoric,* written about 85 BC, encapsulates the 'no-win' situation women found themselves in when it came to adultery and the compromising of *pudicitia.* The author argues that if a woman commits one crime, for example *stuprum*, then she is just as culpable of any number of other crimes, such as poisoning. The strange rationale behind this judgement was that if a woman can bring herself to submit to the foulest of desires then she must be frightened of a lot of people including her husband, parents and so on; such fear leads inevitably to a wish to kill them. Conversely, the woman convicted of poisoning must, by the same token, be an unchaste adulteress because she could only have been driven to poisoning by something as foul as 'filthy desire and out-of-control lust'. Indeed, how could a woman's body remain pure once her mind had been polluted? Men, by the way, were immune from this; they were capable of different forms of evil generated by different passions, but for women, one single passion drives all evil deeds.

Divorce was uncomplicated – it simply required the evaporation of *affectio maritalis* by one or both parties. And, by the end of the Republic, it became relatively common. Evidence for allegedly rampant divorcing comes largely from Seneca, Juvenal and Martial – not the most objective of social commentators – they saw it as yet another sign of permissiveness among women. The woman who marries so frequently doesn't actually marry – she's a legalised adulteress, according to Martial;[26] a whore offends him less than a serial divorcer. Rapsaet-Charlier's study of 562 women of senatorial rank and their marital activity between 10 BC and AD 200 revealed only twenty-seven definite and twenty-four possible divorces, twenty of which were in imperial families, mainly Julio-Claudians.[27] Five of the definites were claimed by one permissive woman, Vistilla, who, Pliny the Elder tells us, had seven children by six different husbands.[28] In Roman divorce, the father usually had custody over the children, a situation which would be a powerful factor in a wife's decision to make the break.

Marriage was often a political expedient – for men. The merry-go-round of political marriage is well-illustrated by a glance at the five wives of Pompey. Antistia was his first wife, the daughter of a praetor called Antistius whom Pompey impressed when defending himself against a charge of possessing stolen goods in 86 BC. Antistius offered Pompey his daughter's hand, and Pompey accepted, but things ended badly; Antistia's father was executed because of his connection with Pompey, and her bereft mother committed suicide. In 82 BC Sulla persuaded Pompey to divorce Antistia so that he could marry his stepdaughter, Aemilia. Aemilia was pregnant by her husband, M. Acilius Glabrio, and reluctant to marry Pompey; she eventually did, but died in childbirth.

Q. Mucius Scaevola was the father of Pompey's third wife, Mucia Tertia, whom he married in 79 BC. Their marriage lasted until 62 BC, and during this time they had a daughter, Pompeia, and two sons, Gnaeus and Sextus. According to Asconius, Plutarch, and Suetonius, Mucia was unfaithful – Suetonius and Cicero allege she had an affair with Caesar – and Pompey divorced her. In 59 BC Pompey married Caesar's daughter Julia, who was already engaged to Q. Servilius Caepio. Caepio took umbrage, so Pompey offered him his own daughter in Julia's place – although Pompeia was engaged to Sulla's son, Faustus, at the time. Julia miscarried soon after fainting at seeing bloodstained clothing, which she had taken to indicate that her husband had been killed. In 54 BC Julia fell pregnant again, but died in childbirth; her infant daughter died a few days later. Pompey's fifth wife was Cornelia, daughter of Metellus Scipio and the widow of Publius Crassus.

In the early days of the republic, serial marriage was, however, rare. Plutarch says quite oddly that divorce was restricted to men divorcing women on certain specific grounds: where the wife poisoned the children, stole the house keys or drank (too much) wine. Where other, spurious, reasons were offered as grounds, the men were punished by confiscation of their property, half of which went to Ceres, the other half to the wife.[28] According to Dionysius of Halicarnassus there were no divorces at all in the first 520 years of Rome's existence.[29] Spurius Carvilius Ruga spoilt it all in 231 BC when he successfully sued for divorce because his wife was unable to bear children and provide an heir – to Spurius and most other Romans, the very point of their marriage. The case is interesting in itself. Apart from blindly assuming that it was his wife who was the infertile partner, Ruga was not required to pay the penalty even though his grounds were spurious; a legal precedent was set, allowing men to divorce their wives with virtual impunity. Later, remarriage was common – given the ease of divorce, high mortality rates and low life expectancy, and the pressure on Romans to be married and produce children.

A dowry (*dos*), certainly among the wealthier classes, was an expected, though not legally required, part of the bride's baggage. By the early empire, around 1 million sesterces payable in three annual instalments was the norm among the wealthier classes. It became the husband's property but was recoverable on divorce, or if the husband died after the death of his father-in-law. Valerius Maximus records that Gnaeus Cornelius Scipio Calvus, while on active service in Spain, requested leave to go home to arrange his daughter's dowry. The Senate was reluctant to allow such a key commander to leave the field and voted a dowry out of the public purse worth 40,000 asses – a small amount compared with later dowries, but significant for the time. The precedent for such public largesse was set around 280 BC when the Senate voted a dowry for the daughter of the famously incorruptible Gaius Fabricius Luscinus Monocularis, whose family was in financial straits.

Polybius tells how Scipio Africanus generously paid the dowries of his two daughters in one-off payments to their respective husbands, Tiberius Gracchus and Scipio Nasica – fifty talents each (about £1.25 million today). In 50 BC, Cicero was unable to find the money to pay the third instalment of Tullia's dowry in her marriage to Dolabella. Cicero toyed with the idea of arranging a divorce and writing off the first two instalments which had been paid. Financial embarrassment came again in 47 BC when he divorced Terentia and had to find the money to repay the dowry; his scheme to remarry and win a new dowry failed when the marriage to Publilia, his well-off ward, ended after a few months. Terentia, however, remarried and lived to the age of 103.

Aemilius Paulus married one of his daughters, Aemilia Paulla Secunda, to a member of the illustrious, though by then not so affluent, Aelia dynasty – Q. Aelius Tubero – giving two pounds in silver dowry from the booty collected after his victory over Perseus of Macedon at the Battle of Pydna in 171 BC.

We need go no further than a more than generous Pliny to realise the importance of the dowry. Twice he generously contributes to the dowries of young brides. Once to the daughter of Quintilianus who needed clothes and a retinue of servants appropriate to her new husband's social standing; the other to Calvina, a relative of his who was deep in debt. As well as contributing 100,000 sesterces to her dowry he paid off her debts, making himself sole creditor, and then wrote off her debt to him. Aulus Gellius records that dowry recovery had become so complicated by the end of the republic that Sulpicius Rufus wrote a book on it. Repayments were made in three instalments unless the husband had been proven adulterous, in which case it was repaid in one lump sum. After Augustus' *Julian* laws a wife found guilty of adultery was punished by exile and a fine equal to half her dowry.

The dowry was not a gift to the husband; its purpose was to help defray the extra costs incurred in accommodating and maintaining the wife and possibly her slaves. The dowry was usually invested in land with only the profits available to spend.

Dowry recovery was, not surprisingly, open to abuse. Valerius Maximus tells how a Caius Titinius, married to Fannia, made a claim to retain her dowry when he divorced her on the grounds of her alleged *stuprum*. The judge, Caius Marius, knew that Titinius had foreknowledge of Fannia's louche behaviour and had only married her in order to procure the dowry. Fannia got off with a nominal fine; Titinius received a fine equal in value to the dowry. Fannia was able to return the favour to Marius when she later concealed him during his flight from Sulla.[30]

Marriage was very much a pragmatic affair: its objective, as we know, was to produce legitimate children, to maintain the birth rate, to ensure the survival of a particular family, to supply the Roman army and bureaucracy, the land and the law with a source of recruits. Even Rome's hedonistic love poets acknowledged the importance of this. Catullus in his wedding hymn urges the wedding night production of sentries to man the frontiers. Propertius is much less enthusiastic; 'why should I breed sons for Rome's triumphs?' he asks, 'No blood of mine will ever produce a soldier.'[31]

Soranus, the Greek physician practicing in Rome around AD 100, says it all when he remarks that women are married for the sake of bearing children and heirs, and not for pleasure and enjoyment.[32] Because she was unable to bear him children, Turia was happy not only to divorce her husband but also to find him another, fertile, wife; she would then act as a sister or mother-in-law in the new *ménage à trois*. Turia's husband was wild with rage at her suggestion,[33] preferring to stay married, even though it would mean the end of his family line. Sulla divorced his allegedly barren wife, Cloelia.[34]

Trimalchio, in Petronius' *Satyricon*, has no such qualms and congratulates himself on *not* divorcing Fortunata because she failed to give him children.[35] Catullus, in his *epithalamium*, tells how you need to have Hymen's blessing in order to produce children – parents cannot rely on offspring without her blessing. Junia, the bride, must be sure to let her husband have sex with her, in case he goes looking for it elsewhere; indeed, Catullus urges the couple to mess around as much as they like and have children as soon as they can.

Suetonius would have us believe that Augustus' many affairs were motivated not through lust but through cunning, using the women to expose the intrigues of their partners, his political opponents. Lust, though, was probably a factor when, out to dinner, he led the wife of an ex-consul from the dining room to their bedroom, and later returned her to the party, her ears burning and her hair all over the place.[36]

In 18 BC Augustus, no doubt all the wiser from personal experience, was sufficiently concerned about the permissiveness in his Empire, particularly the growing infrequency of marriage, the increasing levels of adultery, and the falling birth rate, to introduce the *lex Julia de maritandis ordinibus* and other moral legislation in a bid to reduce adultery, encourage marriage and increase the population. Romans needed to be reminded what marriage was for: it was for producing children.[37] The marriage which ended in the death of one of the partners rather than in divorce had become, it seems, a thing of the past.[38]

Adultery had always been a private affair, a civil matter, usually dealt with within the family; it was now open to the glaring spotlight of public scrutiny. It was illegal to marry an adulteress; under Constantine both parties were sentenced to death.[39] Augustus' own adulterous daughter, Julia, was a notable convict under her father's legislation, and was exiled to Pandateria, modern day Ventotene in the Tyrhennian Sea.

If Augustus had to look for an exemplar of adulterous behaviour then he need go no further than his adoptive uncle, Julius Caesar. Caesar was implicated in a string of adulterous affairs at the highest level: they included Postumia, wife of Sulpicius; Lollia, wife of Aulus Gabinius, Tertulla, wife of Marcus Crassus; Mucia, Pompey's wife. Servilia Caepionis, though, was different – she was the woman he loved, according to Suetonius, and mother of Marcus Brutus. He lavished a pearl worth 6 million sesterces on her and sold off some properties to her on the cheap; the price, according to Cicero, was discounted by one third because Servilia was allegedly prostituting Tertia, her daughter, to Caesar. The armies, too, were up to speed on his adultery in Gaul: 'Men of Rome, watch your wives; we're bringing home the bald-headed adulterer. In Gaul you fucked your way through a fortune, which you borrowed here in Rome.' Foreign queens were among his conquests; they included Eunoe of Mauretania and, of course, Cleopatra VII.

Famous cases of adultery by women resulting in divorce include Pompey vs Mucia, Lucullus vs Claudia and Caesar vs Pompeia after the Bona Dea scandal, not for adultery but for being implicated in a sacrilegious incident which brought ignominy on the state and on the sanctity of the Vestal Virgins – the High Priest's wife must be above suspicion.

Under the new Augustan laws, men lost the right to kill their wives and fathers their daughters; they still could still slay their wives' partners if the transgressor was a slave or freedman and if *in flagrante delicto* in the marital home. Dangerous confusion must have arisen, because fathers were still allowed to murder their adulterous daughters if they killed the adulterer at the same time. Valerius Maximus provides the few recorded cases of women being put to death by their fathers: Pontius Aufidianus, as we know, executed his daughter when she was seduced by her teacher, Fannius Saturninus; Fannius suffered the same fate. Atilius, an ex-prostitute himself, killed his daughter because she was blemished by *stuprum*.[40] The law was amended by Tiberius to put an end to the practice where 'respectable' women registered as prostitutes to facilitate their extramarital affairs.

Aulus Gellius[41] probably summed up the public, or rather male public, mood when he quoted Augustus' speech in support of his legislation in the Senate in 17 BC. 'If we could survive without a wife, citizens of Rome, all of us would do without that nuisance, but since nature has decreed that we neither manage comfortably without them, nor live in any way without them, we must plan for our lasting preservation rather than for our temporary pleasure.' Varro assumes the same air of resignation. 'A husband must either put a stop to his wife's faults or else he must put up with them. In the first case he makes his wife a more attractive woman, in the second he makes himself a better man'.[42]

Naturally, there were efforts to circumvent the legislation: Suetonius says that attempts by men to delay marriage and the birth of children by engagements to young, prepubescent girls were met with stricter legislation relating to subsequent divorces and the length of engagements. Fiancés had been exempt from the penalties paid by bachelors; now Augustus voided betrothals unless the marriage took place within two years. Earlier in his life, Augustus himself (when Octavian) had betrothed his daughter, Julia, to fifteen-year-old L. Junius Silanus, one of Mark Anthony's sons, when she was two years old.

Ultimately the *lex Julia* was unsuccessful; the benefits of childlessness were too great and too attractive.[43] The advantages of having a mistress – a woman of a young man's choosing, not his father's – or of a courtesan, off-limits in the marriage stakes, or of an independent woman from a lower class, were all too obvious and desirable.

CHAPTER THREE

'The Incomplete Woman' and Sexual Medicine

Public medicine as practiced in Rome, particularly from the latter years of the Republic, was actually Greek medicine practiced usually by Greek physicians; before that it was very much a domestic affair – family medicine administered by *pater-* and *materfamilias* largely based on traditional folk remedies.[1]

Graeco-Roman sexual medicine all started with Hesiod in the eighth century BC. He cited a folk tradition which held that men suffered more than women from the effects of heat, diminishing their sexual performance and the production of semen from its sources, the head and knees 'in the draining heat, when goats are plumpest and wine is finest, and women are on heat but men are weak' (*Works and Days* 582–588).

The Hippocratics and Galen then taught that producing semen drained a man, so man had to be careful not to overdo it sexually for fear of depleting his *pneuma*, his life spirit. Sex kills. This self-control in men was to endure throughout the classical period, characterising the axiomatic good and dominant social and political behaviour in a Roman. Women, on the other hand, had cold and clammy bodies, incapable of producing the heat required to produce sperm; instead they had menstrual fluid which formed the basis of new life. Aristotle championed the belief that the female body was inferior to the male: ergo, women were considered inferior to men; incomplete men indeed.

The *Hippocratic Corpus* is a key work in classical medicine: it collects a number of medical treatises dating mainly from the fifth and fourth centuries BC including eleven obsterics and gynaecology subjects out of a total of sixty or so. Among them are *Semen* or *Generation* or *Intercourse; the Nature of the Child or Pregnancy;*

the Diseases of Women; Sterile Women; the Diseases of Young Women or Girls; Superfoetation; the Nature of Woman and *Excision of the Foetus*. Although much of the *Corpus* was written when the Roman Republic was in its infancy, its authority persisted well into the Empire, and beyond.

Diocles of Carystus and Cleophantus both wrote a *Gynaecology*. Herophilos (335–280) produced nine medical books (all lost) including a *Maiotikon* – a midwifery text; he is the father of human dissection and founded the medical school in Alexandria, a centre of excellence which was particularly important around the Mediterranean because the dissection of cadavers was banned on religious grounds in Rome. Only Alexandria had special dispensation to dissect.

Surgeons were generalists with a list which would have taken in fractures and dislocations, trepanning of the skull, cataract operations, maxillofacial surgery, ENT procedures, lithotomy, and obstetrics and gynaecology. Alexander Philalethes was the author of another *Gynaecology*.

Pliny the Elder, who cynically considered medicine to be no more than a down payment on death, reflected the common Roman distrust of Greek doctors and medicine, deploring their greed and the legal impunity under which they worked. Pliny is somewhat disingenuous though; medical science constitutes a key part of his expansive *Natural History* – it covers thirteen out of the thirty-seven of his books. His ambiguity is reflected in his attitude to women, both as medical authors and as sources of medical information. For example, the cure for a rabid dog bite reported by the mother of a Roman soldier wins his approval; on the other hand, the authority of two female Greek medical authors, Elephantis and Salpe, is considered dubious, simply because they disagree on certain matters; best then not to believe them at all.[2] Indeed, Pliny adds, what they write is also told by midwives and prostitutes – which repudiates not only the considerable skills of contemporary midwives but female medical writers in general. Both professions were generally highly respected among fellow scientists and medical professionals.

Hippocrates was not without his critics. At the end of the first century AD the *Gynaikeia* by Soranus of Ephesus was published in which the author disputed Hippocrates' claim that male foetuses incline to the right of the womb, female to the left.[3] Bedside manner and the patient-doctor relationship were covered in the Hippocratic writings; with regard to women, the authors emphasise the close relationship necessary between patient and doctor. With women and girls self-control must be exercised at all times.

The midwives of Rome owe a lot to Agnodice; she was the first professional midwife (*maiae* or *obstetrices*), of ancient Greece, practising around 500 BC when it was illegal in Athens for women or slaves to study or practise medicine. To get round this, Agnodice dressed as a man in her medical lectures. The bad news was that when she qualified, women rejected her (because she presented as a man) until she revealed that she was a woman; a certain Areopagus accused her of corrupting her patients and charged her with practicing illegally. Influential Athenian ladies protested and had the law abolished, after which women were permitted to practise midwifery and medicine, and were paid for it.

Soranus authored twenty or so books on biological and medical science. The *Gynaikeia* was one of the first illustrated medical textbooks; later it was abridged and translated into Latin – probably in the sixth century, by Muscio, who based his *Gynaecia* on it. The first part constitutes what is probably the world's first MCQ book, with questions and answers on anatomy, embryology, childbirth and neonatal care; the second part covers pathology.

Soranus' original establishes the gold standard for finding the best of midwives: she should know theory and practice, including therapy, dietetics, surgery and infection control; she will be calm, reassuring and sympathetic; always sober, as she never knows when she might be called out to an emergency; she will be discreet (as she will share in many secrets of her patients' lives) and she will not submit to vulgar superstition. All very professional, and indicative of the fact that in obstetrics and gynaecology much of the care and treatment was the preserve of the midwife rather than of the doctor; the midwife was, in effect, as much a doctor as a midwife, assuming a high level of literacy and scientific knowledge. We know of Claudia Trophima and Poblicia Aphe who probably met those criteria.[4] The well-named *obstetrix* Hygiae is commemorated on a tombstone by two of her tent mates (*contubernales*) – Marius Orthrus and Apollonius.[5]

Soranus knew what made a good wet nurse too, even though he was a firm advocate of mother's breast is best. She should be between twenty and forty years old, and should have had two or three children herself; she should be big, and of a good complexion. Her breasts should be of medium size, not rigid but soft with no wrinkles, the nipples neither big nor too small; she should be placid, a Greek, and well turned out. This insistence on a calm temperament perhaps betrays a concern regarding the physical abuse of infants; Soranus says that angry women are like maniacs when they drop the babies or handle them roughly just because they cry endlessly. We have a letter from the end of the second century BC advising a new mother on how best to select a competent wet nurse: she should be Greek, modest, clean, alert and sober; she will offer the breast when *she* thinks it's time, *not* when the infant demands; she should be calm and induce a suitably equable environment for the baby, bathing him or her from time to time, not all of the time.[6]

Two contracts for the hiring of wet nurses for foundling slave children have survived from 13 BC in Alexandria. Theodote signs up for eighteen months to provide her pure and unadulterated milk to baby Tyche; if Tyche should die (it proceeds, in a matter-of-fact sort of way) then Theodote will take on another child, agreeing not have sex with her husband nor (in something of a *non sequitur*) get pregnant while she is nursing the infant. Scribonius Largus (around AD 1–50), court physician to Claudius, reinforces the Hippocratic dictum banning abortion and the use of abortifacients.

Galen of Pergamon (b. about AD 129) took on the mantle of expert on all things medical in the second century. Much of his prodigious output is extant – nearly 3 million words in Greek alone, making him responsible for about 10 per cent of all surviving Greek writing. Galen arrived in Rome in AD 162 and lectured, wrote and demonstrated extensively, particularly on anatomy, using the cadavers of pigs and other farm animals, apes and an elephant. His findings were published in a number of books, including *Anatomical Procedures* and *On the Dissection of the Muscles*. In the latter he ascribes musculature to the penis but omits muscles in female genitalia and the womb. Central to his teachings was, in common with his predecessors, the belief that women were inferior to men; how? Because women are physically colder; women have all the bits that men have, the only difference being that in women the parts are internal whereas in men they are external. Women are men turned inside out. Galen believed that women had no need for facial or body hair because they did not need to look impressive in the way that men do (with their beards); neither did women need hair to keep them warm – because they spent most of their time in the house. This, of course, ignores the fact that women did actually go out when they worked in the fields or in shops, or attended the theatre or the games.[7] A later *Gynaecology* was published by Philumenus, at the close of the second century.

Doctors were always up against the ubiquitous amulets, potions and incantations of the fringe and folkey medical practitioners, the quacks, root cutters (*rhizotomoi*), *herbarii,* the practitioners of magic, the *magi* and other charlatans who damaged the reputation of the conventional medical profession. An example of the pseudo-medical paraphernalia comes in the shape of an Egyptian haematite fertility amulet excavated near Welwyn; it bears a picture of a uterus, a scarab beetle and the inscription 'Ororiouth' – the name of the spirit which protected against women's diseases.[8]

Some public baths were alleged to offer healing qualities. For example, at Aquae Sulis (Bath) the temple of Sulis Minerva was a magnet for the sick and infirm. We know that women routinely visited the shrines dedicated to Sulis Minerva there, and other such temples around the Roman world from the discovery of curse tablets, and *ex votos* – models of parts of the female anatomy – breasts in wood, terracotta, bronze and ivory. One such was discovered at Wroxeter showing a case of what is possibly mastitis. Every female body part and organ is represented: female breast and uterus votives probably indicated gratitude for the birth of a child; a large number of male and female sexual organs (compared to an untypically small number of the usually copious hands and feet) may well suggest the prevalence of sexually transmitted infections, for example at the Campetti sanctuary in Veii. The symptoms of gonococcal disease must have inspired some of these male genital votives; they include urethritis, cystitis and urethral stricture, as well as phimosis, hydocele, scrotal varix and testicular cancer. Concentrations of children and pregnant women votives at Massigny-les-Vitteaux near Dijon and of swaddled infants and men and women with exaggerated genitalia at Essarois may be a sign of temples dedicated to fertility and childbirth.

Most doctors were men, but there were many female doctors, *medicae,* lots of them slaves or freedwomen. Theodore Priscianus,[9] in the fourth century AD, dedicated his book on gynaecology to Victoria, the *sweet teacher of my art.* Aspasia was a second-century obstetrician and gynaecologist; we have an inscription referring to a *medica a mammis* – breast disease specialist.[10]

Most medical writers too were men, but there were many female authors. Metrodora was a second-century-AD author of a treatise on gynaecology, diseases of the kidney, uterus and stomach. The uterus was originally thought to have been a mobile organ with all the health problems that that caused, but advances in dissection by Alexandrian times showed it to be fixed and could not move into the lungs, for example. Metrodora is also noted for the exciting advances she made in gynaecological pathology, her expertise in digital examination and the use of the vaginal speculum. Pliny's *Natural History* names female practitioners as sources for his own work: Elephantis, Lais, Olympias of Thebes, Salpe and Sotira. Galen quotes Elephantis' cure for alopecia; she was also the author of a famous book on sexual positions – a Roman *Kama Sutra*. Suetonius tells that Tiberius packed a copy when he left for his debauched retreat on Capri; Martial says it is '[a book] with intriguing new ways of making love'.[11] Aspasia, in the sixth century AD, wrote works on gynaecological surgery and abortion.

Despite the influx of foreign doctors, the copious voluminous textbooks, the exploding advances in medical knowledge and the libraries and medical schools, the gods continued to offer a powerful, persuasive alternative. As we shall see in the chapter on sexuality in religion, there was a divine entity responsible for every stage of life – from conception through to death. The suspicions surrounding the medical profession, the disagreements on the best possible course of clinical action, the cost, and the prospect of enduring surgery and other painful procedures in an anaesthesia-free, septic world would be quite enough to steer the patient away from the doctor towards the gods in a desperate lunge towards a comparatively pain-free, survivable option. The second-century-AD orator Aelius Aristides gives a good example of this when he describes the confusion among his doctors over the best treatment for a huge tumour in his groin. Aristides ignores all the conflicting medical advice and puts his faith in the gods who prescribe a drug – the tumour shrank and all was well.[12]

Much of Graeco-Roman gynaecology centered on the womb, *hystera*, and on woman's ability to bear children – the essential medical difference between man and woman. Hippocrates[13] sums it all up when he asserts, 'Of the so-called women's diseases, the womb is the cause of them all.' The Hippocratic authors believed that women's bodies were made of flesh which was softer and more porous than men's,[14] an example being the female breast in which the woman's nourishment is converted into milk.[15] This porosity was caused by the absorption of moisture in the form of blood, released each month during the woman's period. The concept of porosity is linked to the knowledge that women leak, through the vagina, with menstrual fluid, sexual lubricant, locheal discharge and discharges from various infections.[16]

All manner of advice on sexual medicine was freely available. If you want to produce a boy, rapid thrusting during sex at the end of the woman's period is recommended; for a girl, things should be slightly less vigorous – and somewhat less spontaneous: the Roman should tie up his right testicle and have sex in the middle of his wife's period.[17] Blood clogging up the venous system in the breasts signifies that the woman is going mad – a physiological explanation for the age-old stereotype that women are naturally neurotic, erratic and unpredictable. Menstruation as a purging agent was a good thing, as indeed was epitaxis (nosebleed), which performed a similar role. Amenorrhoea caused all manner of physical and psychological problems; virgins were particularly susceptible, which, it was believed, explains their tendency to hang themselves or jump down wells to their deaths. In essence, the physiological differences between men and women supported the inarguable belief that women were physically and mentally inferior to men.

Empedocles (b. *c.* 493 BC) also believed that men were hotter than women.[18] Aristotle (384–322 BC) taught in *On the Generation of Animals* that men were more perfect than women. Why? Because women were less able than men to produce the heat vital for generation of the species – due to the debilitating effect of menstruation – women were incomplete, deformed males. In contrast to his Hippocratic contemporaries, Aristotle believed that menstruation was not a good thing; he pedalled the long-lasting myth that the womb had two separate compartments – a misconception used to explain the birth of twins: males were born from the right (hotter) chamber, and females from the left, with all its 'sinister' implications. He rejected the Hippocratic belief that hysteria in women was attributable to the movements of the womb and made tentative steps towards an understanding of the Fallopian tubes, largely unrecognised in antiquity. Some 600 or more years later Galen also subscribed to this temperature-based theory and the notion of the incomplete woman.

Herophilos (385–280 BC), in his *Midwifery*, also diverged from the Hippocratics because he believed the womb to be no different from other internal organs. Herophilos highlighted an analogous relationship between the male testicles and the female ovaries, believed that menstruation was the only physiological contribution women made to conception, and considered menstruation to be an illness.[19]

Enemas and pessaries were a common weapon in the armoury of women's medicine, which also often involved remedies made from various potions. Some of these were applied topically via salves and plasters; others were administered internally as fumigants, nasal clysters, enemas or pessaries. Fumigation involved the burning of agents such as human hair, medicinal herbs and bitumen in a pot from which a lead tube was inserted into the woman's vagina. This, of course, was not without its hazards, if Soranus' warnings about the dangers of scorching the vagina are anything to go by.[20] Enemas were inserted for disorders of the bladder, rectum, vagina and uterus – vaginal douches via vaginal clysters were often used. Pessaries were deployed for a wide range of conditions including inducing menstruation, inflammation of the womb, expelling dead foetuses and relieving hysteria.[21] Pessaries were useful in cases of prolapsed uterus,[22] while tents were administered to staunch uterine haemorrhage and suppurating wombs.[23] Celsus pioneered the use of metal tubes introduced into the vagina to deliver medication after operations for occlusion of the vagina. Eviscerated puppies stuffed with spices and cooked were used as fumigants.[24]

One of Celsus' treatments for disease of the womb, based on Numenius, entailed the use of a pessary made up of ¼ denarius of saffron, 1 denarius of wax, 8 denarii of butter, 12 denarii of goose fat, 2 boiled yolk eggs and less than 1 cyathus of rose oil. Other concoctions include pomegranate rind in water for the evacuation of dead foetuses and snails' shells crushed with honey (an antibacterial) for women fitting from diseases of the genitals. Pliny recommended tree moss from Gaul as therapy for gynaecological infections; bramble berries are excellent for gums, tonsils and genitals. When aconite comes into contact with female genitalia the woman dies the same day; a good aphrodisiac was produced by rubbing the genitalia with a donkey's penis that has been plunged seven times into hot oil. Pliny also prescribes calcinated lead in ophthalmic medicines, especially in the treatment of proptosis, bulging eyes – often an indication of hyperthyroidism and Graves' disease – and for ulcers, heamorrhoids and anal fissures, even though he knows full well that the fumes are harmful to dogs. Other ways of increasing the sexual urge involve wearing an amulet made from the right part of a vulture's lung wrapped in a crane's skin; drinking the yolk of five duck eggs mixed with pig fat and honey; and an amulet made from a cockerel's right testicle wrapped up in ram's skin. A lizard drowned in a man's urine had the opposite effect.[25]

Medical instrumentation reflected this clinical progress. Vaginal *specula* were, among other tools of the trade, found in the House of the Surgeon in Pompeii; they would have been used to dilate the cervix in the treatment of hysteria.[26]

Soranus reminds us that it was a Roman wife's first duty to produce children, 'since women get married to bear children and heirs, and not for fun or pleasure'. To this end, Soranus teaches that successful conception is all down to timing. 'The end of menstruation, when the urge and desire for sex is present, when the body is not full nor the partner drunk, after light exercise and a light snack, when the mood is right' – these are the most promising conditions for making babies. Before him, Lucretius had taught that the best position for conception was for the woman to have *coitus more ferarum* – 'to have sexual intercourse like wild beasts do it', or *a tergo*, 'from behind' (*kubra*, in Greek).[27]

Soranus was one of the first, if not the first, to recognise the dangers and risks of alcohol in pregnancy, advising women to be sober during intercourse if they wanted to avoid foetal abnormalites: the soul is afflicted by strange fantasies when the woman is drunk. Women who digest their food readily, do not have loose stools and who are of a good and happy disposition are most likely to conceive. He goes on to offer treatments for excessive morning sickness and pica – a condition which involves eating non-foods such as soil, charcoal, vine stems and unripe fruit. He specified the ideal diet for the pregnant woman and ruled out 'eating for two'. Also out was sex during pregnancy – it leads to superfoetation. Pliny recorded that the best time to conceive was at the beginning or the end of a period; a promising indicator of conception was when traces of drugs used as eye drops appear in the woman's saliva. Soranus too believed that the optimum time for conception was at the end of the cycle, a confusion caused by ignorance of ovulation among the Greeks and Romans.[28]

Today, women enjoy a longer life expectancy than men; for Roman women, however, it was on average just shy of thirty years, somewhat less than that for men. Mortality caused by early childbirth – 'too soon to marry, too soon to carry' – no doubt accounted for some of the difference. Girls could, and did, marry from the age of twelve and, in some cases, may have been subjected to regular sexual activity before menarche, which would typically occur around age fourteen. The serial childbirths that often followed would, over time, have had a damaging impact on a woman's physical and mental health. Add to that dystocia, or difficult labour of one kind or another, haemmorrhage, infection, puerperal sepsis, eclampsia, obstructed labour, thromboembolism, and the fact that precocious sex possibly led to cervical cancer, then there is little wonder that a woman's life expectancy was generally short. There are many funerary inscriptions for women who died in their twenties. Evidence from the Roman cemetery at Poundbury in Dorset may not be conclusive but it shows that fifty-one out of 281 females died in or around childbirth. Pliny the Younger writes about the tragic death of the Helvidiae sisters, who both died in childbirth giving birth to daughters (who survived); 'two great girls cut down in the bloom youth by their own fertility'.[29]

Context is important too; such desperate perinatal mortality figures are by no means confined to the Roman age. Recent statistics show that 90 per cent of adolescent births (2.8 million) in 2006 occured in developing countries where 28 per cent of females gave birth before age eighteen, the age at which a girl is deemed biologically fit for motherhood. In the UK, as everywhere, geographical location and deprivation influence neonatal death; in the most deprived areas infant mortality is 85 per cent higher than the least deprived.[30]

Evidence for maternal mortality, pain in childbirth and a *matrona*'s concern for her offspring is found in an inscription from the end of the first century BC in Egypt. Twenty-five-year-old Dosithea died 'in pain, escaping the pangs of childbirth'. Rusticeia Matrona died in childbirth and from 'malignant fate' at the same age, in Mauretania; she urges her husband to look after their son. Also twenty-five, Daphne, from Carthage, died giving birth; her epitaph records her aching concern for the baby – 'who will feed him, look after him for the rest of his life?' Socratea died of a haemorrhage in childbirth aged thirty-six. This fifteen-year-old died along with her baby giving birth in Tusculum in the first century BC – 'the tomb [holds] two deaths in one body, the [urn] of ashes contains twin funerals'.

Conjecture and ignorance regarding the length of gestation cannot have helped the situation. Aulus Gellius believed that babies could be born in the seventh, ninth and tenth months – but never in the eighth. Strenuous work in the fields and poor diet was the lot of many women and this too must have exacerbated the problem.

Soranus felt very strongly about complicated labour. He dismisses the crude and cruel methods involving such hideous practices as tying the mother to the bed, lifting it up and letting it fall, and shaking the mother violently. Instead, he advocates a reflective approach – calmly assessing the situation and establishing if the causes of the problem are psychological, foetal or physical – and consulting with the midwife. Lubricants, catheters and enemas are deployed as required for the comfort and safety of the parturient, which, he advocates, is paramount.[31]

Popular wisdom held that breech births were to be avoided: much manipulation, therefore, went on to ensure a normal delivery. Pliny declares that breech deliveries are unnatural, and explains why babies born feet first are called Agrippa – *aegre partus* – born with difficulty, and are unlucky. Marcus Agrippa was blighted by lameness: he left us the two Agrippinas who in turn brought Caligula and Nero into the world; Nero too was born feet first.[32] Where manipulation failed a truly sickening array of procedures, embryotomy, came into play to evacuate the foetus as soon as it was presumed dead, to ensure the survival of the mother. Hooked knives were used to dismember the foetus and thus ease delivery; likewise, decapitating instruments enabled the head to be delivered first.[33] Soranus recommended amputating parts of the foetus as they presented, rather than internally, to avoid cutting the vagina with the blade.[34] Unusually large foetal heads were crushed with a cranioclast (a bowed forceps with teeth) or split with an embryotome; both instruments (of *post mortem* torture) are still in use today. Traction hooks were also part of the instrumentation; samples have been found in Pompeii. Their use is described in Hippocrates, and by Celsus and Soranus.[35]

Iberia, it seems, was not the ideal place for a woman to go into labour: Strabo, in his *Geography*,[36] tells us that that when a Spanish woman gives birth, her husband takes to his bed *and she looks after him*. Pliny recommends a way of concluding a protracted labour; what it lacks in expediency it more than makes up for in originality. Get a stone or similar projectile that had been instrumental in killing three living things in three blows – human, bear, wild boar, say – and throw it over the roof of the house where the woman is in confinement; she is then guaranteed to give birth immediately.[37] Potions were available to help in the evacuation of the placenta and in encouraging lactation, as indeed they were for keeping breasts firm or for inhibiting their growth. The ability to delay puberty in girls was a valuable asset in the slave markets where little girls were much in demand.

Infant mortality was on a shocking scale – as high as thirty deaths in every one hundred pregnancies, compared with 9.1 per 1000 in western Caucasian populations today.[38] 30 per cent of all babies died before age one and 50 per cent by age ten; these survivors would then have a 50 per cent chance of reaching fifty. 17 per cent would see seventy. This reveals a lot about the demographics of women in Roman society, and the number of women available for marriage, and for remarriage.[39] The average early-empire Roman woman had to give birth to five babies if she was to ensure the survival of two, and do her bit to maintain the required birth rate.

Pliny passes on some rather unscientific, contentious reasons to explain the very high maternal and infant mortality. Babies born before the seventh month die and only those babies born in the seventh month survive if they are conceived the day before or after a full moon, or during a new moon; eighth month babies are common, but despite what Aristotle says, they are at risk until they are forty days old. For mothers, the fourth and eighth months are the most critical; abortions at that time are fatal. In a normal pregnancy, the ninth day after conception brings headaches, dizziness, blurred vision, loss of appetite and nausea, indicating that the foetus is taking shape. Male foetuses give rise to a healthier complexion in the mother and make for an easier delivery; movements in the womb begin on the fortieth day with male foetuses, for females after ninety days. Babies are particularly vulnerable when they start to grow hair and during the full moon. If the pregnant mother eats too much salt then the baby is born without nails; excessive maternal yawning can be fatal during delivery.

In reality, the main causes of neonatal mortality, death within the first twenty-nine days of life, were insanitary conditions and infections at the birth and trauma; infant morbidity and deaths were often caused by intestinal disorders, particularly enteritis and dysentery. Celsus recorded that the latter was particularly virulent in children up to the age of ten, and in their mothers when pregnant; the unborn baby was also lost.[40] Over-zealous swaddling – where the baby's limbs are tightly confined, causing the heartbeat to slow down to a dangerous rate – along with soiled laundry, and mastication of baby foods by wet-nurses who themselves have an infection, may also have taken their toll. As indeed would goat's and cow's milk containing infectious organisms and used not just by reluctant breast-feeders but by poorer, undernourished women who were unable to breastfeed and could not afford a wet nurse.

Humans have sexual intercourse during pregnancy, and this, the Romans believed, caused superfoetation – carrying more than one foetus at a time. It is, actually, very rare. Pliny the Elder scurrilously cites cases where a woman bore twins and one baby resembled her husband while the other looked like her lover; where a slave from Perconnesus, who had sex twice in one day, produced twins, one like her master, the other like the estate manager; where a mother gave birth after five months and then again at full term; where a woman produced a seventh-month baby and then twins some months later.

Pregnancy could have definite advantages, other than the chance of a healthy child: Julia, Augustus' daughter, is alleged to have said, in a wonderful analogy, that being pregnant allowed her to pursue her extramarital affairs without fear of getting pregnant: 'I never take on a passenger unless the ship is full.' Unfortunately for Julia, another type of ship was to take her into insular exile on Pandateria for her adulterous behaviour. Juvenal, in his sixth satire rant against women, tells us that some women prefer having potent eunuchs or *cinaedi* – to avoid pregnancy and any need for abortion.[41]

Pliny the Younger's wife Calpurnia miscarried; natural sympathy and concern for Calpurnia apart, Pliny, as much as anyone, would have felt the all-round disappointment when so much pressure was on wives to produce a male heir. In his letter to her grandfather, Calpurnius Fabatus, Pliny writes, 'The news that your granddaughter has had a miscarriage will be even sadder for you to hear when you so much wanted a great-grandchild. Being very young she did not know that she was pregnant and so failed to take certain precautions and avoid things she should have avoided. She paid for her mistake with the warning that she had put her life in mortal danger.' The girl's ignorance of her own pregnancy highlights obvious shortcomings in sex education among even more educated families; it certainly demonstrates a failure on the part of the wife's mother, or even the nurse, to provide what today we would consider appropriate care and advice.[42] There is, at the same time, no embarrassment at publicising his wife's medical problems in this way.

Causes of miscarriage can be found in the *Hippocratic Corpus*: carrying too heavy a weight, being beaten up, jumping up into the air (an occupational hazard for dancers), lack of food and fainting, being frightened, loud shouting, flatulence and too much drink. Pliny the Elder disparages the claims of the *magi* when they assert that miscarriage can be avoided if a woman wears the white flesh of a hyena's breast in gazelle leather, along with seven hyena hairs and the genitals of a stag.

Menstruation and the menopause exercised physicians and scientists alike. Celsus tells us that when *menses* ended, much of the protection menstruation afforded women ended with it. Headache and a range of diseases ensued; protection against gout in the feet and gout in the hand disappeared and night vision was impaired while pre-existing consumption became very difficult to treat.[43] A girl's first period will cure her childhood epilepsy. Menstruation, along with other forms of blood discharge such as nose bleeds and therapeutic bleeding, was to Celsus essential for good general health. Soranus recommends that girls surrender their virginity only after the onset of menstruation.[44]

Most writers agreed that menopause occurred between the ages of forty and fifty – but Soranus extended it to sixty and Oribasius had it in the early thirties, particularly for obese women. The *lex Julia* gives a useful indicator of what was thought officially to be the age when childbearing stopped; a woman over fifty was not expected to have any more children and so was exempt from this part of the law.[45]

Dioscorides describes over 100 agents which stimulate menstruation, while Pliny lists over ninety. Pliny addresses the marvellous powers believed to be inherent in menstruation. 'It would be hard to find anything that produces as many amazing effects as menstrual discharge,' he proclaims. The onset of a period during a solar or lunar eclipse spells disaster for the woman, and for any man who happens to be having sex with her during that time. If, however, a woman, during her period, walks naked through a field that is filled with pests, those pests will die as she walks past; he cites Metrodorus of Scepsis as evidence, who says that this is precisely what happened in Cappadocia during a cantharid beetle plague, and that it accounts for the extraordinary fact that women there still walk in the fields with their dresses hitched up above their buttocks. Ironically, cantharidin was to become a popular aphrodisiac in the nineteenth century.

Sprinkling the ashes of menstrual blood onto clothing bleached out their colour and spoilt purple dyes. A menstruating woman will turn grape juice sour, render seeds sterile when she touches them, make vine grafts wither away, dry up garden plants and cause fruit to drop off the tree. Her look will make mirrors cloud over, blunt the sharp edge of steel, and dull the sheen of ivory. If she looks at a swarm of bees, they will all drop down dead; brass and iron will instantly go rusty, and smell disgusting; dogs which lap up the discharge go mad, their bite becomes poisonous and deadly.

Soranus provides a catalogue of physiological changes which take place at the start of menstruation: lethargy, aching, sluggishness, flushes and excessive yawning, nausea and lack of appetite. He advises that each woman do what is best for her during her period: rest, or light activity. Women approaching menopause should ensure that their periods cease gradually, extending them, if necessary, through the use of suppositories or injections. Soranus rejected the view that menstruation was a beneficial, healthy purgative, believing instead that its only use was in facilitating conception. Virginity, on the other hand, was good, as it obviated the stress and trauma caused by childbirth.[46] Roman women, in common with women of other civilisations, used menstrual cloths; a sixth-century-AD philosopher and mathematician gathered some of a woman's used ones to repel an unwanted admirer. The alternative to cloths was to bleed into one's clothes, according to Pliny.[47]

Both Pliny and Dioscorides list various agents which will determine or alter the sex of a foetus. Pliny recommends thistle, hare's testicles, rennet or uterus or a cock's testes for generating male babies.[48]

For normal childbirth, Soranus advises the following sympathetic, patient-centered procedures: oil for injections and cleansing, hot water for washing, hot compresses to relieve labour pains, woollens to cover the mother and bandages to swaddle the baby in and citruses to help the mother regain her strength.

> The midwife should wash her hands in oil and, when the mouth of the womb opens, she should insert the trimmed forefinger of her left hand and rearrange the opening so that the amniotic sac falls forward... three women should be in attendance to reassure the mother, even if they have no experience of childbirth; the midwife should then sit lower down and opposite the mother holding her thighs apart; she should tell the woman behind to hold the mother's anus with a cloth lest it be pushed out with the straining. If the amniotic sac fails to open the midwife should break it with her nails, insert her finger and widen it gradually, taking care that the baby does not drop out.[49]

On delivery the midwife cuts the umbilical cord and the infant is placed on the floor symbolizing contact with Mother Earth; it is encouraged to cry, lifted up, then cleaned and wrapped up and presented to the mother. A grandmother or maternal aunt would then massage the baby's forehead and lips with a finger covered in lustral saliva, a gesture designed to ward off the evil eye.[50] It is at this point that the father would perform the heart-stopping ritual of lifting up the baby, giving his decision as to whether it lives or dies. Those accepted into the family were named, girls on the eighth day, boys on the ninth – after the critical period for infant death had passed. Unwanted babies might be abandoned at the Temple of Pietas or the Columna Lactaria; those with serious abnormalities would be drowned or suffocated.[51]

The Romans recognised the value of mother-infant bonding. Soranus was an enlightened advocate and opposed the common practice of hiring wet-nurses; he did, though, advise new mothers to have a three week period of rest after the birth during which they might employ a wet nurse. He was very clear in his belief that the well-being of the mother took precedence over the child's. Moreover, it was vitally important that a pregnant mother should be very careful what she looks at during her term. Contemplating a fine piece of statuary ensured well-proportioned babies; looking at monkeys, however, produced hirsute infants with long arms. An exquisite example of beauty, or otherwise, in the eye of the beholder.[52]

Multiple births were usually a bad thing, although not in Egypt, where the waters of the River Nile induced fertility. Pliny cites the quadruplets delivered to a lady called Fausta in Ostia on the day of Augustus' funeral; this caused the terrible food shortages which followed. He records the Peloponnesian woman who produced four sets of quintuplets, most of whom survived, and he cites Trogus, who reported seven children born at the same confinement in Egypt.

Soranus also covers the disposal of the placenta, hygienic cutting of the umbilical cord and sound postnatal care for both infant and mother. He deplores the sink or swim practice of the Germans, Greeks and Scythians who plunge their newborns into a vat of cold water – only the fittest surviving.[53] Swaddling, the avoidance of ulceration, bedding, teething and a description of an ancient-world babywalker are all covered in his work.[54] Feeding and the inadvisable temptation to feed on demand, the weakness caused by excessive bathing and what to do when a baby persistently cries are all usefully dealt with.[55] He recommends that weaning begin at around eighteen months or two years – on the basis, no doubt, that he knew that breast milk was one of the most nutritious, and sterile, foods available and an effective weapon in the battle against paediatric disease. Pliny includes breast milk in his list of medicines derived from women which are effective against a whole range of maladies.[56]

Today, hysteria as a diagnosis or disorder is no longer recognised and is now termed 'histrionic personality disorder', linked with conditions such as social anxiety and schizophrenia. Evidently, women have always been particularly prone, hence the cliché 'female hysterics'.[57] Up until the late nineteenth century it was linked to movements of the womb, the *hystera*, presenting as a lack of self-control caused by intense fear or anxiety often related to the imagined disease of a particular body part. Treatment was, for nearly two centuries, pelvic massage – in which the doctor, often a man, stimulated the genitals until the patient, usually a woman, achieved hysterical paroxysm, or orgasm.[58] The condition was thought to have been first recognised around the time of the early Hippocratic writings and endured as a diagnosis right through the Roman era. The Hippocratics never used the term *hysteria*; to them it was *pnix* – suffocation. They taught that the womb became dry if a woman did not have frequent sexual intercourse; infrequency would cause the womb to gravitate towards moister organs, such as the liver, heart, brain, diaphragm or bladder, at which point the woman would faint, lose her voice and become 'hysterical'. The administration of sweet-smelling odours often restored the womb to its rightful place. Failing that, increasingly desperate measures involved binding the woman tightly beneath her breasts, palpating the affected organ, or hanging the woman upside down from a ladder. Plato believed that an animal living inside a woman's womb was responsible for driving the maternal instinct to have children; lack of sexual activity by the woman made the animal restless so it wandered through her body, causing apnea (difficulty in breathing) and other conditions and diseases. Sexual activity relieved the symptoms.[59]

Aretaeus later describes the symptoms of this erratic 'wandering womb'; it is attracted to pleasant smells but is repelled by foul odours, which cause it to rise and suffocate the woman, squashing many of the vital organs into a confined space. In such an emergency the patient must be made to smell stale urine or have perfumed pessaries applied. Pliny thought that black mineral jet was efficacious here. Soranus, who rejected the wandering womb idea, adds that hysteria is preceded by a raft of gynaecological conditions or disorders, including repeat miscarriage, premature childbirth, widowhood, menopause, swelling of the womb and dysmenorrhea. Symptoms include fainting, speechlessness, difficulty in breathing, stridor (wheezing caused by an obstructed airway), grinding of the teeth, bloating of the abdomen, chill, sweating, spasms, and a weak pulse. Generally, the woman recovers if she is calmly laid down, slowly warmed up and refreshed with a sponge. Soranus refutes the efficacy of foul and pleasant smells and tends towards a diagnosis that is akin to today's hysterical conversion disorder.[60]

Galen came very close to establishing a psychological cause for hysteria when he diagnosed a patient demonstrating all the usual symptoms: he established, by deduction, that the cause of her illness was her obsessive infatuation with Pylades, a dancer, and more or less concluded that hysteria was a psychosomatic disorder.[61]

'The Incomplete Woman' and Sexual Medicine   67

Hysteria was especially problematic in virgins and widows. Hippocrates warns that girls who delay marriage suffer nightmares from the time of their first period. This can result in them choking to death: the blood in their womb cannot escape because the cervix is still intact and so it flows back up to the heart and lungs, driving the woman mad. Fever ensues, accompanied by a tendency to suicide brought on by the nightmares; these encourage the women to jump down wells or to hang themselves. Hippocrates' advice is for girls in such a condition to waste no time in losing their virginity; they will be cured if they fall pregnant.[62] Widows, similarly, are cured by sex, or just by climaxing, so that the retained female semen can be released. The inevitable conclusion was that, deprived of sex, a woman would go insane, and the best way to preserve one's sanity was to have sex, and to have it often. A less self-serving Soranus went against this orthodoxy; after experiments on spayed sows and observations of chaste priestesses, he concluded that abstention was the better way.

The received wisdom, though, was that the only real cure open to the 'hysterical' woman was to become pregnant – thus conveniently enabling the woman to fulfil her role as a wife, as well as satisfying her husband's needs for sexual gratification. Hysteria was a naturally occurring outlet for women, a reaction to the *matrona* ideal, when they could cope no more with the pressures that could bring; for some women it was a release from the tedium, the daily grind of being a good, compliant wife and a *matrona*. Hysterical behaviour, of course, was unseemly to the Greek male and to the conservative Roman, and so it was medicalised by men with the prognosis that it could only be cured through regular sexual intercourse and childbirth.[63] It was a truly vicious circle for the Roman woman.

Hippocrates gives us some intriguing gynaecological case studies: a woman from Pheres suffered from idiopathic headache which persisted even after her skull was drained; during her period the headache was less severe. The headaches stopped when she became pregnant, turning that time-honoured excuse for declining sex on its head with suggestions that a headache does not always guarantee a good night's sleep. A woman from Larissa suffered pain during intercourse when she reached sixty, she felt what she thought were severe labour pains after eating lots of leeks. When she stood up she felt something uncomfortable in her vagina, and fainted; a nearby woman pulled out what appeared to be the whorl of a spindle from her vagina. *Lanam fecit* indeed. Hippocrates records that the patient made a full recovery; one wonders if the other woman ever did.

Uterine dropsy, or hydrometra, results in fever, weak periods, swelling in the abdomen and withered breasts: Hippocrates recommends a laxative and immersion in a vapour bath made from cow dung followed by pessaries made from cantharid beetle and then bile; after three days, insert a vinegar douche. If the fever subsides and the stomach softens then the woman should have intercourse. She should drink samphire bark and eat dark peony berries with as much mercury plant, along with raw and cooked garlic – as possible and begin a diet of squid. If later she gives birth she is definitely cured. At the same time, she is definitely poisoned by the mercury. Symptoms of poisoning appear within a few hours including vomiting, pain, gastric and kidney inflammation, inflammation of the cheeks and jaw and drowsiness.

For uterine prolapse the *Hippocratic Corpus* advises garlic, undiluted sheep's milk, fumigation and a laxative, followed by another fumigation of fennel and absinthe and then two pessaries – one of squill, the other of opium poppies. If the woman's periods have stopped then she should drink four cantharid beetles (legs, wings, head removed), and eat four dark peony seeds, cuttlefish eggs, parsley and wine. If her womb nears her liver she will lose her voice, turn a dark colour and her teeth will chatter; a bandage should then be tied below her ribs and sweet wine poured into her mouth while bad-smelling vapours are burnt beneath her womb. This condition particularly affects old women and widows.[64] Soranus recommended surgery for a prolapse that had turned black.

Uterine cancer is rarely mentioned, probably because the symptoms were difficult to differentiate from other conditions or diseases – vaginal bleeding and discharge, periods stopping, for example. Plutarch mentions that cancer of the womb is particularly distressing. Philoxenus of Alexandria, in the mid-first century BC, was something of a cancer surgery specialist and was an exponent of surgical intervention in cervical cancer.[65]

Diseases of the breast receive comparatively little attention. Aetius describes various cancers and their surgical treatment or drug therapies. Hippocrates describes a case of breast cancer where the patient died after the bloody discharge from her nipple stopped. Soranus records in graphic detail a mastectomy performed around AD 100 by Leonides; as with all surgery then it was performed without anaesthetic.[66] Galen tells of the crab-like (*karkinodeis*) swellings which form on a woman's breasts due to retained residues when menstruation is suspended. Dioscorides, Pliny and Celsus all describe various diseases of the breasts, for example swelling, induration, growths (*strumae*) and *carcinomata*.[67]

A case of clitoridectomy, female genital mutilation (FGM), is recorded by Aetius from sixth-century-AD Egypt where, according to Strabo, such practice was common. The feeble justification for it was to prevent the girl or woman masturbating, or to quell the desire for intercourse driven by an unnaturally enlarged clitoris. Paulus of Aegina, a seventh-century-AD urologist, was an expert and describes the procedure in Book 6 of his *De Re Medica Libri Septem*. There is evidence that another form of FGM, female infibulation, was practiced on prepubescent girls, if Strabo and Philo are to be believed. This is where the the labia are removed and the girl's legs are bound to allow the surgery to heal, forming a skin over the vagina; a small hole is made to allow for urination and menstruation. Its purpose then, as now in some societies, was to reassure a husband that he is marrying a virgin.[68] Unlike male circumcision, female genital mutilation was neither deplored nor stigmatised by the Romans.

Malaria was widespread in many parts of Italy and other parts of the empire despite attempts to improve drainage of marshlands and river plains. In a fifth-century-AD cemetery near Lugnano in Umbria almost all of the forty-seven graves contained either infants, neonates or foetuses. The foetuses were from miscarriages, particularly from *primigravidae* mothers, caused by the immune suppression brought on by malaria, and common in women in the final two trimesters of pregnancy. The female anopheles mosquito was thought to be attracted to certain chemical receptors found in the placenta of pregnant women. Empedocles blocked off a gorge in Acragas, Sicily, because it was acting as a funnel for a southerly wind bringing in mosquitoes which introduced placental malaria. Pliny quotes Icatidas, a Greek doctor who taught that malaria in men is cured by having sex with a woman just starting her period.

Plutarch advises men against bathing with a woman: apart from being indecent, some effluvia and excretions from women's bodies are harmful to men. Pliny deplores the vogue for effeminate ointments among wrestlers, hot baths and depilation by women, especially in the pubic region. A graffiti writer from Pompeii shares Pliny's distaste, coming down on the side of non-depilation because it [the unshaven vulva] stays warm and excites the [male] organ.

Sexually transmitted infections would of course have plagued both men and women alike, particularly in a society which freely endorsed men consorting with prostitutes, male and female, and with slaves. Discharges and ulcers are recorded but there is little on infection or contagion. The Campanians, apparently, had a predilection for oral sex, resulting in a high incidence of *campanus morbus* – a facial skin condition, probably a sexually transmitted infection. The Hippocratics, using findings from a dissected inflamed urethra, Celsus and Galen all describe the symptoms of gonorrhoea, referring to it as 'strangury' (painful urination) caused by the 'pleasures of Venus'. Martial and Galen mention anal warts and piles, Celsus and Galen genital warts, and the Hippocratics and Galen describe oral sores which present during menstruation – possibly *herpes zoster*.[69]

Breastfeeding seems to have been a virtue, if the epitaph to twenty-four-year-old Graxia Alexandria from Rome is anything to go by; she is praised for her chastity, and for the fact that she breastfed her sons. Whether this signifies a norm or whether it is exceptional practice, in the light of the middle-class tendency to hire wet-nurses (*nutrices*), it is quite impossible to say. We do know, however, that Tacitus praised German women because they breastfed their own children, an implicit criticism of their Roman counterparts and an appreciation of the nutritional and psychological benefits to both mother and child. Interestingly, in the same paragraph, he deprecates the Roman practice of marrying off daughters at an early age; no German would do that.[70] The philosopher Favorinus, from the second century AD, offers sound arguments why a mother should nurse her own baby, demanding to know why a woman is born with nipples if they are not for feeding her infants. A stranger's milk should be avoided – who knows, the nurse may be from a barbarian country, she may be dishonest, ugly, immodest, a drinker and promiscuous – everything (ugly apart, perhaps) a *matrona* should not be.[71] In the second half of the third century AD a petulant mother in Egypt complains that her daughter has been forced to breastfeed and offers to pay for a wet nurse.[72] Funerary evidence for the *nutrix* comes in the shape of Prima, a freedwoman in the service of Tiberius and wet-nurse to his grand-daughter, Julia Livilla, and Severina from Cologne, who is shown on her tombstone attending to the infant and then giving her the breast.[73]

The breast was considered first and foremost a symbol of nurture and of motherhood. Breast-shaped drinking cups, and representations of breasts have been found among the votive offerings at sanctuaries of Diana and Hercules, some dedicated by wet nurses. Breast milk was sometimes drunk by the elderly, or by those on the point of death. An Etruscan tradition has the goddess Juno offer her breast to Hercules so that he may become immortal. A bedroom wall painting shows Pero offering breast milk to her elderly father who had been imprisoned and sentenced to death by starvation; it bears the legend 'in sadness is the meeting of modesty and piety'. In this *caritas romana* (Roman charity) Pero is discovered by a jailer, but her piety was so impressive that she and her father were allowed to go free.

Valerius Maximus narrates the story in his *Factorum ac dictorum memorabilium* (5, 5, 4, 7); Pliny has a similar story in which a plebeian woman is jailed and nursed by her daughter. A twentieth-century fictional version of Roman charity can be found in Steinbeck's *The Grapes of Wrath* (1939), in which Rosasharn nurses a sick and starving man in the corner of a barn.

Breast milk too had marvellous medicinal qualities: good for chronic fevers, coeliac disease and stomach-ache; poured directly into the eye it repairs ophthalmic trauma. Some say that the milk of a woman who has borne a girl is only effective against spots on the face; the best milk comes from a woman who has given birth to a boy; twin boys is better still, particularly if the mother abstains from wine. It works well when a toad has squirted its fluid into the eye and against toad bites. How common was that? Confusingly, we learn that eye problems are banished for life in patients massaged with the milk of a mother and her daughter together. Ear infections are successfully treated by milk mixed with oil, or warmed with goose grease where there has been a painful blow. Breast milk works well as an antidote for the poison of the sea-hare, of the buprestis beetle and for insanity brought on by drinking poisonous henbane. With hemlock it can be prescribed as a liniment for gout and as an application for pains of the uterus; it is an effective emmenagogue. Lung infections are cured by women's milk; if Attic honey is mixed with it and the urine of a prepubescent child, it will expel worms through the ears. The mother of a boy produces milk which stops dogs going mad.

Women's bodies themselves were a vital source of medicine, a living medicine chest, according to Pliny. Pliny himself considered such medicines to be the product of old wives' tales pedalled by midwives and whores (thereby repudiating again the skill, education and probity we have noted in the midwifery profession). The smell of a woman's burning hair was particularly efficacious:

apart from deterring snakes, the fumes ease the breathing of women choking with hysteria; it cures dry and irritable eyes, as well as warts and sores on babies; mixed with honey it salves head wounds and ulcerative cavities; with honey and frankincense it mends abscesses and gout; with fat it cures cellulitis and staunches bleeding; it is effective against irritating rashes.[74]

Women's saliva makes a good medicine for bloodshot eyes, all the more powerful if the donor has abstained from food and wine for twenty-four hours. A woman's breast-band tied around the head relieves headache.[75]

There is scant evidence of how women fared in terms of mental health. Hippocrates believed erotic dreams to be an indicator of insanity. That women were under considerable social and domestic stress is not in doubt; early marriage, the pressure to produce an heir, managing the household, dealing with slaves, the endless subordination to the husband or father, caring for the children and, in some cases, coping with their husbands' affairs and the abuse, physical and psychological, he may sometimes have handed out, the frustration of not being able to express independence or artistic ability – all of these factors would have caused levels of stress in the Roman woman. A particularly anxious time would have been that one-month post-partum period when mother and baby were both extremely vulnerable and, for some, when the father was deciding the baby's fate – a decision often influenced by the judgment of another woman in the house, the midwife. Women with mental health problems would have been treated in much the same way as men; they were shunned, taunted and often spat at in public. Spitting was thought to prevent the spread of disease and madness. Pliny records how it was customary to spit at epileptics when they are fitting in a bid to throw back the contagion; spitting was a weapon against witches and spitting at anyone lame in their right leg dispelled bad luck. Epilepsy is marginally more common in men than in women but it has implications for women in reproductive health – fertility, puberty, menstruation, for example – so would have had potentially serious social as well as medical consequences when diagnosed in premenopausal women. Caelius is scathing of those practitioners who prescribe for epileptics the binding of limbs or a diet of weasel, smoked brain of camel or the testicles of a beaver – even tickling the patient while a flame is placed close to his or her eyes.

Artemidorus Ephesius was a second-century-AD oneiromancer (diviner of dreams) and author of the five volume *Oneirocritic*. He gives us a rather extreme, and terrible, example of the potential outcome of such stresses on Roman women: a woman dreamt that stalks of wheat sprouted from her breast extending back through her vagina; this occurred after an incestuous episode with her child. She later committed suicide.[76] To the Romans, dreams were very serious phenomena; the erotic dream was termed *oneirogmos* – they saw a physiological link between dream and body in the form of erection and ejaculation. Artemidorus discusses three categories of sexual relations: those that are natural, legal and customary – sex with a spouse, prostitute or slave, or masturbation; those that are contrary to law – incest, notably with a mother, at 1, 79; and those that are contrary to nature – those that can only be dreamed – penetrating oneself and having sex with the gods, or bestiality, necrophilia and 'lesbianism'. Dreaming about touching a woman's genitalia meant that you know her deepest secrets; breasts (as above) were entirely indicative of maternity and child rearing; if a woman dreams of her husband's penis it means that she will give birth to a son; if she dreams of beating her husband she will be an adulteress. Wasting semen through sodomy or fellatio forecasts penury.

Body divination was important too and, like dreams, it had its gender and sexual proclivities. The apparent source is Melampous whose works include *Peri Palmon Mantike*, a treatise on divination by twitches (palomancy), and *Peri Elaion tou Somatos*, a short work on divination by moles – of the dermatological variety. Whole body tremor indicated danger for an unmarried girl, disease for a widow; left ear tremor presaged a reprimand for the girl and a loss for the widow. Oral vibration meant a kiss was in the offing; vibration centered on the top of the head indicated forthcoming marriage for the girl, because Athena was born from the head of Zeus. The thumb was associated with Aphrodite so a vibration there predicted marriage for the girl (as did big toe vibrations) but trouble for the widow. Like the interpretation of dreams, body divination was very male-oriented. A vibrating right testicle indicated a surge in energy and the conception of children; in the left if meant that the favours of a woman were in the offing; in the glans the same promise was in store for a slave.

As for the moles, if a man has a mole over his eyebrow he will marry a virtuous and good-looking woman; similarly a woman with a red mole in the same place will wed a rich and handsome man. However, if the mole is actually on the eyebrow both the man and the woman must avoid marriage as they will end up with five wives or five husbands. A tawny coloured mole on the nose predicted an insatiable sexual appetite leading to adultery – the same for a woman. A mole on the genitalia indicated the birth of a boy in a man, a girl in a woman. The fact that there are nine manuscripts extant for this work gives an idea of its popularity and the credence it commanded.

Hypersexuality – classified today in *ICD-10* as satyriasis in men and as nymphomania in women – appears frequently in the medical authors. Aretaeus denies its existence in women saying that others believe that it manifests, as in men, as a desire for sex; Soranus adds that the 'itching' felt in the genitals which makes women 'touch themselves' naturally increases their sexual urge and causes 'mental derangement' and an immodest desire for a man. His treatment involved bleeding, a liquid diet, refreshing poultices applied to the genitals and avoiding anything which caused flatulence or sexual desire. Theodorus Priscianus termed it *metromania*. The therapy recommended by Rufus of Ephesus included blood-letting, taking honeysuckle seed and the root of the water lily, hot baths and the avoidance of all things erotic. Rufus compares the treatment of female satyriasis with the therapy for spermatorrhea – an involuntary ejaculation of sperm which was thought to occur in both men and women.[77]

Pliny (*NH* 7, 34) notes that the Greeks call excessively tall or small people *ektrapeloi*, 'freaks', but that the Romans have no name for them. Hermaphrodites (*androgyni*) used to be thought of as prodigies, but Pompey changed all that when he made them figures of entertainment, putting them on the stage in his theatre. They were joined in the limelight by such exceptional people as Eutyche, who was later led to her funeral pyre by twenty children – to celebrate the thirty individual babies she had given to the world; by Alcippe, who had given birth to an elephant; and by the slave girl who was delivered of a snake. Sightings of centaurs were not uncommon, it seems; Pliny saw one immersed in honey. Equally unlikely stories include that of a baby born in Saguntum, soon after it was sacked by Hannibal: it took one look around, was not impressed by what it saw, and immediately returned to its mother's womb.

Diodorus, in the late first century BC, described hermaphrodites as 'marvellous creatures' (*terata*), who announce the future, be it good or bad (465). Around AD 500 Isidore of Seville (*Etymolgiae* 11, 3, 11) described hermaphrodites as having 'the right breast of a man and the left of a woman, and after sex can both sire and bear children'. In Roman law, a hermaphrodite was classed as either male or female; there was no third sex. After Pompey made celebrities out of them they had, by Pliny's time, become objects of delight and fascination much in demand in what has been called by Plutarch the 'monster markets' (*Moralia* 520c).

Generally speaking, though, the birth of a hermaphrodite was not good news. The *prodigium* it heralded meant a rupture in the *pax deorum*, peace with the gods. Livy (27, 11) tells us how, in the dark days of the Second Punic War, a four-year-old hermaphrodite caused the *haruspices* to be summoned; they decreed that the child be enclosed in a chest and floated out to sea where it drowned. Another hermaphrodite found in 133 BC was drowned in the local river in another attempt to restore relations wtth the gods.

We have Macrobius to thank for a description of a masculine form of Venus found in a Cypriot cult (*Saturnalia* 3, 8, 2); here, the god(dess) sported a beard and male genitals, and wore women's clothing. The local worshippers, men and women, complemented the deity by cross-dressing. Laevius adds to the enigma when he writes of worshipping 'nurturing Venus, whether female or male'. Often, in sculpture, we find her *anasyrmene*, that is with her clothes pulled up to reveal a penis and scrotum, a gesture that had apotropaic powers.

Pliny is equally insistent on the phenomenon of instantaneous transgender transgression or gender reassignment – it is no dream, he says. In 171 BC a girl from Casinum instantaneously changed into a boy before her parents' eyes; the augurs banished her to an island. Licinius Mucianus records the case of Arescon, a 'man' from Argos who married a man as Arescusa; 'she' then developed a beard and other male features and got married to a woman. There was a similar sighting in Smyrna. Pliny himself saw a bride turn into a man on his/her wedding day. The mother of a boxer, Nicaeus of Byzantium, was born from her mother's adulterous affair with an Ethiopian: the mother had been born white but her son, Nicaeus, one generation later, was born black. Another Ethiopian involved, or the same one? Pliny goes on to assert that certain Indian tribes bear children from age seven and are old by the time they reach forty, while others conceive aged five and die three years later; the children of others go grey immediately after birth. Women who want a black-eyed baby must eat a shrew during their pregnancy.[78]

Equally irrational were the observances of Phlegon of Tralles, an eccentric freedman of Hadrian's. Phlegon's chief work was the *Olympiads*, a sixteen-book history of Rome from 776 BC to AD

137. Other publications included *On Long Lived Persons*, a riveting list of Italian and Roman centenarians culled from the censuses; but it his paradoxographical *Marvels* which interests us here – a half-serious compilation of ghost stories, congenital abnormalites, strange hybrid creatures, hermaphrodites, giant skeletons and prophesising heads. He records, for example, an hermaphrodite from 125 BC who caused such a stir that the *Sibylline Oracles* were consulted; a highly-thought-of slave woman, who, in AD 49, gave birth to an ape; a four-headed child which was presented to Nero; and a child born with its head protruding from its shoulder.[79]

Cornelia is described as the ideal *matrona* by Plutarch in his *Gaius Gracchus*. We know little of Cornelia's early life, other than some unfortunate gynaecology where Pliny the Elder records how she was born with labial adhesion, an inauspicious condition presaging, it seems, the deaths of her two revolutionary sons, Tiberius and Gaius. Pliny notes that for an infant girl to be born with her genitals grown together is unpropitious, as Cornelia proves. Around AD 220 Solinus explains that Cornelia expiated the portent when both her famous sons died. Whatever, some, no doubt, viewed her antenatal condition and the birth of her sons as contrary to divine will.

There are no reported cases of women dying from overexertion during sex, but Pliny reports that both Cornelius Gallus, the first-century-BC poet, and Titus Hetereius died in the throes of sexual ecstacy – with women, he primly adds.

Lucretius, the Epicurean philosopher, gives us a physiological description of sexual function in the male. Physical maturity generates semen, which manifests in wet dreams; seeing a beautiful body, be it a woman's or a boy's, moves semen into the genitals and toward the object of desire. Erection creates an urge to ejaculate with its attendant pleasure. This human sex drive he describes as dumb desire, comparing ejaculation to the blood spurting from a wound. Love is just a by-product which taints sexual pleasure in the same way that life is tainted by the fear of death.[80] Women, on the other hand, are instinctively driven by affection, leading to mutual satisfaction. Falling in love should be avoided by men as it leads to physical, emotional and financial ruin.

Too much semen was a bad thing. Cold baths and avoiding flatulence-causing foods were recommended to limit production.[81] In his *On Semen*, Galen describes semen as a concoction of blood and *pneuma* (the 'vital air' needed by organs to function), formed within the man's spermatic vessels, turning white through heat as it enters the testicles. Too much sex results in a loss of *pneuma* and, therefore, vitality – bad news for some Romans, 'those who are less moderate sexually turn out to be weaker, since the whole body loses the purest part of both substances, and there is besides an accession of pleasure, which by itself is enough to dissolve the vital tone, so that before now some persons have died from excess of pleasure'.[82] Sex kills, again.

Death was not the only outcome of too liberal a dissemination of semen. Before it got to that, mental acuity, masculinity, and a deep manly voice were all compromised [83]. The voice was particularly vulnerable, with singers and actors resorting to infibulation to preserve their voices.[84] Roman doctors, dancers and singers believed that male infibulation protected their voices – infibulation in a man was the clinical practice, literally 'dog tie', of placing a clasp through the foreskin to close the foreskin and draw the penis over to one side. It obviously prevented erections while some believed it resulted in the patient becoming well endowed. It was commonly believed that abstinence from sex also protected the voice, or delayed its breaking. Quintilian taught sexual abstinence for the orator who wished to cultivate a deep masculine voice for court. Galen cautions, though, that too much abstinence leads to a loss of desire and capability – a wrinkling of the testicles as in old men, whereas the blood flow in men having sex often increased desire and a healthy sized set of testicles.[85]

Catullus's fellow new poet, Calvus, slept with lead plates over his kidneys to control his wet dreams. Pliny reports that 'when plates of lead are bound to the area of the loins and kidneys, it is used, owing to its rather cooling nature, to check the attacks of sexual desire and sexual dreams in one's sleep that cause spontaneous eruptions to the point of becoming a sort of disease'.[86]

Lead plates were efficacious in other male sexual disorders: satyriasis, priapism (a chronic erection without a desire for sex) and involuntary ejaculation all benefitted from the laying on of lead plates, or from cupping therapy, or with the use of depilatories.

We have already alluded to the grey area between medicine and the *pharmaka*, the potions and spells dispensed by sorcerers and poisoners. Pliny gives us a lot of detail on the knowledge of pharmacology acquired by men, suggesting that the origins of magic may lie in the early days of medicine.[87] Evidence to support this comes in popular remedies for impotence, plants used as aphrodisiacs, and as poisons.[88]

Mythology plays a part in male knowledge of pharmacology

and raises the question whether or not the negative aspersions on womens' pharmacological knowledge and, indeed, suggestions of witchcraft come in part at least from the mysteries of childbirth, and potions and ointments used by midwives.[89] Criminal misuse of a pharmaceutical is evidenced in the case of Calpurnius Besta, who was accused of rubbing the poison aconite on his wife's genitals.[90] Hemlock was known for its toxic properties, and was used in capital punishments in Athens.[91]

CHAPTER FOUR

Birth Control, Aphrodisiacs and Love Potions: the Need (or Not) for Venus

This chapter discusses the various forms of birth control used by the Romans – from the brutal practice of exposure to barrier methods; it also covers efforts and attempts to encourage sex and love through aphrodisiacs and love potions.

Some girls never had a life. It is true to say that the birth of a daughter was often greeted less enthusiastically than that of a son, if not by the mother then by the father. *Patria potestas* empowered him, by virtue of *ius patrium, ius vitae necisque*, the power of life and death, to kill or sell off unwanted or surplus members of the family. In extreme cases, baby girls were exposed, often, it seems, because of financial hardship: a girl could not always contribute to the household income; she may also require an expensive dowry in the relatively near future.[1] According to the *Twelve Tables* (4, 1), deformed babies of either sex should be disposed of as soon as possible after birth; Dionysius of Halicarnassus[2] alleges that Romulus (in the so-called *Law of Romulus*) ordered Roman citizens to raise all their boys, but only the firstborn girl, unless she was deformed, in which case she too might be killed. Nevertheless, legalised child murder had its supporters and its opponents. To Philo of Alexandria (20 BC–AD 50), the exposure of infants was tantamount to infanticide; he reports cases of strangulation and drowning.[3] Livy, in 207 BC, tells that horrible story of a monstrously deformed child being cast adrift alive in a box, to rid Rome of such a repulsive portent.[4] Suetonius describes a decree in 63 BC that all boys should be exposed; Musonius Rufus in the first century AD deplores child murder.[5] Soranus provided a checklist for midwives to help them determine the newborn disorders for which exposure was permitted.[6] It was not until AD 374 that child exposure was outlawed and infanticide became the legal equivalent of murder. In an earlier bid to curb the practice, Constantine had offered free food and clothing to new parents and legalized the sale of babies, mainly into slavery, in AD 329. However, it was still going on some years later; the skeletons of 100 or so infants were excavated from the bottom of a drain in Ashkelon dating from the sixth century AD.

Hilarion, away on business in Alexandria, writes lovingly to his pregnant wife, Alis, quite adamant that she expose their baby, if it is a girl – the affection he shows Alis makes the demand all the more chilling: 'Please, please look after the baby; I'll send you money if I get paid soon. If you have the baby before I get back let it live if it's a boy; if it's a girl, expose it... how can I forget you? Please don't worry'.[7] Ovid, in the story of Iphis and Ianthe, tells a similar tale. Low-born Ligdus was poor but he had morals and was honourable; his pregnant wife was near her time and he wished her an easy labour, and a boy. 'We can't afford to raise a daughter, they're too much of a burden'. Ligdus was adamant, but happily Iphis, their baby girl, was secretly raised as a boy and was eventually changed into a boy by the gods.[8] Mythology this is, but its message surely reflects real-world practice; significantly, Ovid sees Ligdus as moral and honourable.

Some women were forced to give their girls away or sell them due to abject poverty; one wretched papyrus tells of a widow, Aurelia Herais, who has to surrender all claim to her nine-year-old daughter.[9] Many girls would end up in the slave markets; others would be sold as potential prostitutes. Orphans with nowhere to go were common among the lower classes.[10] Exposure of daughters, along with perinatal mortality – with childbearing telescoped as it was into adolescence and early adulthood – may well have filtered through as a cause of a shortage of childbearing women by the end of the Republic.

Juvenal describes the practice how discarded babies are left abandoned for adoption. Tacitus records that German tribes considered birth control and infanticide to be evil – all very different to contemporary Roman thought.[11] The remains of babies have been found under the excavated floors of houses at Brough-on-Humber (Petuaria).

Due to the high rate of infant mortality, Roman parents

deliberately inured themselves to the harsh fact that their baby might well die, so as to mitigate the grief that normally attends such a tragic situation. The employment of wet nurses, and the knowledge that some Romans 'farmed out' their infants for the first two years or so of their lives, may suggest a degree of parental indifference. Cicero says as much – 'No one pays any notice if he dies in the cradle.'[12] The tombstone of twelve-year-old Julia Pothousa from Arcadia may endorse this; her parents wish that she'd died earlier, before they had grown to love her.

Contraception generally was somewhat makeshift, and toxic. Pliny the Elder, quoting Caecilius, recommended the use of a special amulet: it had to be made from the worms which crawl around in the large head of the hairy spider; if the woman attached it with deer skin and wore it before dawn she would prevent conception for up to one year.[13] Aristotle had advocated smearing cedar oil, white lead or frankincense on the female genitals while the *Hippocratic Corpus* swore by drinking *misy*, dilute copper sulphate. Lucretius taught that women should, after the partner had ejaculated, wriggle their hips to divert the semen – but not all women, not respectable *matronae*, just common prostitutes.[14]

Pliny seems somewhat embarrassed by contraception, no doubt because of the obsessive imperial pressures on women to conceive; he explains it away by his concern to give fertile women some respite from serial pregnancies and childbirth. Non-penetrative or non-vaginal sex can be a form of contraception; graffiti from Pompeii confirms its prevalence, with examples of sodomy and fellatio.[15] Romula sucks her man here, there and everywhere, while Sabina sucks but doesn't get it quite right. Second-century-AD Manetho describes non-penetrative sex as 'breast relief' in his *Forecasts*.[16] Seneca alludes to anal sex taking place on the wedding night, as does Martial, but for him it happens just the once, because nurse and mother stop it becoming a habit; they protest that the bride is his *uxor*, not a *puer* – a wife, not a boy.[17]

Dioscorides was something of an expert; he knew of twenty-four contraceptive potions, three of which were magic, including an amulet made of asparagus. Others involved applying peppermint, honey, cedar gum, axe weed and alum in various concoctions to the genitals. Soranus is equally unromantic. His contraception of choice is stale olive oil, honey or the sap from a balsam or cedar tree applied to the entrance of the vagina – on its own or (alarmingly) mixed with white lead and bunged up with wool. This has a coagulating and cooling effect which causes the vagina to close before sex, and acts as a barrier to the sperm. An alternative method, just as inelegant, involved the woman holding her breath when her partner ejaculates, pulling away so that his semen does not penetrate too deeply, then getting up straightaway and squatting and sneezing before wiping her vulva clean. Dioscorides also recommends using vinegar, olive oil, ground pomegranate peel and ground flesh of dried figs as vaginal suppositories. Things change slowly; olive oil was still being advocated by the Marie Stopes Clinic as recently as 1931, along with other effective spermicides like lemon, alum and vinegar. Douches made from vinegar, alum or lemon juice were still used by the working classes in New York in 1947, and lemons were in use in 1970s Glasgow.

Aetius had a novel approach. He vouched for the liver of a cat inserted inside a tube fitted to the woman's left foot, or a section from the womb of a lioness in an ivory tube. In the fourth century AD, Oribasius recommended a cabbage pessary post-coitus.[18] These methods were hardly discrete or convenient and they certainly demanded consummate foresight and pre-sex preparation. They all tell us that it was up to the woman to organise the contraception – although we do hear, from Pliny, of some male initiatives where spermicides are rubbed onto the penis and goats' bladders are used as a primitive condom. The 'safe' period seems to be unknown, and no one mentions *coitus interruptus,* which may suggest that it was so common and obvious as to not merit comment. Withholding ejaculation was discouraged by Rufus of Ephesus because it damaged the kidneys and bladder; surgical sterilisation only developed as far as experiments on sows, while vasectomy seems to have been performed just on gladiators.[19]

Soranus offers his advice on the strict understanding that contraception is much safer than abortion. For effective abortion the woman should do the opposite to what is recommended for avoiding miscarriage: namely, take brisk walks or horse rides, jump high into the air, massage, or lift weights that are too heavy. He cites the unquestionable example of a flute girl, a slave in his household, whom he instructed to jump in the air seven times and kick her buttocks with her heels. On the seventh acrobatic the foetus fell out, much to the astonishment (and horror?) of the flute girl. Should this physical option fail, the patient should be immersed in a boiled mixture of linseed, fenugreek, marsh mallow, and wormwood, using poultices and fusions of the same. The alternative, pharmacological route, was *phthorion,* an abortive drug. A further option involved taking long baths and eating spicey food; the woman is then bled aggressively and made to take a ride on a horse. A suppository may be inserted, made up from myrtle, snowdrop seeds and bitter lupines, so long as it is not too powerful, and care must always be taken not dislodge the embryo with sharp instruments which may nick neighbouring organs. Uterine sounds or dilators for probing the uterus through the cervix have been excavated at Hockwold in Norfolk and may well have been used to induce abortion.[20]

Two of Ovid's poems clearly show that he was passionately opposed to abortion, particularly if it exposed his mistress's vanity. 'The woman who first set about ripping out her foetus deserves to die midst the carnage she started.' Ovid, mindful of the very real risks, can scarcely believe that the only reason his woman wants an abortion is to avoid developing stretch marks on her stomach; if the mothers in the good old days had done this, the human race would be extinct, he splutters. He questions how a woman can tear out her stomach with sharp instruments or administer terrible poisons to her unborn child. The passage is significant for a number of reasons: these evil toxins are reminiscent of the poisons used by witches and which conjure up an association between abortion and nefarious activity; it highlights, as does the advice from Soranus nearly a century later, the prevalence of backstreet abortions; and it demonstrates the obsession – a modern obsession, Ovid would say – that some women had, as they do now, with self-image, even to the point of endangering their lives in the pursuit of perfection. To Ovid, the whole issue is unnatural: he ends his poem with a salutary warning to the tender girls, – they can have their abortions, but not with impunity – as often as not they too will die along with the unborn child they have murdered. Crowds watching their funeral procession exclaim, *merito!* serve you right! Ovid is only thankful that his girl has got away with it this time – if she does it again, though, let her pay the price! In the second poem he seems too preoccupied with the dangers to be angry; Corinna's life was in the balance, *in dubio vitae,* and he does everything in his power to ensure her recovery.[21]

Ovid was not the only Roman pro-lifer: Juvenal and Seneca both abhorred abortion, as did Cicero, because it reduced the population and wiped out good families. Juvenal talks of the powerful medicines, the *medicamina* and the women who have 'industrialised sterility', killing human life in the stomach. Pliny regarded *abortiva*, abortifacients, to be more evil than poison. Domitian reputedly impregnated his niece, Julia, and arranged an abortion which killed her. Abortion was finally criminalised in the second century AD under Severus.

In the later empire abortion was, for some, inextricably linked to contraception and prostitution, a triad which could only end in death. St John Chrysostom preached in *Homily 24 on the Epistle to the Romans 4*, 'For you, a courtesan is not only a courtesan; you also make her into a murderess. Can you not see the link: after drunkenness, fornication; after fornication, adultery; after adultery, murder?' According to Plautus, abortion was an obvious course for a pregnant prostitute to take, either – as Ovid suggested – by drinking poisons or by using a sharp instrument to puncture the amniotic membrane which surrounds the foetus. Procopius tells us that when she was a prostitute, the Empress Theodora was well versed in the various ways of inducing an abortion.

Medicine, of course, was always caught up in the unquenchable popular taste for the mystical, macabre and chthonic and a preoccupation with the dark arts within the shadier corners of Roman society.[22] Life reflects art and art reflects life: the evidence lies in literature, on excavated curse tables, in papyrology and on tombstones.

By the end of the first century BC, 'sciences' such as magic, astrology, alchemy and daemonology had become mainstream and were established as teachable subjects. Examples are legion. Pliny the Elder records evidence of witchcraft among the Machyles in Africa: apart from being 'bisexual', with one breast female and the other male, they induce drought and child mortality on a prodigious scale.

Sulla's *Lex Cornelia de Sicariis et Veneficis* of 81 BC had made it illegal to administer a love potion or abortifacients. The penalty for the lower classes was hard labour in the mines, while banishment to an island awaited the upper classes, with property forfeited; if the recipient died it was a capital offence.

Curses and charms were popular throughout the Roman period, with women handing them out as well as receiving them. There were restraining spells restraining rivals; retaining spells, retaining the object of desire in the face of competition; obtaining spells, winning the object of desire in the face of someone else's restraining and/or retaining spells; spells which inflicted erectile dysfunction or cured it, provided effective contraception or induced abortion, guaranteed safe delivery or led to pregnancy. Just as sexual medicine is medicalised today, so it was comprehensively magicalised by the Romans.

Birth Control, Aphrodisiacs and Love Potions

Here are a few examples of the 1,600 or so curse tablets which have been found. *Defixiones* reach back as far as the fourth century BC in Greece and were traditionally consecrated to the gods of the underworld. Predominantly a practice of the lower classes, the curses were often provoked by unfortunate events such as commercial disputes, failures in law suits, or unrequited love: they gave vent to the curser's vengeful wrath, malice and vindictiveness. Typically the victim's name was written on a lead tablet, although gold, silver and marble are not unknown; blanks have been found suggesting that there was a steady, ongoing trade. The consecration was made and a nail stuck through the name; this was often followed by the name of the target's mother, to avoid any mistaken identity which would invalidate the curse. Magic words and symbols were added to enhance the chances of success. Some tablets feature a portrait of the victim which is also pierced with nails; the texts were anonymous. In tablets inspired by jilted love, a lock of the intended's hair was sometimes attached. Spells could be deployed to reveal the identity of a rival lover. One involves placing the heart of a hoopoe on a sleeping woman's genitals; another promises that the tongue of a hen placed on her lips or breast will make her spill the beans.

Typical is the *defixio* which brings down all manner of calamity on the recipient. 'May burning fever seize all her limbs, kill her soul and her heart; O gods of the underworld, break and smash her bones, choke her, arourarelyoth, let her body be twisted and shattered, phrix, phrox.'[23] This angry man was leaving nothing to chance. A bitter and broken-hearted Marcus Junius Euphrosynus, obviously torn between grief for a daughter and hatred for her mother, set up a tomb to the eight-year-old daughter, Junia Procula, in the first century AD.[24] On it he curses Acte, his treacherous, tricky, hard-hearted poisoner of a shameful wife, hoping that she gets in the next life as good as she gave in this. He leaves the adulteress a nail and a rope for her neck, and burning pitch to sear her evil heart. A late second-century curse on Rufa Pulica found in an urn along with her ashes in Mentana near Rome lists a number of her body parts: the prurient focus on sexual organs suggests that illicit sex was involved somewhere. Ticene of Carisius suffered a similar *post mortem* fate on a tablet found at Minturnae, south of Rome; her curser wishes that everything she does goes wrong: his catalogue of her body parts is less sexual than Rufa's and quite methodical, running as it does more or less from head to toe. Philo may have had something to hide when he cursed Aristo; he ties up her hands, feet and soul, condemns her to silence and wishes her tongue be bitten off. The wife of Aristocydes curses him and his lovers, hoping that he will never marry another woman... or a boy.

There are more, all intended to scare the life out of anyone contemplating anything which might upset someone else. 'A donkey shall rape him, a donkey shall rape his wife.' Ovid cannot get an erection and blames a witch: 'Maybe it was magic that turned me into ice.' Sentencing to never-ending sexual intercourse was one way of damning a rival, although some, at first sight, may have viewed this curse as a perfect punishment. 'Bring her thigh close to his, her genitals close to his in unending intercourse for all the time of her life.' Less ideal was one of the bluntest, excavated in 2008 at Amathus in Cyprus, from the seventh century AD: 'May your penis hurt when you make love.' Centuries after the sack of Rome and the spread of Christianity it seems that these curses were still going strong.

It was not all fire and brimstone, however. There are occasional examples of love *defixiones* where a lover will invoke chthonic deities to help him win the love of his life. The optimistically named Successus dedicates his wife in a bid to see his love for her requited: 'May Successa burn, let her feel herself aflame with love or desire for Successus.'[25] Plenty of fire but no brimstone here.

The *Greek Magical Papyrus* (or Great Paris Magical Papyrus) offers considerably less romantic, excessively malevolent and obsessively perverted love charms targeted at women; it originates from the fourth century AD, but undoubtedly describes practices which were prevalent much earlier. Some men went to extraordinary, paranoid lengths to ensure the fidelity of their women; the following (*PGM* 4, 296–466) is one of the most notorious and takes a typically prescriptive, recipe form. 'Take wax or clay from a potter's wheel and form it into two figures, a male and a female... her arms should be tied behind her back, and she should kneel.' Directions are then given to write magical words on her head and other parts of her body, including the genitalia, to stick a needle into her brain and twelve others into other parts of her body; tie a binding spell written on a lead plate to the figures, dedicate it to gods of the underworld and leave it at sunset near to the tomb of someone who has died violently or prematurely; invite them to rise from the dead and bring X [the object of the charm], daughter of Y, to him and make her love me. Finally, a litany of instructions follows to deprive the girl of food and drink, sexual intercourse, sleep and health – all designed to make her make love with the curser forever.

Sarapammon invokes a whole pantheon of underworld gods in his perverted efforts to ensure the fidelity of Ptolemais;[26] he asks the daemon Antinous to tie Ptolemais up to prevent her from having intercourse or from being sodomised 'and give no pleasure to any man but me... and let her not eat, nor drink, nor be happy, nor go out, nor sleep with anyone but me... drag her by the hair and entrails until she does not reject me... submissive for her entire life, loving me, desiring me'. This tablet (the Louvre Doll) was found in a vase which also contained a voodoo-type clay figure of a kneeling woman, her hands tied behind her back and body pierced with needles.

This spell, cast by Akarnachthas, was found in Egypt and probably dates from the early first century AD. The ingredients are the egg of a crow, the juice of a crow's foot plant and the bile of an electric catfish from the Nile. These are to be ground up with honey and rubbed on the penis while chanting the following spell: 'Womb of NN, open and receive the semen of NN... let NN love me for all of her life... and let her remain chaste for me, as Penelope did for Odysseus. And you womb, remember me for the whole of my life. If you have intercourse after this, the woman will love you and sleep with no one else.'

The spell on another papyrus aims to render the woman sleepless until she succumbs. 'Take the eyes out of a bat and release it alive. Take unbaked dough... or wax and shape a puppy dog. Put the right eye of the bat into the right eye of the puppy and the left eye of the bat into the left eye of the puppy. Take a needle and stick the magic substance into it. Prick the eyes of the puppy... Pray: I conjure you to... make X lose the fire in her eyes or become sleepless and have no one in mind except me... and love me passionately.' The Papyri were not always heterosexual; one from the second century AD describes a lesbian curse where Heraias brings and binds the heart and soul of Sarapias.[27]

Apples were believed to be especially efficacious at winning over an unobtainable or recalcitrant lover. Throw an apple to your intended (a quince or pomegranate would do just as well); he or she would pick it up and either bite seductively into it or secrete it in her bosom (in the case of a girl). Either way, the message was clear. That is what Acontius did in Ovid's *Heroides* (20 and 21); he threw her the fruit etched with the words, 'I vow to marry Acontius,' and lo and behold, she did! A Great Paris papyrus reinforces this. 'Whichever woman I throw the apple at or hit with it... may she be mad for my love whether she takes it in her hand and eats it or sets it in her bosom... and may she not stop loving me.' (*PGM* 122) The bride on her wedding night was given a quince or an apple to foster fertility, according to Plutarch (*Questiones Romanae* 279f.). Lucian, in his *Dialogi Meretricii* (12, 1, 3036), describes a scene in which one prostitute is put out when her boyfriend flirts with another by throwing her a piece of apple which she kisses and inserts into her cleavage. The apple then is an ice-breaker; prostitutes also use it as an indicator that they are available for business (Aristophanes, *Clouds* 996–997).

Fruit was not the only fertility-giving indicator of sexual availability. A spinning top type toy called the *iunx* also possessed these powers and, as with the fruit, was put to good use with the bride on her wedding night. Examples of *iunges* can be seen on wedding vases and on an Attic pyxis showing a maid of honour (*numpheutria*) magically spinning a *iunx* while the bride does her hair (London E 774). The *iunx* came well recommended from mythology: Simaetha used one in Theocritus while Aphrodite taught Jason to use it while wooing Medea (Pindar, *Pythian* 4, 213–219). Socrates explained to the beautiful, envious Theodote that he was able to attract so many good looking men through his expertise with the *iunx* (Xenophon *Memorabilia*, 3, 11, 16–17).

Related to the *iunx* was the *iunx*-bird, the wryneck, another agent of erotic magic. Aphrodite nailed one to a wheel, like Ixion in the underworld, with a view to transferring the bird's agony to Medea so that it envelopes her and makes her forget her duty to her parents in her obsessive love for Jason.

Eye contact worked as well. The *Greek Magical Papyrus* has one spell (*PGM* 4, 1265–1274) which required the obtainer to stare into their loved one's eyes for seven consecutive days while muttering the name of Aphrodite. He (for the agent was usually a he) may well have bored the woman into capitulation.

A love potion features in Virgil's Eighth *Eclogue* (adapted from Theocritus' *Idylls* 2), where Amaryllis concocts a potion and spells to win back Daphnis. 'By these magic rites I'll try and bring Daphnis back to his senses: all I need now are some spells.' A less than idyllic love potion recommended by the *magi* and scorned by Pliny the Elder involved the wearing of an amulet which contained a hyena's anus.[28]

Erectile dysfunction makes a comical appearance in Petronius' *Satyricon*. Here an old lady, Proselenus, is engaged by Chryseis to cure Eumolpus' impotence with her potions, an amulet and magic stones. His dysfunction originally presented when he was consorting with Circe, Chryseis' mistress; to Chryseis, Circe is nothing but a witch who draws down the moon. Proselenus later returns, her hair in disarray, all in black; she questions if it was a witch who emasculated him and subjects him to a bout of flagellation in the room of Oenothea, priestess of Priapus, god of phalluses. Oenothea comes in, is told by Proselenus that Eumolpus is flaccid, and sets about an elaborate magical process to restore him 'as stiff as a horn'.

Apuleius introduces two witches in his *Metamorphoses*. In the story of Aristomenes, Lucius meets two men in Thessaly, one of whom rubbished the belief that magic can blank the sun, reverse the flow of rivers, freeze the ocean. Aristomenes' old friend, Socrates, was down on his luck and had had an affair with Meroe, an aging innkeeper who possessed magical powers and could do all the things his companion had just scorned, and more.

When one of her previous lovers had been unfaithful to her Meroe turned him into a beaver, the rationale being that beavers, when hunted, bite off their own genitals leaving them lying around as a decoy to put hunters off the scent; the clear intention was for her wayward lover to do likewise. She also changed rival innkeepers into frogs, prosecuting lawyers into rams and condemned the wife of another lover to perpetual pregnancy: unable to give birth, her bump grew to such a size that it looked as though she was carrying baby of elephantine proportions.

Lucian, in a scene from *de Mercede Conductis*, describes two prostitutes, Melitta and Bacchis, employing the services of a Syrian witch to win back Charinis, a former lover. The witch's reputation precedes her; they utter incantations and can make a woman loved, even if she is deeply hated before.[29]

The line between what was considered conventional medicine and malevolent magic potions is often blurred. Pliny gives an example, when he prescribes a potion that makes sex repugnant to women: it involves smearing the genitalia of the woman with blood from a tick that resides on a wild black bull. If she then drinks goat's urine she will find love repellent too. Smearing blood had a similar effect on Faustina, the wife of Marcus Aurelius; she was smitten by a gladiator and finally confessed her passion to her husband. On advice from the Chaldean magic men, the gladiator in question was executed and Faustina was made to bathe in his blood, and then have sex with her husband while still covered in the blood. All thoughts of the gladiator apparently vanished.[30]

Tibullus describes a witch who can confound natural phenomena, call up the dead and call down the stars, creating chaos on land and in the skies; she is well-versed in the evil herbs of Medea, and has tamed the wild dogs of Hecate. Most crucially for Tibullus, though, she has concocted a *cantus*, a spell for Delia, his mistress, which will enable her to deceive her husband. Even if he sees him and Delia in bed together, he will literally not believe his own eyes. Significantly, Tibullus adds that the *cantus* will only work with him; if she uses it while with other men, it will fail to work and all will be exposed.[31]

Lucan's Erichtho is one of literature's most repellent of witches, and an amateur obstetrician. One of her many obscene atrocities involves performing crude caesarean sections on pregnant women whenever a baby is required for the pyre.[32]

Love potion witches feature in Seneca's *Heracles on Mount Oeta*. Deianira, Heracles' wife, is carried away by Nessus, a centaur who, when he attempts to rape her, is shot by Heracles with poisoned arrows. Slyly, Nessus convinces Deinaira that she must make use of his blood as a love potion to keep Heracles true; the potion is given to Heracles but it is, of course, toxic and slowly kills him. Interestingly, the witch notes that it is quite common for women to attempt to save their failing marriages by resorting to magical arts and prayers.[33]

The stereotypical witch is old, ugly, sex-crazed, repellent, squalid and often inebriated. We have the Romans to thank for that – an image which has persisted for centuries and typifies the witch in cultures all over the world. Horace with Canidia and her crones and Lucan's Erichtho are perhaps the most memorable. But it is worth noting that it was not always the case. Circe was attractive enough to get Odysseus into her bed; Fotis in Apuleius' *Metamorphoses*, was a pretty, sexy enough witch, and Dido, although no career witch, was obviously an attractive woman who was able to do for Aeneas what Circe did for Odysseus. Witches and magic generally were feared in Rome and among the highly superstitious Romans: stereotype the witch as a repulsive old hag and you begin to explain and justify to some extent that irrational fear.

Aphrodisiacs, anaphrodisiacs, contraceptives, and abortifacients crop up in both medical texts or pharmacopeia, and in magic handbooks: pharmacology was very confusible with magic potions. Marcellus Empiricus (Marcellus of Bordeaux) in his *De Medicamentis* describes seventy or so sexually-related treatments and typifies the dangerously blurred lines between pharmacology, folky medicine and superstitious magic.[34] A contemporary of

Ausonius, Marcellus had the answer to growths and lesions on the testicles and penis, undescended testes (cryptorchidism), erectile dysfunction, hydrocele (the accumulation of fluid in a sac around the testicle); he could also ensure your woman's fidelity: 'If you've had a woman, and you don't want another man ever to get inside her, do this: cut off the tail of a live green lizard with your left hand and release it while it's still alive. Keep the tail closed up in the palm of the same hand until it dies and touch the woman and her genitals when you have intercourse with her.'[35] And, the *tour de force*, how to make a man a eunuch without recourse to the blade: 'There is a herb called *nymphaea* in Greek, 'Hercules' club' in Latin, and *baditis* in Gaulish; its root, pounded to a paste and drunk in vinegar for ten consecutive days, has the astonishing effect of turning a boy into a eunuch.'[36]

His therapy for enlarged spermatic veins in an immature boy (varicocele) was terrifyingly claustrophobic. 'Split a young cherry-tree down the middle to its roots while leaving it standing, in such a way that the boy can be passed through the cleft. Then join the sapling together again and seal it with cow manure and other dressings, so that the parts that were split may intermingle within themselves more easily. The speed with which the sapling grows together and its scar forms will determine how quickly the swollen veins of the boy will return to health.'[37]

Marcellus also records which herbs[38] were efficacious in inducing menstruation, or to purge the womb after childbirth or abortion; these include abortifacients and may have been used as such.[39] Erectile dysfuntion can be banished by coating the penis with a mixture of honey and pepper to produce an erection,[40] or by boiling a donkey's genitals in oil and using it as an ointment.[41]

CHAPTER FIVE

Buggery, Beasts and Brothels: the Need for *Virtus*

The way we look at sex and sexuality today is very different from how the Romans viewed it; this chapter examines sex and sexuality in Roman men and women, and their attitudes towards it from what we can tell from the available evidence. It covers the Roman sex industry; homosexual Romans, sexual pleasure and sexual deviation, erotica, and 'pornography'.

For the sake of convenience, the terminology we use here is modern; in the ancient world 'lesbian', for example, would have had no homoerotic connotations; furthermore, there are no words in Latin for homosexual or heterosexual. This may suggest that *the difference* between the two did not exercise the Romans in anything like the way it has troubled other societies in the last 2,000 years.

Our twenty-first-century perspective on sex and sexuality is informed by the accumulation of years of baggage loaded onto us by centuries of change – the strictures of the church, the prudish Victorians and the permissive 1960s, to name but three significant changing influences. Rome was somewhat different. The ubiquity of erotica in wall paintings and mosaics, in sex manuals, poetry and plays, in phalluses, on coins and in ceramics would suggest that Romans were somewhat more relaxed and less exercised by the ways of the flesh, accustomed as they were to enjoying having sex around them, even enjoying looking at sex. The shame, embarrassment and secrecy which accompanies erotica or 'pornography' (itself a nineteenth-century term) in many societies today would have been quite alien to them; to the Roman, sex was all probably quite normal, an everyday part of everyday life. There were, of course, exceptions – particularly the stigma attached to oral sex (*os impurum*) and male penetration as the receiving partner, 'lesbian' sex and group sex – but, by and large, sex and sexuality seem to have been relatively unremarkable facets of everyday life. Importantly, the public display of erotica would of course have been seen by women as well as men, and by their children; the love poetry, the plays and the satires were read, heard and watched by literate women as well as literate men. Visual representations of sex, many of them featuring attractive partners of either sex, reflected positive and healthy social attitudes enjoyed by homeowners and their guests alike.

Public nudity, however, was frowned upon in some quarters. Ennius (c. 239–169 BC), quoted by Cicero in his *Tusculan Disputations* (4, 33, 70), declares that nudity is the first step on the road to public shame. Unlike the Greeks, the Romans, until the time of Nero, kept their genitals and buttocks covered up in athletic contests; Cicero sneers at Mark Antony when he appears naked in the Lupercalia, even though the rite demands he be nude. The Romans' anxiety here probably stems from the association, first, of nudity with defeat in battle – defeated enemies were often stripped before they went *sub iugum*, under the yoke – and second, with slaves and servitude, for whom nuditiy was an emblem.

Lucretius (c. 99–55 BC) provides the earliest surviving description of sexuality in Roman literature in his *De Rerum Natura*. This would have had significant influence on elite and literate Romans down the ages. In modern times Yeats read the translation by Dryden and called it 'the finest description of sexual intercourse ever written' (1073–1085).

The phallus, of course, was central to everything sexual. The city of Rome, indeed, has been described (improbably) as being phallocentric with the Forum apparently laid out in the form of a penis and testicles. Egypt provides the earliest evidence of the cult of the phallus where Isis, after Osiris had been dismembered, was unable to find his penis; Isis then fashioned an erect phallus to give to mankind for them to worship. The cult of the phallus spread to Greece and then to Italy.

In Rome, the phallus goes back to the days of Romulus where Plutarch, in his *Romulus*, tells the story of Tarchetius, the cruel king of Alba Longa. A huge phallus rose from his hearth and started flying around the house; oracular consultation revealed that this was actually Mars showing his anger, impatient for Tarchetius to produce a successor to the throne. Mars demanded a virgin for the phallus because the child born of this coupling would excel in virtue, fortune and strength. Attempts by Tarchetius to persuade his daughter to have sex with the phallus failed when she refused; instead he ordered a slave girl to take her place. Romulus and Remus were duly born; Tarchetius abandoned the twins only for them to be adopted by the she-wolf, *lupa*, and nurtured.

The ubiquity of phalluses around Pompeii reminds us of two things: first that Roman society, in every way, was dominated by men and the symbols of manhood; second that the phallus was also a good luck token against evil spirits: it was a defence against the 'evil eye' and was exhibited to ward off the pernicious. Significantly, it was always largely devoid of the shame or embarrassment it evokes in later societies. Hence the Roman phallus could be seen fashioned as wind chimes as well as on street signs, farm carts or buildings, in the shape of loaves, as wine flasks – all to secure good health and good fortune.

The phallus had special significance in aspects of Roman religion. It was an important symbol for the Vestal Virgins who tended the cult of the *fascinus populi Romani*, the sacred image of the divine phallus and male equivalent of the hearth of Vesta. Like the Palladium, Lares, and Penates of Troy and the eternal Vestal flame, the *fascine* were inviolable symbols, emblems of the continuity of the Roman state. Liber, the god of wine, growth and fertility, was the focus each year in the Liberalia for a wooden phallus paraded through Italy and crowned by the most chaste *matrona* to ensure a successful harvest. Plutarch describes the *falloforia* staged by Ptolomy of Alexandria, featuring a procession with celebrants carrying a fifty-metre-long phallus covered in gold. The *falloforia* spread to Greece where processions held in honour of Priapus and Dionysus involved large wooden phalluses. Athenaeus (*Deipnosophistae* 5, 52) ascribes it to Antiochus, King of Syria in a festival in Alexandria in 275 BC which is the last word in extravagance, exoticism and eye-watering sumptuousness.

> In other carts, also, were carried a Bacchic wand of gold, one hundred and thirty-five feet long, and a silver spear ninety feet long; in another was a gold phallus one hundred and eighty feet long, painted in various colours and bound with fillets of gold; it had at the extremity a gold star, the perimeter of which was nine feet.

Antiochus's aim was to exceed in extravagance and opulence the spectacular games held by the general Aemilius Paulus in Macedonia. Lucian (*Calumnies*, 16) points out that not joining in the festivities only led to embarrassing conspicuousness; in the court of King Ptolemy the anti-social Platonic philosopher Demetrius was insulted because he drank water and was the only one who did not don women's clothing during the Dionysia.

Smaller talismans in the shape of a penis and testes, often winged, sometimes fashioned in gold, invoked the protection of the god Fascinus against the evil eye. These charms, or *fascini*, were often worn as a ring or amulet, especially by infants, boys, and soldiers. Priapus, a phallus with a face, was often invoked by couples experiencing sexual problems. Pliny says that the Vestals hung an effigy of the *fascinus* on the underside of a commander's chariot to protect him from envy.

One very important aspect of the sexual images depicted in statuary, mosaics, wall paintings and the sex described in graffiti is that they bring us evidence which for once was not just produced by elite men but by artisans. The wall painters, mosaic makers and scribblers were just as likely to be men, or women, from the lower orders – and, as such, they give a unique perspective into sexuality which is absent from literature or from much of the inscriptional evidence. And there was lots of it. Taking graffiti alone, over 7,500 scratchings have been found in Pompeii; indeed, one graffito found in three separate places says, 'I am surprised, O wall, that you have not collapsed; you have to put up with the tedious words of so many writers!' (*CIL* 4, 1904; 2461; 2487).

Caelius seems to be alone among Greeks and Romans in describing homosexuality as a psychiatric illness. His categorisation survived for two centuries or so: *DSM I* and *II*, the gold standard in the classification of mental disorders, published in 1952 and 1968 respectively, classed it likewise.

The really important difference for the Roman was the dichotomy between the active sexual partner and the passive. The male was, or should be, active, the female, or a man of lower social standing such as a slave or a *cinaedus*, was passive. When a man became a *paterfamilias* it was not just the the power of life and death over his wife, his children and his slaves that he assumed. He also won the right to sodomize his male slaves, but only as an active participant; passivity, or being sodomised, was anathema to the Roman, a sign of depravity and feebleness, something foreigners or barbarians did. Seneca sums the situation up: 'Sexual passivity in a free man is a crime, for a slave a necessity, for a freed slave a duty.' Seneca, though, (*Controversiae* 4, Prologue 10) is quick to point out the humorous side of this when he tells us that *officium* (duty) soon became a witty euphemism for being buggered.

Virtus was the key word in the vocabulary denoting the masculinity of the Roman, indicating at the same time virtue, manliness, military prowess and bravery. A prerequisite of *virtus*, that essential quality of masculinity in a Roman man (*vir*), was that he remained at all times a sexually impenetrable penetrator, and that he thereby maintained his sexual integrity. He could copulate with his women, and his men – but only as the dominant partner. *Virtus* too was imbued with nostalgia – it is what all the Roman ancestors exhibited in the good old days before the tide of effeminate feebleness swept in from Greece and points east. A true Roman was a *virtus* Roman; *virtus* was synonymous with Roman-ness. *Virtus* was the word the true Roman wanted to have on his role of honour up there with all his other *res gestae*. The word soon took on connotations of probity and discrimination; knowing the difference between right and wrong, according to the satirist Gaius Lucilius (c.160–103 BC). Sexual passivity, or being on the receiving end, was most definitely one of the bad things in life, as emphasised by Lucilius in another fragment in which he descrbes freeborn men who made their anus, *scultima*, available for penetration as a *scultimidonus*, or 'arsehole offerer'.

For men, as stated, the shame implicit in penetration by another male goes some way to explain the disgust commonly felt towards lesbians who perform penetrative sex. Penetration was what men do; men could penetrate but on no account should they be penetrated. The *lex Scantinia* of 216 BC had criminalised *stuprum* against a freeborn male minor and penalised adult male citizens who took a passive role in sex with other men. Allowing one's body to be used for pleasure by others in sodomy and oral sex was a sign of weakness, a deficiency of *virtus*. It was fine, however, for a man to indulge with males lower down the social ladder, male prostitutes or slaves, so long as they assumed the penetrative role.

There is ample evidence for male prostitutes selling penetrating services: Hostius Quadra was being penetrated while he watched it all in his mirrors; emperors Nero and Elagabalus scoured the night streets for well-endowed men and Nero accommodated the gladiator Doryphorus (Suetonius *Nero* 29); Plautus refers to it in his *Curculio* (482–484) as does the writer of mimes, Pomponius Bononiensis (fr. 148–149; 151-152 R) and Martial (2, 51; 3, 71; 6, 50). The pseudo-Virgilian *Catalepton* (13, 23–26) refers to sailors on the banks of the Tiber offering the same senior service.

Cinaedus, 'pervert', 'catamite', was the word to describe the person on the bottom, so to speak, in an act of sodomy – the much reviled recipient. He was also associated with adultery and, often as a dancer, was noted for his provocative bum wiggling and his effeminately excessive hair grooming. Aulus Gellius leaves us a description of such a gender deviant in his *Attic Nights* (6, 12), as given by the general Scipio Aemianus: 'The sort of perfumed man who peacocks every day in front of the mirror, trims his eyebrows and prances about with well-groomed beard and depilated thighs.' Nevertheless, the androgynous *cinaedus* did attract the attentions of some women who liked that sort of man. To Justinian the 'man-woman' or effeminate male was disgusting; they 'do unspeakable things' and 'practice this sort of degradation' (*Apology* 1, 27, 2).

To illustrate how common *cinaedus* was and how frequently it was used as an insult or in defamation, there are thirty instances of it in Pompeii graffiti along with 126 references to oral sex, eighty-three references to anal or vaginal penetration and two mentions of *pathicus*. Cunnilingus, often associated with homosexuality, in the Roman world was the licker not the act, as revealed by the discovery of a third-century-AD brick in modern Bulgaria describing Euphiletos as a 'cunt-licker' (*kusthekleikhon*).

Physiognomy had its place in the demonisation of the *cinaedus*. Favorinus of Arelate (*c.* AD 80 – *c.* 160) was a celebrated rhetor but his effeminacy attracted the vitriol of Polemon, his rival, in one of ancient history's most savage (and successful) character assassinations (*Anonymus Latinus* 40; Philostratus, VS 489). As if being born without testicles was not bad enough, Favorinus was 'greedy and immoral beyond all measure', had many feminine features (such as soft cheeks and limbs, abundant hair, and a woman's voice, neck, and walk), and was a 'deceitful magician' and 'a leader in evil and a teacher of it'. Philostratus called him an hermaphrodite. Another victim was the Persian eunuch Bogoas, lover of Darius III and Alexander the Great; Bogoas suffered at the hands of Q. Curtius Rufus. The historian calls him effeminate, sluttish and dissolute; through the Persian governor Orsines he is a whore, a pervert, and lower than a woman.

Polybius reports that homosexuality, and presumably the bisexuality which the Romans could freely enjoy, was prevalent in Rome by the fifth century BC. Lucretius briefly describes homosexuality while Catullus describes it in his Juventius poems. The love poets feature it too, as do Horace and Virgil in the second *Eclogue*. Ovid is a strict advocate of heterosexuality.[1] Phokylides, the early first-century Alexandrian, warns that even animals spurn male-to-male sex and warns women off from adopting the male sexual role (*Sententiae* 190-2); Paul of Tarsus groups effeminates and homosexual men with prostitutes, adulterers and idolators, and promises them that they will not inherit the Kingdom of God (*I Corinthians* 6: 9-10). Tacitus recounts an especially bad outcome for German sodomites: 'They drown [them] in muddy bogs pressing wicker baskets on top of them.' (*Germania* 12, 1-2.) Juvenal praises the up-front homosexual with his honest walk and expressions, as opposed to the moralizing perverts who try to conceal it (2, 8-10; 15-17). According to Lucian, effeminate gays make the best teachers of rhetoric, 'Note the negligent ease of his walk, his neck's willowy curve, his languishing glance; these words are honey, that breath perfume; was ever a head scratched with so graceful a forefinger? And those locks – were there more of them left – how hyacinthine their wavy style; he is tender as Sardanapalus.' (*Rhetorum Praeceptor* 11.) The Christian teacher Clement summed it all up very neatly when he said that he who denies his masculinity by daylight will certainly prove himself a woman at night (*Paed* 3, 30, 20, 3). Indeed, the ascetic early third-century Paul has seen what actually happens to homosexuals in Hell. 'And I saw other men and women covered with dust, and their appearance was as blood, and they were in a pit of pitch and brimstone and borne down in a river of fire.' (*Apocalypse of Paul* 39 trans. M.R. James 1924.) Ausonius encapsulates his confusion with it all. 'Why depilate your buttocks? Unless because the desire to be penetrated (*patientia*) craves the two-man disease, and you're a man in front but a woman round the back.' (*Epigrams* 93, 3, 5-6.)

In the empire, it seems that sexual integrity was less rigorously maintained and harsher sentences were imposed on transgressors, at least in the lower classes. Things changed dramatically in the third century AD when the Christian Marcus Julius Philippus (Philip the Arab, r. 244 to 249) banned male prostitution. By the end of the fourth century, passive homosexuality was punishable by burning and the punishment for a 'man coupling like a woman' was death by the sword under the *Theodosian Code* (9, 7, 3). Justinian (AD 527-65), criminalised all same-sex acts, passive or active; they were deemed 'contrary to nature' and punishable by death.

Homosexuality among the political and military elite has one of its more celebrated exponents in Julius Caesar, and was emulated by Tiberius, Caligula, Nero and Galba at least. According to Suetonius (*Caesar*, 49), while staying at the Bithynian court of

Nicomedes IV, 'he submitted to the king's pleasure'. It was time well spent, however, as Nicomedes later bequeathed his entire kingdom to Rome. Nevertheless, the episode continued to haunt Caesar with repeated innuendo and political slur: Licinius Calvus refers to Bithynia as 'Caesar's buggerer'; Curio describes Caesar as the 'queen's concubine' and refers to the 'whorehouse of Nicomedes' and the 'Bithynian brothel'; to Marcus Brutus, Caesar was queen to Pompey's king. Gaius Memmius describes him as cupbearer to Nicomedes along with other catamites. Cicero reminded Caesar in court while he was defending Nysa, Nicomedes' daughter, that 'it is well known what he gave you and what you gave him'. Even his soldiers joined in the fun, singing a typically ribald marching song during the Gallic campaign: 'Caesar had his way with Gaul; Nicomedes had his way with Caesar; behold now Caesar, conqueror of Gaul, in triumph, Not so Nicomedes, conqueror of Caesar.' Even when he was granted the provinces of Gaul and Illyria by the senate, his exultant boast that he would be 'mounting on their heads', that is, committing oral rape on the enemy, was met with the quip that that would be rather difficult for a woman to do. Caesar shrugged it off by referring to Semiramis and the Amazons as women successful in war.

According to Suetonius (*Galba* 22), Galba had a predilection for older and hard men – unusual in the Romans, who tended to go for the young and pretty. One day, when a favourite of his, Icelus, returned from Spain, he kissed him passionately, begged him to depilate his body hair, and hauled him off.

Caelius called lesbians *tribades* – women who are 'more eager to lie with women than men and in fact pursue women with almost masculine jealousy... they rejoice in the abuse of their sexual powers'. This may reflect a general male homophobia, an antipathy to lesbianism. Caelius is powerless to help. To him the condition is quite incurable; these 'disgraceful vices' are an affliction of the mind, which must be controlled. The situation was hopeless; he believed that homosexuality intensified with age, resulting in 'a hideous and ever increasing lust'.

Tribas comes from the Greek *tribo*, 'I rub', and was a perjorative term from the first century AD; it is defined as 'a woman who practises unnatural vice with herself or with other women', and in Latin, 'a woman who practises lewdness with women'.[2] Other Latin words for lesbian are *fricatrix* (she who rubs) and *virago*. The revulsion felt towards *tribades* stems from the assumption that tribadism entailed penetration (by a dildo, for example) or a large clitoris for penetration; penetration was, in normal circumstances, very much an exclusively male function. Ovid is mystified; he finds it 'a desire known to no one, freakish, novel... among all animals no female is seized by desire for female'. Martial calls Philaenis a *tribas* in the obscene diatribe in which she buggers the boys as vigorously as any man, and performs cunnilingus on the girls. As far as insults go this was extreme and double-edged; Philaenis was not only penetrating like a man, she was licking too – cunnilingus, be it homo or heterosexual, was seen by Roman men as utterly repellent and degrading. Bassa is a similar case; on first sight she appears as chaste as a Lucretia, because she is never implicated with a man, but she is really a *fututor* – a 'fucker', bringing together two *cunni*, pretending to be a man.[3] To Artemidorus, the interpreter of dreams, lesbian sex was as perverted as sex with the gods, with animals and with the dead. For a woman, dreaming of having sex with another woman was a dangerous thing, and not just for her; if she pleasures another woman she will have to share her secrets with that woman; if she is pleasured by another woman she will be separated from her husband or widowed, compensated only by the fact that she gets to learn the other woman's secrets. Stoic Seneca the Younger generalises that women 'satisfy the strangest of sexual tastes, acting as men among men', alluding to their use of dildos for penetration. He believed that homosexuality was *contra naturam*. Seneca the Elder cites a case where a man murders his wife and her lover *in flagrante delicto*, having prudently checked first to establish whether the lover was 'natural' (a man) or 'artificial'– a woman wearing a dildo. We know not which. What we do know from this exercise is that the Romans had no law of adultery when it was committed between women.

Despite all the protests, lesbians there were in Rome and in the wider empire; a Pompeii grafitto (*CIL* 4, 5296) has a woman addressing her lover, another woman, as 'my darling' (*pupula*). Lucian in his *Erotes* (28) invents a rhetorical exercise which aims to establish whether love for a man is better than lover for a woman, or vice versa. The conclusion is non-judgmental either way but the picture painted is truly graphic with its dildos, those 'strange and monstrous tools of lechery without semen'.

Lesbian love is evident from magic spells found in Roman Egypt. These were written down by magicians and paid for by the woman (in this case) who provided the text to influence the object of her desire. The dead person would be invoked while the magician stuck pins in body parts of a doll as mentioned in the spell. The spell, a lead tablet, would be thrown into the grave and left to work its magic. In one, from the third or fourth century AD, found at Hermoupolis, we read,

> By means of the corpse-demon inflame the heart, the liver and the spirit of Gorgonia... with love and affection for Sophia... drive Gorgonia, drive her, torture her body by night and by day, force her to rush around from everywhere and every house... loving Sophia, she surrendered like a slave. (*PSI* 1.28, 12ff.)

A second-century papyrus from Hawara describes a spell to bind two women, Sarapias and Herais (*PGM* 32).

On women and oro-genital sex, Catullus asserts that any woman who has sex with the odious Aemilius would be just as likely to lick the anus of a hangman with diarrhoea.[4] Cicero delivers the most excoriating of insults on Sextus Cloelius when he accuses him of performing cunnilingus on a menstruating woman.

To the fable writer Phaedrus, *tribades*, with their strap-on dildos, and soft (*molles*) men enjoy a deformed pleasure (4, 12, 1–2, 12–14).

A grafitto scrawled on a wall in Pompeii describes lesbian love: 'I wish I could hold to my neck and embrace the little arms, and bear kisses on the tender lips. Go on, baby, and trust your joys to the winds; believe me, light is the nature of men.' Pliny rubbished the *magis*' belief that wearing an amulet of hyena's genitals smeared with honey excited homosexual tendencies.[5]

Two of Lucian's *hetairae*, Clonarion and Leaena, discuss the pros and cons of lesbian sex, indicating that such services were readily available on the streets and in the brothels.[6] They tell of Megilla, a rich woman, who went for Leaena like a man would; both courtesans agree that this was unnatural, commenting that in Sparta they have tribadists just like Megilla who actually look like men. Notwithstanding, Leaena coyly reveals the details of her own seduction by Megilla and her friend Demonassa at a *symposium*; after playing her cithara, Leaena is invited into their bed where they kiss with tongues and squeeze her breasts. Megilla throws off her wig to reveal a bald head and takes on the identity of an athletic Megill*us*, 'husband' to Demonassa. Leaena enquires of Megillaus if she is a hermaphrodite and possesses a penis; she is not and does not, reassuring Leaena that, although she is in fact a woman, she has the desires of a man; she can, therefore, penetrate her (with a dildo, *olisbos*) although Leaena is coyly reticent on further detail here. After a necklace and fine dress have exchanged hands, Leaena is duly penetrated – accompanied by kissing, heavy breathing and obvious enjoyment.

We have already referred to the story of Iphis in the *Metamorphoses*. Ovid describes the prospective lesbian union of Iphis (the girl who had to masquerade as a boy to avoid being exposed) and Ianthe as monstrous, an act unprecedented in nature – no beast does it. Juvenal assails Tullia, a *matrona*, and her lover, Maura, who take it in turns to ride each other: *in...vices equitant.*

One of the poems written by the noblewoman Julia Balbilla, a poetess who was part of the entourage accompanying Hadrian and Vibia Sabina on their trip to the Colossus of Memnon in Egypt in AD 128, may suggest that Sabina and Julia Balbilla were lesbians. The poem is written in the syle of Sappho (born *c.* 630 BC) and opens with the line 'lovely Queen Sabina'. The suggestion, however, remains tenuous at best.

As might be expected, the early Christian writers were not sympathetic and linked lesbianism with whoring. Their homophobia starts with Tatian (an ascetic who eschewed sex of any kind); he described Sappho as a sex-crazed little harlot in his *Address to the Greeks* (33). In Carthage all Tertullian saw around him was *matronae* dressed like prostitutes or *frictrices*. Indeed, he warns against drinking from the same cup as a *frictrix*, a castrated priest of Cybele (assumed to be a homosexual), a gladiator or an executioner. Homosexuals were tarred with the same Christian brush as killers. *The Apocalypse of Peter* (17) reveals that effeminate men and *tribades* spend their time in Hell continually jumping off a very high cliff.

A rare woman's voice can be heard in Juvenal's second satire: Laronia joins the poet to criticise a hypocritical male homosexual, Hispo. To Juvenal nothing is as it first seems; he opens his homophobic attack on these *cinaedi*, pathics, these sad perverts, in grand style, calling them stupid and noting their buggery-induced haemorrhoids. Enter Laronia to lend support, grinning at having found what could be a third conservative, censorious Cato in Hispo (Cato the Younger was the second). She ridicules his effeminacy, invoking the *lex Scantinia* to parry his reference to the *lex Julia de Adulteriis Coercendis*. Look at the men first, they do the worst things, she argues; women don't tongue each other, yet Hispo submits to young boys. Women stay away from mens' matters – litigation, wrestling; on the other hand, men do women's things – they work the wool (that badge of good wifely behaviour), *lanam faciunt*! Laronia's advice to Hispo's girl is to keep quiet about her husband's proclivities and keep taking the jewels. To Juvenal this was all the blindingly obvious truth, and Laronia provided powerful support to his invective.

It is obviously difficult to reconcile this flash of enlightenment towards women with Juvenal's excoriating attack on women in *Satire* Six, where he savagely contradicts much of what he has Laronia say here. The important point is that Laronia's eloquent and reasoned arguments constitute a point of view which Juvenal obviously realised was the sort of thing a woman might say in a situation like this: a woman like Laronia might well be indignant about the hypocrisy and duplicity of men like Hispo, and she, as a *docta puella*, would be quite capable of expressing those views in such a clever way. Laronia is indeed 'used' by Juvenal, but her opinion would seem to be quite plausible and possibly quite representative among certain women of Juvenal's day.

Laronia shows us that when it came to men, women had competition from other men. Lucretius could see the attraction of boys. Ovid, though, was unequivocal. Women make better sexual partners than men; sex with a woman was preferable because of the possibility of mutual pleasure. Plutarch was equally unequivocal: sex with boys is best – perversely, he says that heterosexual sex smacked of effeminacy.[7] In the first century AD, Strato, in the *Greek Anthology*, expresses a preference for boys because girls get little enjoyment from anal sex and are frigid when sodomised. Martial says as much when he rebukes his wife for describing her *culus* as a sphincter when, according to him, she really has two vaginas (*cunni*).

One of the most effective ways for a Roman to publicly denigrate and humiliate another Roman was to accuse him of sexual deviancy, particularly acts of passive homosexuality. Catullus delivers a blistering attack on Mamurra and Caesar (*Carmen* 57); the vocabulary is vivid to say the least, mentioning pervert, faggot, indelible stains, filthy disease, desire for adultery and the abuse of girls. In *Carmen* 16 he reacts badly to accusations of effeminacy because he spends his time penning poetry in days of leisurely *otium* (contrary to *negotium*, business); the penalty for his accusers is oral rape – an expression of Catullus' masculinity, his *virtus*. Martial too threatens rape to underscore his manliness when faced with similar accusations (10, 65), puffing out his hairy chest, as it were. Cicero destroys Mark Antony and Scribonius Curio in his *Philippics* (2, 44–45) with accusations of effeminacy, cross-dressing, male prostitution, pederasty and lust, with Antony even going so far as to steal into Curio's house by night. Just as men attacked women by reference to their sexual *mores*, so did men attack men.

There is plenty of evidence in literature for women taking the initiative in sex and assuming the dominant role. In his description of the sexual frenzy generated by the Bona Dea rites Juvenal describes two aristocratic women vieing with each other, and with the whores, in the torrent of lust that overcomes them; Saufeia and Medullina gyrate lasciviously together. The second-century-BC satirist Gaius Lucilius has an image of a woman grinding corn with her buttocks while Martial describes the famous Gaditanian dancing girl as bumping and grinding so sexily that she could make Hippolytus masturbate. For Lucretius, who took a very pragmatic approach to sexual intercourse, a prostitute will perform in such a way as to give maximum pleasure to her client while a woman writhing on top was simultaneously employing a method of contraception. Wives looking to conceive should avoid vigorous movement since this 'knocks the ploughshare from the furrow and misdirects the sowing of the seed'. As we have seen, Lucretius also recommends 'doggy style' as a good way to conceive.

Apuleius too describes the lubricious movements of the dominant woman, as does Petronius. Horace compares the *meretricula* with a horse rider. The *mulier equitans* appears to have been popular, with the woman 'riding' on top; it was also called the 'Hector horse', as mythological Hector and Andromache allegedly liked sex that way. There are numerous visual representations of the sexually dominant woman, many from the ceramics found in the Rhone Valley dating from AD 70–250: some show the woman to be the soldier in a reversal of the *miles amoris* scenario (*orte scutus est* – 'look out, that's a shield you've got there!'); the man is flaccid. Another medallion has the woman on top with the text *vides quam bene chalas*, 'see how well you open me up'. Others are the victor in the games, *tu sola nica* – 'you're the only victor'. The famous *Navigium Veneris* – 'navigation of Venus', or more loosely, 'cock steering' – medallion is still attached to its original jug and shows a very dextrous man steering his penis into his partner's ample rear, in much the same way as he would manipulate a boat's rudder.

References to the same position in homosexual sex are in Petronius' *Satyricon* and in Juvenal. where the lesbians take it in turn to be on top. Martial describes a wife mounting 'the horse of Hector' while the slaves masturbate behind the bedroom door; Ovid recommends the dominant position for the shorter woman.[8]

The Romans too had their joy of sex. Ovid is of, course, *the* authority on sexual positions (*figurae veneris*), as laid down in his gold-standard *Ars Amatoria*, where he describes numerous ways of copulating.[9] Suetonius tells us that Tiberius was an inveterate collector of sex manuals and owned a prodigious collection of erotic art; his pièce de résistance was a painting of Atalanta giving fellatio to Meleager, a work valued by the emperor at more than a million sesterces.[10] Astrology played its part; according to Julius Firmicus Maternus, an astrologer in the time of Constantine I, the Roman born under Capricorn, Aquarius, Taurus or Cancer was predisposed to clandestine vice or unnatural forms of intercourse, or to being *pathici*.[11]

Sexist and chauvinistic as he was, Ovid does concede that a man should always try and ensure that a woman achieves orgasm, ideally simultaneously with the man. 'But don't you fail your lady, hoisting bigger sails, and don't let her get ahead of you on the track either; race to the finish together: that's when pleasure is full, when man and woman lie there, equally vanquished.'[12]

The *Hippocratic Corpus* says that heterosexual female sexual pleasure is induced by the rubbing on the vulva during intercourse and lasts throughout the act until the man ejaculates. If she is in the mood, as it were, the woman orgasms first; if she is not, then the couple climax together. A woman's orgasm is less intense than a man's, but it lasts longer; sexual intercourse is generally good for a woman's health. The aim of sexual intercourse, though, was conception rather than any pleasure on the woman's part; she was to be consensual at all times.

Masturbation was utterly pointless because it could not result in conception. Women used phallic objects, such as cucumbers, solely to prepare themselves for penetration by their husbands, not for any pleasure; women suffer less frequently with bladder stones because they do not masturbate. An example of masturbating a woman – *cunnum tibi fricabo* – is described in an inscription from Pompeii. For Martial it is low-grade sex – something slaves do – although he does admit to masturbating when he cannot afford a beautiful slave boy: 'my hand relieved me as a substitute for Ganymede'. Lucilius (307 and 959) has a laugh at a personified penis whose girlfriend Laeva (left-hander) wipes away his 'tears'. The left hand was the preferred hand for masturbating, as confirmed by this graffito from Pompeii: 'When my worries oppress my body, with my left hand I release my pent-up fluids.' (*CIL* 2066.)

Martial, fantasising in a poem where he whinges about a wife's coolness towards his sexual advances, alludes to a long tradition of female masturbators, beginning with Penelope and Andromache; in the same epigram he moans about the woman's reluctance to indulge in anal sex, scandalously claiming the traditionally virtuous Cornelia, Pompey's wife Julia, and Brutus' wife Porcia to have been willing participants in the act. We have seen how sodomy was not unknown on the wedding night for some brides. In homosexual sex, some men 'took it like a woman' when penetrated (*muliebria pati*); but when a man sodomised a woman, she played the boy role. Martial (12, 75 and 96) prefers anal sex with boys even though his wife allows him anal sex to keep him happy.

It may be that the *figura veneris* where the woman crouches and lifts her buttocks, the 'lioness', was primarily for anal intercourse; prostitutes who specialised in this were called *culibonia* ('good anal'), although it was probably adopted more as a way of avoiding pregnancy than for client satisfaction.

We have already touched on oro-genital sex; it was much in evidence. *Os impurum*, filthy mouth, was an extreme term of abuse reserved for those who provided oral sex and was used as such with relish by Catullus, Horace, and Martial. Cunnilingus, like fellatio, suggested questionable oral hygiene, anathema to many Romans who held the purity of the mouth in high esteem. The mouth was the vehicle for oratory and declamation; it was the custom to kiss on meeting, so bad breath, also a symbol of moral turpitude through its association with oral sex, was extremely embarrassing. Insults did not come any worse than accusing a man of fellatio with another man. It was indicative of the sexual passivity and receptiveness which was so reviled by the Romans; moreover, it was something older men did when they were unable to get an erection.

The Campanians, as we have noted, had a predilection for oral sex, resulting in a high incidence of *campanus morbus*. Fellatio is privileged with two precise nouns in Latin – *irrumatio* is the action of the penis; *fellatio* the action of the mouth and was obviously a popular alternative to coitus for the clientele of prostitutes. As we have seen, it may also have a contraceptive role, representing an intention to avoid pregnancy, not just in extramarital relationships but also within marriage in a bid to break the relentless cycle of childbearing. Martial, of course, in his frequent references to the act, tends towards the extramarital: we hear of Vetustina's warm mouth and how Thais sucks. In his poem about Galla and Aeschylus he advises that if you are going to do it then you should keep your mouth shut about it, as it were. He accuses Aeschylus of paying over the odds to ensure that the knowledge of his fellatio goes no further; he was, no doubt, mindful of the disgust which attended this sexual proclivity. Suetonius deplores Quintus Remmius Palaemon's predilection for cunnilingus.[13] Galen believed that orogenital sex was unnatural.

The twelve epigrams in which Martial refers to cunnilingus might suggest that the poet was obsessed with the act. He excoriates Nanneius, an inveterate cunnilinguist suffering from lingual dysfunction after contracting a disease of the tongue. So prolific was he that whores preferred to perform fellatio on him rather than kiss him on the mouth because his penis was much cleaner. To Catullus, fellatio had associations with the urinary function of the penis: he refers to 'the repellent spit of a pissed-over prostitute' and excoriates a Celtiberian for brushing his teeth in urine. Martial would have us believe that a nicely scented perfume turns to fish sauce when sniffed by a man whose breath is rank from oral sex. When a *fellator* breathes on a hot cake to cool it down it turns to excrement. Ausonius in the fourth century AD echoes Martial in a blistering attack on Eunus, whom he accuses of licking his pregnant wife's putrid genitals, anxious to tongue the buttocks of his unborn sons: fellatio, antenatal sexual child abuse and incest all in one breath (*Epigrams* 86).

Graffiti proclaims that all the women of Pompeii were 'up for it'. For the ladies, 'Glyco does cunnilingus for two asses'. Martimus, however, is not such a good deal; he does it for four, but will entertain virgins for free – all suggesting a lively trade in male prostitution for the bored housewives of Pompeii.

In art, cunnilingus is usually portayed as one half of 'soixante-neuf'. Some women hired male prostitutes for the specific purpose of getting cunnilingus; one political graffito invites the electorate to 'vote Isidore for aedile; he's the best at licking cunt!' Neverthless, graffiti tells us that a competent *fellatrix* was much in demand. Wall paintings in the Suburban Baths in Pompeii depict cunnilingus; here the beautiful, naked prostitute adopts a dominant role while her fawning, fully clothed male client is something of a comedic figure, indicating the scorn oral sex attracted and the opportunity it gave for parody.

The Romans had a word for forced fellatio, oral rape; inflicting *irrumatio* on another man was a demonstration of virility on the one hand and abject servility of the other for the victim. It is described in the *Priapeia* and in the poems of Catullus and Martial.

It was the punishment of choice inflicted by some husbands whose wives took lovers; after cutting off the adulterer's ears and nose the humiliation was brought to a climax by oral rape.[14] The soldiers of Octavian's army were only too aware of the deep insult tied up in the salvoes they sent towards Antony and Fulvia Flacca Bambula.

Group sex was an occupational hazard, or maybe a business opportunity, for prostitutes. Gallus describes three men penetrating Lyde; Nicarchus, in the first century AD, describes another foursome where the three men draw lots for which orifice they get. One of the scenes at the Suburban Baths in Pompeii shows one man taking a woman from behind while he receives a man standing behind him. Catullus, in *Carmen 56*, re-enacts it, considering it hilarious. Another scene shows a foursome in which a man sodomises another man to whom a woman gives fellatio; another woman performs cunnilingus on her. Tiberius was a devotee. Suetonius gives a description of one of his bizarre events: 'In his retreat at Capri, he put together a bedroom that was the theatre of his secret debauches. There he assembled ... male and female prostitutes, and inventors of monstrous couplings [which he called *spintriae*], so that, intertwining themselves and forming a triple chain they mutually prostituted themselves in front of him to fire up his flagging desires.' The fourth-century-AD poet Ausonius leaves us with a group sex conundrum: 'Three men in bed together: two are committing debauchery (*stuprum*), two are being debauched.' 'Doesn't that make four men?' 'No: the man on either end each counts as a single offense, but the one in the middle both acts and is acted on.'[15]

Women were also attracted by the *cinaedus*, a bisexual, effeminate male. The middle man in the troilism at the Suburban Baths may well have been a *cinaedus*. The *pathicus*, similar to the *cinaedus* but more of a submissive masochist, may have held similar appeal: with *pathici* the woman assumes the role of *domina* and receives cunnilingus.

The Hippocratics contended that whenever a woman became pregnant she had enjoyed the sex during which she conceived; Soranus believed that a woman could only conceive if she was sexually excited – which led him into a corner where he was forced to accept that if a woman became pregnant after being raped then she had, subconsciously at least, enjoyed the violation. Lucretius argued that sex provided mutual pleasure for man and woman – *est communis voluptas* – and that any children conceived would take after the mother whenever the woman took the dominant role during sex. Women, he says, do not always fake sexual excitement – sometimes it is for real. Ovid, in his turn of the millennium *The Joy of Sex*, the *Ars Amatoria*, methodically runs through the various sexual positions a woman should adopt to achieve mutual orgasm with her partner, or if she wants to show off her looks and body to best effect; he also gives handy tips on how to conceal unsightly stretchmarks. Women who cannot climax are encouraged to fake it – convincingly, though, with much flailing about, gasping and rolling of eyes.[16]

Bestiality features prominently in classical mythology and literature, although there is little to suggest that it, in real life, it was any more common in Rome than in any other society. It all starts with the rape of Europa by Zeus masquerading as a bull, as described by Moschus and then by Ovid in the *Metamorphoses*.[17] The Cretan Minotaur was born from the union between a bull and Pasiphae, wife of King Minos, in Virgil – 'crazy, sad girl!'[18] Another famous topic from myth is the rape of Leda by Zeus in the guise of a swan; the significant thing about the swan is that, unlike most other birds, it had an intromittent organ (essentially a penis) which can of course be used for penetration. Images of the coupling is particularly common on oil lamps. But it does not stop with Leda: one lamp from mid-third-century-AD Athens, made by the lamp maker Preimos, shows a woman on a bed with a pony; another from the first century shows a naked woman on top of a crocodile – possibly a humorous swipe at Cleopatra VII (both in the British Museum). Others show women performing with donkeys and dogs. Such images go back a long way: there is a red-figure cup by Epitketos from the end of the sixth century BC showing a maenad being taken by a donkey (in the Naples National Museum). Other early examples of sexual fetishes include a red-figure cup by the Brygos Painter depicting an orgy scene from about 480 BC, in which a woman is beaten with a slipper, and a satyr penetrating a buck on a black-figure cup from about 520 BC. Representations of bestiality almost always involve women receiving excited quadrupeds – only one example of a man penetrating a mammal, a donkey, survives.

We shall see how Nero delighted in dressing up as a wild animal in gladiatorial contests and enthusiastically attacking his opponents' genitals. Martial in his *De Spectaculis* suggests that bestiality was enacted on stage at the inaugural games of the Flavian Amphitheatre in AD 80. The punishment that was death by bestiality was the most terrible of deaths. Martial commends the realism of a re-enactment of the Bull of Pasiphae myth in the arena;

presumably body fluids from a cow on heat were used to arouse and attract the bull to the woman. Pliny records that Semiramis, the ninth-century-BC Assyrian queen, had sex with a horse; Juvenal says that women are so sexed up at the Bona Dea that they will fornicate with a donkey, as a last resort. He also tells us about the actor Bathyllus and the erotic dance in which he dresses up as Leda to have sex with the swan – much to the excitement and arousal of the women watching. Dio has the story of a prostitute masquerading as a leopard to gratify a senator. Apuleius, in the *Metamorphoses*, describes how Lucius, transformed into a donkey, has vigorous, and consensual, intercourse with an insatiable woman who pays Thiasus, his master, for the pleasure.[19] Thiasus sees an opportunity here, and, as noted above, Lucius' next engagement is in an amphitheatre, caged up with a woman condemned to be fed to wild animals; before the spectacle can begin, however, he escapes. No doubt this was not the first telling of a story which would have entertained its audiences down the years, as well as responding to male fantasy regarding female sexual insatiability.

Up until the year 2000 the Gabinetto Segreto in the Museo Archeologico Nazionale di Napoli kept one of the ancient world's worst kept secrets, the famous statue of a satyr copulating with a goat. The censorship dates from when King Francis I of Naples visited Pompeii in 1819 with his wife and young daughter; his tour resulted in him imposing viewing restrictions on the many erotic artefacts on display there, which were then squirreled away or, on site in Pompeii, covered in shutters. Access was confined to persuasive scholars or enterprising young men, prepared to pay the going rate to bribe the guards.

Prostitution in ancient Rome was legal and controlled. Roman men at every social level could visit brothels and pay for sex without incurring the slightest moral approbation. Their wives tolerated it and connived at it: a rest from endless copulation and serial childbirth. At the same time, though, the sex workers were deemed shameful: most were either slaves or former slaves, or if freeborn, were reduced to the despised and stigmatised *infames*, devoid of any social standing or legal protections – a status they shared with actors, dancers and gladiators. Actors were sexually ambiguous because they played the parts of women on the stage, in drag. Sulla had an affair with an actor and Maecenas had an affair with an actor called Bathyllus; it was taken for granted that actresses were prostitutes.

Dancing girls were considered by many to be one step removed from prostitutes – indeed, many dancers probably were prostitutes. Dancing attracted the derision of some men; Sallust scorns the talented and sophisticated Sempronia for her dancing skill. Ovid, though, loves the lubricity of it all while the proud, grieving father of the deceased Eucharis – a celebrated dancer – takes pride in his late daughter's talent. Juvenal, though, is with Sallust: he deprecates the Spanish dancers' movements, calling them worse than those of a prostitute, making other women wet themselves with excitement. On a par with the dancer were the girls who worked in the baths: Martial describes the the *tractatrix* – the masseuse who spreads her practiced (*manus docta*) hand over every limb, the *unctores* (perfumers), *fricatores* (rubbers), *alipilarii* (depilators) and the *picatrices* – the girls who trimmed your pubic hair.

Countless girls and women resorted to prostitution, be they a *hetaera, meretrix, lupa, scortum,* or *fornicatrix* plying their trade, fornicating, under Juvenal's stinking arches, or those urbane courtesans who were so appealing to the equally urbane love poets. Latin, like other languages, has many words and euphemisms for prostitute, fifty or so at least. There is a certain irony in the fact that the legendary founders of Rome, Romulus and Remus, were suckled by a she-wolf, a *lupa*, and that the possibility of selling a baby girl into prostitution undoubtedly saved many from exposure or abandonment.

Propertius tells us that many prostitutes came from Syria (around the Rivers Euphrates and Orontes) and that in Rome they frequent parks and porticos and the Via Sacra; to these haunts we can add the Subura, the Esquiline-Viminal, the Caelian Hill, Juvenal's various arches (particularly around the Colisseum) and the Circus Maximus;[20] a house nearby displays the graffito *hic bene futui* – 'I had a good shag here'. Some whores were peripatetic, escorts or call girls, *scorta erratica*; the lowest were the *diobolariae,* worth two obols, and those who entertained clients among the tombstones. Sex was cheap: the cheapest girls cost the equivalent of a loaf of bread or a glass of wine, while something more exotic cost around two hours pay for an average worker.

The business model often involved working from a rented room and being managed by the much-hated *lena* (madam) or *leno* (pimp). The owner employed a *villicus puellarum*, or manager, who assigned a name to the girl, set her prices, took the money and provided clothing and other necessities. The *villicus* keep a tally of what each girl earned. A plate (*titulus*) over the door of each cell gave the name of the occupier and her price; on the back was the word *occupata*, busy. The cubicle usually contained a bronze or clay lamp, a pallet or cot, over which was draped a blanket which sometimes was used as a curtain. Apart from underneath the arches and in the brothels girls worked in a number of locations including balconies (*pergulae*), taverns (*stabulae*), lodging houses (*diversorium*), cook shops, bakeries (*tabernae*), road houses (*casuaria*) and spelt mills.

Most prostitutes survived in abject poverty, some riddled no doubt with disease; abortion and violence were common companions. Some, however, got rich and made it to the top. Sulla benefitted from the will of a rich whore, while the courtesan Cytheris was always a star, and welcome at all the best dinner parties. Catullus, Gallus, Propertius, Tibullus, Horace and Ovid all loved (and hated in equal measure) these sophisticated ladies.

Prostitutes had a role to play in Roman religion. Ovid (*Fasti* 4, 133–134) tells us that on 1 April prostitutes joined with *matronae* in the ritual cleansing and reclothing of the cult statue of Fortuna Virilis. Usually, respectable women and *infames* such as prostitutes were kept apart and prostitutes were moved aside when a priestess moved through the streets. On 23 April, prostitutes made offerings at the Temple of Venus Erycina, a goddess associated with harlots. According to the *Fasti Praenestini* pimped boys, *pueri lenonii*, were celebrated on 25 April, the day after *meretrices*, high-class female prostitutes. On 27 April, the Floralia, in honour of the goddess Flora and first introduced about 238 BC, gave an opportunity for erotic dancing and striptease by prostitutes. According to Lactantius (*Inst. Divin.* 20, 6),

> in addition to the freedom of speech that pours forth every obscenity, the prostitutes, at the importunities of the rabble, strip off their clothing and act as mimes in full view of the crowd, and this they continue until full satiety comes to the shameless lookers-on, holding their attention with their wriggling buttocks.

Some prostitutes exerted significant political power. Glaphyra was a courtesan from Cappadocia who seduced Mark Antony with her beauty, and, no doubt, her assertive personality; in 36 BC she persuaded him to install her first son, Archelaus, as King of Cappadocia. Antony executed Ariarathes X of Cappadocia, the then king, and replaced him with Archelaus.

You could tell a prostitute by her dress: she did not wear the traditional long *stola* of the *matrona* but a short *tunica* and an often garish (bright yellow or orange) toga – man's wear, and the badge also of an adulteress (Horace *Satires* 1, 2, 63). Bright colours and jewelled anklets were the hallmarks of the prostitute. Sometimes you could tell a prostitute because she had *no dress*, offering her wares in the nude. Nudity suggested slavery: the slave was literally stripped of personal privacy and the private ownership of his or her own body. Seneca describes how a kidnap victim is bought and sold as a prostitute:

> Naked she stood on the shore, at the pleasure of the purchaser; every part of her body was examined and felt. Would you hear the result of the sale? The pirate sold; the pimp bought, that he might employ her as a prostitute.

In the *Satyricon* Encolpius relates how he 'saw some men prowling stealthily between the rows of name-boards and naked prostitutes'. Juvenal tells us about a prostitute standing naked 'with golden nipples' in the doorway of her cell. A tactile Horace explains to us the tangible benefits of the low class whore over the *matrona*:

> The matron has no softer thigh nor has she a more beautiful leg, though the setting be one of pearls and emeralds ... the togaed plebeian's is often the finer, and, in addition, the beauties of figure are not camouflaged; that which is for sale, if honest, is shown openly, whereas deformity seeks concealment ... Ah, what a leg! What arms! But how thin her buttocks are, in very truth what a huge nose she has, she's short-waisted, too, and her feet are out of proportion! Of the matron, except for the face, nothing is open to your scrutiny unless she is a Catia who has dispensed with her clothing so that she may be felt all over thoroughly, the rest will be hidden. But as for the other, no difficulty there! Through the Coan silk it is as easy for you to see as if she were naked, whether she has an unshapely leg, whether her foot is ugly; her waist you can examine with your eyes.

Prostitutes were registered and regulated by the aediles and, from Caligula's reign, paid tax on their earnings equivalent to one client's charge in any given day, even after retirement from the profession. How this was effectively collected remains a mystery, although we do know that the responsibility soon passed from civilian tax collectors to the military – presumably for reasons of security and the benefits of the soldiers' familiarity with the ins and outs of commercial sex. Nevertheless, the tax on whores was still pulling in the cash in the reign of Severus, who directed that all income be used for the upkeep of public buildings so that the filthy lucre did not pollute the treasury. Tacitus records that Vistilia, a lady of praetorian rank who had married six times, confessed to being a prostitute and was charged under the *lex Julia*, which banned prostitution amongs the wives, daughters and granddaughters of Roman *equites*; she was exiled to the island of Seriphos in AD 19.[21]

In that they lived in the household, the concubine, or *paelex*, was an integral part of some Roman families. Festus records the existence of the *paelex* from around the reign of King Numa in the eighth century, where they are forbidden to touch the Temple of Juno – transgressions demanded a loosening of the hair and the sacrifice of a lamb. Scipio Africanus kept a concubine, famously tolerated, indeed rewarded, by his wife Tertia Aemilia; conservative Cato the Censor kept one and eventually married her. At the Imperial level both Domitian and Commodus had them. Plautus, for example through Casina in the *Casina,* and Pliny the Younger (Lutulla) both mention concubinage, *contubernium*, quite casually.

Men had no qualms or conscience regarding visiting brothels. It was perfectly acceptable behaviour and highlights the double standards relating to adultery and infidelity. Horace condones the stinking brothel if it stops men committing adultery with respectable married women.[22] He cites Cato the Censor, who congratulated a man coming out of a brothel; when Cato saw him leaving a few more times after that he protested that he had not intended he live there. Cicero agreed that men buying sex was good for the nation. Anyone who thought it wrong was being a bit harsh and out of step with modern ways; how long has it been wrong to do what is lawful? he demands.[23]

The brothels were open twenty-four hours a day, seven days a week. Higher class establishments had hairdressers available to tidy up after a session while boys stood at the door with bowls for freshening up. Although prostitutes and slave women were fair game, there were strict rules protecting other vulnerable sectors of Roman society. Young boys wearing a *bulla* (a pendant), *matronae*, free-born men and girls from good families were off-limits, protected by the *lex Scatinia* with fines of 10,000 *sesterci*.

The Pompeii brothels are probably the most infamous but a second-century-BC brothel was excavated in 1997 in Thessaloniki, attached to a public bathhouse in the *agora* there. Yannis Stavrakakis describes the excavations by Polyxeni Veleni of the Museum of Thessaloniki in

Archaeology Archive (51, 3, 1998): on the ground floor was a dining room linked to the bath-house; this featured a circular room with twenty-five bath tubs, heated pools, and a round sweating room. Upstairs were the usual small rooms or cubicles and a collection of interesting artefacts, including a large phallus-shaped alabaster vase, jars with phallic mouths, and a dildo with pulsating shaft.

Many brothels did stink, no doubt. They were dark, dingy, dirty and smoky. A number of writers mention the smoke and soot characteristic of the *lupanarium* or *fornix*: Seneca, (*Cont.* 1, 2) says, 'You still reek of the brothel's soot'; Horace, (*Satire* 1, 2, 30), 'except she be standing in the evil-smelling cell of the brothel); Petronius, *Satyricon* 12, 'and the maid, whom he had slighted, and, of course, insulted, smeared lamp-black all over his face'; *Priapeia* 13, 9, 'whoever likes may enter here, smeared with the black soot of the brothel'. Services were listed and illustrated inside and out with name boards; sessions were brief, to say the least, with some clients not bothering to take off their shoes, if the imprints which have been discovered at Pompeii are anything to go by. The girls would stand outside their cubicles propositioning – living advertisements for their visible wares.

Women were often press-ganged into prostitution by ruthless pirates who sold them onto slave markets: a fine example of crime paying. Exposed baby girls and boys would often end up 'on the street', as described by the Christian Justin Martyr (*Apology* 1, 27, 1–5) in a petition to Antoninus Pius. To Justin, the sort of people who did that were just as capable of incest and child sex with their own relations and children, some even castrating themselves to become *cinaedi*, perverts.

Basic contraceptives were used: oils, sanitary rags soaked in lemon juice, various potions and condoms made from animal intestines. Prices were kept low as a matter of policy to ensure that, as with the gladiatorial games and the public baths, being able to afford a whore was within reach of every Roman. Whoring kept the masses happy and subdued – it was part of their bread and circuses. Despite the squalor there were, however, efforts to provide some hygiene, with relays of water collected from fountains for washing down after each client. Some brothels were even connected to nearby aqueducts.

According to Suetonius, Horace, a bit of a voyeur, preferred sex at home to visiting brothels, inviting escorts back to his place where the mirrors in his bedroom literally reflected his sexual activity: *coitus* from every angle. Seneca rants against the perverted Hostius

Quadra, whose house was full of crazy mirrors so that he could view his orgies from distorted angles and penises would look larger than life.[24] Martial knows exactly what he wants from a prostitute: a bargain-basement price and a willingness to take three clients at a time; the older the whore, the less he pays.[25] Juvenal and Strabo describe temple prostitution, sex that was rife in temples such as Eryx in Sicily and at Corinth. Prostitutes also provided a lucrative sideline for low-rent hotels (*tabernae cauponiae*), bars and inns, offering their services as *noctilucae*, night-lights, in the tiny cubicles out the back with their stone beds and straw mattresses. One amusing inscription from Aesernia describes a client paying his hotel bill. The extras included the services of a girl costing eight asses and hay for the mule costing two; the guest protests that it is the mule which is the likely cause of his financial ruin.

Wall painting and graffiti in Pompeii may suggest that the work of bar maids elided easily from serving drinks to serving clients with sexual services.[26] The unimaginative graffito proclaiming that *I fucked the landlady* and the highly imaginative nineteenth-century version of a painting from the Via di Mercurio, now sadly lost, which depicts a well-endowed man taking a barmaid from behind in what looks like a drinking competition, may suggest as much. On the other hand, the former may indicate quite the opposite; perhaps it was scrawled out of spite from hurt male pride, while the latter may just be good advertising. The bronze pygmy with the huge regenerating phallus outside a bar in the Via dell' Abbondanza would indicate that girls (and boys) were available inside. *The Barmaid* (*Copa*) shows how the owner worked both trades, and Horace, on a trip to Brundisium, falls asleep and has a wet dream while waiting for a waitress in an inn. 'Here like a triple fool I waited till midnight for a lying jade till sleep overcame me, intent on venery; in that filthy vision the dreams spot my night clothes and my belly, as I lie upon my back.' *The Aeserman Inscription* gives us the conversation between the hostess and a traveller; the bill for the services of a girl came to eight asses. Paulus Diaconus shows that bakers capitalised on the commercial opportunities afforded by their mills: 'as time went on, the owners of these turned the public corn mills into pernicious frauds. For, as the mill stones were fixed in places under ground, they set up booths on either side of these chambers and caused prostitutes to stand for hire in them, so that by these means they deceived very many, some that came for bread, others that hastened thither for the base gratification of their wantonness.' Festus confirms the practice in Campania: 'Prostitutes were called *aelicariae,* 'spelt-mill girls', in Campania, being accustomed to ply for gain before the mills of the spelt millers.'

The local baths were another popular venue for sex, as well as for bathing and general socialising. In Pompeii the Suburban Baths have a series of paintings depicting a range of erotic scenes which, again, are probably an advertisement for the services offered by the slave girls working there. Nudity among both males and females was the accepted norm although there were reservations about appearing naked in front of children. Initially, bath houses may have offered women a separate wing or a schedule for women or men only bathing. By the empire, though, mixed bathing was quite usual; Hadrian tried unsuccessfully to ban it.[27]

As female providers of sexual services, prostitutes came first, followed by female slaves. Both groups of women were fair game for men, married or otherwise, who needed to satisfy their sexual appetite or demonstrate virility and prowess over women; the prostitute allowed the client to assert his manhood through serial penetration. Paradoxically, though, this provided the whore or slave girl with a degree of vicarious sexual power. The obsession with the erect penis indicated a disturbing vulnerability and anxiety as well as a strength among Roman men; just as it was a mark of potency, so it was an indicator of *another man's* potency – a man who may be consorting with your wife, a man who may even be the father of 'your' children – *horribile dictu*! In around AD 170, Artemidorus wrote in his treatise on the interpretation of dreams that to dream of having sex with one's own female slave was good, 'for slaves are the dreamer's possession; therefore taking pleasure in them signifies the dreamer's being pleased with his own possessions'. Plutarch tells us that Cato the Elder would charge his male slaves for having sex with his female slaves.[28]

Horace's squalid brothel is recalled by Juvenal in his description of the bizarre, incognito nocturnal visits made by Messalina (*meretrix Augusta*) to a whorehouse. Here she habitually prostituted herself, naked and nipples gilded; at the end of the night she is the last to leave, reluctantly, 'with her clitoris still on fire and full of lust'.[29] Elsewhere, in his description of a dissolute dinner party and the entertainment offered by those lascivious Spanish dancing girls, Juvenal compares the scene to a fetid brothel, a world apart from the cerebral evening he prefers with recitations of Homer and Virgil.[30]

Pompeii could boast seven brothels (some say as many as thirty-five), one of them sharing premises with a hairdressers.

Not surprisingly, then, the town is a rich source of graffiti recommending particular prostitutes, and offers all sorts of advice, prices and recommendations: 'thrust slowly'; Candida (a white girl?) hates black girls but can still 'love' them willingly; Myris, good at fellatio; Sabina, not so good; Veneria got a mouth full of semen. Euplia was probably a whore, and an old one at that if this graffito from Pompeii is anything to go by; she has a baggy vagina and a huge clitoris. *Eupl(i)a laxa landicosa*; the price for Attice is sixteen asses. At one time Rome had at least forty-five brothels; one is known (in fiction at least) at Puteoli, or Cumae, depending on where Petronius sets the start of his *Satyricon;* here the hapless Encolpius finds himself among naked whores wearing just their price tags. It is impossible to estimate how many women were active in the sex trade at any one time or in any one place: we can assume, though, that grinding poverty and the vulnerability exposed by slavery will have left many women with little or no choice. Candida may reflect a degree of racial discrimination against black women. Ovid includes them in his *Remedia* 'fifty ways to leave your lover' *Amoris*: think of her as a black woman if she's dusky.[31]

Male prostitutes had a market among rich women. Martial describes Chloe, who extravagantly rewards Lupercus with an endless supply of lavish clothing, jewels and cash; Martial advises caution, however, lest she ends up fleeced and exposed by him. He is decidedly uncomplimentary to Thais; she stinks like urine from a smashed jar, like a randy goat, a putrefied chicken, rancid fish sauce.[32] He also describes how the squalid whore, the *moecha bustuaria*, conducts business among the tombs in a cemetery – a place, as we have seen, she would have shared with others from the lowest rungs of society, including witches and other nefarious practitioners of the dark arts.[33]

Then, at the other end of the spectrum, there were the Lesbias, Cynthias, Delias and Corinnas, who fascinated and frustrated their lovers with their sophistication, erudition, aloofness and unobtainability. We cannot know whether they were all high class, educated prostitutes or simply high class, educated and liberated women. What we can say is that they exhibited characteristics that were the very opposite of those of Roman *matronae* – they exuded excitement, they were obtrusive, extrovert, they were promiscuous and they were often exasperatingly wilful.

Petronius has Chrysis describe how some well-to-do women 'love a bit of rough', how they are aroused even by slaves, donkey drivers, gladiators and actors, even going so far as to lick the wounds of the flogged.[34] Juvenal echoes this *libido* for gladiators in his tirade against women.[35]

Older women attract some of the most extreme disgust, where the vitriol is often associated with sex. Lucilius is repelled by the thought of sexual intercourse during a woman's period;[36] Horace, in a poem reminiscent of those in which he deprecates witches,[37] blames his impotence on his woman's repellent appearance: she smells like a goat, she sweats, and her genitals are shrivelled up. Martial's aged Vetustilla endures a verbal onslaught that is punctuated with references to her sexuality.[38] She too smells like a goat, her breasts sag like a spider's web and her vagina is bone-hard, good only for holding a funeral torch. On the other hand, Ovid's is unable to cure his erectile dysfunction despite his girl's obvious beauty and culture [39]. In the *Greek Anthology* Rufinus typifies the *schadenfreude* when he delights in his *hetaira*'s fall from grace, and beauty: her once proud breasts, fine stature, divine tresses are but shadows of what they once were; ravaged by old age, she now looks like an ape.[40] The god Priapus, in a homily addressed to his uncooperative, flaccid penis, threatens it with the vagina of a hag old enough to have known Romulus; concealed by a sagging belly, this vagina is depressingly cold and cavernous, dirty and covered in cobwebs, a veritable swamp.[41] Publilius Syrus, the first-century composer of maxims, said that old men pursuing affairs was criminal; to Ovid sex and old people was a repellent notion. Age or beauty, though, were no guarantees of good sexual hygiene; one resident of Pompeii found that his beautiful whore was still full of the semen deposited by a previous client, and was sufficiently annoyed by this to record the fact on a wall. Likewise this, from an early-second-century-AD house in southern Spain: 'I nearly froze to death in her cunt.'[42]

Impotence may have been a problem for Martial, given the fact that he raises the issue in nine of his epigrams; Ovid, we have seen, was cursed with it while Tibullus had the occasional problem, and Petronius also mentions it.

Risible it all may all have been to satirists and love poets, the long-lasting loving relationship – usually, but not always, within marriage – was held in high regard and was something to be emulated. We have seen how Augustus bemoaned the passing of the marriage which ended in the death of one of the partners, how it had become a regrettable rarity in the wake of increasing divorce at the beginning of the first century AD. Later, both Pliny and Martial extol the extended marriage: Pliny hopes that his happy marriage to Calpurnia will last forever[43] while Martial wishes that Claudia Peregrina and her husband will go on loving each other well into old age.[44] This is supported by the epigraphical evidence; we see longevity in marriage from Carthage where the husband reaches 102 and the wife eighty,[45] and from Hispania Baetica where the couple are 100 and ninety-nine.[46]

Love is blind – and love makes the lover blind. Lucretius, in his role as *praeceptor amoris*, teacher of the ways of love, describes the blindness caused by love when men simply cannot see reality before their eyes: repulsive women become *deliciae, sheer delights*, and there follows a whole catalogue of false perceptions where the dusky become honey-brown, the stunted a veritable Grace, the buxom a Ceres, the lank a gazelle, the bulky divine. He concludes by deriding the use of perfumes to conceal reality, by ridiculing the locked-out lover – the *paraclausithyron* – and by recommending that men accept that women are imperfect and should just make do with a bad lot. Lucretius recants to some extent later in the poem: despite physical imperfections a little woman, *muliercula*, can still be lovable; she can win love by her pleasantness and her refinement; the sheer habit of life together with her husband can develop into love. Ovid, that master of *praeceptores amoris*, agreed. He too turns the myopia to good advantage: he recommends that a woman's imperfections be disregarded and that the lover substitutes them with positive, euphemistic attributes. The skinny are to be told they are slender, the stunted trim, the cross-eyed divine.[47]

Ovid refers to a number of sex manuals, all now lost, some of which may have been regarded as what we now call pornographic. Many were Greek. An otiose Lucius Cornelius Sisenna translated Aristides into Latin under the title *Milesiae fabulae* around 78 BC; Ovid calls it an anthology of misdeeds full of smutty jokes. The Milesian tale (Μιλησιακά in Greek; in Latin *fabula milesiaca*, or *Milesiae fabula*) had a long history, even by Ovid's day. It is usually defined as a short, erotic story featuring love and adventure. In his dialogue on the kinds of love, *Erotes*, Lucian praised Aristides as 'that enchanting spinner of bawdy yarns'. After the Battle of Carrhae, the victorious Parthians were shocked to find the *Milesiaca* in the baggage of Crassus's officers: 'Surena ... laid before them certain wanton books, of the writings of Aristides, his *Milisiaka*; neither, indeed, was this any forgery, for they had been found among the baggage of Rustius, and were good ammunition with which to supply Surena with insulting remarks about the Romans, who were not able even during war to take their minds off such writings and practices.' The *milesiaca* influenced the racier parts of Petronius' *Satyricon* and Apuleius' *The Golden Ass*, as well as *Cupid and Psyche*. Nearer our time, the medieval *fabliaux* owe much to Aristides: likewise Chaucer's *The Miller's Tale*, some of Boccaccio's *Decameron*, and the *Heptameron* of Margaret of Angoulême.

Women made good sex teachers too. It was not just men who taught the *artes amatoriae*: women contributed to the sex manual publishing programmes. Martial alludes to books by Elephantis in his review of the work of Sabellus; we have seen how she was the author of a famous book on sexual positions – that Roman *Kama Sutra*. Suetonius we know tells that Tiberius packed a copy for reference when he left for his retreat on Capri. Martial recommends the books written by Sulpicia to women and men alike, if they want guidance on how to achieve the perfect marriage – on both sides of the bedroom door. Elsewhere, women lend a helping hand when he recommends that Istantius Rufus has his girl masturbate him as he reads the salacious books of Musaeus.[48]

After the second century AD the Christians put an end to erotic literature, leaving only medical works and theology. Celibacy became the name of the game and the permissibility of sex in marriage even for procreation was questioned by such writers as Tertullian and Clement of Alexandria. The issues surrounding the sexuality of martyrology and sexual torture, notably sexual mutilation involving the female breasts, were debated by Christians.[49]

Two examples are Agatha of Sicily (AD 231–251) and Febronia of Nisibis (AD 284–305). According to Jacobus de Voragine, in his *Legenda Aurea* of 1288, Agatha, who came from a rich and noble family, dedicated herself and her virginity to God. At fifteen she was forced to repel the advances of the Roman prefect Quintianus, who sent her to Aphrodisia, the madam of a brothel. On finding Agatha a somewhat reluctant participant in the business of the house, Aphrodisia complained to Quintianus; he has Agatha put in prison, where her breasts are cut off. She is then then sentenced to be burnt at the stake, but is saved by a timely earthquake and sent to another prison, where St. Peter the Apostle appears to her and heals her wounds.

Febronia of Nisibis was a nun at Nisibis in Mesopotamia. She was persecuted under Diocletian, who offered her freedom if she renounced her faith and married his nephew, Lysimachus, who had been showing tendencies towards a conversion to Christianity. Febronia refused and was tortured; her breasts were cut off and she died. Lysimachus saw her suffering and proceeded with his conversion.

Martial enjoyed a revival in fourth-century Bordeaux, thanks to the poet Ausonius (AD 310–395). Apart from riveting treatises on the occupations of the day (*Ephemeris*) and the workings of a water-powered saw mill, Ausonius has left us with a graphic description of wedding night consummation, the *Cento Nuptialis*. 'Back and forth he plies his path and, the cavity reverberating, thrusts between the bones, and strikes with ivory quill. And now, their journey covered, wearily they neared their very goal: then rapid breathing shakes his limbs and parched mouth, his sweat in rivers flows; down he slumps bloodless; the fluid drips from his groin.' Apart from its explicit eroticism the poem is notable for the way in which Ausonius reworks phrases from Virgil and applies them to his description of sexual intercourse. Ausonius allegedly had an impressive and extensive library of homosexual literature.

The erotic was all around in ancient Rome. Phalluses apart, erotic wall decoration in public buildings and private homes was a cause for concern for Propertius and the effect it was having on impressionable young girls. He deplores the *obscaenae* and the corrupting effect they have on the innocent eyes of girls. He has an agenda, though; what he is really worried about is that the pictures will endgender in them a promiscuity which will not always be to his personal advantage.

Ovid writes to Augustus from exile in Tomis, describing quite casually the wall paintings he has seen there which depict different ways of having sex and sexual positions. In the Pompeiian wall paintings, women are frequently shown playing an equal or dominant role in the sex act; women were not just willing and equal partners here. They would have been just as likely to enjoy the paintings as men, and indeed to assume a matter-of-fact attitude to them. The reception of erotic wall paintings by the Roman man and woman was very different to the reception of the Victorians and later societies, for example, who hid the paintings away from us and kept them locked up for many years.[50]

In Rome, when a sexual act is displayed on a house wall, on a lamp or on a wine jug it becomes part of the domestic wallpaper, accepted as normal by normal people. Mundane objects such as mirrors and jugs, for example on Aretine ware, were often embellished with the erotic, ranging from routine 'courting' to explicit penetration by the erect penis into the vagina.

Propertius deplores the fine clothes, perfumes and hairstyle worn by his girl, recommending instead that her natural beauty be allowed to shine through. He is anxious lest his 'done up' girl attracts undue attention from other men.[51] Ovid had no such qualms; indeed, so important did he consider good grooming and a woman's use of cosmetics that he wrote a book about it, the *Medicamina Faciei*. The *Ars Amatoria* offers advice for girls who are less than beautiful, where Ovid shows a girl how to make the most of shortcomings. He discusses dress, make-up, halitosis, how to conceal bad dentition and even how to laugh discreetly.[52]

Also notable is the casualness with which men describe and enjoy female sexuality and the assumption that a range of female sexual services are there for the taking, be they with a wife, slavegirl or with a prostitute. It reflects, of course, Roman male domination and male promiscuity – acceptable, so long as it was not adulterous. Elite men in the form of poets – didactic and invective – and not so elite men in the shape of graffiti writers are all quick to deride and denigrate the objects of their desires, complaining when they are snubbed by a well-dressed *docta puella*, paranoid that a wall painting will impel their mistress into the bed of another lover, whingeing when denied what some then, and now, might call deviant sex, indignant that a whore smells or that a procuress trains her girls to be meretricious. Lesbians, low-rent prostitutes, and even women generally are vilified in books and on walls – but not on all walls; the graffiti may be fantasist and insulting but the interior decoration sometimes shows the sexual woman on equal or superior terms even with her male partner. Is this the sort of output we should expect from a less privileged, less conservative, more populist and artisanal type of artist who, like the love poets, was not particularly bothered about a *cursus honorum, virtus, stuprum* or chauvinism?

With the exception of the pedastalised objects of desire vaunted by the love poets in literature, women working in the sex trade were marginalised, second-class citizens. In Rome, as anywhere, sex has always been another means by which men exert power and control over women. But there is evidence that women, as wives, mistresses and prostitutes themselves, were increasingly able to exert a degree of independence, influence and power, in and out of bed. This is particularly obvious among the Lesbias, Cynthias, Delias and Corinnas, who are the *dominae* in the *servitium amoris*, unyielding to the *exclusus amator*, vanquishing the *miles amoris* – but it also manifests in the graffiti and in the wall paintings and other depictions where they are represented as active, sometimes dominant, participants in consensual sexual activity.[53]

However, not all public exposure was welcome; women endured their share of public executions. Most of the different methods – beheading, flogging to death, pushing off the Tarpeian Rock, burning alive (vivicombustion), feeding to wild animals or being drowned inside a sack – took place with the victim naked – much to the further delectation of the large crowds which had been summoned to these spectacles by a fanfare of trumpets. As a concession to modesty, however, women escaped the extra humiliation of very public exposure and were executed in private. Even when a Pontifex Maximus scourged a Vestal Virgin for letting the flame go out, he did so behind a curtain. The curtain would have been little consolation to those women who were sentenced to death by strangulation; they were, according to Tacitus and Dio Cassius, raped by the executioner beforehand.[54]

Women's breasts do not seem to have always held the fascination or attracted the fetishism they have in later societies. Indeed, it seems that small was beautiful, with the ideal size being comparable to an apple.[55] Martial scoffs at large breasts, while the much-maligned elderly woman was usually described as being ugly and had pendulous breasts.[56] Large breasts were popular features in Roman comedy, part of the stereotyping of ugly women. In Plautus' *Poenulus* (line 1,416), a flute girl is written off as unattractive because her cheeks and her breasts are too big – puffing out the cheeks while blowing a wind instrument was considered a sign of ugliness. On the other hand, we find, by contrast, in Plautus's *Casina*, *edepol papillam bellulam* – 'By Pollux, what lovely little tits!'[57]

Catullus and Ovid do allude to the erotic appeal and erogenous nature of breasts. Ovid likes to touch nipples ready for squeezing, while Catullus, in his wedding hymn, observes that the bride's 'tender nipples' will keep a husband interested and encourage the birth of children and a lasting marriage.[58] We read in Achilles Tatius's *Leucippe and Clitophon* from the early second century AD that 'her breast when it is caressed provides its own particular pleasure'.[59] Of the Augustan elegists, Propertius observantly associates breast development with girls reaching an age at which they can 'play', while Tibullus notes that he can get a flash of a woman's breast when she wears loose clothing.[60] In the third century BC, Manetho in his *Aegyptiaca*[61] told that breast relief, thrusting the penis between a woman's breasts to ejaculation, was enjoyed by men born under the conjunction of Venus, Mercury, and Saturn. Breasts are covered up often, even in the most explicit wall paintings, by the breastband or *strophium*.

Breast-baring and the beating of breasts had religious and military significance. In war it accompanied appeals for mercy by women in conquered cities as a powerful indication of woman's nurturing role.[62] Servius explains its function as an accompaniment to grief as producing milk to nurture the deceased.[63] Julius Caesar saw breast-beating among the Celts during the siege of Avaricum, when the mothers exposed their breasts and held out their hands in an appeal for the women and children to be spared. Tacitus noted a more belligerent, perhaps erotic, function among German women, who bared their breasts to encourage their reluctant men into battle.[64]

We have already seen how erotic wall paintings decorated some houses. Valerius Maximus describes what seems to be something like a private sex club in 52 BC:

> [Metellus Scipio] established a whorehouse in his own house, and pimped out Mucia and Flavia, each of them notable for her father and husband, along with the aristocratic boy Saturninus. Bodies in shameless submission, ready to come for a game of drunken sex! A banquet not for honouring consul and tribunes, but indicting them![65]

Cicero accuses Verres, Piso, and Antony of converting his bedrooms into *stabulae* with cubicles for prostitutes and his dining room into *popinae*, a kind of takeaway.[66]

Throughout this chapter we have noted the male Roman's insistence on sexual superiority and domination: he must be the penetrator, the active and potent sexual force, for only then can his *virtus*, his manliness, power and virtue, be demonstrated and exerted. Sexual prowess was also a metaphor for national power, pride and dignity, for *Romanitas* – the quintessential quality of being a Roman. This is well illustrated in the theatre Pompey built in 55 BC and dedicated to Venus Victrix, the *Theatrum Pompeium*. It was a kind of ancient version of London's South Bank: in addition to the theatre, columned porticos surrounded a large garden complex of fountains and statues with a covered arcade housing galleries of art and sculpture, much of which was plundered by by Pompey on his campaigns.[67] The significance of this lies in the dichotomy between male and female, the strong and the weak; exhibitions included portrait galleries of female writers and of courtesans, freakish births that had served as prodigies and war omens.[68] Intellectuality and culture are represented as feminine and Hellenistic, while war and politics are unmistakably Roman and masculine. Fourteen subdued nations are represented as women in ethnic or barbarian attire. We can recognise similar monuments throughout the Roman world: for example, the Sebasteion at Aphrodisias and the altar of the Sanctuary of the Three Gauls at Lugdunum (modern Lyon); coins show conquered lands and peoples as women: Roman military might is victorious over the effeminate losers and the vanquished. At Aphrodisias we see a heroically nude Claudius subduing Britannia, her right breast bare, and Nero hauling away a slain Armenian, reminiscent of the defeat of the Amazon Penthesilea by heroic Achilles. The coins depicting *Iudaea Capta* have on the verso a female personification of the Jewish nation mourning and captive, minted by Vespasian after the destruction of the Second Temple of Jerusalem in AD 70 by Titus. The female is possibly a depiction of the prophecy of Isaiah 'For Jerusalem is ruined, and Judah is fallen... Thy men shall fall by the sword and thy mighty in the war. And her gates shall lament and mourn, and she being desolate shall sit upon the ground.'[69]

Sex and sexuality are well and truly gendered throughout the Roman world; sexual conquest and domination were unmistakeable metaphors for Roman imperialism and Romanisation.[70]

CHAPTER SIX

Sex in the Afternoon: the *domina* and Her Love Slave

Some genres of Roman literature is full of references to sex and sexuality – something that should come as no surprise: we have already established that sex generally did not carry the stigma and embarrassment with which subsequent societies have imbued it, rendering it taboo. This chapter looks at how far Roman literature may reflect sex and sexuality in wider Roman society, and the struggles the love poets in particular had to get their women into bed.

It is difficult to assess just how far the dramas of Plautus and Terence reflect actual Roman experience since the plays are coloured by Greek *mores,* as portrayed in Menander and other playwrights of the New Comedy. If, then, Titinius, Plautus or Terence were to raise a laugh then they would surely have drawn their characters with traits and mannerisms recognisable by their audiences through their own everyday experience; their plots would reflect aspects of Roman life and their characters would be recognisable as regular Romans.[1] The prologue to the *Poenulus* is a case in point, where Plautus plays to a strictly Roman audience; here he rebukes the *matronae* for their irritating way of laughing, and then requests that the wet nurses do not bring in their bawling babies.[2] These comedies are particularly important because they shed light on aspects of non-elite Roman family life; unlike much of the rest of the literary evidence, they describe domestic situations in the lower classes.

Anna Raia has counted the appearances of women in Plautus.

The 54 women in Plautus' plays – and there are 61 if we count the seven women who are discussed but never appear – can be grouped into five stereotypes: the *puella* or young maiden, the *matrona* or married woman, the *meretrix* or courtesan, the *ancilla* or handmaid, and the *anus* or old woman. The comedies feature: eleven *puellae*, four of whom are invisible; thirteen *matronae*, two of whom are never seen; nineteen *meretrices*, one of whom doesn't appear; twelve *ancillae;* and five personages who fit the category of the *anus*.[3]

This compares with 154 male roles. Three of the plays have no speaking female parts at all: the *Captivi, Pseudolus,* and *Trinummus.* Reasons for the imbalance may be that Plautus was mirroring the restrictive social situation of women in Greece; that he was reflecting the subordinate position of women in his own society; or that it was simply easier to limit female characters from a production point of view because actors in Rome were always men. A combination of all three of these reasons may be responsible.

New Comedy prototypes displayed characteristics and behaviour redolent of Roman society that would be familiar to the audiences.[4] The prostitute, *meretrix,* is no exception. The whole gamut of prostitute types show up in Plautus' plays: the, naive, the novice and the one-man *meretrix*, as exemplified by Philaenium in the *Asinaria*, Pasicompsa in the *Mercator* and Philematium in the *Mostellaria*. The busy, sophisticated prostitute who spends her day working or working at working, with her make up, fine clothes, dinner parties, bathing and clever conversation, is represented by Gymnasium in the *Cistellaria*, Erotium in the *Menaechmi* and Acropolis in the *Epidicus* – these women are the closest we get to the frustrating and exasperating women who were later to excite the love poets of the first century BC. Finally, there are the whores way past their best, the *lenae*, procuresses, who now spend their time further corrupting their already corrupted young charges, much to the disgust of Propertius and the like.

In Plautus, Alcmene, the wife of Amphitryo in the *Amphitryo*, is a very complex character. She exhibits characteristics of the chaste girl, *pudica puella*, the *amans amica*, the loving girlfriend, the *matrona irata*, the angry wife and, in her adulterous affair with Jupiter, the *meretrix*. Plautus probably draws on the ideal, *univira matrona*, from his own Rome. Her (unsuspected) dalliance with Jupiter is one of the few descriptions of physical love in Roman literature as articulated by a woman; her dignified protestations of fidelity to Amphitryo on his (real) return embody the essence of good matronly behaviour, indignant as she is at being thought otherwise. Alcmene is indeed a paradox: Plautus has her passionately vocalise her love in a loud, ostentatious way that was at odds with good matronly decorum and, for that reason, objectionable to men; he then has her proudly list her credentials as a good *matrona*.

Plautus died in 184 BC. The eloquence of Alcmene may be seen as a precursor to the much freer expression found a few years later in Terence, and may be indicative of how quickly things were moving on in Roman society in that short time. Chremes, the *paterfamilias* in the *Andrea*, puts his daughter's happiness first when it comes to the choice of a husband; Antipho in the *Phormio* marries a young girl because he loves her, against the wishes of his father and despite the fact that she has no dowry, and is an orphan from a family of no standing. In the *Hecyra, The Mother in Law*, we have a play whose action is monopolised by women: two mothers-in-law, a courtesan and a pregnant daughter(-in-law)/wife.

The late Republic saw a growing independence among increasing numbers of better-off women, allowing them more freedom outside the home. At the same time a number of male poets were able to eschew the traditional *mos maiorum*, rejecting the *cursus honorum* for a life of *otium* in which they could while away their time penning poetry and pursuing the objects of their affection. Among these coteries we can recognise such poets as Licinius Calvus, Varro of Atax, Valerius Cato, Furius Bibaculus, Helvius Cinna, Cornificius, Ticidas and, most famously, Catullus. Collectively, they went under the name of *poetae novi, neoteroi* or *Cantores Euphorionis*.[5] Traditionalists regarded this otiose lifestyle as frivolous and un-Roman. *Otium* was the opposite to *negotium* – the business.

In the *Amores* (1, 5), Ovid describes perfectly another hot summer's day of *otium*, stretched out on his couch, shutters half-open, letting in just enough light to protect a girl's modesty with Corinna on her way in her loose, flowing dress. She arrives and feigns resistance – but as Ovid tears off her clothes, she yields.

Like Sallust's Sempronia, the women pedastalised by the love poets, their *doctae puellae*, were diametrically opposed to the *matrona*; they were anything but modest, discrete, *univira*, compliant or chaste – they were decidedly not *univirae* and it seems unlikely that between them they produced very much wool. The poets allowed themselves to be dominated by these women, their *dominae*, even to be enslaved by them in *servitium amoris*. Their *cursus honorum* was *militia amoris,* their role in the *domus* and the *familia* bore little resemblance to *patria potestas*; they languished locked-out on the doorstep, *exclusus amator*.

Propertius opens his anthology with a poem which leaves no doubt about his predicament: he is a slave to his love for Cynthia, a state of servitude which colours much of the remainder of the poems. Tibullus too is under the yoke (1, 9; 1, 10 etc.), but his enslavement to Delia is physical as well as emotional (1, 5); he invites branding as a real slave and penetration by the sword – a huge phallic capitulation of his male pride, masculinity and *virtus*. Ovid too surrenders to penetration when he is pricked with Cupid's arrows in the opening poem of the *Amores*, but manages to reverse the malady in I, 7 when he reasserts his masculinity and strength with a slap in the face for his mistress. He is a man again: *io, forti victa puella viro est!* The slave to love is just as capable of handing out physical abuse as he is subservience in language which is reminiscent of the *miles amoris*.

As champion of the *mos maiorum* and despiser of things Greek, Cato the Elder (234–149 BC) had spoken out sternly against what he saw as a period of moral decline and the erosion of the sturdy principles on which Rome had lain her foundations.[6] He identified the growing independence of the women of Rome as an ominous ingredient in this.[7] The defeat of Hannibal at Zama in 202 BC, the victory over the Macedonians at Pydna in 168 BC and the final extinguishing of the Carthaginian threat in 146 BC all allowed Rome to relax more and encouraged an unprecedented influx of Greek and eastern influences and luxuries into a receptive Rome.[8]

Marriage *cum manu* had more or less died out, leaving women to marry in a much freer arrangement where love and affection were sometimes nothing more than a fortunate by-product;[9] divorcing was easy and adultery was on the increase. Widowhood, free marriage and divorce often left women better off financially; certainly they could often live more independently.[10] The social climate is well, if not hypocritically, summed up by Horace writing about Rome around 28 BC. He describes how the traditional Roman *familia* and *matrona* were now corrupted; he talks of how 'generations rich in sin first sullied marriage, families and the home' and then focuses on the *matura virgo* who loses no time perfecting Greek dancing and other blandishments. She fantasises about illicit love – and at drinking parties indiscriminately and casually seeks out young adulterers; the lights are left on so that her husband, who is taking payment for her services, can see it all whether she's cavorting with a Spanish sailor or a door-to-door salesman – 'the buyer of her pricey shame'.[11]

It is in such an environment that Catullus and the love poets flourished in the final days of the republic and the early years of the empire. Their urbane and sophisticated women could mix with whomsoever they chose at the games, at festivals, at dinner parties or in the theatre, enjoying, if they so chose, a degree of sexual freedom not dissimilar to that enjoyed by a *meretrix*, a prostitute, but with little of the social stigma.[12]

On a typical lazy day, *dies otiosus,* Varus invites Catullus to come over and meet his girlfriend: first appearances show her to be elegant and well-mannered; however, a later indiscretion on her part which embarrasses Catullus renders her silly and annoying. On another occasion Flavius' reticence about his girl leads Catullus to assume that she is 'common and a bit rough', 'a fever-ridden slag no less'. When he invites himself over to Ipsithilla's place for an afternoon of sex he sarcastically and sycophantically calls her 'my delight, my clever one'.[13] Both Quintia and Ameana fall short: Quintia is indeed fair, tall and she holds herself well, but beautiful, *formosa,* she is not, because she lacks charm and wit; Ameana cannot talk posh. As for Caecilius' girlfriend, she has begun reading his *Magna Mater* and is fired with passion for Caecilius as a result. To Catullus, she is thereby more refined than the Sapphic Muse.[14]

It is Lesbia, though, for whom Catullus reserves the highest praise: Claudia Pulchra Prima (b. 94 BC), wife of Metellus Celer – brother of Publius Clodius Pulcher – and mistress of Catullus. She was also a lover of Marcus Caelius Rufus', the friend whom Cicero defended against charges of attempted poisoning and, in doing so, destroyed Clodia's reputation, such as it was, calling her, among other things, the 'Medea of the Palatine'.[15] Lesbia, though, has the *venustas* and *salis* Quintia lacks, and *Veneres* – 'grace, elegance and charm'; this, and physical beauty – adds up to total beauty. Lesbia has literary talent; she can identify the 'best bits of the worst poet', as she demonstrates when she hands back the dreadful annals of Volusius, 'pure unsophisticated doggerel, complete crap'– *pleni ruris et infacetiarum annales Volusi, cacata charta*.[16]

At the end of the first century BC Propertius describes Cornelia, the daughter of Scribonia and wife to Lucius Aemilius Paullus,

Augustus' stepdaughter. She can boast excellent credentials as a *matrona*: dutiful daughter, dutiful wife and dutiful mother, the ideal role model for her children. All the fine, matronly qualities are here – her life was faultless from beginning to end. 'Nor did my lifestyle change; it was blameless throughout, I lived respected between both torches (namely marriage and funeral).' Cornelia is just the sort of woman to pose as cover girl for Augustus' moral legislation, the *lex Julia de maritandis ordinibus*. She is the opposite of Cynthia, Propertius' decadent mistress; Propertius enumerates traditional *matrona* qualities to highlight, by comparison, the unconventional and outrageous behaviour of Cynthia. Cornelia, though, in the eyes of Propertius, is a somewhat empty character who lives a proper but uninteresting life, following her own *cursus honorum* to the letter; to him she is a victim of Roman tradition who, despite her obvious intelligence and attractions, lived a rather submissive, confined life.[17] For Propertius, Cynthia is a much more exciting prospect.

Not for Tibullus the cosmopolitan life of a Catullus or a Propertius; he, 'in his madness', actually desires a bucolic lifestyle, embracing *rus* (as opposed to *urbs*) rather than sneering at it, as was the convention – 'I'm going to live in the country, and my Delia will be there to look after the fruits of the earth.' He describes a way of life more befitting a country *matrona*, which sees Delia sitting at home in the evening surrounded by seamstresses who, one by one, fall asleep working away at the loom. This itself is remimiscent of Lucretia, that paradigm of *matronae*, sewing away in the half-light when others were out partying.[18]

For Horace, who was writing about the same time as Propertius and Tibullus, any appreciation of female artistic accomplishment is largely limited to the floor shows put on by the dancing girls at the drinking parties he attended. Damalis is leered at remorselessly, Lyde is summoned to play her lyre and Neaera is required to sing – all as warm-up acts before the sex with their lusting audience. Phydile is dismissed as simply *rustica*;[19] Licymnia is praised for her sweet singing, Chloe is skilled on the cithara and is good at gentle dance rhythms while the lyres of Lydia and the *scortum* Lyde are much in demand, as are Phyllis and melodious Neaera for their singing, and Tyndaris for her lyre-playing and singing.[20]

Paradoxically, Horace is at his most scything with 'the grown up girl [who] delights in being taught the Greek movements and is coached in seduction; all she thinks about now is illicit sex from head to toe', 'dancing today, adultery tomorrow'.[21] Horace probably summed up the usual male attitude, an attitude exemplified by Scipio Africanus, who was flabbergasted by the increasing popularity of dancing among girls and boys; dancing was so Greek, not at all Roman. Sempronia, we have observed, was vilified by Sallust because she danced like a professional. On the other hand, Cornelius Nepos later admonished Romans for their xenophobic assumption that other cultures could not possibly like dancing, just because Romans despised it and consigned it to the *demi monde* [22].

Ovid is even less particular: to him a woman is urbane if she affects the resilience of the famously 'raped' Sabine women, if she is bookish – or if she is common, if she attracts by virtue of her *simplicitas:* if she is any or all of these things, she is fine by Ovid. Shy girls, coquettish girls, tall girls, small girls, fashionable girls, frumpy girls, blonde girls, black girls – girls, girls, girls – they are all the same to Ovid. In the same poem, however, he does single out the attractions of a woman who is literate and critical, who can sing, play the lyre and dance well. 'This girl sings sweetly, she has good range… this one thrums the tricky strings with practised thumb – who could not adore such clever hands? This one delights in the way she moves, her arms following the rhythm and her soft hips twisting with subtle skill.'

Ovid confirms this in the *Ars Amatoria*.[23] The obsession with, and admiration for, dancing girls and singers flew in the face of traditional Roman convention. Dancers to many, Horace included when it suited him, were but one short step up from prostitutes, ancient world lap dancers.

Ovid, however, is useful: he can advise where to find all types of girls, including sophisticated ladies – the games, for example, are literally crawling with smart women, confirmation that the educated woman was out and about and generally much sought after. He acknowledges that some women appreciate good oratorical style and oratory, and he himself consorts with women who are clever enough to value his poetry – not least Corinna. He advises his fellow men to get educated, because women appreciate intellectual gifts in a man more than they do good looks.[24] He recommends that men read widely in the Greek classics and in modern literature, suggesting clearly that women were similarly well read and enjoyed bookish discussion. Later in the poem, though, he qualifies this when he admits that *doctae puellae* are rather thin on the ground and that, generally, poetry is held in low regard. Clever women do exist, though, and many aspire to culture; women can be seduced by verse or a piece of declamation, be they clever or stupid.[25]

This is Ovid as *praeceptor amoris* – a teacher of love, or 'agony aunt'. In Books One and Two he teaches men; in Book Three, women. He is working for both sides: his advice to women covers social etiquette and sexual technique, all designed to maximise the pleasure for both parties [26]. Unfortunately for Ovid, *praeceptor amoris* as a profession was not exclusive to men. While the love poets were busy admiring the intellectual and artistic talents of their women, an altogether less salubrious type of education was being provided in the seedy Roman *demi-monde*. The bawd had a role to play as *praeceptrix amoris*, instructing her girls in seduction and meretricious exploitation.

Propertius' Acanthis poem is an example of the rancour these women excited. The poet spits out a litany of invective and abuse, expressing outrage that the *lena* has scuppered his chances of any sexual progress with his girl. It starts savagely, setting the tone for what is to follow: a catalogue of all the unhelpful advice the girl has received, all freighted with Propertius' disgust. Acanthis recommends a wholly mercenary attitude, dishonesty and deceit, withholding sex, jealousy – it gets personal for the poet in Propertius when she scorns poetry and music as worthless gifts.[27] She sabotages Propertius' best weapons – his intellect and his verse.

Sulpicia was that rare thing, a woman poet whose work has survived, a true *docta puella*; the six elegies in which she describes her love for Cerinthus constitute one of the very few surviving examples of poetry composed by a Roman woman.[28] Just as her male contemporaries, Tibullus and Propertius, lived a somewhat dissolute life, free from the shackles of the *mos maiorum* and the *cursus honorum*, so too did the coquettish Sulpicia, liberated from the modesty and chastity expected of the *matrona*: she loves a party – *pecasse iuvat*.

There was also Sulpicia Caleni, a poet who lived during the reign of Domitian and who is praised by Martial. Her poems, only two of which survive, are based on her personal experience of married life, particularly her sex life with husband Calenus; Martial declares that these poems are required reading for wife and husband alike and the key to a happy, one man, one woman marriage: all the wives, all the husbands are reading Sulpicia.[29] Another Roman *Joy of Sex*.

She, a *univira*, teaches pure and honest love, 'messing about, teasing and having fun'. Sappho, no less, would have learnt something from her as teacher. In the fourth century AD her reputation is still sufficiently alive for Ausonius to describe her work as salacious, her manner prim; the less liberal Sidonius Apollinarus in the fifth century includes her in a list of earlier poets whom he will *not* be imitating.

Rome's national poem, the *Aeneid*, showcasing the exploits of national hero Aeneas in his challenge to found Rome, is not without its sexual interest. The Dido episode in Book 4 is a pivotal point in the poem where Aeneas tarries with the Carthaginian queen, makes love to her in a cave and then deserts her in preference to his national responsibilities. Aeneas thus consigns Dido to a list of forsaken heroines which was already quite long by the beginning of the first century AD. To Dido the affair constituted something approaching a marriage – *coniugium* – but to Aeneas, nothing of the sort, as he sailed off over the horizon. Dido's tragic response is to end it all on a funeral pyre midst the magical incantations of a Massyllian prophetess. He Trojan sword is described in phallic terms as it penetrates her – to Dido the sex was a source of shame, a crime – *culpa* – generated by naked desire [30]. She of course was dispensable in the great Roman scheme of things but, as a woman scorned, was able to exact a terrible revenge on Rome in the shape of two of the three Punic Wars.

There is more sex, but on a divine scale, in Book 8. Here, Venus and Vulcan make love; the ekphrasis as depicted on Vulcan's shield illustrates Rome's often bloody past and predicted future through the wars in which it subdued neighbouring nations, and the internecine civil wars of the first century BC.[31]

We have seen how the Romans viewed their own sexual conduct. Respect for the *matrona* and inculcation of the matronly ideal; criminalisation of adultery with a freeborn married woman; taboos surrounding the passive role and penetration in oral and anal sex. According to many, including Cato the Younger and Horace, this is how sexual conduct used to be: civilised, proper and discreet, family and nation building. Now it was all adultery and exotic permissiveness – it needed Augustus to put a brake on all the corruption with his (largely ineffective and hypocritical) moral legislation. The stain of licentiousness was one of the prices paid when exotic practices flowed in from the east. All something of an exaggeration, no doubt, as the evidence for sex in the city that was Rome and its expanding empire largely comes from elite males with prejudices and axes to grind.

However, given these caveats, we can still look at how the Romans viewed the sexual practices of the nations and cultures they came into contact with, and how far their own perceptions on the domestic situation was reflected in their views on sex outside the city and empire of Rome.

Writers in the Roman period tell us much about the cultures and societies with whom the Romans came into contact – some of it is plain, curiosity-satisfying, educative and informative, explicating how, for example, the Germans differ from them in various cultural, physical and social ways. Some of it, on the other hand, is xenophobic and exclusive, prurient even – highlighting what are seen as oddities, fetishes or vices. Descriptions of the sexual practices of other cultures fall into both camps.

Polygamy and the sharing of women – and public sex outdoors – were of course contrary to Roman practice and law, but the Romans could, nevertheless, concede some benefits, particularly in the sensible attitude to complicated paternity issues. Julius Caesar, for one, is not censorious when describing the arrangements among the Britons whereby the man who took the woman's virginity was decreed the father of the multitude of children resulting from free love. He did believe, however, that half-naked bathing among the Germans led to promiscuity although he commended them on their belief that sexual activity weakened the body and that their abstinence was responsible for their physical prowess.[32] Diodorus Siculus gives us a measured description of the Fish-eaters, the *Ichthyophagi* on the Red Sea coast: they walk around naked in herds, like cattle, and share their women and children; the good thing about them, according to Diodorus, was that they source their food and their women locally so there was none of that corrupting imported luxury and pleasure which plagued and polluted Rome.[33] However, when it comes to Ireland, Ierne, Strabo reports that the men there eat their dead fathers and have sex in public with their mothers and sisters.[34] He adds that the Arabs shared their women between the men of the family and placed a staff against the tent door to indicate when a woman was busy: all good and well for the man (especially if he was on the woman's side of the door) but one woman got round this assumption on her sexual availability by placing a stick there even when she was alone.[35] Strabo records the story of Menander's Thracian who admits that Thracians are sexually incontinent, accounting for their many wives.[36] Diodorus tells how the Celts ignore their beautiful women in preference to wild homosexual orgies.[37] Juvenal famously describes one Greek from whose lust no one in the house is safe: *matrona*, virgin daughter, son, son-in-law, even grandmother.[38] Ammianus Marcellinus identifies the lustful barbarian among the Saracenes, the Gothic Taefalians (for boys) and the Parthians.[39] He also reported that the Huns had sex in their wagons. So what?

It was by no means all unbridled sex, though. Indian sages lived lives of abstinence and taught restraint to their male and female pupils;[40] Indian ladies did not come cheap: Arrian, writing in the early second century AD, believed that the only way to seduce an Indian woman was to buy her an elephant.[41] Valerius Maximus has the uplifting story of the good looking Etruscan Spurinna who disfigured his face to deter the attentions of women. This is in direct contrast to the sex-mad, permissive Etruscans described by the Greek Theopompos.[42] Polybius, Livy and Plutarch all praise the wife of a Galatian chieftain's wife who unsuccessfully rejected the attentions of a Roman centurion; after he had raped her she killed him and spent the rest of her life chastely with her husband.[43] We have already met Martial's matronly Claudia Rufina; she of British stock, a barbarian, but nevertheless a Latin at heart. She is fertile, *univira* and looking forward to her childrens' marriages.[44] Conversely, Graeco-Egyptian Cleopatra VII was a *fatale monstrum*, a doom monster, according to Horace, and the revolutionary Boudica not much better in the eyes of Tacitus and Dio who tell us that Boudica accused the Romans of pederasty.[45] Tacitus, elsewhere, compares German *mores* favourably with those currently prevailing in Rome; despite the fact that German women bare their breasts, he praises their monogamous society and the fact that they do not marry just to satisfy male sexual desire, and that their wives are faithful and chaste – just like Romans used to be.[46]

Polygamy is deplored by Cicero among the Persians and Assyrians, by Lucan in the *Pharsalia* and Justin among the Parthians.[47] Other writers see the benefit of creating a pool of male citizens; Strabo says as much, with regard to the Persians and the Brahmin philosophers in India.[48] Diodorus Siculus appreciated the benefits of polygamy to the Egyptian economy[49] while Ammianus Marcellnus counterbalanced criticism of Persian polygamy with the concession that they eschewed luxury and were masculine despite their effeminate appearance.[50]

Moreover, early-third-century-AD Athenaeus confirms for us that it was not just barbarians who were rapacious and sex-crazed. He gives us the report that the hubristic and luxury-addicted Tarentines in Southern Italy forced captured Iapygian boys, virgins and *matronae* into temples, stripped them naked and raped them in public.[51]

Literature, then, seems to have caught the prevailing sexual mood very well, reflecting a growing liberalism among men and women in the crossover years between republic and an increasingly permissive early empire. The comic playrights, Plautus and Terence, Romanised their makeovers of Greek originals while the love ports, starting with Catullus and his coterie, described a freer, more independant class of woman who could be enjoyed in an extramarital, unmatronly relaxed environment. The sexual practices of the nations with which the Romans came into contact were examined either as a source of curiosity or interest, and with prurience and xenophobia in equal measure.

CHAPTER SEVEN

Cross-Dressing, Transsexualism and Same-Sex Marriage

This chapter looks at transvestism or cross-dressing, gender identity disorder, same-sex marriage, and attitudes to them as well as the attitudes to eunuchs, castration and circumcision. We have already touched on the two instances where Julius Caesar was involved in cross-dressing: apparently, aged twenty, he lived the life of a girl in the court of King Nicomedes IV, and was later referred to behind his back as 'Queen of Bithynia', 'every woman's man and every man's woman'. Suetonius describes his long-fringed sleeves and loose belt as unusual, prompting Sulla to warn, 'Beware of the boy with the loose belt.'

A more famous case of transvestism occurred when Publius Clodius invaded the women-only rites of Bona Dea *chez* Julius Caesar to seduce Pompeia, Caesar's wife; he, Clodius, was dressed as a woman. Cicero prosecuted him for *incestum*, and ridicules him thus: 'Take away his saffron dress, his tiara, his girly shoes and purple laces, his bra, his Greek harp, take away his shameless behaviour and his sex crime, and Clodius is suddenly revealed as a democrat.' Tiberius apparently dressed up as a woman during his debaucheries on Capri; Caligula showed up at banquets dressed as Venus. Ulpian declares that to dress up as a woman only attracts scorn; he gives another example of transvestism when he describes 'a certain senator accustomed to wear women's evening clothes', who was disposing of the women's ware in his will. Long before that the playwright Accius (170–86 BC) refers to a father who secretly wore 'virgin's finery'. In a rhetorical exercise set by the elder Seneca, a youth is gang-raped while out wearing women's clothes in public; unfortunately for him, this was all part of a dare rather than any desire for sexual pleasure.[1]

A tragic example of a woman's transvestism occurred in AD 39 during the reign of Caligula. Gaius Calvisius Sabinus had been accused of *maiestas* in AD 31 after the fall of Sejanus, but he had survived; now he was under suspicion by Caligula. Cornelia, his wife, was in the habit of watching soldiers during exercises; less innocently, she visited sentries at night, dressed up herself in military uniform and offering her services. One such night she was caught *in flagrante* in the headquarters. She and Sabinus committed suicide.

Philo of Alexandria describes transsexuals in the early days of the Empire as

> taking every possible care on their outward adornment, they are not ashamed even to employ every device to change artificially their nature as men into women... Some of them... craving a complete transformation into women, have chopped off their penises.

Later that century Manilius wrote that they

> are obsessed with their bedizement and good looks; to curl the hair and lay it in waving ripples... to polish the shaggy limbs... Yes! and to hate the very sight of (themselves as) a man, and long for arms without growth of hair. Woman's robes they wear... (their) steps broken to an effeminate gait.' An impatient Juvenal asks, 'But why are they waiting? Isn't it now high time for them to try the Phrygian fashion and to make the job complete – take a knife and lop off that superfluous piece of meat?

Full of remorse after kicking his pregnant wife, Poppaea Sabina, to death, Nero seeks out a surrogate who resembles her – and finds Sporus – not a woman but a young man. Nero's people then castrate the ex-slave and the couple marry. Sporus joins Nero in bed with Pythagoras, who nightly played the role of husband in their troilism. Sporus routinely accompanied Nero decked out as his empress, even making one of his favourites, the powerful Calvia Crispinilla, Sporus's 'mistress of wardrobe'. Tacitus calls her Nero's 'tutor in vice'. A disgusted Tacitus has left us his thoughts on the earlier wedding between Nero's wine servant, Pythagoras and Nero:

> He stooped to marry himself to one of that filthy herd, by name Pythagoras, with all the forms of regular wedlock. The bridal veil was put over the emperor; people saw the witnesses of the ceremony, the wedding dower, the couch and the nuptial torches;

everything in a word was plainly visible, which, even when a woman weds, darkness hides.

This all took place at the banquets of Tigellinus, where another nauseating spectacle took place; Nero, draped in the skins of wild animals, was released from a cage and mutilated the genitals of men and women who were bound to stakes. Later, another freedman, Doryphorus, took on the role of groom and would penetrate Nero, his bride, to the accompaniment of wailing virgins being raped.[2]

The 'Phrygian fashion' Juvenal refers to is the Phrygian cult of Cybele, which was introduced into Rome during the republic and led by the Phrygo-Roman god, Attis. The priests were eunuchs who had castrated themselves and were known as Galli. This ritual castration took place during an ecstatic celebration called the *Dies sanguinis*, or 'Day of Blood'. The Galli wore women's clothes and a turban, together with necklaces and earrings. Their hair was long, and bleached, and they wore heavy makeup. They performed dances to the accompaniment of pipes and tambourines, and ecstatically flogged themselves until they bled.[3] Catullus in *Poem 63* describes the emasculation of Attis under the intoxicating influence of Cybele:

> Roused by rabid rage and mind astray, with sharp-edged flint downwards dashed his burden of virility. Then as he felt his limbs were left without their manhood, and the fresh-spilt blood staining the soil, with bloodless hand she hastily took a tambour light to hold, your taborine, Cybele, your initiate rite.

'He' seamlessly becomes 'she' in the aftermath of his self-inflicted castration.[4]

Dio records that that Domitian (r. AD 81–96) hated his brother, the previous emperor, Titus, so much that 'although he was in love with a eunuch named Earinus, he decreed that, from now on, no-one in the territory ruled by Rome should be castrated. And so he insulted Titus, who had also been strongly attracted to castrated boys.'[5] Martial and Statius both 'celebrate' Earinus in their poetry.[6] Martial applauds Domitian's legislation against castration, 'stolen manhood sliced away by the craft of a greedy slavemonger', and the child prostitution which often accompanied it – 'free to swipe a kid from his mother's breast and set him hawking for filthy money'.

Nero's same-sex marriages were probably the most famous in the Roman world, but there are others recorded in the literature. Martial describes a wedding ceremony in which bearded Callistratus weds rugged Afer; to all intents and purposes, it reflects a traditional wedding ceremony right down to the last detail, the only difference being that there will be no children – once the very point of a Roman marriage. 'Are you still not satisfied Rome? Are you waiting for him to give birth?'[7] Juvenal is appalled by the aristocratic Gracchus' behaviour in marrying a socially inferior cornet player, or perhaps he was 'playing the straight horn', Juvenal cuttingly ponders. Again, all the traditional details are there – dowry, wedding dress, veil, banquet – but the poet, like Martial, makes the point that there will be no children – no bad thing, according to an acerbic Juvenal.[8] Although neither may be best qualified to comment objectively, both poets deplore what they see as the rubbishing of the fine old Roman institution of the wedding ceremony. We cannot know how common same-sex marriages were, but it seems they were frequent enough to warrant comment by the poets of the very early second century AD.

It all came to end, legally at least, when same-sex marriage was outlawed in AD 342 by the Christian emperors Constantius II and Constans.

> When a man 'marries' in the manner of a woman, a 'woman' about to renounce men, what does he wish, when sex has lost its significance; when the crime is one which it is not profitable to know; when Venus is changed into another form; when love is sought and not found? We order the statutes to arise, the laws to be armed with an avenging sword, that those infamous persons who are now, or who hereafter may be, guilty may be subjected to exquisite punishment.[9]

To the Romans, castration, eunuchs and circumcision were barbaric, despite the best efforts of the Galli and Elagabalus to convince otherwise. Castration was more to be pitied than deplored. Diodorus mentions it in relation to the Troglodytes (3, 23, 2; 33, 7). Ammianus Marcellinus blames Semiramis for introducung such an unnatural practice (14, 6, 17); Lucian pities the castrated Galli and tells the story of the man who castrated himself to avoid the advances of his queen (*De Dea Syria* 19–27). To the Neoplatonic philosopher Sallustius, circumcision smacked of cannibalism and incest; he associated the snip with the Massagetae who 'eat their fathers' and the Persians who 'preserve their nobility by begetting children on their mothers'.

By the end of the first century AD, bans against castration had been enacted by the emperors Domitian and Nerva in a bid to stop the burgeoning trade in eunuch slaves. Hadrian may have outlawed circumcision on pain of death, while Antoninus Pius exempted Jews and Egyptian priests from the ban. Origen Adamantius (AD 184–253) reports that only Jews were allowed to practice circumcision while Constantine freed any slave who had been subjected to circumcision; in AD 339 circumcising a slave was punishable by death. According to Eusebius,[10] Origen reputedly castrated himself, after contemplating the book of Matthew.[11] If the thought of circumcision was loathsome to the Romans, it would be intriguing to know what they thought of the procedure to reverse circumcision. Some Jews resorted to a surgical procedure (epispasm) to restore the foreskin and cover the glans 'for the sake of decorum' and to make themselves less conspicuous at the baths or during athletics. Celsius describes how to raise the prepuce from the penis with a scalpel (and a steady hand), stitching the foreskin to its rightful place with a threaded needle. Apparently it was neither painful nor accompanied by much bleeding.[12] Martial refers to circumcision four times, all of them disparagingly.[13]

CHAPTER EIGHT

Bacchanalian Orgies and Vestal Virginity

Sexuality was central to Roman religion; Roman religion was central to the Roman state. Cicero sums up the role of sexuality in Roman civilisation perfectly when he says, in his *De Officiis*, 'For since the reproductive instinct is by naturally common to all living creatures, the first union is that between husband and wife; the next, that between parents and children; then we find one home, with everything in common. And this is the foundation of civil government, the nursery, as it were, of the state.'

As stated, a crucial and vital element of the state was state religion. The duality of male and female was central in all of this; the Dii Consentes were a council of deities comprising male-female pairs. Livy lists them as Jupiter–Juno; Neptune–Minerva; Mars–Venus; Apollo–Diana; Vulcan–Vesta; Mercury–Ceres. The Flamen Dialis and Rex Sacrorum state priesthoods were held jointly by a married couple. The Vestal Virgins had their flame and their sacred phallus – representing sexual purity, *pudicitia*, in the female and male progeneration. Marriage and families were expected of the men who served in the various colleges of priests.

Roman religion was constructed on and around an extensive and incestuous pantheon, where the gods and goddesses governed and controlled everything that happened to Romans in the Roman world, in their current life and in the next. All aspects of love, sex and sexuality were amply represented by the deities, male and female, in that pantheon. Everyone had recourse and access to these divinities; the Romans and their allies could see them all around – painted on walls, erected in statuary, stamped on their coins, laid out in mosaics on the floor. For those who could read, they could learn about them from, for example, Homer's *Odyssey*,

Lucretius' *De Rerum Natura,* Cicero's *On the Nature of the Gods,* or Ovid's *Metamorphoses*; if illiterate, then theology or mythology could be read to them verbatim or communicated in stories; they could watch their antics on the stage, comedic or tragic; the Roman would also see his or her gods at countless festivals and in temples – in short, Roman gods were omnipresent and ubiquitous. Both Cicero and Virgil say so: 'God covers all things: the earth, the open seas and the vast skies.'[1]

Ceres and Vesta were closely associated with *castitas*, sexual purity. Ceres' torch symbolises the purity of the bride at her wedding; she is also a goddess of motherhood. The opposite of *castitas* was *incestum* – something which defiles purity. As we shall see, Vestals were charged with *incestum* when their virginity was compromised; Clodius Pulcher was accused of *incestum* when he sacrilegiously gatecrashed the festival of Bona Dea. Incest as we define it today was just one of the many manifestations of *incestum*. Julius Caesar was troubled by a dream he had in which he committed incest with his mother; all was well, though, when the dream interpreters prophesied that this meant he would rule the world, and revealed that his mother was in fact the earth, mother of all, and not just the rather more mundane Aurelia Cotta. In the empire, Julia Domna, wife of Septimius Severus, was accused of incest with her son, Caracella, after her death in AD 217, by the historian Herodian and in the *Historia Augusta*.

Tragedy provided fertile ground for incest. Seneca, in the *Oedipus, Medea* and *Phaedra,* reworks the Greek originals, laying much greater emphasis on the criminality of this deviant behaviour; to the Greeks it was just a disease. This presumably reflects the seriousness with which incest was regarded in Roman society; incest was *nefas* – not right, religiously or otherwise.

State religion had become rather staid, dilapidated and impersonal by the end of the Republic.[2] Varro, in 47 BC, was so concerned by this decline and indifference that he thought he had better write it all down before it was forgotten altogether. His *Human and Divine Antiquities* contains sixteen books describing the festivals, rites, priests, temples, divinities and institutions. Ovid, too, lists the various festivals and liturgies in his *Fasti*. Within the religious malaise, a woman's religion was considered irrelevant; on marriage women were expected to renounce their personal religion and follow their husband's. Priesthoods, sacerdotal responsibilities and Sibylline Books were mainly controlled by men.

The state pantheon featured numerous deities dedicated to

every conceivable aspect of conception, puberty, sex, gynaecology, childbirth and the like. *Fortuna Virginalis* looked after virgins and it was to her whom young girls turned and dedicated their togas when they reached physical and sexual maturity around the age of twelve. They proudly exchanged it for the *stola*, the garb of a *matrona*. Diana too was responsible for pre-nuptial girls in her guise as Diana Nemorensis, named after her most celebrated shrine at Nemi.[3] Ovid tells how girls crave her help in marriage and childbirth. She is also adopted by girls who died before they were married, offering their grieving parents solace with an image of their daughter hunting in the afterlife.

Fortuna Primigenia of Praeneste came next after marriage, the goddess of mothers and childbirth, whom women shared with men in her capacity as goddess of virility, material wealth and financial success. Indeed, as Augustine observes, the bridal chamber seems to have been rather overcrowded with well-intentioned divine intervention. Mutunus Tutunus, related to Priapus, was a phallic deity on whom virgins practised before consummating their marriage; Lactantius says, 'Brides sit on this god's organ to make the first offering of their virginity.' The Church Fathers were appalled by what they saw as a dereliction of viginity; Arnobius says that Roman matrons were taken for a ride (*inequitare*) on Tutunus's 'awful phallus' with its 'immense shameful parts'. His temple on the Velian Hill was visited by women wearing veils, according to Festus. Both words in the god's name are slang for penis.[4]

Augustine has more; wedding night sex is meticulously controlled down to the very last detail.[5] Virginiensis, or Cinxia, is there to loosen the bride's girdle, along with Subigus, who yields the bride to the groom; Prema, goddess of the sex act itself, attends, as does Inuus or Pertunda, who helps with penetration; Venus provides the passion and Priapus the erection. Juno is the goddess for women's sexual function and has a multifunctional role in marriage: as Iterduca she is specifically responsible for leading the bride to the groom's house and, as Unxia, oversees the annointing of the bride; she is a bridesmaid, as Pronuba, and performs a midwifery role as Lucina. Janus opens the way for the semen to enter, leading, hopefully, to conception, while Saturn looks after the semen. Consevius is the god of insemination; Liber Pater enables the man to ejaculate; Libera does likewise for the woman.[6] Mena (Juno) produces menstruation, which in the pregnant mother is diverted to feed the foetus. Fluonia is Juno, who keeps the nourishing blood in the womb. Vitumnus gives the foetus life; Sentinus or Sentia develop cognition in the newborn.

Venus, of course, is goddess of love, of *matronae* and marriage, and, at the other end of the social spectrum, of prostitutes. Liber is the god of wine, growth and fertility: each year a wooden phallus representing the god was carted through various towns of Italy, Lanuvium being the most famous, and crowned by the most chaste *matrona* to ensure a successful harvest and to avert the evil eye. His female equivalent, Libera, is closely associated with Ceres.

Priapus we have met; he was a fertility god who first came to Italy in the third century BC, allegedly the son of Aphrodite and Dionysus – a potent, potentially explosive combination in any culture. One of his roles was, as a statue in the Roman garden, to ward off thieves or in fields, vineyards and gardens – as a crop enhancer or a bird scarer – and on chariots, like a modern 'go faster' sticker. Priapus was everywhere – an indication of how strongly Romans of both sexes felt about male power, virility, procreation and sex. He turns up over doors, outside businesses, in paving stones, on amulets and at windows. Priapus, the phallus, was integral to and necessary for Roman society – he carried none of the shame, embarrassment or stigma he brings to modern societies. The *Priapea* is an anthology of poetry which deals with phallic sexuality; in one poem, Priapus threatens anal rape against any would-be thief. Upsetting Priapus might result in impotence, or perpetual sexual arousal from which there was no relief or release; Priapus once laid a curse on a thief which ensured he had no recourse to women or boys to relieve his erection; the thief eventually burst.

As we have seen the phallus, or *fascinum,* was much more than a sexual symbol; it was a catch-all charm against the evils of magic, often worn as an amulet – hence its ubiquity and its presence in all manner of public places. The phallus, and its champion, Priapus, were designed to raise a laugh – a proven remedy against demons and the evil eye. A large number have been unearthed in Pompeii and we can assume that this would be the case in the Roman world generally. The phallus, we have seen, was even worshipped by Vestal Virgins; Priapus was often invoked by couples experiencing sexual problems.

Servius Tullius, the sixth king of Rome, reputedly owes his birth to a mock bride and a phallus. The exceptionally beautiful and modest Ocresia was captured at Corniculum, and became a slave, working for Tanaquil, wife of Tarquinius Priscus. One day, she was ordered to pour wine on the embers of a fire left burning for the household gods: a phallus rose spectacularly from the ashes. Tanaquil told Ocresia to dress as a bride and sit on the hearth;

she was penetrated by the phallus, a representation of Vulcan, and subsequently gave birth to Servius Tullius.[7]

Mater Matuta was the *univira*'s special deity; she was, therefore, exclusive to respectable *matronae*. This is demonstrated by the rite which involved introducing, then expelling, a lowly slave girl amid a fusillade of physical violence and abuse. Ovid gives us all the details.[8] Fortuna Virginalis had links with Mater Matuta; their temples were built close to eachother in the Forum Boarium in Rome and they shared the same dedication day, the Matralia, June eleventh. Aunts, who held their sisters' children during the ceremony, were also protected by Mater Matuta. There was a connection with the cult of Pudicitia Patricia (Patrician Chastity) also templed in the Forum Boarium; this contained a veiled statue, touchable only by *univirae*. Livy records that in 296 BC the patrician Verginia was excluded from the cult because she had married a plebeian. Verginia indignantly responded by founding the corresponding cult of Plebeian Chastity, *Pudicitia Plebeia*, tartly reminding the religious authorities that plebeian *matronae* had the same ideals, the same *pudicitia* as their patrician counterparts. The following year, however, a number of *matronae* were convicted of adultery; this led to the dedication of the temple of Venus Obsequens – Venus the Compliant – which stood as a permanent, official warning to women to watch their ways. The cult of Fortuna Muliebris was also exclusive to *univirae*, established in 491 BC after the demonstration of woman power which dissuaded Coriolanus from attacking Rome at the head of the Volsci. The women's reward was a temple dedicated to Fortuna Muliebris built on the site with the rare right to sacrifice there.

Fortuna Virilis, or Fortuna Balnearis, was also involved in the sexuality of women. 1 April each year saw women invading the mens' baths; it seems that the celebration was confined to plebeian women, possibly even just prostitutes and other such socially inferior women. For some men this was all a bit decadent, so the *Sibylline Books* were consulted; they recommended that adulteresses receive a permanent warning, with the establishment in 215 BC of the cult of Venus Verticordia – the Heart Changer – also celebrated on 1 April at the Veneralia, and attended by Vestal Virgins. Verticordia promoted fidelity and harmony in marriage, the essence of *univira*-ness, the opposite to carnality and prostitution. Her statue was dedicated by Sulpicia, wife of the Senator Q. Fulvius Flaccus, the most *pudica matrona* in Rome, chosen by a committee of 100 of the most chaste Roman *matronae*. Statues of Verticordia were ritually washed and garlanded; the *matronae* then bathed, adorned themselves with myrtle and drank a concoction of milk, honey and poppies – all to sex themselves up for their husbands and revivify their marriages.

We cannot know how effective these cults were in inculcating real *pudicitia* and matronly values and virtues in Roman women. Juvenal would have us believe that they were spectacularly unsuccessful and describes how the desecrating Tullia and Mauria would stop their litters to urinate on the Temple of Pudicitia; this 'is where they piss, filling the goddess' statue with their long streams'.[9]

Despite all this attention to and patronage of the minutiae of sex and sexuality, the new religions percolating into an increasingly inclusive Rome must have seemed that much more exciting. Official Roman religion was essentially founded on and catered for an agricultural society. For example, Jupiter made the crops grow with his rain and sun; Saturn encouraged sowing; Ceres promoted growth. As Rome's overseas possessions increased and more of the world was Romanised, as Rome itself became more urbanised, then, with the syncretisation of exotic and mysterious foreign gods and goddesses, traditional religion gradually lost much of its relevance to Roman life and culture. It became boring and unappealing, and so men and women turned to and embraced the new, oriental, mystery religions which invaded Roman society. With the exception of Mithraism, which was exclusively for men, these cults, particularly the cult of Isis, offered women an active role in the priesthood; the cults could be personalised and customised to meet the needs of individuals, and because their eschatology often enshrined birth and rebirth, they seemed to offer hope of life after death, immortality. They often spoke of fertility, an obvious attraction to women.

But there were those who deplored these new religions. In vivid contrast to the more relaxed and objective account by Plutarch,[10] Juvenal launches an excoriating attack on the patrician women performing the rites of the Bona Dea, describing them as drunken maenads, crazed with desire for sex. 'This urge, if it cannot be satisfied by an *adulter*, will be sated by the *adulter*'s son, or by slaves, or the man who brings the water; if all else fails they will allow an ass to take them in the arse.'[11] Bona Dea first appeared in Rome around 272 BC, during the Tarentine War. She was associated with chastity and fertility, and with the protection of Rome; as Fauna she could prophesy the fates of women. She had the luxury of two festivals: one at her temple on the Aventine; the other at the home of the Pontifex Maximus, as desecrated by Clodius Pulcher *chez* Julius Caesar. Her Aventine cult, in which a blood sacrifice took place on May first, was re-dedicated in 123 BC by the Vestal Virgin Licinia, but this was annulled as unlawful by the Senate; Licinia was later charged with unchastity and entombed.[12]

Although Bona Dea was celebrated by men and women alike,[13] in the domestic rite which took place on December third, all males were banished, even male animals and pictures or statues of males. Only *matronae* and the Vestal Virgins were present; the Vestals brought in *Bona Dea's* image from her temple and a meal of sow's entrails was eaten, sacrificed to her on behalf of the Roman people, and sacrificial wine. The fun lasted all night with female musicians, games and wine, euphemistically called 'milk', from a 'honey jar'. This was not a feeble attempt to conceal clandestine drinking; rather, the ritual came about when Faunus, married to the Good Goddess, caught her drinking surreptitiously and beat her to death with a myrtle branch. Myrtle was also associated with Aphrodite and with sex; as such it was alien to the rites and banned. The *matronae* refrained from sexual relations in the run up to the festival to maximise purity. According to Cicero, any man caught observing the rites could be punished by having his eyes poked out.[14]

Bona Dea owed a lot to the all female Thesmophoria – a Greek cult which celebrated the the rape of Persephone by Hades and her fecund restoration on earth; it deployed sexuality in its promotion of fertility. Greek matrons assembled to encourage Ceres to provide a good harvest; to this end they used pastry in the shape of genitals and indulged in obscene banter. A piglet was sacrificed – the same word is used as slang for female genitalia. The Bona Dea shared many of the unique characteristics of the Thesmophoria: female exclusivity, aphrodisacs, elite *matronae*, sexual licence enhanced in the form of alcohol.

Bona Dea was jealously protected by its adherents, so when the high profile rites of 62 BC were infiltrated by a high profile man, the ensuing scandal was huge, not least because Caesar's mother, Aurelia Cotta, Pompeia, his wife, his sister, Julia, and the Vestals were all there. According to Juvenal, any sexual propriety that remained in Rome in 62 BC evaporated that night: Publius Clodius Pulcher sacrelegiously gatecrashed the rites which were being held at Caesar's house, that year's Pontifex Maximus. Juvenal describes Pulcher as the 'lute girl with a penis'. The scandal led to Caesar divorcing Pompeia; her very prescence implicated her, and Caesar's wife must not be under suspicion.

The Nonae Caprotinae, in honour of Juno Caprotina, took place on 7 July and were exclusively celebrated by and for women, particularly female slaves. They ran about hitting themselves with fists and with rods. One derivation has it that, after a damaging siege by the Gauls in the fourth century BC, various unscrupulous neighbouring Latin tribes demanded Roman women in marriage, on threat of destroying the vulnerable and weakened city. A slave-woman, Tutela, along with other slave-women dressed as *matronae*, approached the enemy armies, and, pretending to be out on a hen night, got the Latins drunk. When the soldiers were sleeping it off the slave-girls relieved them of their weapons, and Tutela climbed a fig tree – a symbol of fertility – to wave a torch signalling the Romans to attack.

The Lupercalia took place in February. Here women offered themselves up to be ritually whipped with goatskin to promote fertility, banish sterility and ease childbirth; the Vestals handed out *mola salsa*. Plutarch describes various other rites. In the Bacchanalia, for example, frenzied women go straight for the ivy and chew it to bring on 'a wineless drunkenness and joyousness; [it] has an exciting and distracting breath of madness, deranges persons, and agitates them'.[15] Initially, the cult of Bacchus was exclusively female, and notorious only for the frenzy and shrieking of its adherents, the beating of drums and the clashing of cymbals. It had huge popular appeal even before men were admitted; Livy described its spread as an epidemic that excited the sexual emotions in women.[16] Officially, it was regarded as an unsettling conspiracy against Rome but originally, it was relatively harmless, with daytime rites three times a year and *matronae* as priestesses; we know from Cicero that nocturnal rites were illegal, as was initiation, except in the rites of Ceres.[17] Things changed dramatically when a priestess called Paculla Annia started initiating men and the rites were moved to night time and took place a frequent five times every month. The heady mix of wine, darkness, women and then men was explosive, with *orgia* on a grand scale involving hetero and homosexual sex, and providing a platform for perjury, forgery, poisoning and murder. The initiation of men was seen as a conspiracy to remove them from the sanctity of the *familia* and of the state.

It all came to a head in 186 BC when Publius Aebutius happened to be persecuted by his greedy stepfather who, with the boy's mother, Durenia, conspired to dispose of him by enrolling him in the Bacchanalia, a sure-fire death sentence. Aebutius' girlfriend, Hispala Faecina, a reforming prostitute who had witnessed the orgiastic rites as an initiate, was horrified when she heard this and dissuaded Aebutius from joining up. Such was the notoriety of the cult and the hazards involved: ritual male rape was routine and any opposition resulted in summary sacrifice. Aebutius reported the matter to the consul, Spurius Postumius; Hispala, understandably reluctant at first, eventually agreed to reveal all, taking up residence in Postumius's house for safety. According to Livy, 7,000 Bacchantes were prosecuted under the *Senatus Consultum de Bacchanalibus*, many of whom fled Rome or committed suicide.[18] A manhunt ensued, and imprisonments and executions followed. Many of the convicted women were handed over to their *paterfamilias* for the family to dispense justice; most of the Bacchic shrines in Rome and throughout Italy were then destroyed. The whistle-blowers were handsomely rewarded, a measure of the deep concern the rite caused the authorities and of their determination to stamp it out.

The temple of Carmenta may owe its origin to women who refused to sleep with their husbands, pending the repeal of a law prohibiting them from riding in horse-drawn vehicles. Carmenta was the patroness of midwives; she also invented the Roman alphabet, although it remains doubtful that there is any connection between the two. Hyginus records that she altered fifteen letters of the Greek alphabet to make the Latin alphabet, which her son Evander introduced into Latium.[19] Women who sacrifice to Rumina, responsible for breastfeeding as the she-wolf which suckled Romulus, do so with milk and not wine because Rumina knows that alcohol is harmful to babies.[20]

Rumina was by no means on her own; the Roman maternity suite was as crowded as the bridal suite. Alemona presided over the foetus; Nona and Decima were responsible for the ninth and tenth months of gestation; Parca or Partula watched over the delivery. At the birth, Parca establishes the extent of the baby's life in her guise as a goddess of death called Morta. The *Prophecy of Parca* indicated that the child was a mortal being; Egeria delivers the baby. Postverta and Prosa avert breech birth, considered unlucky; Lucina is the goddess of the birth; Diespiter (Jupiter) introduces the infant to the daylight; Vagitamus opens the baby's mouth to emit the first cry; Levana lifts the baby from the ground, symbolising contact with Mother Earth; Cunina looks after the baby in the cradle, protecting it from malevolent forces and magic; Statina gives the baby energy; Candelifera is the nursery light, kept burning to deter the spirits of darkness that would threaten the infant in the crucial first week of birth, and to banish the bogey-women

– child-snatching demons such as Gello. The *Fata Scribunda* were invoked – the *Written Fates* – which was a ceremonial inscription of the child's new name. The giving of a name was as important as the birth itself; receiving a *praenomen* established the child as an individual with its own fate. Potina allows the child to drink, Edusa to eat; Ossipago builds strong bones, Carna healthy muscles, defending the internal organs from witches; Cuba is there to ease the child's transition from cradle to bed; Paventia deflects fear from the child; Peta attends to its first demands; Agenoria bestows an active life; Adeona helps it learn to walk. Iterduca and Domiduca watch over it as it it leaves the house for the first time and returns home again; Catius Pater makes children clever; Farinus teaches children to talk; Fabulinus gives the child its first words; Locutius helps it to form sentences; Mens provides intelligence; Volumnus makes the child want to do good; Numeria is there for counting, Camena for singing; the Muses bestow an appreciation of the arts, literature, and sciences – and so it went on, with a host of spirits – or gods – attending every single stage of life and death.

Some of these cults encouraged religious ecstasy, fuelled no doubt by the herbs and alcohol liberally available at the ceremonies. The wine and aphrodisiacs did much, in turn, to fuel establishment fear and suspicion and the 'inappropriate' involvement and behaviour of women thereat. We only have to look at the divine inspiration exhibited by the Cumaean Sibyl in Virgil's *Aeneid* (Book 6) to appreciate how close, in aspects of her divine possession, religious ecstacy comes to orgasm.

The hearth was literally the *focus* of the Roman household, traditionally tended by the daughters of a family. Vesta was the goddess of the hearth, traditionally attended by virgin priestesses, the Vestal Virgins, who kept the sacred flame alight in the Temple of Vesta. This flame symbolised the nourishment of the Roman state. Any Vestal careless enough to allow the flame to go out was whipped; tending the flame occupied each Vestal for around eight hours every day. Vesta was also associated with agricultural productivity and with fertility. The Vestals' virginity embodied the safety of Rome: Rome was safe while their virginity remained intact; when it was violated, Rome was under threat.

During the Vestalia, donkeys were celebrated to mark their valuable role in the making of bread. The donkey was Vesta's saviour when Priapus attempted to rape her: this accounts for the presence of a donkey in some depictions of the goddess. Its sexual prowess forms part of the paradox that surrounds the Vestals, as is the phallus which is sometimes shown in the flames of their fire. The fact that Vestals, as virgins, enjoyed privileges reserved for married women, *matronae*, and for men, highlights even further the sexual ambiguity of their status and throws into relief their vulnerability and the fragility of their reputation.

The last known *Vestalis maxima* was Coelia Concordia, appointed in AD 380. The Vestals were finally disbanded in AD 394, but not before ten or so had been entombed alive, the awful penalty for a Vestal who lost her virginity (*incestum*), or was suspected of having lost it. The entombment took place in a cellar under the Campus Sceleratus; the male partner was flogged to death in the Comitium like a slave, *sub furco*. The rationale behind entombment and the slow death was that Vesta would still have time to rescue the 'Virgin' if she were innocent. Vesta never did. Plutarch graphically describes the solemn process where the condemned Vestal is bound and gagged and carried to her subterranenan prison in a curtained litter; she is unbound and, after a prayer, the Pontifex Maximus puts her on a ladder which leads to the small chamber below. The ladder is hauled up, the entrance closed and covered with earth. The chamber has a bed, lamp, bread, water, milk and oil. To Plutarch this is the most shocking spectacle in the world; when it occurs it is the most horrific day Rome has ever seen.[21]

Vestal Virgins sometimes took the blame when catastrophe struck: for example, their alleged *incestum* was held responsible for the slaughter that was the Battle of Cannae in 216 BC.[22] Two Vestals, Opimia and Floronia, were duly convicted; one was entombed, the other committed suicide. Lucius Cantilius, the secretary of the Pontiffs who had deflowered Floronia, was beaten to death.

The Vestal Virgins were the stuff of legend and provided a fertile source of copy for the historians. One Vestal, Aemilia, let the flame go out, provoking questions about her chastity; she reacted by praying to Vesta and threw a cloth onto the cold embers; when this burst miraculously and spontaneously into flame all questioning ceased. Tuccia endured the same calamity but absolved herself by fetching a sieveful of water from the Tiber without losing a single drop.[23]

Domitian had his doubts over the moral rectitude of the Vestal Virgins: he brought a number to trial in AD 83 and AD 90 in a bid to improve the moral climate – particularly as it seems the Vestals had lost their moral compasses under Vespasian and Titus and were running what was virtually a brothel. In AD 83 the Oculata sisters and Varronilla were given the option to commit suicide while their lovers were exiled; seven years later, Cornelia, the Chief Virgin, was condemned to the living death that was entombment, while her lover was whipped to death.[24]

Vestal Virgins were sometimes sacrificial lambs in games of political intrigue. In 114 BC three were charged with *incestum* and running a brothel. One was convicted, and the other two were condemned the following year after a retrial was demanded by Sextus Peducaeus, who accused the Pontifex Maximus, L. Metellus Delmaticus, his political rival, of partiality.[25] In 73 BC two Vestals were embroiled in the Catiline conspiracy: Fabia, the half-sister of Terentia, Cicero's wife, was accused of having an affair with Catiline, while Licinia was similarly accused of consorting with Crassus, her cousin. Both were acquitted.[26] In AD 215 Caracella seduced a Vestal and had her entombed, and two others for good measure. In AD 220 Elagabalus divorced his wife and married a Vestal, Aquilia Severa, after arranging special dispensation for her to renounce her vows of chastity.[27]

They allegedly had wondrous powers too. Pliny tells us that even in his day some people believed that a Vestal Virgin could root a runaway slave to the spot with one glance, provided he was still within the city of Rome.[28]

The ancient Roman festival of the Lupercalia also had its puzzling paradoxes. It too had erotic overtones. Its typical role was as a purification and fertility rite but it also marked the important passage for young Roman men and women as they moved from youth and took on the full responsibilities of Roman citizenship. Ovid clearly demonstrates this crucial stage in the Hercules-Omphale episode in his *Fasti* in which the poet explains why the Luperci are traditionally naked.[29]

The initiates, Hercules and Omphale, indulge in a spot of cross-dressing; Hercules puts on Omphale's clothes, and Omphale dresses up in typically Herculean lion skin and wields his club.[30] This presumably symbolizes the one-ness, the union, between the couple; like the young celebrants of the Lupercalia, Hercules and Omphale are moving on to a new level in society.

Why do the Lupercali run naked? Because of the unsuccessful rape attempt on Omphale by Pan, that randiest of half-goats and symbol of fertility. It seems that Omphale's clothes were the problem – Pan was unable to get through them and penetrate her: to prevent such a calamity ever happening again, Pan insisted that the Luperci always be naked. Why were women initiates whipped? The origin of this tradition, according to Ovid, lies in Romulus' concern over the fertility of the Sabine women he and his compatriots had recently abducted. They were simply not producing the babies the Romans had hoped for. Juno's bizarre advice was to allow the sacred goat to penetrate the Italian mothers.[31] Women initiates were whipped by their young men in the belief that it not only promoted fertility but made for easy delivery and conception. The penetration was symbolised by tearing of the skin from the lashings rather than by any bestial penetration – not something most husbands or fathers would have welcomed.

Further sexual overtones lie in the fact that Livy says that the god of the Lupercal is none other than Inuus, the god of copulation.[32] Etymologically, the name Lupercal shares a connection with *lupus*, 'she-wolf', one of the many Latin words for a prostitute. The legendary founders of Rome, Romulus and Remus, were of course raised by a she-wolf; Servius believes that Mars raped the twins' mother during the Lupercal, making her pregnant with Romulus and Remus.[33]

The Lupercalia took place between 13 and 15 February, marking renewal and rebirth for the coming year. It was in two parts: the first took place where Romulus and Remus were suckled by the she-wolf – the Lupercal. Here priests sacrificed a goat and two male dogs (noted for their strong sexual instinct[34]) and smeared their blood on the foreheads of the young men at the altar, the Luperci. The skins of the animals were cut into strips for use as those whips. The second stage involved the Luperci running around naked and lashing the women with their goatskin thongs The most famous celebrant was Mark Antony, whom Cicero denigrated in his description of him as 'naked, oiled and drunk'.[35]

Suetonius, in his life of Augustus, tells that *matronae* would have initially bared their backs to receive the whipping but after 276 BC were completely naked. Augustus stopped beardless young men from serving as Luperci because of their sexual attraction to women.[36]

CHAPTER NINE

Raping the Romans

Ovid teaches that women like rough sex (*vis*). They enjoy being forced against their will and they actually love their violators; for the rape victim, forced and violent sexual intercourse is a blessing, while the woman who is unmolested remains dejected and unwanted. In Ovid's *Ars Amatoria,* when a woman says no, she really means yes.[1]

Roman law defined *raptus* (or *raptio*) as a kidnapping or abduction, and not the sexual violation we associate with our word, rape – derived, of course, from *raptus. Raptus* usually involved the abduction of an unmarried girl from her father's household, seized from his *patria potestas*, either consensually or as a kidnapping. Forced sex was usually expressed as *stuprum,* with the addition of *cum vi* or *per vim*, with violent force. *Raptus ad stuprum* was abduction with a view to committing a sex crime; it later emerged as a legal distinction in the late Roman Republic. The *Lex Julia de vi publica*, dating probably from Julius Caesar's time, defined rape as forced sex against 'boy, woman, or anyone'.

We have seen how the rapes of Roman legend were instrumental in the very foundation of Rome and the establishment later of the republic. The rape of the Sabine women was a nation building exercise, and the rape of Lucretia, which resulted in the overthrow of the monarchy, reflected rape as an expression of unbridled lust and was tantamount to tyranny.[2] Much later in the 50s BC, Lucretius condemned the act of rape as primitive behaviour beyond the realms of a sophisticated civilisation like Rome, describing it as 'a man's use of violent force and imposition of sexual urge'.[3]

The law differentiated between victims of rape. Rape could only be committed against good Roman citizens; if a slave was raped (and they often were) then then violator would only be prosecuted for damaging the owner's property under the *Lex Aquilia*.[4] Prostitutes or people in the entertainment business fared equally badly, as they were *infames* and had no legal protection in Roman law; you gave up any rights when you sold your body, stepped onto the stage or into the arena, in effect, surrendering your right of protection from sexual abuse or physical violence.[5] Men who had been raped 'by the physical force of robbers or of the enemy in war' were, however, exempt from *infamia*.[6]

Under Diocletian (r. AD 284–305) the position was

> The laws punish the foul wickedness of those who prostitute their modesty to the lusts of others, but they do not attach blame to those who are compelled to *stuprum* by force, since it has, moreover, been quite properly decided that their reputations are unharmed and that they are not prohibited from marriage to others.

A woman could bring her own charges against her alleged rapist in the courts. Cicero defended a client on a charge of the gang rape of an actress, pleading that this was normal behaviour with those in the entertainment business.

Crimes did not come much more serious in Rome than the rape of a freeborn male (*ingenuus*) or a female virgin; it was up there with parricide and temple robbing.[7] Rape was a capital crime, despite the fact that execution generally was an infrequent penalty under Roman law.[8] Acquittal would render the prosecutor liable to a charge of *calumnia*, malicious prosecution.

Women victims fared less well under the Christian emperors. Constantine redefined rape as a public offence rather than a private wrong.[9] He decreed that if the girl had consented, she should be punished, as an accomplice, along with the male 'abductor', by being burnt alive. If the act was not consensual she was still considered an accomplice, 'on the grounds that she could have avoided the situation by screaming out for help'[10] She was punished by being disinherited, regardless of her parents' wishes; any marriage resulting was legally void.[11]

St Augustine overturned the centuries old symbolism and the accepted interpretation of the suicide of Lucretia. He questioned if her decision to end her life was an admission that she had secretly encouraged the rapist, while Christian apologists saw her as having committed the sin of involuntary sexual pleasure.[12]

We began the chapter by noting Ovid's view of how women victims see rape – shocking by today's standards, but ours are not the standards of Ovid's day. Ovid, of course, was something of a chancer, who purported to like his women wherever he could find them – a bit of a lad who set himself up as a guru on women and sex, and an authority on how to get both. To assert that all women always wanted sex (and, therefore, could not be raped) was part of his mantra, to him and his readers a truism and an aphorism. Ovid, of course, had books to sell and an audience to please; his posturing will have gone down well among sections of his male readership. Moreover, Ovid, like any other educated Roman, would have grown up reading stories of rapes, of both men and women, which appeared in earlier literature and, particularly, in Greek and Roman mythology. For example, Leda was raped by Zeus slyly masquerading as a swan; Cassandra was raped by Ajax in the temple of Athena in Troy; Chrysippus was violated by his tutor Laius; Antiope too was raped by Zeus, this time in the guise of a satyr; beautiful Medusa was raped by Poseidon in the temple of Athena – Athena punished her by rendering her terrifyingly ugly. Philomena was raped by her brother-in-law, Tereus, who told her to keep quiet about it and cut out her tongue when she was defiant; all was revealed, however, on a tapestry woven by Philomena. This incensed Procne – Tereus' wife, and sister to Philomena – who killed their son, Itys, boiled him and served him up to Tereus – now a cannibal as well as a rapist [13]. The daughters of Leucippus, Phoebe and Hilaeira, were abducted and raped by Castor and Pollux. This is not mythology for mythology's sake; the myths are didactic and each came into being and were developed over centuries for a reason, to explain one thing or another about the meaning of life.

Philomena is a good example; her story tells us something more. She loses not only her virginity but her power to speak as well, and, in the end, her human-ness when she is turned into a nightingale. She is not alone: Arethras is raped and morphs into a dove, Callisto becomes a bear, Io changes into a cow and Daphne becomes a bay tree. Caenis is the most tragic of all; she is raped by Neptune and is so distraught that she pleads to become a man to avoid ever enduring rape again. That rape dehumanises is the inescapable message Romans would have taken away from these didactic myths.

Livy demonstrates that the very foundation of Rome stemmed from a rape – the rape of the Sabine women. They may actually have been 'abducted', but raped they presumably were once the Romans 'got them home', so to speak, given that they were coerced in the first place and, in many cases, already had husbands. Violated Lucretia was held up as a paragon of feminine virtue and the paradigm on which every true Roman *matrona* should model herself; the male duplicity and atrocity she suffered attracted universal Roman disgust and her suicide was seen as an emblem of her *pudicitia*. Lucretia was implicated in the ending of the Roman monarchy, Verginia in the resolution of the Conflict of the Orders, the one raped, the other dying at the hands of her father to avoid inevitable rape. The rape of supremely virtuous Roman women was inextricably tied up with major constitutional change, a supreme price to pay for such momentous changes.

Rape is frequent in the comedies of Plautus and Terence but it is often used just as a dramatic device, a means to an end, to further the plot and bring about the denouément. The audiences for these plays had paid to have a laugh; the playwrights wrote their plays to effect this. Both parties would have suspended any usual, everyday thoughts on the odium associated with rape. There is little concern for the ethics of raping or of the physical and psychogical trauma endured by the victim. In Plautus' *Aulularia* Lycanides rapes Phaedria and shows scant remorse. Eunomia excuses the violation with having had too much to drink. In the *Cistellaria* and the *Truculentus* rape is simply a device. Terence, for whom three of his six surviving plays deal with rape, however, is more sympathetic towards the victim. In the *Hecyra,* Pamphilus rapes Philumena on a visit to his mistress Bacchis. In the *Adelphoe* Aeschinus rapes a young girl when drunk. In the *Eunuchus* Chaerea disguises himself as a eunuch to enter Thais' house and rape the girl she has brought up. Chaerea is quite remorseless: jubilant that he has raped the girl.

Ovid's view, and that of hs literary and 'historical' hinterland, would suggest an equally casual attitude to rape and its human consequences; an attitude reflected, no doubt, in the real world, despite the apparent seriousness of the crime – but only when committed against freeborn women. This chauvinism reinforces the Romans' insistence on male domination, of *vir* eliding into *virtus* – male strength and power equalling virtue – and the submissiveness of his compliant women.

Male rape seems to have been relatively prevalent. The raped man was exempted from the further indignity of *infamis* and all the stigma and loss of rights this involved. In the second century BC even a man with a dubious reputation could expect protection in law against rape.[14] The rape of a freeborn male (*ingenuus*) was

Above: **1.** A bedroom scene from a mosaic in a villa at Centocelle from the early first century AD.

Below: **2.** A typical tombstone showing man and wife, in this case Publius Aiedius Amphio and his wife, Aiedia. Located in the Pergamon Museum, Berlin.

3. The Venus Mosaic comes from the floor of a fourth century AD Roman villa discovered in Rudston, East Yorkshire in 1933 by a farmer. Venus is naked; she wears bracelets on her arms and in her right hand the apple she won in the Judgement of Paris. Venus is nearly always shown with a mirror. The half-human, half-fish figure next to her is Triton, a reference to her birth out of the sea.

4. A wedding scene from a third-century-AD sarcophagus found in the Via Latina. The husband and wife take centre stage and join hands with Juno Pronuba between them. (Courtesy of Museo Nazionale Romano in Palazzo Massimo)

5. A 1932 advert by Lucky Strike, American Tobacco Company, from the days when smoking was still good for you. It associates the natural rawness of the cigarettes with the actions of the Romans when they abducted the Sabine women in their nation-building exercise (!).

Left: 6. A hairpiece from a Roman woman found in a sarcophagus which contained a lead coffin and gypsum; presumably the hair was preserved because it was treated before burial. Two cantharus-headed hair pins are still in position. (Courtesy of York Museums Trust YORYM 1998.695 [ID 1131])

Right: 7. The Temple of Vesta – home of the Vestal Virgins in Rome.

8. Pavel Svedomsky's *Hareme*. (1885)

9. Young ladies in what look like bathing costumes in Piazza Armerina, Sicily. (Photo courtesy of AndanteTravel)

10. The abduction of Europa by Zeus disguised as a bull; from Kos.

11. Slaves dressing a lady: one with mirror, the other loosening her hair. Part of a first-century marble relief from Neumagen-Dhron on the Mosel. (Noviomagus Trevirorum)

Left: 12. The impressive Priapus of Lampsakus now in the Archaeological Museum of Ephesus. It was found in one of the rooms of a brothel there. *Right:* 13. An example of a *sopio*: Priapus – Mercury at Pompeii, in the Naples Archaeological Museum. A *sopio* was a sexualised caricature with an abnormally large penis.

14. Europa riding the bull, in the Naples Archaeological Museum from Pompeiii AD 79.

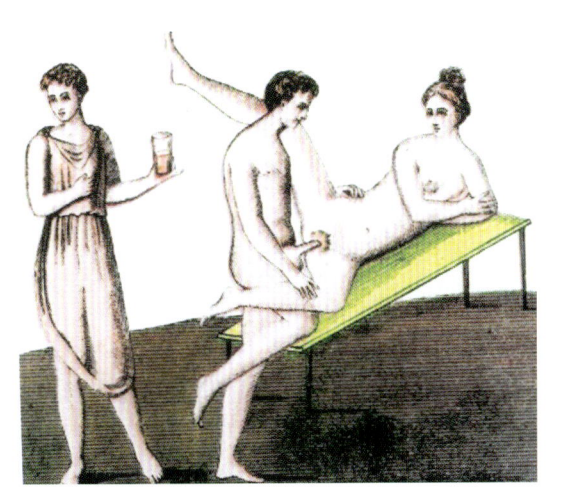

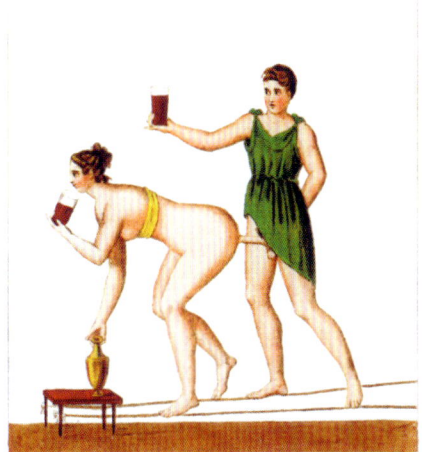

Left: **15.** An erotic scene from Pompeii, hidden from public gaze for many years in the 'Secret Cabinet' but now available to view in the Naples Archaeological Museum. It shows a handsome cubicular slave, feigning modesty, bringing drinks to the copulating couple. The double digit gesture may have indicated cuckoldry, so the sex was extramarital, but it is more likely to be a sign to avert witchcraft. It, along with others, was copied and published in *Musee Royal de Naples* in 1871 by Colonel Famin. The originals are now sadly lost. *Right:* **16.** The ultimate drinking game?. Another of Colonel Famin's erotic scenes, this one from a bar in Pompeii's Via di Mercurio (V, 10, 1): 'The actors in it, placed on two outstretched ropes, caress each other without losing their equilibrium, and drink without spilling a drop of the liquor contained in their glasses … obscene to a degree.'

17. Leda and the Swan from Paleaepaphos, third century AD.

18. Erotic motifs such as these were very popular on clay oil lamps; this collection is in the Berlin Pergamon Museum.

Left: **19**. A satyr consorting with a young woman; in the Lady Lever Gallery, Port Sunlight.

Right: **20**. Young satyr and maenad, mythological symbols of sexuality, from a mosaic found in the house of the Faun in Pompeii.

Below: **21 & 22**. A terracotta breast and womb – it was common for models of body parts to be left at sites of healing in thanks for recovery.

23. A childbirth scene from a terracotta relief in the Museo Ostiense. (Inv 5204)

24. NAVIGIUM VENERIS – the 'navigation of Venus' shows a dextrous man performing some very skilful navigation. (Courtesy of the Gallo-Roman Museum of Lyon; © J.-M. Degueule, Gallo-Roman Museum of Lyon Inv. 1999.5.82. *CIL* 7645)

Left: **25**. A black Ethiopian slave carrying water vessels above. strigils suggesting female genitalia on a mosaic found in the entrance to the caldarium in the House of Menader in Pompeii.

Right: **26**. Phallic satyrs released from the Gabinetto Segredo.

27. Women on top: an erotic scene from Pompeii on the east wall of Room X in the House of the Vetii.

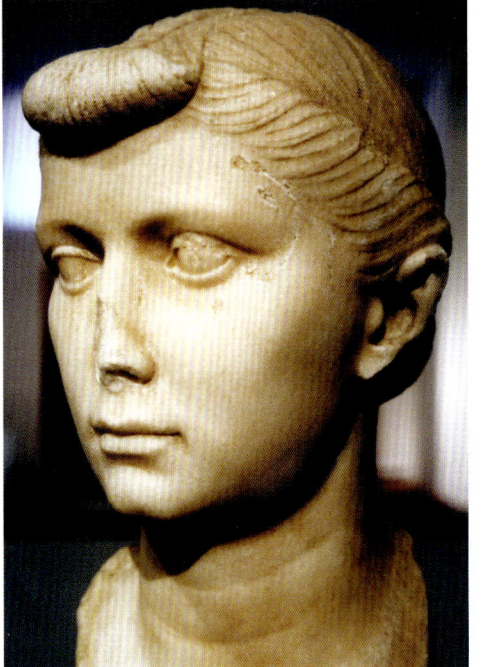

Above: **28.** Votive offerings including penises, breasts, and a uterus – in the Naples Archaeological Museum.

Left: **29.** Julia, the wayward daughter of Augustus – a bust from Baeterrae now in the Musée St Raymond, Toulouse. (With kind permission of Musée Saint-Raymond, Toulouse © J.-F. Peiré)

Above left: 30. Cimon and Pero, offering breast milk to her ageing father in an act of Roman charity. In the Naples Archaeological Museum; photograph by Stefano Bolognina.

Above right: 31. Woman breastfeeding in the presence of the father. Detail from the sarcophagus of Marcus Cornelius Statius, who died as a young child. *c.* AD 150. (Photo by Marie-Lan Nguyen from *A History of Infant Feeding: Part I: Primitive Peoples, Ancient Works, Renaissance Writers*)

Below: 32. Gladiators in the arena from the Curium Mosaics in Limassol, Cyprus. The gladiators aroused passions amongst some female spectators.

Above: **33**. An erotic scene from Pompeii, showing what Lucretius termed *a tergo*. Lucretius had taught that the best position for conception was for the woman to have *coitus more ferarum* – 'to have sexual intercourse like wild beasts do it', or *a tergo*, 'from behind' *(kubra*, in Greek).

Below left: **34**. *Julia Exiled on Ventone* with time for reflection on her fornication (1885), without men or drink – by Pavel Svedomsky (1849–1904).

Below right: **35**. Aphrodite and Priapus in the Naples Archaeological Museum, from Pompeii AD 79.

Above left: **36.** Aphrodite as Hermaphroditus in the Lady Lever Art Gallery, Port Sunlight. *Above right:* **37.** Antinous in the Lady Lever Art Gallery, Port Sunlight. A second century AD sculpture in the style of the early classical period, about 450 BC. *Below:* **38.** Pan uncovering Hermaphrodite in the Naples Archaeological Museum, from Pompeii AD 79.

39. The empress Theodora, from a mosaic in Ravenna.

40. A sestertius minted in AD 79 in Vespasian's reign depicting *Iudaea Capta*, a female personification of the Jewish nation as captive, minted after the destruction of the Temple of Jerusalem in AD 70. The coin graphically symbolises Roman sexual conquest. (Classical Numismatic Group)

just as serious as the rape of a *materfamilias* and was a capital crime. The *Lex Julia de vi publica* defined rape as forced sex against 'boy, woman, or anyone'.[15] We have noted that it was a capital offence for a man to abduct a freeborn boy with a view to having sex or to bribe the boy's chaperon. Negligent chaperons could be prosecuted.[16]

The twelve sexual violations recorded by Valerius Maximus include six cases of male rapes.[17] As we have seen, Seneca the Elder sets a hypothetical case in which a youth is gang raped by ten other boys; the assumption always is that the ten will be prosecuted. In their defence it was noted that the victim was dressed as a woman at the time.[18] If you found your wife in bed with another freeborn man you could rape him with impunity, if you so desired.[19] Apart from the physical and psychological revulsion some men would have felt at the prospect of anal rape, it could be even worse if subjected to oral rape, (*irrumatio*). For the Roman, passive penetration of the oral kind was a double hammer blow to his *virtus* and *Romanitas*. On the other hand, though, Seneca's Hostius Quadra (the mirror loving voyeur we have already met) has no qualms about any of this. He delighted in watching himself in his mirrors being taken from behind and in the mouth simultaneously; his deviant behaviour was always performed with the lights on, as it were, and he even went so far as to have paintings done of him having sex of one kind or another. Seneca's description is, of course, a moralising rhetorical exercise tagged onto a section on halos, rainbows, meteors and other atmospheric lighting, masquerading under an expatiation on mirrors and reflected light, but the theme was obviously of sufficient social and moral moment to justify inclusion in this technical lesson. Quadra would happily indulge in troilism with a man and a woman, dispensing that other social shame, cunnilingus, while being buggered: 'all my organs are involved in lechery' he jubilantly proclaims.

Perhaps the most celebrated description of oral and anal rape is in Catullus' *Carmen 61*:

Fuck you, boys, up the butt and in the mouth, you queer Aurelius and you fag Furius! ... because you happen to read about 'many thousands of kisses', you think *I'm* not a man? Fuck you, boys, up the butt and in the mouth![20]

Interestingly, Catullus extends the concept of oral rape to his own political circumstances, and those of his two friends, Veranius and

Fabullus, in *Carmen* 28. He, like his friends, had been metaphorically 'fucked' by the generals Memmius and Piso (*irrumasti*). Given the stigma attached to oral rape and passivity this description indicates deep bitterness on the part of Catullus at the hands of Memmius and Piso and his vicarious empathy with Veranius and Fabullus who had been similarly shafted with similar treatment. It must have been bad.

Sexually, children were strictly off limits and were protected in law from predators. Freeborn boys and girls wore the *toga praetexta*, a purple-bordered toga that told everbody that the wearer was inviolable, to keep off.[21] It was wrong (*nefas*) to use obscene language in front anyone sporting the *praetexta*.[22] Cato the Elder said that when talking in the presence of his son he tried to speak as though Vestal Virgins were in the room.[23]

Freeborn Roman boys also wore the *bulla*, an apotropaic amulet which incorporated a phallic talisman (*fascinum*) inside a gold, silver, or bronze locket, or in a leather pouch – another indication that the boy was off limits.[24] Girls wore the *lunula*, a crescent moon amulet. We know that the rape of a freeborn boy was a capital crime under the legislation protecting freeborn boys from predators.[25] At the trial of the dissolute Quintus Apronius, Cicero accuses Apronius of dancing naked at a banquet in front of a boy wearing the *praetexta*.[26] Quintilian rebukes parents of his day for parading their mistresses and male concubines and their inappropriate behaviour in front of their children – evidence of a general malaise in society.[27]

Rape then was something literate Romans grew up with. It was there in the mythology for all to hear and read, but as something that was uncivilised and dehumanising. It was there in the early history or legend as a metaphor for significant constitutional change which came at a terrible price for Lucretia and Verginia. Depending on where you stood on the social ladder, you were protected in law with extreme penalties handed down to those found guilty. Likewise *matronae*, married women and minors were protected and off limits. Slaves and other unfortunates could not be raped as they were, in law, property or outside the law. The comic playwrights used rape as a dramatic device; Catallus leaves us in no doubt as to the seriousness implicit in inflicting anal and oral male rape; Ovid tell his (male) audience what they want to hear: that raping a woman is simply satisfying an erotic need in the victim. War rape and gang rape of women, boys and men by the military was par for the course amongst rampaging and victorious armies – not least in the aftermath of sieges.[28]

CHAPTER TEN

The Power of Sex: In Bed with a Soldier

Wherever there is power, wherever there is war, then sex is never far away. Powerful men and women can often transmit a sexual attraction. Horace reminds us that from time immemorial, even pre-Helen, 'cunts were an abominable *casus belli*' (*Satires* 1, 3, 107): *nam fuit ante Helenam cunnus taeterrima belli causa*. In war, rape is frequently a terrible by-product of victory, of the subjugation of enemy territory or of the raising of a siege; war permits and fosters horizontal collaboration and fraternisation with the enemy.

A dubious sexual reputation, alleged or real, was frequently used to defame and denigrate an enemy both in the courts and the senate and outside. This was a powerful weapon when men were anxious and unnerved by powerful women intruding in their exclusive world. We have seen how Cicero slandered Clodia and made her the 'Medea of the Palatine', a witch by any other name. She lives in a red light district (*Pro Caelio* 15, 37), lives the life of a whore (*meretricia vita*, 20, 49–50), lives off the earnings of a *meretrix*, (1, 1); has whorish habits (*meretricius mos*, 16, 38); mention of her kisses, the way she walks and her embraces add to the sordid picture. Clodia never recovered.

Sallust did a similar hatchet job on Sulpicia, one of the Catiline conspirators. He writes that she exhibited a boldness worthy of a man; she was well-married with children; she was literate, musical and a good dancer, she was good company and made good conversation. But marriage and motherhood apart, she displayed none of the qualities expected of the conventional *matrona*; she was impulsive, louche, highly sexed, a perjurer, an accessory to murder, a liar and a spendthrift (Sallust, *Catilina* 25).

Women were also prey to what we might call defeminisation by male writers. Brave, clever and generally outstanding women must owe some of their achievement to manly qualities – they could not possibly have done what they did just by being women. Apart from Sempronia's 'boldness worthy of a man' we hear of Ummidia Quadratilla from Pliny the Younger (7, 24): this grandmother is *viridis* – spritely, unusual in such an old woman. When Porcia, Brutus' wife, defiantly and bravely swallowed hot coals after her husband's death in 43 BC, Valerius Maximus said that 'her woman's spirit was equal to her father's manly death'. He also cites the capable lawyer Maesia of Sentium, who, in 77 BC, conducted her own defence and, through her forensic expertise, secured her own acquittal – Maesia became known as Androgyne because she had succeeded and excelled in the work of a man, rather than of a woman. Juvenal, in his excoriating sixth *Satire* against women, deplores the woman who assumes the role of the (male) grammarian and parades her knowledge of Virgil or Homer at the dinner party; so great is the force of her verbiage that it silences *grammatici, rhetores, causasdici* – even other women. In short, the woman who wants to be *docta* and *facunda*, the pedant and the know-it-all, is a *monstrum* who should just go away and be a man.

Of powerful women, Plutarch describes a certain Praecia – a beauty and a wit – who was instrumental in helping Lucius Licinius Lucullus win the governship of Cilicia in 74 BC, and subsequently the much sought-after command against Mithridates.[1] Praecia, though little more than a prostitute according to Plutarch, had a reputation as something of a fixer and wielded great influence and power. She began an affair with the equally influential, and dissolute, Publius Cornelius Cethegus, arch-enemy of Lucullus'; she was soon dictating everything Cethegus did: 'nothing important was done in which Cethegus was not involved, and nothing by Cethegus without Praecia'. Lucullus saw his chance and proceeded to insinuate his way successfully into Praecia's affections to the extent that Cethegus was soon backing Lucullus for the governorship.

The ambitious and assertive Fulvia Flacca Bambula (*c.* 83 BC – 40 BC), is infamous for gleefully and sadistically pricking the decapitated Cicero's tongue with a hairpin; she took exception and revenge after Cicero had insinuated that Mark Antony, her third husband, only married her for her money.[2] Cicero's head was on public display in the Forum after his proscription in 43 BC.[3] Velleius Paterculus records that she 'was creating general confusion by armed violence' and that Octavian's troops tied obscene messages to stones and fired them directly at Fulvia. Two were aimed at her clitoris, with the unmistakeable suggestion that she was a tribade, a lesbian;[4] Fulvia and Antony were invited to open their arses wide to receive the projectiles. They in turn responded by calling Octavian a cock-sucker and wide-arsed, suggesting that he too was open to penetration – the ultimate insult for a freeborn man. Martial preserves for us the lascivious epigram which Octavian reputedly composed for Fulvia:

> Because Antony is shagging Glaphyra, Fulvia has decided that my punishment will be that I shag her too. Me fuck Fulvia? What if Manius begged me to bugger him? Would I? I think not, if I had any sense. 'Fuck or fight,' she says. Doesn't she know that I love my prick more than life itself? Let the battle trumpets sound!'[5]

Martial's Octavian is implying that the ensuing civil war was caused because Fulvia was put out by his rebuffal.

Fulvia was not the only sadist in town. Pomponia, the widow of Cicero's brother, Quintus Tullius, and sister of Atticus was even more sadistic; when Philologus, the freedman who betrayed the Ciceros, was brought to her she ordered him to cut off strips of his own flesh, cook them and then eat them. This was according to Plutarch, in his biography of Cicero (49).

Many men were absent from home for increasingly long periods of time and for much of their careers, due to the exigencies of military service and provincial administration. Augustus banned soldiers from marrying, except those from the ruling classes. Partners were considered concubines and they and their children had no legal status. The ban was in place right up to the time of Septimius Severus, when it was repealed in AD 197.[6] Officialdom, though, obviously connived at the relationships which were formed with local women; on discharge the soldier and his partner were granted the right of marriage as citizens, and any children were awarded citizenship. Aulus Caecina Severus adopts an extreme view in a speech from AD 21, as recorded by Tacitus, but it contains within it the arguments which no doubt moulded the regulations relating to accompanied postings. Severus gets on with his wife and they have had six children together. Why? Because women encourage extravagance in peacetime and weakness during war; they are feeble and tire easily; left unrestrained they get angry, they scheme and boss the commanders about; he cites instances of women running patrols and exercises, how they attract spivs and embrace extortion.

We only have to look to Scipio Aemilianus to see that Severus' attitude was not all chauvinism or just plain spoiling the party. In 134 BC while fighting Numantia, Scipio expelled 2,000 prostitutes from his camp in order to restore discipline, if not morale.[7]

One of the fascinating Vindolanda Tablets from around AD 100 shows that wives of officers clearly did accompany their husbands abroad; Claudia Severa sends a birthday party invitation to her sister Lepidina asking her to make her day by coming on 11 September. The body of the letter is written by a scribe but the postscript is written by Claudia and is the oldest example of a woman's handwriting in Latin in existence.[8]

Homosexual behaviour among soldiers not only violated the rule against intercourse with another freeborn man, but also meant that the penetrated soldier's sexual, and therefore military, dominance was seriously compromised as, depending on how you looked at it, rape and penetration were emblems of military defeat. According to Polybius, a soldier who had been penetrated would pay the ultimate penalty of being bludgeoned to death.

Effeminacy in the ranks got a number of soldiers off the hook, or else proved that looks can be deceiving, even when camouflaged in uniform. The fabulist Phaedrus tells the tale of a hulk of a soldier in Pompey's army who was brought up on a charge of robbing the supply train. He had cultivated a girly voice and gait and, as a result, won a reputation as a *cinaedus*; this got him off the charge and, when he was permitted to fight again, he did so with success and bravery and was duly decorated by Pompey. Suetonius tells how two soldiers who pretended to be *pathici* or *cinaedi* were implicated in a plot to assassinate Domitian; the other conspirators were executed but not these two because the emperor could not believe that such effeminate perverts could only be quite inept. Such was the reputation of *cinaedi* in military circles.[9]

Salvian, Bishop of Marseilles (c. AD 439–50), knew a thing or two about the behaviour of conquering armies. The treatment Marseilles received during the four times it was overrun by invaders may account for some of the bitterness when he compares Vandal with Roman.

> Certainly the Romans of noble birth made effeminacy a regular practice. What more have I to add? Not one of the Vandals was polluted by the incest of the effeminate Romans about him. Certainly, effeminacy had long been considered by the Romans as a virtue rather than a vice, and those men thought themselves

models of manly strength who had put others to the basest uses. For this reason the attendant boys, who once followed the soldiers, were given as a reward for services well performed on campaign, the privilege of being shamefully used as women, since they had proved themselves brave men. What a crime was this! (*De Gubernatione Dei* 7, 20).

The younger soldier was never safe, it seems, not just from his enemy but also from predetatory senior officers.[10] Plutarch, in his life of Marius, tells how a legionary called Trebonius was habitually sexually assaulted by his superior officer, Gaius Luscius. Trebonius reacted on one occasion and was hauled before a tribunal for murdering Luscius; however, he was able to call witnesses to attest that he had never prostituted himself or accepted gifts in exchange for sexual favours. He was acquitted and decorated for defending his masculinity and freeborn male integrity. The *De Bello Hispaniensi* mentions a Roman officer who engaged in regular sexual activity with his concubine. We hear from Valerius Maximus of Gaius Laetorius Mergus, who came on to his adjutant during the Samnite Wars and was subsequently tried in a civilian court on a charge of *stuprum*, illegal sexual advances on a freeborn boy. Mergus committed suicide. Valerius is much more concerned about the effect on the unit than he is on the well-being of the young soldier, or, for that matter, Mergus.[11]

Juvenal cautions about the dangers facing young, fresh-faced recruits and advises they stay off the perfume, exaggerate their masculine features and refrain from removing nostril or armpit hair.[12]

CHAPTER ELEVEN

Gladiator Adulator

The amphitheatres around the Roman world and the spectacular games held within were associated with sex on a number of levels. First, Ovid recommends the games as *the* best place to pick up a sophisticated lady; the place is crawling with them.[2] Valeria 'accidentally' met with Sulla there, and later married him. However, unless you were a Vestal Virgin or a member of the imperial family, you were subjected to a pecking order when it came to seating in the amphitheatre or the theatre; women, along with slaves and foreigners, found themselves stuck high up at the back, while men enjoyed seats at the front allocated according to their rank. Second, some women were physically attracted to some of the bronzed and muscular gladiators who performed in the arenas, occasionally as celebrities in their own right. And third, by the same token, some men would have found the bouts fought by *gladiatrices*, women gladiators, erotic and sexually exciting.

This chimes with Ovid's assertion that some elite women were partial to 'a bit of rough', and with Petronius in his *Satyricon* who has Chryseis describe how some well to do women burn with desire for men of the lower orders: 'There are some women, you see, whose lust is triggered only at the sight of slaves or messenger boys with their tunics belted right up high. Gladiators in the arena, a mule driver covered with dust, an actor in the shameful exposure of this performance – that's what it takes to get some females heated up. My mistress is one of this tribe: her taste goes fourteen rows back from the reserved seats and looks for a lover at the fringes of the mob.' They even going so far as to lick the wounds of the flogged. Juvenal includes this distasteful *libido* for gladiators in his tirade against women.[1] Martial wrote of Hermes, the famous gladiator,

'Hermes spells riches for the ticket touts'. Some women bribed guards to allow them access to the gladiator billets. As we shall see, Elagabalus 'married' his blond-haired chariot driver, Hierocles

The gladiator, although usually a slave and on the lowest level of Roman society, was something of a fascinating paradox with magical qualities. His blood was used as a remedy for impotence, an aphrodisiac, and any sensible bride would have her hair parted by a spear to ensure a fertile married life – ideally one which had been dipped in the blood of a defeated and dead gladiator. Medical authorities had it that drinking a gladiator's blood or eating his liver cured epileptics.

Ironically, given that they were considered *untermenschen*, some gladiators won admiration for their bravery, and for their willingness to die – true Roman qualities, *Romanitas* indeed, and indicative of the *virtus* to which every man, every Roman worth his salt, aspired to. Despite their lowly station, some became celebrities and were depicted in mosaics and sculptures, on lamps and tombstones: graffiti was scrawled by them and about them: 'Celadus the Thracian, thrice victor and thrice crowned, the young girls' heart-throb' and 'Crescens the Netter of young girls by night.'[3] Gladiators were all the rage. But, even in victory, a gladiator remained what he was: *infamis* and a slave, unable to escape his ranking alongside criminals, whores, actors, dancers and similar dregs. The paradox and irony was not lost on Tertullian:

> Men surrender them their souls, and women their bodies, too ... On one and the same account, [men] glorify them and degrade and diminish them – indeed, they openly condemn them to ignominy and the loss of civil rights, excluding them from the senate house and rostrum, the senatorial and equestrian orders, and all other honors or distinctions of any type. The perversity of it! Yet, they love whom they punish; they belittle whom they esteem; the art they glorify, the artist they debase. What judgment is this: on account of that for which he is vilified, he is deemed worthy of merit!

In the second century AD Calpurnius Flaccus ranked gladiators below slaves: 'There is no meaner condition among the people than that of the gladiator.'[4]

Despite it all, they still won the admiration and adulation of some women in the crowds: the gladiator was what the Roman lady yearned for, what her husband, son and brother surely envied.

The elite gladiator exuded virility: archaeological evidence for the sexualisation of gladiators has been found in the shape of a multitude of objects depicting phalluses: a phallus-shaped terra cotta gladiatorial helmet; a stone relief from Beneventum, showing a heavily armed gladiator in combat with a huge penis. The very word *gladius*, sword, carries unmistakeable sexual connotations and is sometimes slang for penis. The famous bronze figurine from Pompeii shows a menacing gladiator using his sword to fend off a dog-like beast which is growing out of his huge erect penis. Five bells are suspended from his body: everyone woman's perfect doorbell.

Juvenal spits out the sorry tale of

> Eppia, the senator's wife, [who] ran off with a gladiator ... And what were the youthful charms which captivated Eppia? What did she see in him to allow herself to be called "a she-Gladiator"? Her dear Sergius had already begun to shave; a wounded arm gave promise of military discharge, and there were sundry deformities in his face: a scar caused by the helmet, a huge wen upon his nose, a nasty humour always trickling from his eye. But then he was a gladiator! It is this that transforms these fellows into Hyacinths! It was this that she preferred to children and to country, to sister and to husband. What these women love is the sword: had this same Sergius received his discharge, he would have been no better than a Veiento[5].

Excavations in the armoury of the Pompeii gladiatorial barracks unearthed eighteen skeletons in two rooms, presumably of gladiators; but they were not alone. There was also the bones of a woman wearing gold and expensive jewellery, and an emerald-studded necklace; she clearly was not there to serve the rations...

We have seen that while the performance arts *per se* were held in high regard by the Romans, those who performed them – dancers, actors, musicians and gladiators – were despised. Dio's disgust in describing members of the elite classes actually performing on stage and in the amphitheatre is palpable.[7]

Women gladiators shared their particular stage with an elephant walking on a tightrope – at games arranged by Nero in honour of his mother, Agripinna the Younger, whom he had recently murdered. Tacitus is just as outraged: 'Many ladies of distinction, however, and senators, disgraced themselves by appearing in the amphitheatre'.[8] The fact that these were rich women and had no need of extra money suggests that they did it for the adrenalin, the sexual high, it gave them. Dio tells of another spectacle when Nero, entertaining the king Tiridates I of Armenia, gave a gladiatorial show featuring Ethiopian men, women, and children.[9] Petronius describes a woman who fought from a chariot just like the male *Essedari*, possibly armed with bow and arrow.[10]

Women gladiators were just one of many variations on a theme used to keep the baying crowds entertained. In the hundred-day games put on by Titus they competed with a battle between cranes and one between four elephants – just a handful of the 9,000 beasts slaughtered in one single day, 'and women took part in despatching them'.[11] They must surely have participated in Trajan's games in in AD 108 which lasted 123 days and in which 'eleven thousand or so animals both wild and tame were killed and ten thousand gladiators fought'. Martial, in his *De Spectaculis*, describes women battling in the arena, one dressed as Venus herself. Another overcomes a lion: 'Caesar, we now have seen such things done by women's courage.'[12] Domitian put on 'hunts of wild beasts, gladiatorial shows at night by the light of torches, and not only combats between men but between women as well' and, Dio adds, 'sometimes he would pit dwarfs and women against each other'.[13] Statius sums it all up: 'Women untrained to the *rudis* take their stand, daring, how recklessly, virile battles!'[14] The *rudis* was the wooden sword given to a gladiator when he was freed after a series of conspicuous victories.

Juvenal sardonically describes 'Mevia', hunting wild boars in the arena 'holding her spear, breasts exposed'. Elsewhere, he was scathing:

> How shameful is a woman wearing a helmet, who shuns femininity and loves brute force... If a sale is held of your wife's effects, how proud you will be of her belt and arm-pads and plumes, and her half-length left-leg shin-guard! Or, if instead, she prefers a different form of combat how pleased you'll be when the girl you love sells off her greaves!... Hear her grunt while she practises thrusts from the trainer, wilting under the weight of the helmet.[15]

Nicolaus of Damascus mentions women gladiators.[16] Nero dealt with annoying senators by threatening to have their wives thrown into the arena to do combat.

In AD 19 a *senatus consultum* from Larinum stated that elite women cannot appear on the stage or become gladiators. In AD 11 an attempt to ban senators and women performing in amphitheatres and on the stage were unsuccessful.[17] The law decreed that 'no female of free birth of less than twenty years of age and for no male of free birth of less than twenty-five years of age to pledge himself as a gladiator or hire out his services'.

Nearly 200 years later in AD 200, Septimius Severus barred any female from fighting in the arena, μονομαχεῖν. Dio reports that 'women took part, vying with one another most fiercely, with the result that jokes were made about other very distinguished women as well. Therefore it was henceforth forbidden for any freeborn woman, no matter what her origin, to fight in single combat.'[18] This came about after Severus' visit to the Antiochene Olympic Games, where he would have seen traditional Greek female athletics. His attempt to impress the mob in Rome with a similar extravaganza was met with derision from the crowds in the Colisseum.

A second-century-AD marble relief from Halicarnassus (modern Bodrum) in Turkey (now in the British Museum) shows two women, Amazon and Achillia, fighting as gladiators. They are heavily armed like a *secutor* (a chaser of the *retiarius*, net man), with greaves and the right arm protected and carrying a large oblong shield; their hair is cropped in the style of a slave and their breasts are bare. Such a spectacular must have been important for it to commemorated in this way. An epigraph from Ostia praises Hostilianus as the first to 'arm women' in the history of the local games.[19]

In September 2000, the Museum of London announced that they had discovered the grave of a female gladiator, from the first century AD – the first ever to be found. A piece of red pottery has been discovered with the inscription VERECVNDA LVDIA LVCIUS GLADIATOR, 'Verecunda the woman gladiator, Lucius the gladiator'.

It seems likely that female gladiators came to the arena by a number of different routes. Some would have been slaves, coerced by their masters, the *lanistae*; others would have volunteered and received the requisite training in the gladiator schools; others still may have just been thrown in there as a punishment: *damnati ad gladium* – 'damned to the sword'. Women would not have faced men; rather, as we have seen, they would fight from chariots with the bows and arrows characteristic of the Amazons, *mulierem essedariam*, Diana and Atalanta; alternatively, they may have been pitched against dwarfs.

The female gladiator with her breasts revealed would have an erotic impact on the male members of the audience, heightened by the arousing appearance of a woman wealding a weapon – something a typical Roman woman obviously never did, except for a handful of military exceptions or when a woman stabbed a man in a domestic setting. Women trained in combat were usually foreign women from foreign lands – this exotic mystique must have stimulated further the sexual overtones of the spectacle and the libido of the male spectators. Ovid, we know, says that the games were the place to pick up a woman, and that the sight of a female leg, rarely seen outside the home, was exciting; the half-naked, weapon-wielding female gladiator would have been more exciting still.[20]

CHAPTER TWELVE

Bad Language: Roman Sexual Vocabulary

Latin is exceptionally rich in words describing all aspects of Roman sexuality and sexual activity. The nuances and differences in, for example, words for prostitutition, copulation and genitalia are frequently captured by a precise word to leave the reader or audience in no doubt as to what the author – be he poet, orator, playwright, historian or graffiti scrawler – really meant. This chapter will describe and discuss some of this colourful and, to some, shocking, vocabulary.

Amor, *cupido* and *libido* are all used for sexual love with *cupido* more analogous to 'desire' and *libido* to 'lust'. *Amor* too has these sexual connotations: the rapist Sextus Tarquinius 'burns with lust', *amore ardens*, while a benevolent prostitute is capable of loving, non-sexual, devotion (*amatus*) at Livy 39, 9, 6. *Venus* is also used as a metonym for sexual love. The bright lights of racy Baiae were synonymous with *libidines*, *amores* and *adulteria* according to Cicero in his *Pro Caelio* (15, 35).

Submitting oneself to penetration was, as we have observed, highy reprehensible and socially unacceptable. The verb used is often *pati*, associated with Greek *paschein*. The Julian law stipulated that any male who willingly 'submits' (*patitur*) is a criminal (Julius Paulus, *Opinions* 2, 26, 13). Theopompus of Chios found it hard to believe that the Etruscans had no problem with being the passive partner, *paschontas* (*FGrHist* 115 F 204).

Stuprum was a central legal concept in Roman sexual *mores*.[1] Translatable as illicit sexual intercourse, criminal debauchery, fornication or sex crime, it impinges on *incestum* and describes what was going on when adultery was committed. Our word 'incest' is but one translation of *incestum*, the main use being to denote 'unchastity'. In its association with *raptus*, *stuprum* signifies rape: *raptus ad stuprum*: abduction with the intention of committing a sex crime. In Roman law, *raptus* meant abduction; the legendary 'rape' of the Sabine women was a bride abduction in which the sexual violation came later, *cum vi* or *per vim* – with force.

At the other end of the spectrum was chastity, *pudicitia*, as idealised by the perfect Roman *matrona* and by the good Roman who was in control of himself. *Pudicitia* did not entail abstinence from sexual actitivity but sex in appropriate measures: for virgins none at all; for wives, sex exclusively with the husband, and for a man, sex with whomsover he wished so long as it was not with another man's wife or as a passive homosexual. Synonymous with *pudicitia* are *castitas* and *castus* – 'chastity' and 'chaste' or 'pure'. Abstention from sex in the run up to a festival, for example the Bona Dea, ensured purity (*castimonia*). In his *Life of Numa* (10, 1), Plutarch describes the Vestal Virgins as being in a state of *hagneia* for thirty years, the Greek equivalent to *castitas*. Seneca deplored the absence of *pudicitia* in the youth of his day (*Controversiae* 1 Pref. 9): 'They are born lifelong spineless weaklings, attacking the *pudicitiae* of others and casual with their own.' Livy has the venerable Lucretia describe her rape as a loss of *pudicitia*, *amissa pudicitia* (1, 58, 7).

As in other languages, there are numerous words descibing the various types of prostitutes and aspects of prostitution. This profusion helps to give an idea of how prevalent it was in Roman society and the manifold forms it took. To act as a prostitute is *scortor*, very popular with Plautus. *Glubo* often describes a whore as one who 'rips you off'.

Aelicariae, baker's girls, were girls who worked outside temples selling their bodies and small cakes in the shape of male or female genitalia for sacrifice to Venus or Priapus. *Amasiae* were girls who combined work with Venus worship; *ambubiae* were professional singers with a sideline in prostitution. *Ancillae ornatrices* were maids who helped whores tidy themselves up, fix their hair and make up in between customers; the *aquarii*, water boys, served the wine in brothels and fetched the water for washing. The *blitidae* worked in taverns; they took their name from the cheap wine (*blitum*) sold there. *Bustuariae* were low-rent prostitutes who prostituted themselves in graveyards or between funerals.

The Roman military was no different from any other army on the march: their camp followers, or Roman comfort women, not only gave sex but had to to cook, dress wounds, mend clothes or clean the camp. The *casuaria* was a roadhouse, which usually had a brothel round the back. *Citharistriae* and *cymbalistriae* were harpists and cymbal players who whored on the side; the *copae* were serving girls cum prostitutes or slave-girls; the *delicatae* were posh courtesans, some of whom were also actresses. *Diobolares* were at the other end of the price list – cheap streetwalkers who charged a mere two obols. A *diversorium* was a boarding house which rented rooms out to prostitutes while *dorides* were visiting escorts; *famosae* were like *delicatae*. A *fellatrix* was a woman who specialized in fellatio and usually worked in bath houses. *Forariae* worked out in the country while *fornicatrices* plied their trade underneath the arches of public buildings and aqueducts; (hence our 'fornication'). *Gallinae* ('hens') were to be avoided: they combined prostitution with robbery and extortion (cash-and-dash) and were often pimped by professional robbers. A *leno* was a brothel keeper; a female brothel keeper or madam was a *lena*. *Lupae* ('she-wolves') were streetwalkers who attracted clients by howling like wolves, apparently, and a *lupanar* was a brothel. *Mimae* combined miming with prostitution; *noctiluae* ('nightwalkers') walked the streets late at night but *nonariae* ('nine o'clock girls') were only allowed to work from 9 p.m. until dawn; *pergulae* worked from balconies, usually high-class *meretrices*. A *proseda* leased a room in a *lupanar* and a *quadrantariae* charged a pittance. *Meretrix*, *scorta erratica* and *scortum* were other names for harlots; a *stabula* was a one-roomed brothel where sex took place in public view. *Tabernae* were bakeries with rooms or cellars rented out to prostitutes; a *tugurium* was a very low-rent hut used by streetwalkers. *Turturillae* ('pigeon houses') were large pigeon coops frequented by whores, particularly by transvestite male prostitutes. *Venerii* were priestesses of Venus who taught sexual techniques to courtesans; a *villicus* was the cashier at a brothel, who took the money and fixed the prices. If you were a concubine you were a *paelex* or a *concubinusla*. Galba had a *concubinus* called Icelus (Suetonius, *Galba* 7, 22, 1).

The penis too is blessed with a plethora of words describing it and its functions; there are no fewer than 120 or so. Many of these words describe the penis as a weapon, an aggressive instrument of combat and conflict which, of course, is consistent with the Romans' obsession with sexual power and domination. We have seen, too, how the military adorn slingstones with graffiti suggesting a penis-like function when they hit the anus, clitoris or vagina of the intended target. Fulvia and Antony are, of course, the most famous targets of the *glandes Perusinae* at the Battle of Perusia against Octavian's army.

Pride of place for the most common obscene word for penis is *mentula* – a word which Martial attempts to elevate to respectability, although his own obscene use of it forty-eight times rather undermines his argument.[2] Cicero avoids it even when expatiating on obscene language,[3] but Catullus deploys it eight times, most notoriously as a nickname of sorts for Mamurra – 'dickhead'. Not surprisingly, it appears twenty-six times in the *Priapea*, eighteen times in graffiti from Pompeii and three in the *Graffiti del Palatino*. *Verpa* was more caustic and offensive, denoting an erect penis with foreskin drawn back, fresh from vigorous sexual activity. *Verpa* is used once each by Catullus and Martial, and in the *Priapea*.[4] *Virga* too, branch, rod, stake or beam, and *vomer*, plough, were both used in a metaphorical sense as were *vena* (vein), *penis* and *cauda* (tail) and *nervus* (tendon). An ironic poem (28) in the *Priapea* contrives to use *mentula* in conjunction with two more choice profanities: 'I'd rather die than use obscene and improper words; but when you, Priapus, as a god, appear with your balls (*colei*) hanging out, it is right for me to speak of cunts (*cunni*) and cocks.'

A *sopio* was an obscene caricature with a huge, Priapus-like penis; Catullus uses it (37) as a threat – 'I will draw *sopios* on the front of the tavern' – and it turns up in a rather disgusting graffito from Pompeii: 'whoever drew these *sopios*, let him eat shit! (*merdas*)'. The grammarian Sacerdos leaves us an unflattering reference to Pompey: 'whoever is not ashamed and blushes is not a man, but a *sopio*'.

Pipinna was infantile slang for the penis; Martial (11, 71) deeply insults Natta with 'Natta sucks the pee-pee of his athlete. By comparison, Priapus is a eunuch'. The word to get an erection is *arrigere*, as in Suetonius, *Augustus* 69.

Testicles are *testes*, the Latin for 'witness', and may derive from the ancient ritual of swearing oaths on the male genitalia with the menacing implication that false oaths might result in infertility and with it the end of the family line. Our 'testicle' comes from the diminutive *testiculum*. The obscene alternative was *coleus*. It features in what was probably an unedifying proverb: 'when an old man lies down, his testicles cover his arsehole'.

Precisely where a penis penetrated was very important to the Romans, and where it penetrated determined which of two words was to be used. *Pedicare* describes insertion in the anus and comes from the Greek παιδίκω, itself from παῖς (child). *Irrumare*, on the other hand, means to insert one's penis into another person's mouth for sucking, and comes from the Latin word, *ruma*, for teat. A male who sucks a penis is as a *fellator* or *pathicus*. As we have seen, a *pathicus* translates as a 'fag' or 'faggot', someone who also had a predilection for being penetrated; Catullus cites Julius Caesar as an example (*Carmen 57*, 1–2). Brothel graffiti gives us *fellare*, to perform fellatio (*CIL* 4, 2259) while in Petronius's *Satyricon* (23) we have the metaphoric *super inguina mea...moluit,* 'he worked on my groin for a long time but to no avail'. Dreaming of oral sex gave no escape. Artemidorus of Daldis teaches that the man who dreams of performing 'the unmentionable' on a man or a woman he knows will hate that person thereafter because they can no longer kiss; if he dreams he performs it on someone he does not know then everyone will come to harm apart from those who make a living from their mouth, for example, flute players, trumpeters and orators. If he allows a child to perform the act on him, he will bury that child. (*Interpretation of Dreams* 1, 79).

The standard obscenity for the female genitalia is *cunnus*, corresponding to our highly offensive 'cunt'. Martial uses it liberally, more than thirty times, Catullus once, and Horace three times; it appears too in the *Priapea* and as graffiti. Women in particular refer to their genitalia as *porcus*, 'pig'; Varro believes this to derive from the sacrifice of a pig to Ceres in wedding rites.[5] Other agricultural and horticutural metaphors include fields, gardens, and meadows; the image of 'ploughing' the 'furrow' also features. Others still, with varying levels of vividness, include cave, ditch (*fossa*), pit, bag, vessel, door, hearth, oven and altar.

Cicero in his *Brutus* (154) explains why in Latin 'with us' is rendered *nobiscum* rather than the expected *cum nobis;* run the two words together and you hear *cunno bis,* 'a pair of cunts'. French has the same problem with *qu'on*, which sounds like *con* (cunt) and gets round it by adding *l'* to form the less ambivalent *que l'on*. Helen's 'cunt' is described by Horace by synecdoche as the cause of the Trojan war (*Satires* 1, 2 and 1, 3).

Ovid in the *Ars Amatoria*, is alone in referring to a woman pleasuring herself through genital stimulation. Martial is disparaging of female genitalia, describing one woman's vagina as 'loose... as the foul gullet of a pelican'; he compares the vagina to a boy's anus.[6] The obscene word for clitoris was *landica*, found in the *Priapea – misella landica,* 'poor little clit' – graffiti and in Martial and Juvenal.[7] One of those Perusian sling bullets was destined for

Fulvia's clitoris, *Fulviae landicam peto*. Martial familiarises us with the lesbian who wields her sizeable clitoris as a penis.

Lucilius refers to penetrating a 'hairy bag' when he has to contend with pubic hair; depilation was the norm in men and women.[8] A graffito from Pompeii pronounces that 'a hairy cunt gives a much better fuck than one which is smooth; hairy makes steamy and wants cock'.[9]

Papillae is the word of choice when the love poets refer to breasts in an erotic sense. Ovid speaks of malleable nipples (*habiles papillae*), his desire to fondle the breasts of his mistress and to have inserted his left hand in her 'sheath'. Propertius is up against his mistress's nipples when he tustles with her naked.[10]

We have already noted *tribas*; it comes from the Greek *tribo*, I rub, and is defined as 'a woman who practises unnatural vice with herself or with other women', and in Latin, 'a woman who practices lewdness with women'. Other Latin words for lesbian are *fricatrix* (she who rubs), and *virago*. There is no precise word for homosexual, male or female, in Latin. *Hetairistria*, 'woman-lover', is a Greek word used by Lucian in his *Dialogues of the Courtesans* (5, 2).

'I fuck' is *futuo* – not always obscene, as it is used as a commercial verb for sex between a prostitute and her client. Cicero never uses it; Martial does forty-nine times and Catullus seven. A fragment from Plautus may suggest that it was one of the sexy words used by women during the wedding night seduction – the *nupta verba*.[11] It springs to the lips of the military-minded Fulvia in her confrontation with Octavian: 'Either fuck me or let's scrap it out.'[12] Pompeii graffiti written by men and women (sixty-five uses have been found) demonstrate its casual use to give an impression of power, gratification and availability. There are a number of highly descriptive derivatives: *perfututum* means 'totally fucked', and *defututa* 'shagged out'; *fututio* is 'a fucking' while *fututori* is a 'fucker'. Catullus describes a *puella* (41) as *defututa* and a penis similarly fucked (29). In 32, Catullus refers to nine successive fuckings, *fututiones*. Graffiti gives us *fututa sum hic* ('I got fucked here', written by a woman) and this from prostitutes: *Felix bene futuis* ('Lucky man, you fuck well') and *Victor bene valeas qui bene futuis* ('Victorious, best wishes to one who has fucked well'). What better advertisement?

Ceveo and *criso* defy precise translation into English. *Criso* is what a woman does during sex: bumping, grinding or riding on a penis; *ceveo* is the homosexual equivalent – the actions of the passive, receiving partner.

To bugger is *pedicare*, usually male, but not always. It is used aggressively for forced penetration or as a general obscenity as in 'fuck you!' Anus was *culus* with metaphors including *ficus*, fig, and *anus*, ring. Martial describes a *cūlus aeni*, 'the bronze arsehole', as on a statue.[13] The less offensive *clunes* were buttocks.

We have already met Priapus and Mutunus. Suffice to add the conversation Horace has with his penis, his *mutto*.[14] 'What do you want? Surely you're not demanding a grand consul's granddaughter as a cunt?' *Mutuniatus* appears in Martial and in the *Corpus Priapeorum* to describe a well-hung male.[15]

Latin indeed was very precise when it came to erotic, ovscene and sexual vocabulary; not however, as precise as ancient Greek which can boast a single noun for the humiliating act of thrusting a radish up the anus as a punishment for adultery. The incriminating word is *rhaphanidosis* and was coined by Aristophanes in *The Clouds*, line 1,083, 'what if he gets buggered with a radish and his pubic hair plucked out with hot ashes?' Catullus was obviously familiar with the practice, adding a fish for good measure, when in Poem 45 he asserts *percurrant raphanique mugilesque*, 'both radishes and mullets will run you through'.

PART TWO

In Bed with the Emperors, and an Empress or Two

CHAPTER THIRTEEN

Augustus' Women: Flawless, Faithful and Fornicating

This chapter looks at the various women who populated the life of Octavian, later Augustus, first emperor of Rome: mother, wives and daughter – very different women with very different sexual complexions.

Atia Balba Caesonia (85–43 BC) was the niece of Julius Caesar and mother of Augustus. Tacitus describes Atia's matronly virtues and the reverence in which she was held: 'You offended her if you swore in her hearing or misbehaved in any way; she was meticulous in her management of the children's duties, their leisure and their play time.'[1] Suetonius is equally reverential in his description of the prodigies which accompanied her pregnancy and the birth of Octavian. Quoting as his source the *Theologumena* of Asclepias of Mendes, he tells how Atia visited the temple of Apollo one night and fell asleep; a serpent came and went. When she woke she washed, as she would after making love with her husband, and discovered an indelible tattoo of a serpent on her body. Thereafter, she avoided the public baths out of embarrassment. When Octavian was born he was thus considered to be the son of Apollo. During her confinement Atia dreamed that her internal organs were raised to the stars and spread over all the Earth; Octavian later dreamed that the sun rose from between Atia's thighs.

Livia Drusilla was born on 30 January 58 BC; she married Octavian, was the mother of Tiberius, his successor, was paternal grandmother of the emperor Claudius, paternal great-grandmother of Caligula, and maternal great-great-grandmother of Nero. Tiberius, Augustus' stepson, was born in 42 BC after a pregnancy in which Livia, anxious for a boy, divined the sex of her baby by keeping a hen held against her breast, passing it to a nurse to maintain the warmth whenever necessary. A cock was born of the hen; Livia had Tiberius.[2]

Livia would have met Octavian in Rome when she was about six months pregnant with Nero Claudius Drusus, her second child by her then husband, Tiberius Nero. Dio says that Livia and Octavian were having an affair in 39 BC; they were betrothed in the autumn of that year. At the time Octavian was married to Scribonia. His first wife was Clodia Pulchra, whom he returned to her mother, Fulvia, still the virgin she was the day he married her and something of a disappointment. Octavian, reputedly smitten by Livia, divorced Scribonia on the day that Scribonia gave birth to their daughter, Julia.[3] Suetonius, in his *Life of Galba,* describes how the couple tried to mitigate the potential scandal caused by their unseemly haste to wed by peddling the tale that their relationship was sanctioned by a divine omen: while *en route* to her country villa in Veii an eagle, the bird of Jupiter, dropped a white hen chick into Livia's lap – it was holding a sprig of laurel in its mouth. According to Dio, Livia saw significance in this sign; she kept the chick for breeding and planted the twig in her garden. Remarkably (because white hens were thought to be sterile), the hen gave birth to a number of white chicks. A grove of laurels sprang up and subsequently, all *triumphatores* cut laurel from the trees for their triumphal wreaths.[4] The fable had obvious symbolism. It neatly suggested that the marriage was divinely sanctioned and the haste was imperative; it (wrongly) portended fertility in Livia, and it associated the couple with military victory. Dio, however, suggested an alternative, more prosaic explanation: that Livia had the power of the emperor, not a hen, in her lap.[5]

In 40 BC Scribonia had been forced to divorce her second husband, Publius Cornelius Scipio, so that Octavian could marry her. The rationale behind the marriage to Scribonia was to forge a political alliance with Sextus Pompeius. The marriage may always have been doomed because Octavian, reputedly, was irritated by Scribonia's constant nagging over his infidelities. In this respect she failed the test of the true *matrona*, who was expected to turn a blind eye to a husband's peccadillos.

Octavian and Livia married on 17 January 39 BC. The omens at the time of the marriage were not good, however: the ancient hut of Romulus burnt to the ground; the statue of Virtus fell flat on its face; Magna Mater was rumoured to be angry with the Romans, causing panic among the people.

There then followed fifty-two years of marriage in which Livia, from the start, acted in consort with her husband, advising him on policy decisions while running her own affairs. At the same time, though, she was very much the role-model *matrona*, dressing modestly in the *stola*, working the wool, wearing little jewelry, her hair conservatively done, often in *nodus* style with its old Republican overtones as championed by Octavia, her sister-in-law; she attended to the relatively modest household on the Palatine, striving for a child, an heir for her husband and for Rome.

Octavian probably was, from the start, attracted to what Tacitus describes as Livia's affability, her *comitas*; Tacitus and Velleius Paterculus describe Livia's *forma*, her beauty, and Tacitus adds that Octavian was motivated by passion, 'by desire for her body'.[6] This, in time, settled down into what we might assume to be love and affection: even Suetonius concedes that Augustus' love for Livia was 'special and enduring'. That she was a powerful force there is little doubt: Scribonia complains of her no little power, power in the political rather than an erotic sense, while Tacitus hints at coquettishness when he reports that she was not an unwilling player in Octavian's seduction. Seneca calls her *maxima femina*,[7] all woman.

Livia, nevertheless, was level headed and rational. Dio records how she pardoned a number of men who had been sentenced to death for inadvertently appearing naked before her; Livia explained that to a modest and chaste *matrona* naked men were no different from statues, and just as unsexy. On the other hand, a letter from Mark Antony to Octavian, reported by Suetonius, would suggest that Livia had much to put with: Antony asks Octavian why he is so exercised and obsessed by his affair with Cleopatra when Octavian has presumably already slept with Tertullia, Terentilla, Rufilla, Salvia Titisenia and the rest of them. Not that Antony was a shining example of virtue: Cicero, admittedly grinding his axe, accuses him of hiring what we would call rent boys at the astonishing price of 100,000 sesterces and holding all-male orgies with special boys in the villa he rented from the corrupt Verres. Suetonius tells us that Livia was party to scandalous behaviour: she was present at the notorious and decadent Feast of the Divine Twelve, and was apparently involved in procuring virgins for her husband to deflower, well into his old age.

When he was not being pilloried for his adulterous activities, or hypocritically legislating against adulterous behaviour among the common herd, Augustus was being accused of effeminacy and homosexuality – not unusual in itself as this was a popular way of discrediting a political or military rival. It is interesting, though, to see it extending right to the very top of government and into the very seat of ultimate power. Pompey accused him of being effeminate, while Mark Antony alleged, again according to Suetonius, that he had bought his adoption by his uncle, Julius Caesar, with sexual favours; Antony's brother, Lucius, adds that Augustus paid Aulus Hirtius 300,000 sesterces for sex with him while he was in Spain and that he was in the habit of applying hot nutshells to his legs to soften his hairs. Most embarrassing of all, though, must have been the time at the theatre when the actor playing the priest of the Cybele delivered the excruciating line, 'See how an effeminate rules the globe with his finger!' Digital gesturing was yet another sign of effeminacy.[8]

We have already noted Seneca's disgust at the growing effeminacy he detects in the youth of his day. Young men are dull, half-asleep all the time and intent on pursuing the evil that is singing and dancing. They plait their hair and speak like women. They are nothing short of 'soft' (*Controversiae* 1 Pref. 8–9).

The usual *deliciae* – naked, young, pretty boys kept for entertainment in the imperial household – included one Gaius Julius Prosopas, whom Livia shared with Livilla until his death at the age of nine. Dio tells of an amusing incident where Livia had a conversation with a *delicia* at a banquet soon after she was engaged to Octavian. They were always loquacious, cheeky youngsters who were expected to be rude, risqué and impertinent; Seneca informs us that they had special training in abuse and impudence and were always regarded as witty, but never gave offense. This particular *delicia* told Livia, who was reclining with Octavian before their marriage, that she was in the wrong place as her husband, Tiberius Nero, was somewhere else in the room.[9]

Julia Augusti, or Julia Caesaris, was the only blood child of Octavian, and the only child from his marriage with Scribonia. Julia's role as a pawn in her father's games of political intrigue began early, at age two, in 37 BC when she was part of a deal between Octavian's friends, Gaius Maecenas, Marcus Vipsanius Agrippa and Mark Antony.[10] Julia was engaged to Antony's ten-year-old son, Marcus Antonius Antyllus.[11] As things turned out, circumstances dictated otherwise and the engagement was called off when Antony was defeated by her father at the battle of Actium. Julia was later betrothed to Cotiso, the King of the Getans with whom Augustus was trying, unsuccessfully as it turned out, to forge an alliance against Mark Antony; according to Antony,

Augustus was to marry Cotiso's daughter but it all went wrong when Cotiso joined Antony.[12] In 25 BC, aged fourteen, Julia married her cousin, seventeen-year-old Marcus Claudius Marcellus, tipped to be Augustus' successor.[13]

Fate again intervened. Two years after the death of Marcellus in 21 BC Julia was dealt her next move in the political powerplay when she was married off to Agrippa, her father's friend and ally; she was now eighteen, and Agrippa was forty-three.

But things started to go wrong when Julia began to assert her own individuality, reacting, no doubt, to the oppressive childhood she had endured, the increasingly liberal society around her and her father's sexual hypocrisy, evident in his private life and in his legislation. Her next marriage, the unhappy marriage to Tiberius, was to make matters so much worse. In the meantime there were reports of Julia's serial adultery with Sempronius Gracchus, described by Tacitus as a persistent adulterer, and rumours of an unhealthy relationship with her stepbrother, Tiberius. Suetonius describes Julia's, and her sister's, behaviour as 'all kinds of vice'.[14] In 12 BC Agrippa died suddenly in Campania. Augustus moved quickly and, as soon as Julia, still in mourning, had given birth to Agrippa Postumus, betrothed Julia to Tiberius.[15]

The fifth-century writer, Macrobius shows us[16] a thirty-eight-year-old Julia in Julia's world: a world of putting on makeup ready to hit the town, tweezing grey hairs, going to gladiator fights in the company of trendy young men, dressing provocatively. Macrobius describes her coquettish behaviour: 'One day she stood before Augustus wearing a daring costume which upset her father although he kept quiet; the following day she came in dressed much more modestly, at which he expressed his delight that she was now dressed appropriately for a daughter of Augustus.'

Julia wittily responded by saying that today she dressed for her father, yesterday for her husband. Her modish dress sense was, of course, in direct contrast to the simple, modest homespun clothing Augustus was trying to promote to his subjects and which Livia, her step-mother, wore. In reply to those people who wondered why she did not conform to her father's apparently moralistic behaviour she pointedly answered that 'he forgets that he is Caesar but I never forget that I am Caesar's daughter'. Julia was very much her own woman. When asked how her children all resembled Agrippa despite her wayward behaviour, she, as we have already noted is alleged to have quipped that being pregnant allowed her to pursue her extra-maritial affairs without fear of getting pregnant: 'I never take on a passenger unless the ship is full'. Unfortunately for Julia, a somewhat less accomodating ship was later to take her into insular exile on Pandateria.

Augustus could only take so much. He had to choose between his responsibility to Rome or to Julia. He first denounced Julia and her permissive behaviour to the Senate; and then he had her arrested for adultery and treason and annulled her marriage. Her very public fornication was the last straw and reflected very badly on him, on the state and on his ability to govern the state. To a sensationalist Velleius Paterculus, a storm erupted in Augustus's *domus*, 'disgusting to describe, repellent to remember'. Augustus had found out about his daughter's all too public fornication: 'Julia... scandalously left nothing lustful or lavish undone that a woman could when prostituting herself, and quantified her good fortune by her dissolute sin, claiming she could rightfully do whatever she liked.'

According to Seneca, whose vocubulary and imagery is even more immoderate, Julia's sins were, for Augustus, 'sores', which when excised, felt as if he was cutting off his own limbs, limbs which, Tityos-like, kept growing back. Julia's nocturnal adventures had even involved prostitution and, ironically, sex on the statue of Marysas in the Forum – a symbol of liberty and freedom of speech. More galling for Augustus must have been the report that Julia regularly fornicated on the very rostra on which he had delivered his moral legislation, which, among other things, criminalised adultery with a sentence of island exile. And so did Julia arrive on the island of Pandateria.

Julia may not have been totally without male company on her island, though, if Suetonius's story[17] that she gave birth to a child there is to be believed; Augustus, exercising his rights as *paterfamilias*, had the baby exposed.

Velleius Paterculus describes Julia as 'stained by sex or excess', adding a list of her lovers.[18] Seneca says she had 'adulterers by the herd'; Pliny the Elder calls her 'the epitome of licentiousness' with her night time frolics on the statue of Marsyas which groans under the weight of her lewdness. Dio Cassius records 'night time orgies and drinking parties in the Forum, even on the Rostra'. Seneca reminds us that the Rostra was the very place where Augustus had delivered his moral legislation, restoring family values and outlawing adultery, the *Leges Juliae*; Julia had chosen to prostitute herself there.[19]

CHAPTER FOURTEEN

Capricious Depravity with Tiberius

If we needed a 'role-model' for the depravity allegedly exhibited by Julia then we need look no further than Tiberius, Augustus' successor and stepson, Liva's son. Livia had pushed relentlessly for Tiberius to succeed Augustus, and when she succeeded she continually meddled in affairs of state where she, by Roman convention, had no business meddling. This irked Tiberius no end, a man who, despite his proven expertise as a military commander, had little or no interest in politics or empires, or even in ruling empires.

'Saturnine' is one word which defines him, a mood brought on by his mother's constant interference and by the forced termination of a very happy marriage. This unhappy event was imposed on him by Augustus (and Livia) to clear the way for him to marry Julia, his stepsister, for purely political reasons. 'Depraved' is another defining epithet: we already know about the allegations of impropriety with Julia, cross-dressing, group sex, his prodigious library of sex manuals and his notorious pederasty. According to Suetonius and Tacitus, there was more, much more.[1]

Unable to tolerate an increasingly suffocating Rome and his mother's controlling influence any longer, Tiberius deserted the capital in AD 26 and took himself to Capri in self-imposed exile, leaving the satanic Sejanus to run the empire more or less as he pleased. Tiberius had found the splendid isolation he had long craved, but he was never isolated, except perhaps in a geographic sense. Suetonius tells of the sex club he had specially built as a seedy venue for his clandestine depravity and how he had trawled his empire looking for girls and young men expert in unnatural copulation (*monstrosi concubitus*). He called them his *spintriae*, turning him on with their troilism. Aulus Vitellius, one of the short-lived emperors of AD 79, is rumoured to have been one of the *spintriae*. He was seduced on Capri by Tiberius while an adolescent – his virginity was lost in order to help his father along his *cursus honorum*.[2] The most obscene paintings and statues were all around in ante-rooms, with ready references written by the famous sex writer Elephantis of Egypt on hand for consultation.

Outside in the woods he had boys and girls role-playing, dressed up as Pans and nymphs pleasuring each other in the caves. In the sea, Tiberius played a particularly odious game in which trained little boys, his *pisciculi*, 'minnows', chased him and got between his legs to lick and nibble at him. Even breastfeeding babies were not safe from his deviant behaviour and debauchery; he made them suck away at his breast and in his groin.

We know about Tiberius' painting by Parrhasius, which he had in his bedroom depicting Atalanta giving fellatio to Meleager. Once, while performing a sacrifice, he took a fancy to the boy carrying the incense carrier and his brother trumpeter: both were sodomised and when they protested he broke both their legs. Tiberius's cruel misogyny knew no bounds; one unfortunate victim was a woman called Mallonia, whom he seduced. When she showed him just how repellent she found him, he had her followed by informers and, inevitably, she ended up in court. He railed at her, demanding an apology; she went home and committed suicide, but not before delivering another invective against the 'foul-mouthed, hairy, stinking old man' – or, put another way, 'the old goat goes for the mother goat with his tongue.'

Tacitus corroborates Suetonius' account of these disgusting days. He describes the emperor's sojourn on Capri as being spent shamed by the evil deeds and depravities into which he had hurled himself. He had corrupted and destroyed the innocence of the children of freeborn citizens; so unnatural was his depravity that some of his activites had no Latin words to describe them and had to be coined. He even used slaves as predators and for stalking and procuring victims, rewarding the complicit and threatening those who resisted; violence and force was shown to uncooperative parents, happy to treat them as you would a prisoner of war – with rape and murder presumably.

Exotic cults from the east of the empire had been percolating into Rome, threatening the authority of and compliance to established state religion. The Bacchanalia was a case in point; the cult of Isis was another; it spread through the Roman empire like wildfire and was viewed with considerable concern by the authorities. Anti-Isis fever reached its peak under Tiberius after a scandal involving a well-to-do *matrona*, Paulina, and the equestrian Decius Mundus. The priests of Isis had convinced Paulina that Anubis, the Egyptian god, wanted to have sex with her in the temple; Anubis, of course, was played by none other than Decius Mundus, who had paid off the priests to assist him in his scheme. 'Anubis' had sex with the gullible Paulina but the tactless equestrian made the fatal mistake of bragging about his conquest. Word inevitably reached Tiberius; Mundus was exiled, the priests were crucified and thousands of Isis worshippers were expelled from the city to Sardinia.[3.]

With Livia, a bullying, meddling mother, and a wife whom he loved but was compelled to divorce for a third wife he resented, Tiberius was best with issues which jaundiced his relationships with the women in his life. We have noted how in 12 BC Augustus betrothed Julia, his stepsister, to Tiberius, and soon had her married to him.[4] But Tiberius was already happily married, so he was forced to divorce Vipsania Agrippina, who was pregnant with their second child. Vipsania had been betrothed to Tiberius at birth when Tiberius was ten years old; they married in 19 BC. The divorce took place in 11 BC, 'not without considerable pain' on Tiberius' part, and was a constant source of anguish to him for the rest of his life. One day Tiberius saw Vipsania in the street and became so distraught that measures were taken to prevent it ever happening again. Suetonius records that despite a happy start to the marriage with Julia 'living in harmony and with mutual affection', Tiberius soon came to loathe her; the feeling was mutual.[5] By 6 BC, he and Julia had separated.

CHAPTER FIFTEEN

'The Whore Augusta', Incest with Caligula and Claudius, and Nero's Necrophilia

Caligula assumed the title of emperor in AD 37 on the death of Tiberius. According to Suetonius, incest between Caligula and his sisters was a long-running, regular, public occurrence, even in the presence of his wife. Indeed, his grandmother, Antonia, once caught him in bed with Drusilla when they were staying at her house.

Abuse of power and sexual abuse went hand in hand. Caligula seduced Ennia Naevia, the wife of Macro, the commander of the Praetorian Guard and an ally. He promised, in writing, that he would marry her when he became emperor. In AD 37, heightened concerns about his succession may have prompted Caligula's marriage to Livia Orestilla; they soon separated on grounds of her infertility. His cavalier attitude towards women had unsavoury implications for any woman who had the misfortune to stray into his orbit; it explains, or perhaps is a result of, his alleged incestuous relations. In his *Caligula*, Suetonius records that he actually appropriated Livia Orestilla at her wedding to Gaius Piso, carting her off to his palace; two years after her peremptory dismissal, he banished her for allegedly returning to Piso.

The rich and beautiful Lollia Paulina was his next victim; Caligula was attracted to her because someone happened to mention that Lollia's grandmother had been beautiful. Caligula made Lollia divorce her husband, Publius Memmius Regulus. Six months later he divorced her, because she too was supposedly barren; he then sentenced her to eternal celibacy, forbidding her to have sex with any other man.

His homosexual conquests included Marcus Lepidus, Mnester the actor and Valerius Catullus, a senator who boasted loudly that he had buggered Caligula and was exhausted by the emperor's sexual voracity. 'He is said to have been inflamed with an unnatural passion for Marcus Lepidus Mnester, an actor in pantomimes, and for certain hostages; and to have engaged with them in the practice of mutual pollution.' Pyrallis was one of the many prostitutes he had an affair with. His malicious sadism shone through when he kissed the neck of a mistress or wife, declaring that the lovely neck could be severed the minute he gave the order. Caesonia was threatened with torture to elicit from her just why he loved her so much. Dressing up in women's clothes was a regular habit.

Marriage never got in the way of an affair. He continued to have sexual intercourse with his sister Drusilla after her wedding: 'When she was afterwards married to Cassius Longinus, a man of consular rank, he took her from him, and kept her constantly as if she were his lawful wife'. Particularly humiliating was his habit of inviting colleagues and their wives to dinner; he would have the wives parade in front of him, manhandle them and choose which ones to seduce. After the sex was over he would degrade the husband and wife with comments on how the wives performed and descriptions of intimate physical features.

Caligula married Milonia Caesonia in AD 39; Suetonius says that she was neither beautiful nor young, but she was fertile, having had three children from a previous marriage. She was extravagant and louche, but Caligula seemingly loved her, showing her off before his troops, parading her dressed up in combat uniform and a shield. He even made her deport herself, naked, before his friends. 'He loved with a most passionate and constant affection Caesonia, who was neither handsome nor young; and was besides the mother of three daughters by another man; but a wanton of unbounded lasciviousness.'

Caesonia gave birth to their daughter, Julia Drusilla, one month after their wedding – he refused to call Caesonia his wife until she had given birth. Julia was entrusted to Minerva for her education; Caligula never had any doubts that she was his child, as her violent temper and habit of trying to scratch out the eyes of her friends convinced him of his paternity. He established an imperial brothel on the Palatine, populating it with respectable, and reluctant, *matronae* and freeborn young men, pulling in clients from his tours round the city.

In AD 38 Drusilla, Caligula's sister, died of a fever. She had been

Caligula's favourite and her death hit him badly. Hereafter, his attitude towards Livilla and Agrippina, the other sisters, cooled markedly; Caligula was replaced in their beds by his catamite friends. In AD 39 the two girls devised a plot to assassinate him, with the help of Drusilla's widower and their cousin, Marcus Aemilius Lepidus. This became known as 'The Plot of the Three Daggers'. The plot failed, and the three conspirators were accused of *incestum*. At Lepidus's trial, Caligula denounced Agrippina and Livilla and produced spurious letters, supposedly written by them, revealing their plans for murder. Lepidus was executed by having his throat cut, while the two sisters were exiled to the Pontian Islands, Pontia and Pandateria – the third generation of imperial women to enjoy such solitude.

However, Caligula did not survive for much longer. He, Milonia Caesonia, and their daughter, Julia Drusilla, were murdered outside a theatre in January AD 41, in a conspiracy led by Cassius Chaerea. Julia's brains were dashed out.

Two other men who had come under suspicion after the attempted 'Three Dagger' coup were the prodigiously cruel prefect of the Praetorian Guard, Ofonius Tigellinus (*c.* AD 10–69), and Lucius Annaeus Seneca, Seneca the Younger (*c.* 4 BC–AD 65). Like Lepidus, both also shared the dubious distinction of allegedly having affairs with Caligula's sisters Agrippina Minor in AD 58 and Livilla in AD 41, for which Seneca had been exiled by Claudius to Corsica. In AD 39 Tigellinus was banished when he was found guilty of adultery with Agrippina and Livilla. Two years later he was recalled by Claudius. To complicate matters further, Tigellinus is also alleged to have had affairs with Domitius and Marcus Vinicius – the husbands of the two princesses.

Valeria Messalina was the third wife of Claudius, paternal cousin of Nero, second cousin of Caligula, and great-grandniece of Augustus. Claudius declined the Senate's offer to honour Messalina with the title of Augusta; fifty years later, Juvenal alluded to this when he described Messalina as 'the whore Augusta' ('*meretrix Augusta*'), itself an allusion to Propertius' description of Cleopatra as the 'whore queen', '*meretrix regina*'. To Dio, Messalina was little more than 'an adulteress and harlot ... for in addition to her shameless behaviour in general, she at times sat as a prostitute in the Imperial palace, and compelled other women of the highest rank to do the same.'[1] It was not long before a very insecure Messalina began her campaign to eliminate potential obstacles to her son's succession. That son was Britannicus.

The first to go was Pompeius Magnus (AD 30–47), the husband of Claudius's daughter Antonia, who was stabbed while in bed with a favourite catamite.[2] However, Messalina went too far when, in the same year, she ordered the execution of the celebrated Decimus Velerius Asiaticus, lauded as the first Gaul to win a consulship. He was the husband of Lollia Saturnia, the sister of Caligula's third wife, Lollia Paulina; his immense wealth allowed him to purchase and develop the sumptuous gardens of Lucullus, the renowned general, politician and gourmet. Messalina coveted these gardens, and was similarly motivated by jealousy towards the beautiful Poppaea Sabina (the mother of Nero's wife), with whom Asiaticus was having an affair. Sabina was also a rival to Messalina's own affections for Mnester, the famous Greek dancer. Asiaticus was arrested by Publius Suillius Rufus while holidaying in Baiae, and was accused of adultery with Poppaea, bribing the army (therefore treason), and, worst of all, of effeminacy – the humiliating and derogatory opposite of *virtus*, that true badge of Roman manhood. Messalina was able to persuade Claudius that executing Asiaticus was the only option; Asiaticus duly opened his veins, concluding resignedly that he was the victim of 'a woman's guile' (*fraus muliebris*). Poppaea committed suicide soon afterwards.

The elimination of Asiaticus – without trial – was a serious miscalculation on Messalina's part. This, alongside the animosity aroused by the greedy bullying of Suillius and the order to exile Polybius, won the empress no friends and considerable unpopularity. Polybius was one of Claudius's freedmen, a reliable and faithful researcher; he was eventually executed for alleged crimes against the state, trumped up by Messalina when he outstayed his welcome as a lover.[3] On the other hand, Lucius Vitellius, an ally of Agrippina the Younger's, managed to attach himself to the court of Claudius.

Suetonius tells the strange story of Vitellius' shoe fetish; he would beg Messalina to allow him to remove her shoes, whereupon he would secrete one of them in his clothing, removing it from time to time to kiss it. This was not Vitellius' only paraphilia; he was also in the habit of mixing the saliva of a freedwoman mistress with honey, before using it as a lotion for his neck and throat.[4]

Messalina's greatest and most bizarre *faux pas*, however, was her bigamous marriage to Gaius Silius (born *c*. AD 13) in AD 48, and then allowing the couple's plot to kill Claudius to be discovered. According to Tacitus – who was himself astonished by the fantasy of it all – her adulterous affairs had become so routine and casual that she drifted, trance-like, into 'unheard-of lust'.[5] Messalina forced Silius to divorce his wife, Junia Silana. The lavish wedding of Messalina and Silius was marked by 'prodigious infamy' complete with a bridal gown, witnesses, sacrifices, a wild Bacchanalia of a party, and breakfast. It all took place while an oblivious Claudius was at Ostia.[6] The disarmingly naïve plan was for Silius to adopt Britannicus, so that he and Messalina could rule on behalf of her son until he came of age; he was then aged seven. Tiberius Claudius Narcissus exposed their sham marriage and their plot to kill Claudius, using two of Claudius's mistresses, Calpurnia and Cleopatra, as messengers. Narcissus was another of Claudius's freedmen, and wielded great influence in the imperial court. Like the other freedmen, Narcissus would have been particularly stung and unnerved by the treatment meted out to Polybius; Messalina's clumsy machinations had lost her the invaluable support of the freedmen surrounding the emperor.

Meanwhile, furniture and possessions were coming out of the imperial palace destined for Silius's house, while an infatuated Messalina showered him with gifts. The partying and fantasy came to an abrupt end, however, when Messalina realised that she had been betrayed by Narcissus. Claudius reacted to the news of the coup with incredulity, asking repeatedly if he was still emperor. Understandably, he was both incandescent and intractable. In desperation, Messalina invoked her children and enlisted the support of Vibidia – the influential chief Vestal Virgin – who demanded that Messalina be allowed to plead her case. The farce was heightened further when Messalina attempted to forestall the returning emperor and win sympathy by hitching a lift on a cart full of garden rubbish.[7] Of course, the cuckolded Claudius was having none of it – although, under pressure from Vibidia, he promised Messalina that he would attend to the matter the following day, while she reflected on the enormity of her stupidity and cupidity in the appropriated gardens of Lucullus.

By now Claudius was 'on fire, exploding with threats'. The guard was briefed, and proceeded to arrest and execute Silius and other complicit *equites*. Mnester, in an attempt to escape any blame, showed Claudius' men the whip marks from Messalina's flagellation, but was not spared – after all, he was a dancer, *histrio*, and how could a dancer be pardoned when so many illustrious men were dying? Likewise, Sextus Traulus Montanus who one night had suffered the indignity of being summoned for sex and then immediately dismissed by a capricious Messalina, was also executed. Perversely, Suilius Caesonius was spared because

Messalina had forced him to play the role of a woman in a squalid orgy. Claudius presumably thought that he had suffered enough.

Messalina was joined in the gardens by her mother, Domitia Lepida the Younger – this was an extraordinary act of *pietas* and matronly behaviour on her part, considering the gulf that had divided them for many years. Desperate and angry letters were written, while copious amounts of wine helped Claudius to calm down and adopt a more lenient attitude to his remorseful wife – he was now describing her sympathetically as 'the poor woman'; anger was now giving way to love (*amor*), and the fear, according to Tacitus, was that he would submit to 'memories of the conjugal bed'.[8]

Narcissus saw this and realised that the whole affair could rebound on him. He moved quickly; Claudius's soldiers arrived in the gardens, Domitia Lepida advised her daughter to commit suicide. Messalina did not have the courage, and botched the attempt; she was then run through with a soldier's sword. Claudius received the news while dining and reacted with indifference, continuing his feast. Suetonius, to illustrate Claudius's 'absent-mindedness and myopia', adds that Claudius actually asked where Messalina was when she failed to turn up for dinner that night.

Juvenal was savagely censorious of Messalina, and must take some of the responsibility for the scandalous reception Messalina has endured down the ages. Pliny the Elder, who was less cynical and possibly more objective, also had his part to play, as of course did Tacitus and Dio. Messalina was easy prey for Juvenal; to him, she was the *meretrix Augusta*, stealing out of the imperial bedchamber, while Claudius slept, for a night on her back on a mat in a brothel. According to Juvenal, she wore a hood and a blonde wig to conceal her familiar, recognisable black hair, and checked into her personal cell in a fetid whorehouse. There she prostituted herself, using the working name 'Lycisca' ('Wolf Bitch'). She stuck out her belly, indicating, 'The stomach you were in, noble Britannicus.' Juvenal states that Messalina was always the last of the girls to leave, staying until the very last minute, with 'her clitoris still burning and stiff with lust'; to Juvenal, the clitoral erection betrayed Messalina's penis envy. She may have been worn out by the men, Juvenal records, but she still went home unsated, taking the stench of the brothel back to the imperial bed with her.[9]

In *Satire 10*, Juvenal revisits Messalina in a reference to her sham marriage to Silius and the catch-22 decision he had to make: refuse the marriage and he would die, but to accept was also a death sentence.[10] Pliny the Elder gives us the unedifying story of Messalina's epic orgy, in which she challenged a veteran prostitute to a twenty-four-hour sex marathon. The empress won with a score of twenty-five partners – an average of just under one client per hour.[11] The context in which this appears is an expatiation on the mating of animals, and Pliny's revelation that man is the only animal for which copulation is insatiable – Messalina's victory provides the evidence. Tacitus lists twelve of her distinguished equestrian lovers, who paid for their lust with their lives. Dio describes Messalina's group-sex sessions, attended by the husbands of the women involved; those who complied were rewarded, but those who declined to prostitute their wives were murdered. Messalina concealed these orgies from Claudius by providing a ready supply of slave women for his bed.[12]

Agrippina the Younger was born in AD 16 near modern Cologne, a great-granddaughter of Augustus, sister of Caligula, niece *and* fourth wife of the emperor Claudius, and mother of the emperor Nero. Pliny the Elder tells us that Agrippina the Younger had a double set of canines in her right jaw – a rare dental condition but, because it was on the right, a good omen.[13] Approximately 2 per cent of adults have supernumerary teeth. Apart from this, all we know of Agrippina's physical appearance is that she was attractive. Tacitus notes that she is beautiful; he rather spoils the picture by adding that she was also depraved. Dio describes her as beautiful (*kale*)[14], while we also know that Nero – in a macabre post-mortem scene – found her corpse to be beautiful [15]. Her succession of lovers probably confirms that she was physically and sexually attractive. Agrippina was in good shape for most of her life; aged forty-three, and after a night's feasting, she was able to swim for her life in the March seas of the Bay of Naples when the attempt on her life ended in shipwreck.

Agrippina gave birth to a son in December AD 37 – her only natural child. She called him Lucius Domitius Ahenobarbus; later, he would become better known as Nero. Suetonius tells of numerous omens, the most significant of which was that the baby was bathed in a shaft of morning sunlight, even before his father could make the traditional symbolic gesture of touching him on the ground to symbolise his crucial connectivity with earth.[16] Chaldean astronomers gave Agrippina some very good news, that Nero would one day be emperor; but there was bad news too – he would also kill his mother. Agrippina was quite unphased and replied, 'Let him kill her, just so long as he is emperor.'

Suetonius was contemptuous of Domitius, Nero's father, calling him loathsome in every way imaginable. It is not difficult to see why he detested him: Domitius' atrocities included murdering a freedman of his when he refused to drink as much as he was ordered to. He also deliberately whipped up his horses and ran over a boy in a village on the Appian Way; and, in the Forum, knocked out the eye of an equestrian when the equestrian publicly criticised him. He was a notorious cheat, swindling bankers and, as Praetor, charioteers of their prize money; he was a serial womaniser: Tiberius charged him with treason, adultery and incest with his sister, Domitia Lepida the Younger (born 10 BC)... but Caligula saved him.

The good fortune promised by the fortuitous shaft of sunlight was cancelled out by the breech delivery that Agrippina endured, a bad omen. Pliny the Elder wrote that breech deliveries were unnatural, and explains why babies born feet first are called Agrippa or Agrippina – they were born with difficulty (*aegre partus*)[16] Marcus Agrippa was the only child thus born to come of any good, but even he was blighted by lameness; worse, his legacy was the two Agrippinas, who left Caligula and Nero to the world. When Domitius was congratulated on the birth of his son, he ominously quipped that anything born to himself and Agrippina was bound to be a despicable danger to the public.[17]

According to Suetonius, Agrippina tried to seduce the noble and wealthy Servius Sulpicius Galba, the future Emperor, and draw him away from his wife, Aemilia Lepida. But no match could tempt him; not even Agrippina, who blatantly went for Galba even though her husband had recently died and Lepida was still very much on the scene. Lepida's mother rebuked her in front of a crowd of *matronae*, even going so far as to give her a good slap for her impudence.[18] Galba's dynastic credentials were impeccable, and just in case anyone doubted this, he carried around with him a copy of his family tree, going all the way back to Jupiter.

In the meantime, Agrippina was now having an affair with Marcus Antonius Pallas (born *c*. AD 1), a former slave of Antonia Minor. He was another of Claudius's trusted freedmen advisors, in charge of the treasury. Apart from influencing both Claudius and Agrippina, Pallas initiated the law which allowed a freedwoman who married a slave to keep her freedom (so long as the slave's master agreed), a law for which he received much acclaim. He had failed to take Narcissus into account who was planning to bring about Agrippina's downfall by revealing her affair with Pallas to

Claudius. Narcissus had joined forces with Britannicus, Nero's rival for the succession.

The imperial household was in chaos – who was to be Claudius's next wife, his fourth?[19] Claudius vowed to remain celibate after the Messalina bigamy fiasco, even promising his guards, presumably with tongue-in-cheek, that they must kill him if he broke his word. That, of course, did not happen, but he did have the law changed to allow uncles to marry nieces – paving the way for him to wed Agrippina, a relationship which, until the timely change in the law, was blatantly incestuous. This scandal was made worse by Claudius's inappropriate references to his new bride as his daughter and foster-child, born and bred on his lap. To Tacitus, the union represented the acme of Agrippina's depravity; in the *Octavia*, attributed to Seneca, the nurse describes the imperial marriage bed as the font of all evil, and their marriage as illegal and lamentable.[20]

The contest for Claudius's hand generated a seething pit of intrigue at Rome. The intensely competitive contenders were Lollia Paulina, championed by the wealthy freedman Gaius Julius Callistus, secretary responsible for justice and law, and Agrippina, backed by Pallas. Narcissus tipped Aelia Paetina, who had already had the misfortune of being Claudius's second wife.[21]

Tacitus records that Agrippina, described as 'unyielding in her hatred' abhorred Paulina, showing her nothing but odium and hostility. Paulina had enjoyed something of a reputation for extravagance and ostentation; Pliny the Elder[22] records how she wore the best part of her inheritance to a dinner party one night, decked out, Cleopatra-like, in 40 million sesterces worth of jewels. In case anyone doubted the value of her jewelry, she made sure to carry the receipts with her available for inspection.[23] At around the same time, another noble woman, *inlustris femina*, Calpurnia, was exiled for ten years because Claudius offended Agrippina when he praised her beauty. Agrippina only stopped short of having her executed when she realised that Claudius had no serious designs on her.

Aelia Paetina, the wealthy owner of a pottery, had married Claudius in AD 28, and in AD 30 their only child was born: Claudia Antonia. By AD 38 Claudius had divorced Paetina for 'slighter offences' significantly 'slighter' than the offences of scandalous unchastity and suspected murder committed by his first wife, Plautia Urgulanilla, whom he had married in AD 9. Her daughter, Claudia, was born five months after her divorce from Claudius: she was the illegitimate daughter of Claudius's freedman, Boter.

Claudius repudiated the baby and left her, naked, on Urgulanilla's doorstep.

Their son, Drusus, was betrothed to one of the daughters of Sejanus, but he died when he choked on a pear which he had playfully thrown up in the air and caught in his mouth. Yet more scandal followed in AD 24, when Urgulanilla's brother, Plautius Silvana, threw his wife, Apronia, out of a window to her death. She was preceded by two failed betrothals: the first was to Aemilia Lepida, which broke off after her mother, Julia the Younger, was disgraced in AD 8; the second was to Livia Medullina, who died on her wedding day.[24]

As we have seen, Agrippina made use of her charms to seduce Claudius. Her position as a niece allowed her a unique intimacy in which the lines between avuncular affection and sexual gratification were very blurred. Suetonius tells of the kisses and caresses she deployed to impassion Claudius; more crucially, however, Claudius would have seen that Agrippina brought political benefits. She had ancestries in both the Julian and Claudian dynasties – the former through her mother, and the latter through her father, the ever-popular Germanicus, who was grandfather to Nero. Marriage to Agrippina would clearly eliminate the inconvenient Julio-Claudian rivalry that was rife, and make his regime more palatable to the troublemakers in the Senate.

Agrippina eventually prevailed, and Claudius married her on 1 January AD 49 – after the sycophantic Lucius Vitellius the Elder had secured a vote in the Senate recommending that Claudius marry again. According to Tacitus, the union between Claudius and Agrippina was confirmed by 'rumour and by their illicit love'.[25] Vitellius argued that Agrippina had all the credentials for an imperial wife. She could look after Claudius's 'domestic concerns' and be his 'companion in good times and bad, in whom he could confide his most intimate thoughts and to whom he could entrust his little children'. Agrippina, he went on, had a fine and famous lineage; she was fertile and she was morally impeccable, the perfect *matrona*. Vitellius won the day, the law against incest was amended (the scandalous amendment was not repealed until AD 342), and the couple married, with great celebration among the fickle senators.[26]

Soon after her wedding to Claudius, Agrippina had Paulina arrested on spurious charges of witchcraft – more specifically, consorting with Chaldean astrologers and magicians, and consulting the oracle of Apollo at Colophon about her marriage. Despite a sham eulogy on her fine lineage by Claudius, her property and most of her wealth was summarily confiscated and she was exiled. Claudius was led to believe that she was a public danger (*perniciosa*), and that her potential for criminal activity had to be expunged. Paulina was later forced to commit suicide, on Agrippina's orders; she must have taken something of a beating as well, because when her head was brought back to Rome, Agrippina could only identify it by Paulina's dentition – which had identifiable abnormalities like her own.

According to Dio, Agrippina now had Claudius exactly where she wanted him. For Tacitus, their marriage was historically pivotal, as it altered the whole complexion of the Roman state; in effect, all Romans now obeyed a woman. Agrippina did not make a laughing stock of Rome through her lubriciousness as was the case with Messalina, but she did rather worse by imposing a masculine kind of servitude, *quasi virile servitium*. Once again we see powerful qualities in a woman interpreted as male characteristics. In public, Agrippina was strict and somewhat superior – but privately, with Claudius, she was chaste unless she could use *impudicitia* as a shortcut to power. She was extremely venal, on the pretext that the accumulation of wealth was necessary to support her reign. The attempts by Claudius to make incest respectable by changing the law, then later punishing Silanus and Junia Lepida for the same offence, were seen as hypocritical and risible.

However, the Senate was beginning to have concerns about Agrippina's power. According to Tacitus, this is when things started to go wrong for Agrippina. AD 54 was a bad year for the omens. Tacitus records how a blood-raining comet was seen (often a warning of the death of a king or queen) and standards and tents burst into spontaneous flame, struck by lightning. Bees swarmed around the pedestal of the Capitol, babies were delivered half-human and half-beast, and a pig was born with the claws of a hawk. Every official office suffered a death: one quaestor, one aedile, one tribune, one praetor, and one consul died. In the same year, it was recorded by Phlegon that a Syrian woman in Mevania in Agrippina's service turned into a man the night before her wedding.[27] However, what terrified Agrippina the most was when a drunken Claudius tactlessly let slip that it was his fate to suffer his wife's shameful acts and then to punish her for it. Tacitus records it as 'it's my fate to suffer my wife's fornication', whereas Suetonius neatly transcribes it as 'all my marriages were unchaste, but not all were unchecked'. Frightened by this, Agrippina resolved to act quickly.[28]

Agrippina's jealousy drove her to murder Domitia Lepida – sister of Gnaeus Domitius Ahenobarbus, mother of Messalina, and grandmother of Britannicus. Domitia had unwisely considered herself to be as much of a celebrity as Agrippina and, as Tacitus states, little separated the two in terms of beauty, age, or wealth. Indeed, they were both notoriously immoral and violent women. The burning issue, however, was their competition with each other over Nero; Lepida tried blandishments and indulgence to win him over, while Agrippina was harsh and threatening. Lepida had to be disposed of, for womanly reasons (*muliebribus causis*) – she was charged, and sentenced to death, with the attempted murder of Agrippina through magic, and with keeping unruly slave gangs in Calabria. Narcissus, ever the champion of Britannicus, looked on in horror, seeing Agrippina as more repellent now than Messalina ever was; she was totally without honour, modesty, and chastity. He retired to Sinuessa through ill health.

Agrippina now saw her chance to murder Claudius and install Nero on the imperial throne: the only question was the type of poison to use. Anxious that Claudius might recant on his death bed and rehabilitate Britannicus if a slow-working poison was used and aware that an aggressive, instantaneously acting toxin would be incriminating, she compromised with a venom that would drive him insane before delivering a slow death. Locusta, a lady proficient in pharmacology with a criminal conviction hanging over her head for poisoning, *veneficii damnata*, was enlisted. The poison was prepared; it was to be administered by a eunuch, Halotus, a regular dish taster. Tacitus says that a particularly juicy mushroom was smeared with the poison but failed to be effective; a terrified Agrippina called in Claudius' physician, Gaius Stertinius Xenophon, who was in on the plot, so that he could introduce a poisoned feather into Claudius' throat, pretending to make him vomit. Suetonius, too, subscribes to the mushroom theory telling how Nero later quoted the Greek proverb which describes mushrooms as the 'food of the gods' – *cibus deorum*. What exactly killed Claudius is open to speculation; fungi, of course, are unpredictable things and it may be that Claudius died of an accidental poisoning, malaria or natural causes. Whatever the cause, Nero, Agrippina's sixteen-year-old son, was now Emperor of Rome.

Suetonius records (*Nero* 26) that Nero's celebrated descent into lust, greed and notorious cruelty was a gradual development. Nevertheless, it was not long before he was donning a cap as a sort of disguise and doing the rounds of the cookshops by night looking for trouble and whores, assaulting people and looting markets, the spoils from which were sold off back in the palace. Once he was nearly killed by a senator whose wife he had assaulted. His public banquets were frequented by prostitutes plying their trade; his river boat shuffles down the Tiber or at Ostia or Baiae were noted for the pop-up taverns he had set up full of respectable women who played the part of whores and solicited him as he sailed past. The Vestal Virgins did not escape his clutches; he raped one called Rubria.

History seemed to be repeating itself. Just as Livia fell out irrevocably with her son, Tiberius, then so did Agrippina with Nero. A freedwoman called Claudia Acte was the catalyst for the rift between Nero and his mother. Nero much preferred this exciting young girl, who satisfied his adulterous desires, to his noble and virtuous wife Octavia, whom he had grown to despise. At the same time, to make the situation worse, two fashionable young men-about-town insinuated themselves into Nero's life – Marcus Salvius Otho (the future emperor) and Claudius Senecio.

Tacitus tells us that when Agrippina found out about Acte, she, predictably, raged as only a woman or a mother can, incensed at having to compete with a former slave girl and at the prospect of having a maid as her daughter-in-law.[30] The nastier his mother's reproaches, the more Nero burned with love for Acte, until the power of that love began to turn him against Agrippina. He took solace in Seneca and Annaeus Serenus, who had been complicit in Nero's affair from the start – even to the extent that Serenus had posed as Acte's lover, in order to divert suspicion. Nero was so besotted with Acte that at some point during their three-year affair he expressed a desire to marry her; he had a family tree fabricated which showed how her ancestry was linked with King Attalus of Pergamum, and he bribed some ex-consuls to swear to her royal birthright.[31] Agrippina soon realised the futility of her inflexibility, and adopted a more indulgent and generous approach. She offered Nero and Acte the use of her bedroom, plied him with gifts, and admitted that her earlier severity had been intemperate.

Too late; Agrippina was now isolated, and easy prey to anyone seeking revenge. One such predator was Junia Silana. We have already seen how she was embroiled in Messalina's plot to murder Claudius, and how she was forced to divorce her husband, Gaius Silius. Junia was noted for her lineage, her looks and her lascivious behaviour and had once been a friend of Agrippina. However, this friendship soured when Agrippina deterred the noble Titus Sextius Africanus from marrying Junia – Agrippina gossiped that Junia was a loose woman, and 'past it'. Tacitus says that Agrippina had no designs on Africanus herself, but rather she was trying to keep her friend, the childless (and heirless) wealthy widow out of the grasp of an obvious bounty hunter – probably because she had an eye on her friend's legacy herself. Junia did not appreciate Agrippina's uncharacteristic altruism, and saw her chance for revenge.

Her plot entailed accusing Agrippina of inciting Rubellius Plautus, son of Tiberius' granddaughter Julia, to overthrow Nero, marrying him, making Plautus Emperor and taking over Rome together. Paris, a regular and usually jovial visitor to Nero's chamber at that time of night, was deputed to tell Nero this sorry tale. Nero was terrified; his immediate reaction was to murder Agrippina and Plautus and remove Burrus, a noted ally of his mother, from his position as head of the Praetorian Guard. A frightened Nero was keen to kill his mother – but others, Seneca and Burrus in particular, advised caution: Agrippina would indeed be executed if found guilty but she must be allowed, and seen, to defend herself; moreover, there was only one accuser in the case and he was not particularly reliable: in short, it was getting late, they had enjoyed a convivial evening and it was all getting a bit out of hand and silly.[32]

Agrippina got her defence: Burra and Seneca visited Agrippina the following morning and read the charges for her to deny, or to confess and suffer the penalty. She responded with her usual ferocity, demanding to know how Junia could possibly know how a mother feels, spitting out that parents do not change their children as often as disreputable women like Junia change their adulterous men. She proceeded then to discredit all the guilty parties, winning Nero's permission to reward her supporters and wreak vengeance on her accusers. Paris, however, escaped punishment: he was too prominent and popular a player in Nero's nocturnal debaucheries. Altogether, a remarkable display of Agrippina's power over Nero, even at a time when the relationship between mother and son was at its lowest ebb.

In AD 58, Agrippina and Rome were threatened by another *impudicitia*, in the person of Poppaea Sabina. Tacitus tells us that she was a woman who had everything – everything, that is, apart from honesty.[33] She inherited glory and good looks from her exceptionally beautiful mother; she was rich, and a *docta puella*. She preached modesty but practiced salaciousness. She was something of a recluse, but when she did go out she wore a veil – either to tantalise men or to accentuate the allure of her beauty. She cared nothing for her reputation, and made no distinction between married men and adulterers; she never lost control of herself, and she was never controlled by a man. Where there was a chance of personal advancement, her lust came to the fore. Nero composed a poem which celebrated her striking auburn hair, triggering a fashionable new hairstyle among the women of Rome. Her predilection for bathing in asses' milk also started a craze, as did 'Poppaea's Cream' – an anti-aging lotion which eradicated wrinkles. According to Dio, Poppaea believed it when someone told her that in milk 'lurked a magic which would dispel all diseases and blights from her beauty'.[34]

Poppaea was first married to Rufinius Crispinus; they had a son together. She later had an affair with the libertine Otho, Nero's very good friend, which ended in divorce for Crispinus and a sham marriage to Otho. Tactlessly and annoyingly Otho would praise Poppaea to the Emperor, ever reminding him of her beauty and elegance, endlessly going on about her nobility and fine looks. Nero and Poppaea were already having an affair themselves and when Nero came to claim her back, he was refused access in a highly comedic scene in which the emperor of Rome was reduced to little more than a locked-out lover – that pathetic stock character of the Latin love elegists, the *exclusus amator*. She coquettishly led him on, coaxing him, 'I'm a married woman; you still love Acte, your servile concubine.'[35] He grew more and more frustrated. Poppaea emphasised the difference between the fine lifestyle she enjoyed with her one-of-a-kind Otho, and Nero's grubby, low-life, servile relationship. Otho was soon removed from the scene, posted to a governorship in far-off Lusitania to contemplate his tactlessness.[36]

The following year, in AD 59, Nero's passion for Poppaea grew all the more intense. She had hopes of marrying the emperor, but realised that this was unrealistic while Agrippina was still around. Accordingly, she set about nagging him, accusing him of being under his mother's thumb. An artful adulteress, she cited her own beauty, lineage, fertility, and sincerity in contrast to his mother's arrogance and greed. Poppaea's aim was persuade Nero to assassinate his mother, paving the way for him to then marry her. According to Dio, Seneca also urged Nero to commit matricide.[37]

Dio describes Poppaea's extravagance, narcissism and vanity: she shod the donkeys which pulled her carriage with golden shoes, and had milked daily 500 asses that had recently foaled so that she could bathe in their milk. One day, she caught sight of herself in a mirror and thought that maybe she did not look quite so beautiful; she then prayed that she would die before she passed her best.

Agrippina was not to be outdone. Tacitus records how Cluvius relates that Agrippina, in a bid to compete and maintain her influence, would dress up provocatively at around midday and offer up her body to Nero, who was already drunk by that time.[38] However, the lascivious kisses and shameful caresses did not go unnoticed; Seneca enlisted Acte's help, believing that only a woman could help against another woman's blandishments. Acte told Nero that his disgraceful incest was public knowledge, that Agrippina was glorying in spreading it about, and, crucially, that it was weakening his position with the Praetorian Guard. Tacitus believes that Agrippina fully understood the enormity of her incestuous actions and knew exactly what she was doing: such perverted lust was only to be expected from a woman who had indulged in *stuprum* with Lepidus and then Pallas, and had married her own uncle. Rumour had it that Agrippina and Nero had sex every time they shared a litter, proven by the state their clothes were in when they emerged onto the street. Suetonius adds that Agrippina was later deterred from further incest with Nero by her enemies, who gossiped that having sexual relations with him would only make him harder to tame and more despotic.

Nero obviously missed the sex with Agrippina. His reaction was to find another woman who looked exactly like his mother. He found one and, according to Dio, 'when he toyed with the girl herself or displayed her charms to others, he would say that he was wont to have intercourse with his mother.'

By now Agrippina, perhaps fearing the worst, began to spend more time at her villas outside Rome at Tusculum and Antium. Nero had had enough of his meddlesome mother and determined to murder her, the only question being whether it be by poison, sword or some other violent means. Like Tiberius before him, he had threatened to abdicate and go into exile on Rhodes; he had her pestered with irritating law suits and he hired mobs to jeer loudly and insultingly outside her house – the anti-social behaviour was all to no avail. Any plot was fraught with problems, not least Agrippina's paranoid but prudent habit of taking prophylactic antidotes against poisons.

Shipwreck and sabotage were the answer. Anicetus, commander of the fleet at Misenum came up with the ingenious idea of building a ship with a section which would fall away at sea and throw Agrippina overboard. Dio says that the idea was inspired by a ship Anicetus had seen in the theatre which automatically split in two, let out some animals, and then came together again, quite seaworthy. A similar vessel was built while Nero showered his mother with flattery and devotion to put her off her guard. The festival of Minerva, the Quinquatria, at Baiae was chosen as the time and place; the special boat, built in Agrippina's honour and magnificently decked out, was placed at her disposal. However, Agrippina got wind of the plot and travelled to Baiae by litter. After an extended banquet at which a good time was had by all, Nero dutifully escorted his mother to the vessel which she boarded with her attendants, Crepereius Gallus and Acerronia Polla. Everyone was happy that Nero and Agrippina had seemingly been reconciled. Then, at a signal, the lead-lined canopy collapsed into the boat, killing Gallus outright. Acerronia and Agrippina survived this, but the boat did not sink as planned and the crew had to scuttle it. Acerronia pretended to be Agrippina and screamed for help; she was battered to death by oars and poles, while the injured Agrippina was able to swim to safety; she was picked up by some boats.[39]

Suetonius' version is even more melodramatic; he says that Nero was irritated by his mother's overbearing behaviour and made three attempts to poison her but was thwarted by timely antidotes and she survived. Nero then attempted to crush her with a mechanical ceiling suspended over her bed. When this failed because of a tip off, he had a collapsible boat built on which the cabin would fall in on itself, or it would be shipwrecked when boats rammed it. In the event Agrippina sailed to Baiae in her own boat; a collision was deliberately staged in which her galley was damaged. For the return journey, a happy Nero escorted her to the quay where he kissed her breasts before she boarded the custom-built boat which had been offered on account of the damage to her own galley.

Dio's version is that on reaching Bauli, Nero gave a series of sumptuous banquets over several days at which he entertained his mother 'with every show of friendliness... he embraced her at the close of dinner about midnight, and straining her to his breast, kissed her eyes and hands, exclaiming, 'Strength and good health to you, mother. For you I live and because of you I rule.' Though the ship parted asunder and Agrippina fell into the water, she did not perish. Notwithstanding that it was dark and that she was glutted with strong drink and that the sailors used their oars against her with such force that they killed Acerronia Polla, her companion on the trip, she nevertheless reached shore safely.[40]

A detachment of armed men arrived at Agrippina's house, broke down the door and entered her bedroom, where she waited with one maid. The maid deserted her. Agrippina declared that Nero was not to blame in the boating incident, stating, 'But if you have come here to commit a crime, I believe my son is not involved, he would not murder his own mother.' One of the officers smashed her on the head with a club; when the other drew his sword to finish her off, she shouted, 'Strike my womb!' (*ventrem feri*) – a dying reference to Nero. Dio is more explicit: '... she knew for what they had come, and leaping up from her bed she tore open her clothing, exposing her stomach, and cried out, 'Strike here, Anicetus, strike here, because this bore Nero!'[41]

Tacitus believes that some sources insisted that Nero then displayed an unhealthy interest in his mother's corpse; Nero ran off to look at the murdered body, fondling the limbs, finding fault with other parts, taking a drink when he got thirsty. For Dio, the suggestions of necrophilia are more opaque, but just as sinister:

> ... the deed was so monstrous that he was overwhelmed by incredulity; he therefore desired to behold the victim of his crime with his own eyes. So he laid bare her body, looked her all over, and inspected her wounds, finally uttering a remark far more abominable than even than even the murder. His words were: 'I did not know I had such a beautiful mother.'[42]

It comes as no surprise that the omens were not good. One woman gave birth to a snake, while another was struck by lightning while she was having sex with her husband; the sun went out, and the fourteen districts of Rome were struck by lightning. Nevertheless, after a triumphant return to Rome, Tacitus tells us that Nero '... then immersed himself in all sorts of debaucheries, from which hitherto a kind of respect for Agrippina had not exactly restrained him, but had modulated his behaviour'.

Nero was not averse to physically abusing his wives. He had tried to strangle his first wife, Octavia, on three occasions. This politically contrived marriage bored him; he loathed her because she was popular and the daughter of an emperor, so he divorced her on the grounds that she was barren. Poppaea Sabina her rival, however, was not satisfied; Tacitus tells us how she had one of Octavia's slave girls denounce Octavia for adultery with an Alexandrian flautist called Eucaerus. 'Witnesses' refused to condemn her, even under torture. As we know, one such brave witness was Pythias, a slave girl who stood up for Octavia under interrogation and torture; she defiantly spat in the face of her interrogator, Tigellinus, when he questioned Octavia's virtue, exclaiming, 'My mistress's [vagina] is cleaner than your mouth!'[43] Octavia was banished to Campania under military guard.

Poppaea urged Nero to finish off Octavia, so he bribed Anicetus to allege that he had been having an affair with Octavia. Nero announced that Octavia had plotted to take over the fleet by seducing Anicetus, and that she had undergone an abortion (conveniently forgetting his charge of infertility) to hide her libidinous behaviour. Nero exiled her to Pandateria, where she was told of her impending death a few days later. Octavia invoked the name of Agrippina, but to no avail. She was tied up and her veins were cut, and to speed things up she was placed in a very hot bath. Her head was presented to Poppaea in Rome.[44]

Nero later kicked Poppaea to death when she was heavily pregnant; she had complained of being ill, and had had the temerity to scold him for returning late from the races. Tacitus says that she was buried in the Mausoleum of Augustus; her body was not cremated (according to Roman custom), but was stuffed with spices and embalmed in the Oriental way.[45]

The aftermath of Poppaea's death led to even more psychotic and unbalanced behaviour in Nero. He missed Poppaea so much that he kidnapped and debauched a woman who resembled her; later, he had a boy called Sporus castrated since he also resembled Poppaea, and he abused him as a wife. In time, although he was already 'married' to Pythagoras (a freedman), he also 'married' Sporus, in Greece. Tigellinus gave the eunuch away at the sham wedding; Nero provided a dowry, and laid on the wedding ceremony. His wedding to Pythagoras in AD 64 also took place in full regalia, with Nero wearing a bridal veil, with dowry, marriage bed, and torches all on public view. Now Nero had two men in his bed – Pythagoras played the role of his husband, and Sporus that of his wife. The latter was called 'lady', 'queen' and 'mistress'.

Antonia, Claudius's daughter, was selected to take Poppaea's place, but she refused. Her defiance led to her execution on a charge of attempting a coup. Nero raped Aulus Plautius and then killed him, declaring that Agrippina could now come and kiss his successor – Nero believed that she had conducted an affair with Plautius, and had backed him in a takeover bid for the throne. Nero had Poppaea's son from an earlier marriage, Rufrius Crispinus, killed by the boy's own slaves while he was out fishing – the pretext was that Rufrius had been playing 'generals and emperors' – this was seen as treasonable. Nero drove Seneca to suicide in

AD 65, and poisoned Burrus with a toxic cough medicine. Seneca planned for his wife, Pompeia Paulina, to die with him, but she survived her suicide attempt when Nero's henchmen interceded and administered an antidote.

The later Flavian emperors were serial divorcers, and adulterous too, as was Domitian's wife Domitia. Vespasian (r. 69–79) married Flavia Domitilla, who had been the mistress of Statilus Capilla; when she died he turned to Antonia Cenis, a former mistress whom he could not marry because she was a freedwoman – but they lived together as man and wife. She was the secretary of Antonia Minor, mother of the emperor Claudius and, according to Dio, was blessed with a prodigious memory. She wielded considerable influence with the emperor, carrying out official imperial business on his behalf and making herself very rich into the bargain through selling governorships, procuratorships, generalships and priesthoods. Vespasian's younger son, Domitian, despised her because she was not one of the family.

Vespasian was the first emperor to tax public lavatories, a move which was unpopular not just with the Romans but with his family – when the money came Vespasian smelled it and announced that it carried no offensive odour. French public urinals are called *vespasiennes* to this day. When a woman approached him to say that she loved him, he took her to bed and paid her 400,000 sesterces – accounted for as Vespasian's Seduction.

According to Suetonius, Vespasian's son, Titus (r. 79 –81), had an affair with Domitian's (his brother) wife. Domitia Longina denied it, asserting that if it had happened then she would have boasted about it.[46] After serving in Britannia and subduing the revolt led by Boudicca, Titus returned to Rome and married Arrecina Tertulla, daughter of a former prefect of the Praetorian Guard. She died in AD 65, at which point he married the distinguished Marcia Furnilla, whose sister was Marcia, the mother of the future emperor Trajan. Her family was involved in the opposition to Nero, the failed Pisonian conspiracy of AD 65. It seems likely that Titus divorced his new wife because of her family's involvement. He had married her for political expediency but this political hinterland spoiled it all. Titus never remarried.

Titus was a distinguished soldier and statesman but he was also deparaved to an inordinate degree. Catamites and eunuchs were everywhere, while androgynous young dancers swirled around him; it was the role of some of these eunuchs to drink his sperm. Titus entered the orbit of Queen Berenice, the Jewish Cleopatra and daughter of Herod Agrippa I; she was ruler of Chalcis in southern Lebanon with her brother Herod Agrippa II, King of Judaea, with whom she had, according to Juvenal, an incestuous relationship. Berenice first married one of her father's allies at the age of thirteen but was soon widowed. She then married her uncle Herod, king of Chalcis and bore him two sons before his death in AD 48; Berenice was twenty years old. King Polemo II of Pontus, king of Cilicia, was her next husband but, according to Juvenal and Josephus the Jewish historian, he failed to satisfy her and she returned to Agrippa to satisfy her licentiousness; Polemo had even gone to the trouble of getting circumcised for her. In AD 70, Titus showed up to recapture Jerusalem after which the couple lived together in Rome as man and wife. Senatorial opposition and the antipathy of his father forced Titus to choose between Berenice and the succession: he chose the latter. He died of malaria in AD 81.

Domitian, Vespasian's second son (r. AD 81 to 96), was forever harassing other mens' wives. As a young boy he had been something of a homosexual libertine: one of his famous affairs was with Claudius Pollo; another was with the future emperor, Nerva.

In AD 70 Vespasian had tried to arrange a dynastic marriage between Domitian and the daughter of Titus, his virgin niece Julia Flavia Titi. Domitian declined to take her as his wife, but was only too happy to seduce her once she had married T. Flavius Sabinus. Domitian made her pregnant and arranged the abortion which allegedly killed her. Julia was deified and her ashes were mixed with Domitian's on his death and secretly smoked by an old nurse in the Temple of the Flavians. Domitian had then insisted on marrying Domitia Longina, and even persuaded her husband, Lucius Aelius Lamia, to divorce her so that he could marry her himself. He later had Lamia executed for treason when he mentioned to Domitian, who had praised his voice, that he had given up sex and gone into training. Imperial confiscation of other men's wives was common practice: Augustus, when Octavian, appropriated Livia, pregnant with Julia; Caligula took both Lollia Paulina and Ceasonia from their husbands; and Nero deprived Otho of Poppaea.

Domitia herself had an affair with the actor Paris; Domitian reacted by murdering Paris and divorcing and exiling Domitia, despite the fact that he was conducting the affair with niece Julia at the time. The abortion and the reason for the exile are most probably examples of historians economising with the truth in order to vilify; her exile was more likely due to the fact that she failed to provide an heir. However that may be, Domitian could not bear to be separated and retied the knot with Domitia, who resumed her role as empress.[47]

As we know, Domitian had issues with the Vestal Virgins and their chastity – which he considered to have been compromised. He sentenced the Oculata sisters, Varronilla and the chief Vestal, Cornelia, to death as part of a programme of puritanical reforms intended to restore the moral health of Rome. Other extreme measures in AD 83 included making himself perpetual Censor and censoring libellous poetry, banning mime and dancing to eradicate their opportunities for satire, removing an ex quaestor from the senate because he was an avid dancer and actor; he removed the right of disgraced women to travel in litters, to receive legacies and inheritances, and he erased the name of an equestrian from the jurors' lists because he had taken back a wife whom he had previously divorced and accused of adultery.[48] Adultery was punishable with exile after he revived the *Lex Iulia de Adulteriis Coercendis*. Homosexual acts with boys of free birth were banned on penalty of death, as was castration, possibly to irritate Titus, who had a predilection for eunuchs. Castrated youths could no longer be sold to brothels, while those who predated the law were assigned minimum prices to deter such sales. Martial is quick to illuminate Domitian's hypocrisy in all of this, keeping, as he did, eunuchs in his palace while banning them in the empire.

To Domitian, Suetonius' 'man of excessive lust', sexual intercourse was 'bed-wrestling', which gives an idea perhaps of how physical he liked his sex to be.[49] Domitian was apparently very sensitive about his baldness, which he disguised by wearing wigs; he wrote a book on haircare, perhaps as a form of therapy. Nevertheless, he got his own back by habitually depilating his mistresses; he also frequently went swimming with common prostitutes.

Domitian was the first to introduce topless female gladiators into the arena, following this with female athletes at the games. The women gladiators were pitched against dwarfs to satisfy the Romans' fetish for and fascination with combatants with physical deformities. Women afflicted by scoliosis and other disabilities were popular as concubines and populated many a harem. The attraction of male dwarfs was in their outsized genitalia; Roman *matronae*, apparently, would go and watch them when they trained naked. Augustus kept a dwarf called Lucius; Caligula allowed his dwarfs to decide whether their able-bodied colleagues lived or died. Some parents deliberately stunted their childrens' growth by twisting or breaking their bones – life as a dwarf could be very lucrative. On the downside, however, they were much in demand by magicians, who disembowelled them live, using their intestines in their prognostications.

The big-penised dwarf anticipated the growth in popularity of the pygmy from the late first century BC: black, stunted and, again, (stereo-) typically sporting a large penis. Like the dwarf, the pygmy was employed to cause laughter and therefore protection against chthonic agents. They had sex outside, sometimes on boats, were homosexual as well as heterosexual and became very popular on frescoes, notably in Pompeii.

Jews and Christians fared particularly badly under Domitian, according to the fourth-century writer Eusebius of Caesarea.[50] Perhaps Domitian's most horrific act was when he was determined to rid himself of suspected conspirators. Suspects were subjected to a novel form of eye-watering torture which involved injecting fire into their genitals, chopping off their hands for good measure. The ignominy suffered by others when they were forced humiliatingly to confess to acts of passive sodomy was paltry by comparison.

Twenty-five years after Domitian's assassination, and despite the *damnatio memoriae* imposed by the Senate, Domitia loyally still referred to herself as 'Domitia, wife of Domitian'.

CHAPTER SIXTEEN

Hadrian and Antinous: A Man Worth Dying For

The emperor Hadrian (AD 76–138) reigned from 117 to 138. Apart from his impressive achievements as a military commander, as restorer of the magnificent Pantheon in Rome, and as the builder of the famous wall in Britannia, Hadrian is also renowned for his humanism and for his love of things Greek. This philhellenism embraced a close homosexual pederastic relationship with the Bithynian Antinous. His grief at Antinous' death is recorded in the *Historia Augusta*: 'During a journey on the Nile he lost Antinous, his favourite, and for this youth he wept like a woman'.[1] Details are scarce and speculation has been endlessly rife, but it seems that Antinous' committed a form of non-military *devotio* whereby he sacrificed himself for Hadrian. Whatever, he was deified by the Greeks on Hadrian's command both as a god and as a *heros* – a deified mortal; he was said to have articulated oracles which were most likely composed by the emperor himself.

The relationship probably started around AD 128 when Antinous joined Hadrian's retinue on a tour of the empire. They went together to the annual Eleusinian Mysteries in Athens; Antinous was with him when Hadrian killed the Marousian lion in Libya. It was in October 130, on a voyage down the Nile, that Antinous died.

Apart from the deification, Hadrian founded the city of Antinopolis near to where Antinous died; it became a cultic centre for the worship of Osiris-Antinous. Hadrian also instigated games in commemoration of Antinous, which took place in Antinopolis and Athens.

Royston Lambert gives what is probably a reasonably accurate description of the relationship: 'The way that Hadrian took the boy on his travels, kept close to him at moments of spiritual, moral or physical exaltation, and, after his death, surrounded himself with his images, shows an obsessive craving for his presence, a mystical-religious need for his companionship.'[2]

Pederasty was very much a Greek thing. In ancient Greece it carried none of the moral or fiercely anti-social connotations it has in the west today. Indeed, it was so prevalent that it has been called 'the principal cultural model for free relationships between citizens' in classical Greek society.[3] Furthermore, 'a certain kind of sexual relationship ... was considered by many Greeks to be very important for the cohesion of the city: sexual relations between men and youths... Lycurgus even gave them official recognition in his constitution for Sparta'. For centuries, pederasty had been socially acceptable among Greece's citizen classes: the older *erastes* (aged between twenty and forty) embarked on a a caring sexual relationship with an *eromenos* (aged between twelve and eighteen), assuming responsibility for their education. The age-range when boys entered into such relationships was about the same as the age when Greek girls married, usually to husbands much older. Boys, however, were typically wooed and could choose their partner, while marriages for elite girls were, as in Rome, arranged for financial and political reasons at the behest of the father.

In Rome, pederasty is frequently mentioned in the literature. We find it in Plautus' *Casina* (449–70), an example of how the master has free access to both female and male slaves. Cicero is censorious regarding the Greek and Spartan practice in his *De Republica* (4, 3–4). Virgil describes pederasty, the love between Corydon and Alexis, in his second *Eclogue* (1–27); there are shades of it between Pallas and Aeneas, and between Nisus and Euryalus in the *Aeneid*. Tibullus refers to pederasty in three of his *Elegies,* the Marathus cycle. Horace recommends slave boys (and girls) as convenient relief for a 'hard on' (*Satires* 1, 2, 116–118). Ovid prefers sex with women on account of mutual orgasm (*Arts Amatoria* 2, 683–4). Philo is appalled: pederasty is all the rage, including passive penetration, and should be punished with death (*De Specialibus Legibus* 3, 37–42). It features in the *Satyricon* (85–87) when Eumolpus feigns disgust but takes the good-looking boy of his host to the gym; Trimalchio was his master's *delicias* for fourteen years (75); Statius describes the love between Ursus and the slave Philetus (*Silvae* 2, 6, 35–58); Martial's wife protests in envy that she too has an anus when she catches her husband sodomising a slave boy (11, 43); Martial tells her to stop pretending she has two cunts. Dio Chrysostom (7, 151–2) deplores those lustful men who have got bored with sex with women and sneak over to the men's quarters and corrupt the boy recruits. For Juvenal a boy is better than any wife (6, 28, 34); Tacitus tells us about the slave of Pedanius Secundus who killed him out of jealousy over an *exoletus*, a ripe male (*Annals* 14, 42, 1) while Strato, the second-century-AD poet from Sardis, delights in young boys from the age of twelve (*AP* 12, 4). A teenage Marcus Aurelius expresses his undying love for his teacher, Fronto (*Ep. Add.* 7, 1). Lucian's Charicles and Lycinus expatiate on the benefits of sex with boys over women, concluding that pederasty should be the preserve of the wise (Lucian, *Amatores* 26, 27); the novelist Achilles Tatius concedes that sex with young men is becoming norm, giving their frankness and handsome bodies as superior to women (2, 35); Paul, the lawyer around AD 220, agrees with Philo that pederasts whould be punished with death, as should any chaperons who had been bribed (*Digest* 47, 11, 1, 2).

The Egyptian Athenaeus warned Stoic philosophers off unnatural pederasty and pretty boys in his *Deipnosophistae* (605d) – the Stoics allegedly retained 'boys' until they were twenty-eight; their hypocrisy is exposed when Athenaeus points out that they should not call others *kinaedoi* when they go around with boyfriends who shave their cheeks and bottoms. Nemesianus, the Carthaginian poet, warns boy lovers to be patient with them and put up with their sulks (*Eclogue* 4, 56–9). John Chrysostom echoes his near namesake when he calls the spread of pederasty, and its apparent acceptability, an incurable disease and the filthiest of all plagues in his *Against the Opponents of the Monastic Life* (3, PG 47, 360–2). Ausonius called pederasts a corruptor of 'the entire boyish sex, a digger at the back door of perverse Venus' and the poet Lucilius in particular a 'stealthy boy shagger' (*Epigrams* 77, 5–8').

We know that Tiberius was an evil pederast; it is, however, the emperor Trajan who is perhaps the most famous. Pliny is not phased by it in the slightest: Trajan was to him free from vice; Dio says that it did no one any harm. Trajan's reputation was alive and well 200 years later when Julian II quipped that Jupiter should watch out lest Trajan's ghost steal his Ganymede from him.[4] History does not record how the emperor's wife, Pompeia Plotina, dealt with all of this; she presumably accepted it, as one did, and did not allow it to spoil a happy marriage. Indeed Plotina, an ardent Epicurean philosopher, no doubt had more than enough to think about: she has gone down in history as a champion of more equitable taxation, better education, helping the poor, and injecting greater tolerance into Roman society.

Hadrian would have been attracted by Antinous's intelligence as well, and by their shared love of hunting. Hadrian wrote both an autobiography and erotic poetry which would have included references to his favourites. None of these works are extant but we can assume that Antinous features in both.

The years 127 to 130 were taken up almost completely by the two men in travelling, starting in Picenum and Campania from where they returned to Rome to lay the foundation stone for a temple of Venus and Rome. North Africa was next, then Corinth and Athens, where they were joined by Sabina. Here they attended the Great Mysteries of Eleusis, and possibly Antinous was initiated into the position of *epoptes* in the Telesterion. From there they went to Antioch, visiting Syria, Arabia, and Palestine. Here Hadrian's suspicions regarding Judaism and Jewish culture intensified and he is said to have banned circumcision and replaced the Jewish Temple with a Temple of Zeus-Jupiter. From there, they sailed to Alexandria where they paid homage at the sarcophogus of Alexander the Great. By now Hadrian was beginnng to attract criticism and scandal regarding his sexual activities, not least his relationship with Antinous.

In Libya the two men hunted down the Marousian lion which had been terrorising the locals. During the confrontation Hadrian saved Antinous' life before killing the beast. Hadrian made the most of the publicity potential and cast bronze medallions celebrating the event, urging historians to write about it, and commissioning the philosopher Pancrates to compose a poem on it. A tondo was produced depicting the incident and later placed on the Arch of Constantine.

In autumn AD 130 the retinue embarked on a trip down the Nile; at Hermopolis Magna, Antinous fell into the river and drowned. How it happened is unknown but when Hadrian announced his death, gossip and rumour rampaged through the empire speculating that Antinous had been killed intentionally. Another rumour had it that Antinous had died after castrating himself in a futile bid to retain his youth and his attraction to Hadrian. This is unlikely as Hadrian was firmly opposed to genital mutilation of any kind and because Antinous was too old anyway for it to have any physical benefit.

Human sacrifice, or *devotio*, is another possibility, subscribed to by Dio some eighty years later.[5] In the Rome of the time it was widely held that the death of one man could promote the health of another: by dying, Antinous may have believed that he was prolonging the life of Hadrian, who was not a well man at the time. There was also an Egyptian tradition in which sacrificing boys to the Nile during the October Osiris festival ensured that the river flooded to its full capacity, particularly important in 130 as the previous two years had seen floods insufficient to fertilise the valley.

Hadrian named a star after Antinous, and the rosy lotus that grew on the banks of the Nile became the flower of Antinous. He also was known as a conqueror of death, to the extent that his name and image often appeared on sarcophagi. Caroline Vout has observed that there are more sculptures of Antinous than of any other figure in classical antiquity except Augustus and Hadrian.[6] Royston Lambert believes that the sculptures of Antinous 'remain without doubt one of the most elevated and ideal monuments to pederastic love of the whole ancient world', describing them as 'the final great creation of classical art'.[7]

Vibia Sabina (AD 83–c. 136) was Hadrian's wife; she was a strong-willed woman and this may account for their reputedly unhappy marriage. They had no children but did adopt two sons. If Hadrian knew the details about Sabina's alleged affair with Suetonius, the famous historian and his very own secretary, then this too cannot have helped the relationship.[8] Hadrian was away a lot and obviously at one time during the marriage was far more interested in Antinous than he was in Sabina.

Hadrian was, it seems, bisexual, if we are to believe the reports of his numerous adulterous affairs with the wives of other men. Bizarrely, Vibia rebukes Antinous for not doing enough to keep Hadrian from straying towards married women. She allegedly complained that Hadrian treated her like a slave and that she avoided getting pregnant to avoid visiting on the world a child from so dreadful a man. Hadrian complained that she was moody and obstreperous and that he would have ditched her were he a private citizen.[8] Nevertheless, these sources are notoriously unreliable and the fact that Sabina was often with Hadrian on his many tours, the coins he minted celebrating her, the protection he gave her in the Suetonius affair, and her apotheosis – the first such depiction of a woman on a relief in Roman art – may suggest a much more harmonious marriage.[9] No matter what, Sabina would have had to tolerate the innate sexism in Roman society which permitted a friend of Hadrian's to say in response to his wife's complaints about his infelicities, 'Let me have my fun; to be a wife is an honour, not a pleasure.'[10]

CHAPTER SEVENTEEN

Faustina and the Gladiator's Bloodbath; the Vile Corruption of Commodus

Annia Galeria Faustina Minor or Faustina the Younger (*c.* AD 130–175) was a daughter of Antoninus Pius and his empress Faustina the Elder, and wife to her maternal cousin Marcus Aurelius. Like Vibia Sabina she was denigrated by later historians, despite having lived, it seems, a creditable life and having enjoyed a happy marriage. Indeed, giving birth to and raising thirteen children in twenty-three years would have left her with little time to philander, slaves or no slaves to help. On her death, a grieving Marcus Aurelius honoured her with burial in the Mausoleum of Hadrian. She was deified: her statue was placed in the Temple of Venus in Rome and a temple was dedicated to her. Halala's name was changed to Faustinopolis and Aurelius opened charity schools for orphan girls called *Puellae Faustinianae* or 'Girls of Faustina'.[1] The Baths of Faustina in Miletus carry her name.

However that may be, Dio and the *Historia Augusta* both report that Faustina ordered deaths by poison and execution, and instigated the revolt of Avidius Cassius against her husband. The inevitable adultery smears to be found in the tabloid *Historia Augusta* implicates sailors, gladiators, mime actors and various senators.

Marcus Aurelius never remarried as a widower, preferring instead to take the daughter of Faustina's maid as a mistress, and thus avoid his children putting up with a stepmother. However, even Julian II admitted that the widowed emperor went beyond what was expected in his grief, even though Faustina was 'not even a virtuous woman'. Sextus Aurelius Victor alleged that she used to cruise the beaches of Campania picking up the sailors who worked naked there. Her son, Commodus, was alleged to have been fathered by a gladiator. Lucius Verus, her son-in-law, was rumoured to have shared her bed, and died for the pleasure at the hands of Faustina. Marcus Aurelius seems to have been remarkably relaxed and philosophical about the whole matter; on discovering the affair with the gladiator, he consulted soothsayers, who recommended he have the gladiator slain so that Faustina could bathe in the blood and then have sex with him.[2] On another occasion, the emperor found his wife having breakfast with a lover and promptly promoted him.[3]

It seems that the enormously successful and wealthy Herodes Atticus may have been responsible for starting the scurrilous accusations against Faustina. Apart from a reputation for abusing his slaves and humiliating his disabled son, he was not beyond character assassination and the humiliation of anyone who had the temerity to cross his path.[4] In AD 160 he was charged with murdering his eight-months-pregnant wife, Annia Regilla; a slave had been ordered to beat her to death.[5] Feigning grief, he was acquitted.

Faustina and Atticus went back a long way, and there was no love lost between the two: she would remember how he beat her father one day in a fracas on Mount Ida and Regilla, her relation and childhood friend, would have talked about the abuse she received from her husband.[6] During one law case Faustina pleaded with Marcus Aurelius to hear the Athenian defendants out; this he did, much to the chagrin of Atticus, who insulted Faustina by moaning that he had been 'sacrificed to the whim of a mere woman and her three-year-old child'. He then proceeded to denigrate Marcus Aurelius.[7]

In his *Meditations*, the emperor confesses that he 'has been blessed with a wife so obedient, so affectionate, so genuine'.[8]

The controversy surrounding the paternity of Commodus is given further impetus by the son's dissolute and degenerate character. Commodus was the tenth of thirteen children produced by Marcus Aurelius and Faustina – the only son to survive. After a period of joint rule with his tolerant and sagacious father, Commodus reigned between AD 180 and 192 and in that time displayed behaviour that would have matched the debauchery of Tiberius.

We have the sensationalism of the *Historia Augusta* to thank for much of the detail relating to the monstrous and debauched life of

Commodus; he delegated many of the affairs of state to one of his prefects, Perennis, so that he could focus on his degenerate lifestyle: 'Even from his earliest years he was base and dishonourable, and cruel and lewd, defiled of mouth, moreover, and debauched.'[9] He was in the habit of visiting brothels and taverns at night. Evidently, he ran a harem of 300 girls and women and 300 boys, some of whom were probably kidnapped. He killed his sister Lucilla, after banishing her to Capri for her part in a conspiracy against him; this was organised by one Pompeianus, who was having an affair with Lucilla and her mother.[10] He raped his other sisters, had an affair with a cousin of his father, and named one of his concubines after his mother. When he caught his wife in the act of adultery, he banished her, and later put her to death. His concubines were raped in front of him; he was 'not free from the disgrace of intimacy with young men, defiling every part of his body in dealings with persons of either sex'.[11] Many of Commodus' endless atrocities had a distinctly sexual flavour to them: among his retainers were men whom he renamed after the genitals of both sexes and whom he woud kiss in public; one of these was a man with a penis larger than that of most animals, whom he called Onos because he was hung like a donkey. He treated Onos with great affection, made him rich and appointed him to the priesthood of the Rural Hercule.[12]

By 192 Rome and the senate had had its fill of Commodus' corruption, his Herculean impersonations and his demeaning obsession with the world of the gladiator with his many public displays in the arena.[13] A plot was hatched in which Marcia, one of his concubines, was to administer poison in some beef to Commodus. This failed when he vomited up the poison, but his survival was only momentary; Narcissus, the emperor's wrestling partner, strangled him. Commodus joined Domitian as the recipient of a *damnatio memoriae*.

Hadrian had adopted the father of Lucius Verus with a view to him succeeding as emperor of Rome. Lucius Verus himself was adopted by Antoninus Pius in AD 138 and ruled jointly with Marcus Aurelius from 161 – 169. The *Historia Augusta* is our only extensive source for his life, and it is from this that he quickly won a reputation not only for 'the licence of an unbridled life, but also by adulteries and by love-affairs with young men'. He allegedly set up a cook shop (notorious haunts of prostitutes) in his home, where he held banquets and had

all manner of foul persons serve him... and that he so rivalled

Caligula, Nero, and Vitellius[14] in their vices as to wander about at night through taverns and brothels with only a common travelling-cap for a head-covering, revel with various rowdies, and engage in brawls, concealing his identity the while; and often, they say, when he returned, his face was beaten black and blue.[15]

Rumour had it that he had a relationship with his mother-in-law, Faustina and that she murdered him by having poison sprinkled on his oysters, because he had revealed the affair to her daughter.

Another unhealthy relationship distinguished the reign of the emperor Caracella, who ruled from 198 to 217 with his father, Septimius Severus, until his death in Eboracum, modern York. His joint rule with his brother Publius Septimius Antoninus Geta was a disaster and culminated in the murder of Geta, of his former cousin and wife Fulvia Plautilla after exile on Lipari, of his daughter and other members of the family of his former father-in-law Gaius Fulvius Plautianus.

The *Historia Augusta* gives us the unlikely story of Caracella's incest and subsequent marriage to his mother, Julia Domna: she was by repute a very beautiful woman, and one day she carelessly showed 'a considerable part of her person' in Caracella's presence. Caracella said, 'I should like to, if I might,' whereupon Julia replied, 'If you wish, you may; are you not aware that you are the emperor and that you make the laws and do not receive them?' They had sex and Caracella contracted a marriage, 'and to fratricide he added incest, for he joined to himself in marriage the woman whose son he had recently slain'.[16]

CHAPTER EIGHTEEN

Elagabalus: 'An Unspeakably Disgusting Life'[1]

Sex and scandal feature prominently throughout the life of Elagabalus (AD *c*. 203–22), a notorious transgressor and deviant, beset by gender confusion and depravity.

His real name was Marcus Aurelius Antoninus Augustus but he is usually known as Elagabalus or Heliogabalus, and was emperor from 218 to 222. Elagabalus was Syrian, the second son of Julia Soaemias and Sextus Varius Marcellus. The name Elagabalus comes from the god, Elagabal, for whom the young Elegabal served as a priest in his mother's hometown of Emesa (modern Homs in Syria). Only after his death was he called Elagabalus.[2]

Elagabalus became emperor at the age of fourteen, in the wake of some adept scheming on the part of his grandmother (and Caracella's maternal aunt), Julia Maesa, in AD 217. That year, the reigning emperor, the dissolute Caracalla was assassinated and replaced by his Praetorian Prefect, Marcus Opellius Macrinus. Julia Maesa, in exile, wasted no time in stoking a rebellion among the *III Gallica* legion to have Elagabalus declared emperor on 8 June 218, at the Battle of Antioch. The pretext was that Elagabalus was the illegitimate son of Caracella. Elagabalus began his reign as he intended to go on, with a total disregard for Roman religious convention and sexual taboos.

Elagabalus had a short life, but a consistently active sex life. He was married at least five times; he showed favour to his many male lovers, and prostituted himself around the imperial palace. For example, Elagabalus tried to have one lover, the charioteer Hierocles, declared Caesar, while the athlete Aurelius Zoticus was appointed to the influential, and convenient, position of Master of the Chamber, or *Cubicularius*.[3] To Elagabalus, Hierocles was his husband and reputedly declared, '[I am] delighted to be called the mistress, the wife, the Queen of Hierocles.' Had Hierocles succeeded in becoming Caesar he would have been successor to the imperial throne. However, Hierocles was executed, along with other members of the court, when the emperor was deposed in AD 222. Apparently he was anally abused with a sword.

Before all that, though, it was not long before Elagabalus started to alienate the Praetorian Guard, the Senate, and his subjects. At first, the unpredictable and volatile Elagabalus got on tolerably well with Julia Maesa and Julia Soaemias, his mother. He allowed them access to the senate, the first women to be (officially) permitted there,[4] and both were honoured with senatorial titles: Soaemias became *Clarissima,* and Maesa *Mater Castrorum et Senatus* ('Mother of the army camp and of the Senate').

Other women fared less well. Even the Vestal Virgins were not safe; he married the Vestal Virgin Aquilia Severa, in a bid to produce 'divine children'.[5] A more shocking and flagrant breach of Roman religious law and convention could not be imagined. It was the ultimate in hubris and impiety, in treason even. The traditional punishment for a Vestal who misplaced her virginity was the agonisingly slow death by live entombment.[6] Religious symbolism may have led Elagabalus to marry Severa; Elagabalus was an adherent to the eastern sun god El-Gabal and, by marrying Severa, he was forging a union between the sun god and Vesta. The 'marriage' was soon annulled and Elagabalus wed Annia Faustina, a less controversial bride. The extremely wealthy Faustina had recently been widowed when her late husband, Pomponius Bassus, was executed for subversion and treason. Faustina did not last long and was divorced so that her short-lived imperial husband could return to the lapsed Vestal Virgin, claiming that the original divorce was invalid.

Elagabalus naturally wanted to become the high priest of his new religion; to achieve this he had himself circumcised.[7] More sacrilege and iconoclasm followed when he removed some of the most sacred and revered relics of traditional Roman religion to the Elagabalium, including the symbol of the Great Mother, the fire of Vesta, the Shields of the Salii and the Palladium; no other god could now be worshipped without Elagabal.[8]

Elagabalus' first wife was the noblewoman Julia Cornelia Paula, Empress of Rome from 219–20, then divorced so that her husband could marry the Vestal Virgin, whom it is alleged Elagablus forced into marriage and raped.[9] His affairs with Hierocles and Aurelius

Elagabalus: 'An Unspeakably Disgusting Life'

Zoticus, however, seemed to have been pursued with much greater enthusiasm than any of his heterosexual marriages.[10] Indeed, according to the *Historia Augusta*, Elagabalus actually married Zoticus at a lavish ceremony in Rome.[11] He was now applying eye make up, depilating body hair and wearing wigs before prostituting himself in taverns, brothels, even in the imperial palace.[12] Dio gives the sordid details:

> Finally, he set aside a room in the palace and there committed his indecencies, always standing nude at the door of the room, as the harlots do, and shaking the curtain which hung from gold rings, while in a soft and melting voice he solicited the passers-by. There were, of course, men who had been specially instructed to play their part. For, as in other matters, so in this business, too, he had numerous agents who sought out those who could best please him by their foulness. He would collect money from his patrons and give himself airs over his gains; he would also dispute with his associates in this shameful occupation, claiming that he had more lovers than they and took in more money.[13]

Herodian adds that make up was a regular feature.[14]

The Historia Augusta, if it is to believed, gives us a startling insight into the emperor's perverted sense of humour:

> the recipient of lust in every orifice of his body, he sent agents looking for men with large organs to satisfy his passions. He put a dancer-cum-actor, Cordius, in charge of the Praetorian Guard, and a barber, Claudius, of the grain supply. The size of a man's organ often determined the post he was given. He would often lock his friends up when they were drunk and suddenly, in the night, let in lions and leopards and bears – surreptitiously rendered harmless – so that when they woke up they would find at dawn, or what is worse, at night, lions, bears and panthers in the same bedroom as themselves. Several of them died as a result of this.[15]

He opened the bath of Plautinus to the public in order to attract men with unusually large penises. He scoured the whole city searching for *onobeli*, those who were inordinately well endowed, hung like a donkey. Mythology could not escape his indecency:

> He used to have the story of Paris played in his house, and he himself would take the rôle of Venus, and suddenly drop his

clothes to the ground and fall naked on his knees, one hand on his breast, the other on his genitals, his buttocks projecting meanwhile and thrust back in front of his partner in depravity.[16]

Things went a step further when he offered huge amounts of money to any physician who could give him permanent female genitalia or, in the words of Dio, 'to contrive a woman's vagina in his body by means of an incision'.[17] Dio also alludes to castration when he tells us that a physician was asked to employ his skill to make him bisexual by means of an anterior incision.

Elagabalus seems to have been partial to child sacrifice, collecting 'children of noble birth and beautiful appearance', and employing magicians to perform daily sacrifices so that he could examine the children's internal organs and torture the victims.

Credit where it is due, though. The emperor obviously saw what was coming to him and even had a suicide tower built 'with gilded and jewelled boards spread underneath in front of him ... saying that even his death ought to be costly and of an extravagant pattern'.

On 11 March AD 222 Elagabalus and his mother, Julia Soaemias, were butchered by the Praetorian Guard. Dio takes up the lurid story:

So he made an attempt to flee, and would have got away somewhere by being placed in a chest, had he not been discovered and slain, at the age of eighteen. His mother, who embraced him and clung tightly to him, perished with him; their heads were cut off and their bodies, after being stripped naked, were first dragged all over the city, then the mother's body was cast aside somewhere or other while his was thrown into the [Tiber].[18]

Many of Elagabalus's friends and colleagues were then murdered, including Hierocles. His sacrileges were reversed. Women were again barred from the Senate and *damnatio memoriae* was applied. As we have seen, Gibbon was no fan, and indignantly highlights just one of many instances of the emperor's decadence; the effeminate wearing of silks:

Two hundred years after the age of Pliny, the use of pure, or even of mixed silks, was confined to the female sex, till the opulent citizens of Rome and the provinces were insensibly familiarized with the example of Elagabalus, the first who, by this effeminate habit, had sullied the dignity of an emperor and a man.[19]

Despite the *damnatio*, many works of art and literature have been spawned by the emperor's memory. He lives on in the Spanish word *heliogábalo*, which means 'a person subsumed by gluttony'.

Elagabalus was succeeded by Severus Alexander, his cousin, who reigned from AD 222 to 235. As a thirteen-year-old emperor it is hardly surprising that he was dominated by his grandmother, Julia Maesa, and his mother, Julia Avita Mamaea. Julia was a virtuous woman, scandal-free and devoted to the education of her son. Alexander married three times, most famously to the sixteen-year-old Sallustia Orbiana, *Augusta*, whom he married in AD 225, a union arranged by Alexander's mother. However, when Orbiana received the title of *Augusta*, Mamaea became increasingly jealous and resentful. He divorced and exiled her in 227. The second wife was Sulpicia Memmia, from one of the most ancient patrician families in Rome. Alexander fathered no children with any of his three wives.

In complete contrast to Elegabalus, Alexander dismissed all eunuchs from his service and commanded that they should serve his wife as slaves, reducing their number and removing them from all duties in the palace except the care of the women's baths. He used to say that eunuchs were the third sex of the human race, one not to be seen or employed by men and scarcely even by women of noble birth. When one of them sold a false promise in his name he ordered him to be crucified along a busy road frequented by slaves.[20]

Alexander strove to reverse some of the debauchery established by his cousin. He forbade mixed bathing – which had been outlawed previously but then allowed by Elagabalus. He imposed taxes on procurers, whores and catamites with the income used to restore the theatre, the Circus, the Amphitheatre, and the Stadium. He wanted to ban catamites altogether but desisted in case it simply drove the practice underground.[21] He banned women of dubious reputation from attending the levees of his mother and his wife. All dwarfs, both male and female, idiots, catamites who had good voices, every kind of entertainer at table, and actors of pantomimes were made public property; those, however, who were useless were assigned, each to different towns for support, so that no one town might be burdened by too many beggars. The eunuchs were given to his friends, with the proviso that if they did not return to honest ways, it would be lawful to put them to death without authority from the courts. Women of ill repute, of whom he arrested an enormous number, he ordered to become public prostitutes. He later deported all catamites, some of whom were conveniently drowned by shipwreck in transit.[22]

Alexander tried hard to reduce the luxuries that had stifled Rome for centuries. He sold all his jewels with the proceeds going to the public treasury, saying that men had no need of trinkets, and that the women of the royal household should be content with one hairnet, a pair of earrings, a necklace of pearls, a diadem to wear while sacrificing, a single cloak ornamented with gold, and one robe with an embroidered border, not to contain more than six ounces of gold. He set a fine example for good men to follow while his wife was an exemplar for *matronae*.[23]

Dexippus of Athens tells us that Alexander married the daughter of Macrinus and that he gave this man the name of Caesar. However, when Macrinus tried to kill him Alexander not only put Macrinus to death but also divorced his wife.[24] When he heard about a soldier mistreating a woman he made the soldier take her on as a slave and look after her.[25]

The *Historia Augusta* gives us another dissolute emperor: Gordian II is said to have serviced twenty-two concubines and fathered four children from each of them.[26] His stamina won him the nickname 'Priam' after the notoriously fertile King of Troy, or Priapus, for obvious reasons.

CHAPTER NINETEEN

Theodora: Slut or Saint?

Theodora (*c.* AD 500–48), the wife of Justinian I and powerful empress of the Byzantine empire, acted as a virtual co-regent with her husband. Procopius is our main source for her life, but perplexingly we have three wildly varying accounts from him in three separate works. *The Wars of Justinian* is complimentary and describes a brave and influential empress; Procopius' *De Aedificiis*, *Buildings of Justinian,* is a panegyric which show Justinian and Theodora as a pious couple.[1] But it is his *Anekdota* ('unpublished works') or *Secret History*, published a thousand years later, which is of interest to us. When he wrote it, Procopius was disenchanted, depicting Justinian as cruel, greedy, wasteful and generally useless. As for Theodora, Procopius describes a woman who is vulgar and characterised by unquenchable lust – quite unrecognisable from his portrayals in the earlier works. To Procopius the couple are demons with disembodied heads which float around the palace by night. He nevertheless concedes that Theodora was not unattractive, if a little short and wan in complexion.[2] The considerable delay in publication suggests that Procopius never intended this work to be published.

Corroboration of a kind comes from the Syriac historian John of Ephesus, when he describes Theodora as 'coming from the brothel'. Apparently, she was something of an authority on different types of abortion and disposed of any number of unwanted and unintentional children.[3]

Theodora's mother was an actress and a dancer; her father, Acacius, was a bear trainer at the hippodrome in Constantinople. this marked the family out as *untermenschen*, socially equivalent to adulterers and prostitutes. John of Ephesus and Procopius concur that when she was young, Theodora from an early age followed her sister, Comito, who was something of a star, into work in a Constantinople brothel and later became an actress performing mime and obscene burlesque. One of her star roles was as Leda in a stage production of *Leda and the Swan*; this involved performing almost in the nude (total nudity was banned), and lying on her back while other actors scattered barley on her groin.[4] The barley was then picked up by geese (as Zeus) with their beaks. Inviting fellow actors to copulate with her on stage was another party piece. Procopius relates with some distaste that in the early days Theodora was still too young to provide routine sexual intercourse but prostituted herself as a young boy, offering anal sex to her clientele, which included slaves. In time she became a low-class whore, one of 'the dregs of the army', stripping off at the drop of a hat. Perfecting 'novel ways of intercourse' was a specialty, as was her enthusiastic participation in group sex at dinner parties. Ten or more young men in succession were easily accomodated; once these had been exhausted she moved on to their slaves, up to thirty at a time. Still her lust remained insatiable. She would often stand up in front of guests and lift up her dress to reveal her genitalia, complaining that Nature had only given her three orifices and that the holes in her nipples should be larger so that she could 'devise another variety of intercourse in that region'. According to Procopius, 'with such lasciviousness did she misuse her own body that she appeared to have her private parts not like other women in the place intended by nature, but in her face!'

After travelling around the Mediterranenan from the age of sixteen, taking in Libya, Alexandria and Antioch, she returned to Constantinople in AD 522. In Libya she consorted with a certain Hecobolus 'in order to serve him in the most revolting capacity'. In Antioch she met a famous ballet dancer, Macedonia, whose day job was informer to Justinian. Procopius tells how Theodora apparently told Macedonia about a dream she had in which she would come back to Constantinople where the Lord of the Demons would seduce her, marry her and give her limitless riches.[5]

The reality was not quite so glamorous. Arriving back in Constantinople she renounced her former libidinous lifestyle and took on rather more matronly work as a wool spinner in a house near the imperial palace. By this time she had converted to Monophysitism, a non-orthodox Christian doctrine.[6] Her alleged beauty, wit and amiable ways attracted Justinian, then heir to the throne of his uncle, Emperor Justin I. Annoyingly for Justinian,

Roman law prohibited government officials from marrying actresses, a law which empress Euphemia fully supported. Justin had bought Euphemia as a slave when she was called Lupicina, with its overtones of *lupa*, suggesting that she was also a prostitute, adopting the respectable name of Euphemia when she became empress. However, Justin repealed the inconvenient law in 525 after Euphemia had died, allowing Justinian to marry Theodora and adopting Theodora's illegitimate daughter.[7] The law erased Theodora's past reputation and restored her *pudicitia*, a *damnatio memoriae* in reverse. Erasure of a more sinister kind followed when Theodora's alleged affair with her slave, Areobindus, was discovered; she had him flogged and he disappeared from the scene.

Procopius is quite incredulous that such a woman could rise from the lowest and most depraved of backgrounds to become empress of Rome. Justinian had the pick of all the women in his empire and could have selected 'for his bride the most nobly born woman in the world… thoroughly acquainted with the claims of modesty, and had lived in an atmosphere of chastity … and still a virgin – or, as they say, firm-breasted'; instead he chose to 'consort with a woman double-dyed with every kind of horrible pollution and guilty over and over again of infanticide by wilful abortion'.

Procopius suggests that it was sheer lust which attracted Justinian to Theodora, but it seems that there was more to it than that. Theodora was desperate for another child and when the archimandrite Mar Saba visited Constantinople in 531 she pleaded with him that she might conceive; he insensitively refused, dashing her hopes when he declared that any son she bore would be a greater disaster for the empire than the Monophysite emperor Anastasius.[8] Theodora never did conceive.

After acquitting herself brilliantly during the Nika riots in 532 by urging her dithering husband (now emperor) with a stirring speech to stand and fight the rebels instead of fleeing, she, according to Procopius, grew excessively haughty.[9] Court protocol was an obsession, with the relationship between emperor-empress and senators and others reduced to something approaching master to slave:

> They were kept waiting in a small, stuffy room for an endless time. After many days, some of them might at last be summoned, but going into her presence in great fear, they very quickly departed. They simply showed their respect by laying face down and touching the instep of each of her feet with their lips; there

was no opportunity to speak or to make any request unless she told them to do so. The government officials had sunk into a slavish condition, and she was their slave-instructor.[10]

Gibbon's assessment is something of a backhanded compliment, and a swipe at Procopius and his followers: 'Those who believe that the female mind is totally depraved by the loss of chastity, will eagerly listen to all the invectives of private envy or popular resentment, which have dissembled the virtues of Theodora, exaggerated her vices, and condemned with rigour the venal and voluntary sins of the youthful harlot.'[11]

Nevertheless, despite the reputation – real or exaggerated – Theodora never forgot her roots and the prejudice she had suffered as a young girl; her work for women's rights was extensive and commendable. She championed laws prohibiting forced prostitution and closed down brothels. She established a convent on the Dardanelles called the *Metanoia* (Repentance), a kind of refuge where ex-prostitutes could be rehabilitated and support themselves. She also extended the rights of women in divorce and property ownership, equating a woman's rights here to a man's, brought in the death penalty for rape, banned the exposure of unwanted babies (usually girls), gave mothers some rights of guardianship over their children, criminalised the killing of a wife who committed adultery and legislated that a lover must receive three witnessed written warnings before he could be killed with impunity. From AD 390 widows were allowed to be guardians of their children and grandchildren if they did not remarry and if there were no other legitimate male guardians. A woman could no longer be put into prison where she might be raped by male guards; if she had to be locked up then she should be sent to a convent. The ante-nuptial donation, a counter-dowry given by the husband to his wife, should be equal in value to the dowry.

According to Procopius, a veritable saint? A saint, maybe, in the version given in *Buildings of Justinian*. A reading of the *Secret History* gives a very different picture of the woman: here Theodora is said to have 'rounded up' 500 prostitutes, 'incarcerating them in a convent', leading to suicides as prostitutes tried to escape 'the unwelcome transformation' to a life of chastity.[12] According to Victor of Tunnuna, Theodora died of what was probably breast cancer in 548, aged forty-eight. Justinian was distraught.

Flavius Belisarius (*c.* AD 505–65) was a successful general and faithful supporter of Justinian, largely responsible for suppressing the Nika riots with the massacre of 30,000 rebels in the hippodrome at Constantinople. Procopius served as his secretary and advisor between AD 527 and 540. His wife, the duplicitous Antonina, brought with her a reputation even worse than Theodora's, and was alleged to have had an affair with her adopted son, Theodosius. Sex often took place in front of the slaves with Antonina 'a slave to her lust'; even when Belisarius caught them in the act he was unwilling to believe what he had seen with his own eyes. Theodora and Antonina were long-standing friends. Antonina was a schemer and a fixer of the first order, playing a prominent role in the downfalls of Pope Silverius and John the Cappadocian, 'making Silverius appear a pro-Gothic traitor' and implicated John 'in a conspiracy to gain the throne'.

Procopius bluntly sums up Antonina's dubious backgound. Both her father and grandfather were charioteers, and

> her mother was one of the prostitutes attached to the theatre ... [Antonina] having in her early years lived a lewd sort of a life and having become dissolute in character, not only having consorted much with the cheap sorcerers who surrounded her parents, but also having thus acquired the knowledge of what she needed to know, later became the wedded wife of Belisarius, after having already been the mother of many children.[13]

In time the cuckolded Belisarius arrested Antonina on evidence provided by bedchamber servants but was unable to bring himself to exact punishment – due, according to Procopius, to Antonina's skillful use of the black arts. The informants were deemed to be lying: Antonina had their tongues cut out and their bodies chopped up; the body parts were dumped in the sea. Theodora eventually restored Theodosius to a grateful Antonina, but not before she had whipped Photius, her son, half to death for concealing him. Unfortunately, Theodosius died soon after of dysentery.[14]

Primary Sources Cited: Greek [Gk] and Latin [L] Authors

Achilles Tatius (*fl.* second century AD) *Leucippe and Clitophon* [Gk]
Aelius Aristeides (AD 117–181) *Roman Oration; Hieroi Logoi* [Gk]
Ammianus Marcellinus (AD 325/330 – after 391) *Res Gestae* [L]
Anonymous (*c.* 85 BC) *To Herennius on Rhetoric* [L]
Anonymus Latinus
Appian (late first century AD – 160+) *Bellum Civile* [Gk]
Apuleius (late second century AD) *Metamorphoses* [L]
Aristaeus (early third century AD) *Deipnosophistae* [Gk]
Aristophanes (*c.* 446 – *c.* 386 BC) *Clouds*
Aristotle (385–322 BC) *Historia Animalium* [Gk]
Arnobius Sicca (*fl.* 290] *Adversus Nationes* [L]
Arrian (*c.* AD 95–175) *Indica* [Gk]
Artemidorus Ephesius (second century AD) *Oneirocritica* [Gk]
Athenaeus of Naucratis (*fl.* end second century AD) *Deipnosophistae* [Gk]
Augustine of Hippo (AD 354–430) *De Civitate Dei; Confessions* [L]
Aulus Gellius (*c.* AD 125 – after 180), *Noctes Atticae* [L]
Aurelius Victor (end of fourth century AD) *Epitome de Caesaribus* [L]
Ausonius (*c.* AD 310 – *c.* 395) *Epigrams; Cento Nuptialis* [L]
Caesar, Julius (100–44 BC) *De Bello Gallico* [L]
Caelius (fifth century AD) *On Chonic Diseases* [L]
Calpurnius Flaccus (second century AD) *Declamations* [L]
Cato the Elder (234–149 BC) *De Re Floria* in Aulus Gellius *frag 57*
Catullus (*c.* 84–54 BC) *Carmina* [L]
Celsus (before 47 BC) *De Medicina* [L]
Chrysostom, Dio (*c.* AD 40 – *c.* 115) *Orations* [Gk]
Chrysostom, John (*c.* AD 347–407) *The Type of Women Who Ought to be Taken as Wives; Homily 24 on the Epistle to the Romans; Against the Opponents of the Monastic Life* [Gk]
Cicero (106–43 BC) *Ad Atticum; Ad Familiares; Brutus; De Divitatione; De Haruspicum Responsis; De Legibus; De Officiis; De Oratore; De Re Publica; In Catilinam; Oratio de Doma Sua; Philippicae; Pro Caelio; Pro Murena;*

Primary Sources Cited: Greek [Gk] and Latin [L] Authors

Tusculanae Disputationes; In Verrem; Pro Cluentio; Post Reditum in Senatu; Pro Planco; Verrine; Parad [L]
CIL in *Corpus Inscriptionum Latinarum* (Berlin 1863)
Clement of Alexandria (AD 182–202) *Paedagogus* [Gk]
Codex Theodosianus (AD 438) [L]
Columella (AD 4 – c. 70) *De Re Rustica* [L]
De Bello Hispaniensi (40 BC) [L]
Dio, Cassius (AD c. 155–235), [Gk] *Historia Romanae*
Democritus (c. 460 – c. 370 BC) *Paegnia* [Gk]
Diodorus Siculus (*fl.* between 60 and 30 BC) *Bibliotheca Historica* [Gk]
Dionysius of Halicarnassus (c. 60 BC – after 7 BC) *Roman Antiquities* [Gk]
Dioscorides (AD 50) *De Materia Medica* [L]
Euripides (c. 480–406 BC) *Andromache* [Gk]
Eusebius (fourth century AD) *Historia Ecclesiastica* [Gk]
Festus (*fl.* late second century AD) *Epitome; Nothum* [L]
Gaius (*fl.* AD 130–180) *Institutiones* [L]
Galen (AD 130–200) *On the Divisions of the Medical Art; On the Usefulness of Parts of the Body; On the Seed; On Prognosis; De Simplicium Medicamentorum Temperamentis* [Gk]
Greek Anthology [Gk]
Heliodorus *Aethiopica* [Gk]
Herodian (c. AD 170–240) *History of the Empire from the Death of Marcus Aurelius* [Gk]
Hesiod (*fl.* 750 and 650 BC) *Works and Days* [Gk]
Hippocrates (*fl. c.* 460 – c. 370 BC) *Aphorisms; Natura Mulierum; On Virgin; Epidemics* [Gk]
Historia Augusta (fourth century AD) [L]
Homer (c. 850 BC) *Odyssey* [Gk]
Horace (65–8 BC) *Epodes; Odes; Satires* [L]
Hyginus (c. 64 BC – AD 17) *Fabulae* [L]
Isaiah
Isidore of Seville (d. 636) *Etymolgiae* [L]
John of Ephesus (c. AD 507 – c. 588) [Syriac]
Josephus (AD 37 – c. 100) *Jewish Antiquities* [Gk]
Justin Martyr (c. AD 155–157) *Apology* [L]
Justinian (AD 529–534) *Institutiones* [L]
Juvenal (*fl.* early second century AD) *Satires* [L]
Lactantius (c. AD 240 – c. 320) *Institutiones Divinae* [L]
Livy (59 BC – AD 17) *Ab Urbe Condita* [L]
Lucan (AD 39–65) *Bellum Civile* [L]
Lucian (c. AD 125 – after 180) *De Mercede Conductis; Affairs of the Heart; Calumnies; Rhetorum Praeceptor; De Dea Syria* [Gk]
Lucilius (c. 180–102 BC) [L]
Lucretius (c. 99 – c. 55 BC) *De Rerum Natura* [L]
Macrobius (*fl.* fifth century AD) *Saturnalia* [L]
Marcellus of Bordeaux (early fifth century AD) *De Medicamentis* [L]
Marcus Aurelius (AD 161–180) *Meditations* [Gk]
Martial (c. AD 40–100) *Epigrams; De Spectaculis* [L]
Matthew
Milesiaca

Modestinus (*fl.* AD 250) [L]
Naevius (270–201 BC) *Bellum Punicum* [L]
Nepos, Cornelius (*c.* 110 – *c.* 25 BC) *Noctes Atticae; De Viris Illustribus* [L]
Nicolaus of Damascus (*c.* 64 BC) *Athletica* [Gk]
Orabasius *Ecloga Medicamentorum*
Origen Adamantius (AD 184–253) [Gk]
Ovid (43 BC – AD 17) *Fasti; Tristia; Metamorphoses; Ars Amatoria; Amores; Remedia Amoris* [L]
Paul (Saul) of Tarsus (*c.* AD 5 – *c.* 67) *Timothy; Opinions; Edict; Digest; Sent. Recept; Corinthians; Apocalypse of Paul*
Persius (AD 34–62) *Satires* [L]
Petronius (*c.* AD 27–66) *Satyricon* [L]
Philo (*c.* 20 BC – AD 40) *Questions and Answers on* Genesis; *De Specialibus Legibus* [Gk]
Philodemus (*c.* 110 – *c.* 40 BC) *Palatine Anthology*
Philostratus (*c.* AD 172–247) *Lives of the Sophists* [Gk]
Phlegon of Tralles (*fl.* second century AD) *Miracles* [Gk]
Phokylides (*fl.* 544–541 BC) *Sententiae* [Gk]
Pindar (*c.* 522–443 BC) *Pythian Ode* [Gk]
Plautus (*c.* 254–184 BC) *Bacchae; Curculio; Aulularia; Mercator; Captivi; Truculentus; Poenulus; Cistellaria* [L]
Pliny the Elder (AD 23–79) *Historia Naturalis* [L]
Pliny the Younger (*c.* AD 61–113) *Epistulae* [L]
Plutarch (*c.* AD 45–125) *Romulus; Brutus; Caesar; Cato Maior; Cato Minor; Cicero; Gaius Gracchus; Lucullus; Moralia; Numa; Quaestiones Romanae; Tiberius Gracchus; Themistocles; De Fort. Rom.; Mulierum Virtutes; Marius* [Gk]
Polybius (*c.* 204–122 BC) *Histories* [Gk]
Pomponius Bononiensis (*fl. c.* 90 BC) *mime writer* [L]
Pomponius (first century AD) *On Sabinus* [L]
Priapea *Virgilian Appendix* [L]
Priscianus, Theodore (fifth century AD) *Euporista* [L]
Procopius (AD 500–560) *Wars of Justinian; Buildings of Justinian; Secret History* [L]
Propertius (50–45 BC – 15 BC) *Elegies* [L]
Quintilian (*c.* AD 35–90) *Institutiones Oratoriae* [L]
Rabi Eliezer (first/second century AD) *Ketubot*
Sallust (*c.* 86–35 BC) *Bellum Catilinae* [L]
Salvian, Bishop of Marseilles (*c.* AD 439–50) *De Gubernatione* [L]
Seneca, L. (*c.* 4 BC – AD 65) *Ad Helvia; Ad Marciam; De Beneficiis; Octavia; De Matrimonia; Declamations; De Ira; Heracles on Mount Oeta; Natural Questions; Phaedra; Dialogus* [L]
Seneca, M. (54 BC – *c.* AD 39) *Controversiae* [L]
Servius (late fourth century AD) *On Virgil; On Georgics* [L]
Soranus (*fl.* AD 100) *Gynaikea; Leonidas* [Gk]
Statius (*c.* AD 45 – *c.* 96) *Silvae* [L]
Strabo (64 BC – *c.* AD 24) *Geography* [Gk]
Strato (*c.* AD 120) *Greek Anthology*
Suetonius (*c.* AD 69–140) *Augustus; Caligula; Claudius; Domitian; Galba; Julius Caesar; Life of Horace; Nero; Otho; Tiberius; Vitellius; Ad Gramm.; Titus* [L]

Tacitus (AD 56–118) *Agricola; Annals; Dialogus de Oratoribus; Germania; Histories* [L]
Tatian (*c.* AD 120 – *c.* 180) *Address to the Greeks*
Terence (*fl. c.* 170–160 BC) *Hecyra, Adelphoe; Eunuchus* [L]
Tertullian (third century) *On the Apparel of Women; Ad Nationes; Apolegeticus; De Spectaculis*
Theopompus of Chios (*c.* 380 – *c.* 315 BC) [Gk]
Tibullus (*c.* 55 – 19 BC) *Elegies* [L]
Ulpian (*c.* AD 170–228) *Digest; Regulae; On the Edict; De Ritu Nupt.* [L]
Valerius Maximus (AD 14–27) *Memorable Deeds and Sayings* [L]
Varro (116–27 BC) *De Lingua Latina; Human and Divine Antiquities; On Agriculture* [L]
Velleius Paterculus (*c.* 19 BC – *c.* AD 31) *Historiae Romanae* [L]
Virgil (70–19 BC) *Aeneid; Eclogues* [L]
De Viribus Illustribus (first half of fourth century AD) [L]
Xenophon (*fl.* 371 BC) *Memorabilia* [Gk]

Notes

Introduction

1. Rabbi Eliezer, *m. Ketubot 5*, 6. Rav at *yketubot 5*, 8, 30a–b.
2. Cicero, *De Legibus* 3, 3.
3. Valerius Maximus 2, 9.
4. Plutarch, *Cato the Elder* 17; Cicero *De Re Publica* 4,6; Dionysius of Halicarnassus 20, 3; Livy *Periochae* 14, 39, 4; Plutarch *op. cit* 18; Aulus Gellius, 4, 8; 4, 12; Pliny, Natural History 18, 3. Dionysius 20, 3; Livy 7, 2. See Fantham, *Stuprum: Public Attitudes and Penalties for Sexual Offences in Republican Rome*, 121; Richlin, *Not before Homosexuality: The Materiality of the cinaedus and the Roman Law against Love between Men*, 556. The emperor took the job on during the empire.

1 Love, and Being a *Matrona*

1. *CIL* 6, 11602.
2. *CIL* 1, 1007.
3. Allia Potestas *CIL* 6, 37965. Ulpia Epigone Museo Gregoriano Profano, Vatican 9856. Port Sunlight: the Funerary Altar of Pedana, inv. LLAG 12.
4. *CIL* 6, 29580.
5. *CIL* 6, 18817; 6, 29436; *L' Annee Epigraphique* 1922, 48.
6. *CIL* 6, 9499.
7. *CIL* 13, 1983; *CIL* 13, 2182.
8. Seneca, *de Matrimonio* 72–7.
9. *CIL* 8, 11294 found in Algeria. *CIL* 3, 3572.
10. Catullus, 62, 63–70.
11. *CIL* 6.1527, 31670. Valerius Maximus, *Memorable Deeds and Sayings* 6,7,1–3.
12. Tacitus, *Agricola* 4.2–4; translation H. Mattingley, *Tacitus, The Agricola and the Germania*.
13. Tacitus, *Dialogus de Oratoribus* 28.
14. Quintilian *Institutiones Oratoriae* 1.1. 6–8, 15–17, 20; Cornelius Nepos, *Fragmenta 1–2 de Viris Illustribus*.

15. Livy, 10, 2, 7–8.
16. *CIL* 10, 6009.
17. Martial, 11, 53.
18. Statius, *Silvae* 3,5.
19. Martial, 9, 30.
20. Quintilian, *op. cit.* 6, *Preface* 4 and 5.
21. Pliny the Younger, *Epistulae*, 6, 7; see also a similar refrain in 7,5 and Pliny's concern about his wife's illness in 6,4.
22. Seneca, *op. cit* (frag. 58 Haase 1872); Tacitus *Annals* 15, 63.
23. Ovid, *Fasti* 2, 720–758.
24. Pliny, 3,16 3–6.
25. Martial, 5, 34; 10, 61.
26. Pliny, 7,19. Tacitus, *Histories* 1,3.
27. Tacitus *Annals* 16, 34.
28. Pliny, 6.24.
29. Plutarch, *Brutus* 13 and Dio 44, 13–14. See also Valerius Maximus *op. cit.* 4.6 and 6.7 on brave and faithful wives; Appian *Bellum Civile* 4, 39–40 and Tacitus, *ibidem*, on brave wives in the civil wars.
30. 4, 6, 5.
31. Tacitus, *Annals* 6, 29; 16,10.
32. *ibid* 6, 40.
33. *ibid* 6, 29.
34. *ibid* 15, 63, 2–4.
35. *ibid* 16, 34.
36. Pliny, *op. cit* 3, 16, 7–9.
37. Valerius Maximus, *op. cit*, 6.7. 1–3.
38. Quintilian, *op. cit.* 8, 5, 16.
39. Appian, *op. cit.* 4. 39–40.
40. Dio Cassius, *op. cit* 62, 13.4.
41. Sallust, *Catilina* 25. See Balsdon, *Roman Women* 47–49 for the controversy surrounding Sallust's description of her.
42. Plautus, *Curculio* 35–38. Augustine, *Confessions* 9,9.
43. See Grmek, *Les Maladies* 214–225.
44. Seneca, *ad Marciam* 1, 1; *ad Helviam* 16, 5.
45. Livy, 34.2.1, 2; 8–11, 14.
46. Plutarch, Cato *Maior* 8,4; *Life of Themistocles* 18.
47. Plautus, *Aulularia* 498–550.
48. Valerius Maximus 9, 1,3.
49. John Chrysostom, *The Type of Women Who Ought to be Taken as Wives* 4; Livy 34, 3, 3; 34,7.
50. Philo, *De Specialibus Legibus* 172–175. Translation by C. D. Yonge: *A Treatise on Those Special Laws Which Are Referrible to Two Commandments in the Decalogue, the Sixth and Seventh, Against Adulterers and All Lewd Persons, and Against Murderers and All Violence,* (London 1854).
51. Plautus, *Bacchae* 41.
52. Cicero, *Pro Murena* 12, 27.
53. Martial 8, 12.
54. Cicero, *Att.* 15,11.
55. Cicero, *ad Fam* 14, 4–6.
56. Plutarch, *Cicero* 20. Ovid, *Tristia* 4, 10, 69ff.

57. Ovid, *Ars Amatoria* 1, 31–32; Martial 1, 35, 8–9; Valerius Maximus 8, 3. Seneca, *Declamations* 1.
58. Livy 1, 57–60.
59. *ibid* 1, 58,7.
60. See Edwards, *Death* 180ff.
61. Livy 3, 44–48; Dionysius of Halicarnassus 11, 35, 4.
62. Plutarch *Gaius Gracchus* 4,3; 19, 1–3. Translation by Ian Scott-Kilvert in *Plutarch, Makers of Rome*. Valerius Maximus 4, 6, 1.
63. For the snake anecdote see Cicero, *de Divitatione* 1,36, and 2,62; Pliny, *op. cit.* 7, 122; Valerius Maximus *op.cit.*; *Viribus Illustribus* 56, 16.
64. Plutarch, *Tiberius Gracchus* 1, 6.
65. Plutarch, *Gaius Gracchus* 4, 3, trans. Bernadotte Perrin (Cambridge, MA: 1921) with adaptions. 17. For Cornelia's fecundity see Pliny, *op. cit.* 7, 57 and Seneca, *ad Helviam* 16, 6; Pliny, *op. cit.* 7, 57.
66. Suetonius, *Augustus* 73,1; 64,2.
67. Balsdon, *op. cit.* 270 and note 59.
68. Ovid, *op. cit.* 3, 817–820.
69. Columella, *praef* 1–3; 7–9.
70. Aelius Aristeides, *Roman Oration* 71b.
71. Petronius, *Satyricon* 37, 67.
72. Cornelius Nepos, *De Viris Illustribus praef.* 6.
73. Columella, 12, 3.
74. Ulpian, *Regulae* 11. 1, 21,27,28. Also Cicero, *Pro Murena* where he asserts that women require guardians because of their inferior intellect.
75. Gaius, *Institutiones* 145, 154. See Gardner, *Family* 241ff.
76. Justinian, *Institutes* 1, 9.
77. Cf Chalmers, 24–25; 30ff.
78. Caesar, *Bellum Gallicum* 5, 14.
79. Dio 77, 16, 5.
80. See P. Dubois, Slavery (2009) in G. Boys-Stones, *The Oxford Handbook of Hellenic Studies* (Oxford), 316–327.
81. Martial 4, 13; Juvenal 11, 146ff; Ammianus Marcellinus 28, 1, 49.
82. *CIL* 6, 7296; 6, 9976; 8, 20084 cf *CIL* 6, 6, 6335 and 6358.
83. Tacitus, *Annals* 14, 42, 1.

2 Marriage, Divorce and Adultery

1. Livy, 34, 7, 12.
2. Paul, *Opinions* 2.19, 2–2, 6–9; 2,20,1; *Edict* 35, 1.
3. Dio, 54, 6, 7.
4. Aulus Gellius *Noctes Atticae* 10, 10; Egyptian post-mortems provided the evidence, apparently.
5. Gaius *Institutiones* 1, 108–119; Servius on Virgil, *Georgics* 1,31; Aulus Gellius, *op.cit.* 3,2,12f.
6. *Digest* 25.7.4 (Paul).
7. 22,3,1.
8. Ulpian, *On the Edict* 35.
9. Pomponius, *On Sabinus* 5.
10. Balsdon, *op. cit.* 184–185 and his notes 44–53.

Notes

11. Tacitus, *Annals* 15, 37, 8f; Suetonius, *Nero* 28,1. Juvenal 2, 117ff.
12. Juvenal, 6, 300.
13. Servius *Ad Virgil, Aeneid*, 1, 37.
14. Valerius Maximus 2,1,5.
15. Pliny, *NH* 14,89; Polybius 6, 11a; Plutarch *Questiones Romanae* 6.
16. Valerius Maximus, 2,1,6.
17. Dio, 54, 16, 7.
18. *CIL* 1,1221.
19. *AE*, 1971, 534.
20. See Harkness, *Age at Marriage*.
21. *BGU* 1052.
22. Plutarch, *Cato Maior* 17.
23. Plautus, *Mercator* 823–9.
24. Ovid, *Amores* 3,4,37.
25. Plutarch, *Moralia* 145A. For Julia Mamaea see Herodian 5, 3, 10; 5, 7, 3.
26. Martial, 6,7.
27. Rapsaet-Charlier, M. –Th. *Ordre Senatorial*.
28. Pliny, *NH* 7,5.
29. Plutarch, *Romulus* 22.
30. Dionysius of Halicarnassus, 2, 25, 7.
31. Catullus, 61, 71–73; Propertius 2,7,13f.
32. Soranus, *Gynaecology* 1, 34,1.
33. *CIL* 6, 10320.
34. Plutarch, *Sulla* 3, 2.
35. Petronius, *Satyricon* 74.
36. Suetonius, *Augustus* 62, 63, 69.
37. Plautus, *Captivi* 889: 'liberorum quaerundorum causa ei, credo, uxor data est'
38. *CIL* 6. 1527 rara sunt tam diuturna matrimonia, finita morte, non divertio in...nobis. Paul, *Sent. Recept* 2, 26,4; *Digest* 48,5,30.
39. Valerius Maximus, 6, 1, 3 and 6.
40. Aulus Gellius *Noctes Atticae* 1,6,2; 1,17,4.
41. Malcovati, fr 6.
42. Tacitus, *Annals* 3.25.
43. Pliny, 2,20.

3 'The Incomplete Woman' and Sexual Medicine

1. Greek doctors: see Flemming, *Medicine* 50. Pliny, *NH* 29, 21; 29, 8, 16–18; 29, 6. Martial, 8, 74; 1, 47. Aristaeus, *Deipnosophistae* 666A. Galen, *On the Divisions of the Medical Art* 2.
2. Pliny, *Natural History* 25, 6, 17–18.
3. Soranus, *Gynaikeia* 1, 45 (CMG 4, 31, 26ff) and Hippocrates, *Aphorisms* V.
4. *CIL* 6, 9720; 9723.
5. *CIL* 6, 6647.
6. *Thesleff* 123–124.
7. Galen, *On the Usefulness of Parts of the Body*, 14, 6–7ff; hair: *idem*, 11,14.
8. See Jackson, *Doctors* 106.
9. *Euporista* 3, 1, 13.
10. Baader, *Spezialarzte* 233, footnote 62.

11. Suetonius *Tiberius* 43, 2; Martial 43, 1–4.
12. Aelius Aristides, *Hieroi Logoi* 1, 61–68.
13. *Places in Man* 47.
14. *Diseases of Women* 1, 1.
15. *Glands* 16.
16. Carson, p. 153.
17. *Superf.* 31.
18. *Frag* A81, B65, B67.
19. *UP* 14, 6–7. For Herophilus: Soranus, 3,3; 1, 29; Galen, *On the Seed* 2, 1. Soranus 1, 2–4. Pliny, *op cit* 7, 67.
20. Pliny *NH*, 26, 90; Soranus, *Gyn* 4, 14–150.
21. Celsus *de Med* 5, 21, 1; Pliny *op. cit* 26, 90, 152–158.
22. Soranus, *Gyn* 4, 38.
23. *op. cit.* 3, 41.
24. *de Med* 7, 28, 2; *Mul* 230.
25. Pliny, *op. cit.* 7, 33; 24, 27; 117–118; 27, 4; 27, 262; 34, 169. Celsus, *de Medica* 4, 27; 5, 21; Pliny, *op cit* 30, 41.
26. See Jackson *op. cit.* 92–93 for details, including a technical description from a contemporary of Soranus', Archigenes of Apamea, via Paul of Aegina, 6, 73.
27. Lucretius, 4, 1290.
28. Aulus Gellius, *Noctes Atticae* 3, 10, 8; 3, 16; Pliny the Elder, *op. cit.* 7, 38–43, 48–49.
29. Pliny, *Epistulae* 4, 21.
30. *Population Reference Bureau* 2006 and Bliss: bliss.org.uk.
31. *Gyn* 4, 7; 8.
32. See Suetonius, *Nero*.
33. Celsus *de Med* 7, 29, 7.
34. *Gyn* 4, 2.
35. Celsus, *op. cit.* 7, 29, 4–5; Soranus, *Gyn* 4, 12.
36. 3, 14, 17.
37. Pliny, *NH* 28, 9, 42.
38. Soren, *Excavations* 482.
39. See Jackson, *op. cit.* 103–104. Treggiari: *Roman Social History* 45–46.
40. Celsus, *de Med* 2, 8, 30–31.
41. Julia: Macrobius 2,5,9 (trans. A. Richlin). Juvenal 6, 366–348.
42. Pliny, *Ep* 8, 10.
43. Pliny, *NH* 28, 99. Hippocrates, *op cit* 1, 1, 25.
44. Celsus, *de Med* 2, 7, 7; 6, 6, 38; 2, 8, 7 and 25.
45. Oribasius, *Ecloga Medicamentorum* 132, 1.
46. *Gyn* 1, 33; 1, 29–30.
47. Soranus, *op. cit.* 1, 24. Pliny, *NH* 28, 23. On menstrual cloths, see Croom, *Running the Roman Home* 96–97.
48. Pliny, *op cit* 27, 23, 85.
49. *NH* 20,99, 263; 25, 54,97; 30,43,123; 25,18,39.
50. Aristotle, *Historia Animalium* 583A; Hippocrates *Natura Mulierum* 98; *Muliebria* 1, 76. Dioscorides *de Materia Medica* 3, 34; 1, 77,2; 3, 130; 5, 106, 6. Lucretius, 4, 1269–1278. Pliny, *op. cit.* 29, 27, 85. Soranus, *op cit* 1, 60, 4; 1, 61, 1–3; 1, 64, 1–2, 1, 65, 1–7. Aetius, 16, 17. See Hopkins, *Contraception*.
51. Seneca, *De Ira* 1, 15, 2.
52. Soranus, *op. cit.* 1, 89

53. *ibid* 2, 6.
54. *ibid* 2, 45.
55. *ibid* 2, 38; 30; 40.
56. *ibid* 2, 47; Pliny, *NH* 28, 21. Peek 1233; *CIL* 8, *Supplement* 20288; *CIL* 8, 24734; Peek 1871; *CIL* 14, 2737; *ILS* 8451. Soranus, *Gyn* 2, 18–20; 11, 19 (translation adapted from Temkin); Plutarch, *Moralia* 3C–D, also recommended maternal breast feeding. Tacitus, *op. cit.* 20.
57. See King, *Once upon a Text*.
58. See Maines, *The Technology of Orgasm*.
59. *Tim.* 91a–c.
60. *Gyn* 3. 29. See *DSM-IV* and *ICD-10* for definitions.
61. Galen, *On Prognosis* 6.
62. Hippocrates, *On Virgins* 8, 466–70.
63. See Jackson, *op. cit.* 89–90.
64. See Jackson, *op. cit.* 89–94 for uterine disorders.
65. *Mor.* 518d. Galen, 13, 539.
66. Hippocrates, *Epidemics* 5, 101; Soranus, *Leonidas* quoted by Aetius, 16, 44. Aetius, 16, 115.
67. See Jackson, *op. cit.* 90–91.
68. See Bryk, *Circumcision*, 271. Strabo, 17, 25. Philo, *Questions on Genesis* 3, 47.
69. Celsus, 4, 28; Galen *Nat. Mul.* 109; *Epid.* 3, 7. Martial 1, 65, 4; 7, 71. See Fenton, *The Late Roman Infant Cemetery*. Grmek, *Les Maladies*; Younger, *Sex* 184. Horace, *Satires* 1, 5, 62.
70. *CIL* 6, 19128. Tacitus, *Germania* 20.
71. Aulus Gellius, *Attic Nights* 12, 1.
72. *P. Lond* 951 verso.
73. *CIL* 4352.
74. See Bonfante, *Nursing Mothers in Classical Art*, 174ff. Soranus, *Gyn*, 2, 18–20. Breast *vota* were also dedicated at healing sanctuaries for those seeking a cure for mastitis and other breast diseases, some of which may have been cancer. Pero: Valerius Maximus 5,4,1. Aulus Gellius, 12, 1.
75. *P. Lond* 951 verso. Breastfeeding: Pliny, *NH* 28, 73, 123. See also Richlin, 'Pliny's Brassiere' in *Roman Sexualities* 204–205.
76. Artemidorus, 5, 63.
77. For nymphomania see WHO *ICD-10*; Gourevitch, *Women Who Suffer*.
78. Diodorus Siculus 4.6.5. Isidore of Seville, *Eytmologiae* 11.3. 11. Pliny, *NH*7, 33; 36; 51; 30; 23. Shrew: *NH* 30, 134.
79. Phlegon, *Marvels* 10, 28.
80. Lucretius, *De Rerum Natura*, 4, 1030–57; See Brown, *Lucretius on Love and Sex*, 62–63.
81. See Dugan, *Preventing Ciceronianism*, 403–404.
82. Galen, *De Semine* 1.16.30–32.
83. See Hanson, *The Restructuring of Female Physiology at Rome*, 267; *Priapea* 78 and *CIL* 12, 6721(5), one of the Perusine *glandes*.
84. Martial, 7, 82; 9, 27, 11, 75; 14, 215. Juvenal 6, 73, 379.
85. Quintilian, *Institutio Oratoria* 11, 3, 19. Aristotle, *History of Animals* 781a, 21–27; Celsus, *On Medicine* 7, 25, 3.
86. Pliny *NH* 34, 166. See also Galen, *De Simplicium Medicamentorum Temperamentis ac Facultatibus*, Kuhn, 12, 232. *Ibid, De locis Affectis*, Kuhn, 8, 450–451.

87. Pliny, *NH* 30, 2.
88. Pliny, *NH* 24, 157; 25, 154; 28, 99,262.
89. Pindar, *Pythian* 3, 46, 54.
90. Pliny, *NH* 28, 97, 100, 102; Euripides, *Andromache* 29–35, 155–60.
91. Pliny, *NH* 27, 4.

4 Birth Control, Aphrodisiacs and Love Potions: the Need (or Not) for Venus

1. For infanticide see Brunt, *Roman Manpower*, 148–154.
2. 2,15.
3. Philo, *de Specialibus Legibus* 3, 114–115.
4. Livy 27, 37.
5. Suetonius, *Augustus* 94,3; Musonius Rufus, *Reliquae* 80f.
6. Soranus, *Gynaekia*.
7. *P. Oxy* 744. *The Gnomon of the Ideologue* (41 and 107) provides for male foundlings – *children of the dung heap* but there is nothing for females.
8. Ovid, *Metamorphoses* 9, 669–684; 704–706. The *Codex Theodosianus* 11.27.1 in AD 315 makes provision for state assistance for families who are driven to expose or give away their children on account of poverty.
9. *P. Oxy* 1895. Private charity, or alms, existed too, as shown on a monument from around AD 175 in Sicca, North Africa (*CIL* 8, 1641). It bequeaths the interest on a 1.3 million sesterces donation for the feeding and upkeep of 300 boys and 300 girls, in perpetuity (replaced when girls reached thirteen and when boys were fifteen).
10. See the plangent papyrus letter from a young girl, Tare, from Apamea in Syria, to her aunt, appealing for someone to take her in, *'all alone in a strange land'*. *P. Bour.* 25.
11. Juvenal 6, 602–608. Tacitus, *Germania* 19. Soranus, *op cit* 1, 67–69; 17, 4, 9. For infant burials in Roman Britain, see Allason-Jones, *Women in Roman Britain* (1989) 42ff. Monkeys etc: Soranus, *op. cit.* 1, 55; 1, 49, 1, 54, 1, 39.
12. Pomeroy, *Goddesses* 164–165 points out the short-sightedness of these policies, delimiting as they do the supply of child bearers and their male offspring, much needed for the army; the comparison with Spartan policy is stark. See Golden, p. 155. Cicero, *Tusc.* 1, 39, 93; *IG* 5, 2, 43.
13. *NH* 20,99, 263; 25, 54,97; 30,43,123; 25,18,39.
14. Aristotle, *Historia Animalium* 583A; Hippocrates *Natura Mulierum* 98; *Muliebria* 1, 76. Dioscorides *de Materia Medica* 3, 34; 1, 77,2; 3, 130; 5, 106, 6. Lucretius, 4, 1269–1278. Pliny, *op cit* 29, 27, 85. Soranus, *op cit* 1, 60, 4; 1, 61, 1–3; 1, 64, 1–2, 1, 65, 1–7. Aetius 16, 17. See Hopkins, *Contraception*.
15. *CIL* 4, 107.
16. *CIL* 4, 4185; Manetho, *Forecasts* 4,312.
17. Seneca, *Controversies* 1, 2, 22. Martial, 11, 78.
18. In Oribasius, 68.
19. Pliny, *NH* 8, 209.
20. See Rouselle, *Body Politics* 308 and Kapparis, *Abortion*.
21. Juvenal 6, 595–597; Seneca *Helv.* 16, 1. See also Ovid, *Fasti* 621–624; *Heroides* 37–42; Cicero, *Pro Cluentio*, 2–4.
22. Pliny, *op cit* 25, 7, 24–25. See Gardner, *Law and Society* 158–159 for the legal

Notes

implications. John Chrysostom, *Homily 24 on the Epistle to the Romans* 4; Plautus, *Truculentus* 179, Ovid *Amores* 2, 14. Procopius, *Secret History* 9, 20.
23. Ziebarth 24, 1–4, 1042ff.
24. *CIL* 6, 20905; trans. R. Lattimore.
25. *ILS* 8751; *IG* 3,3,97, 34–41; *CIL* 10, 8249; *IG*, 3,3, 78; *SEG* 27, 1717.
26. Suppl Mag, 47.
27. *CIL* 8, 12507; *PGM* 36, 283–294; 1, 83–87; 1, 167–168; 32.
28. Hyenas: Pliny, *op cit* 28, 106. Virgil, *Aeneid* 6, 71–74. Dionysius of Halicarnassus, *Roman Antiquities* 4, 62, 5–6. Virgil, *Eclogue* 4, 6, 24, 31.
29. Lucian, *de Mercede Conductis* 4. The translation is by C. D. N. Costa.
30. Pliny, *op. cit.* 28, 256. Marcus Aurelius, 19.
31. Tibullus 1, 5, 37–56; 1, 2, 42–66.
32. Lucan, *de Bello Civili* 6, 419ff.
33. Seneca, *Heracles on Mount Oeta* 449–472.
34. Marcellus of Bordeaux, *De Medicamentis* 33.
35. *ibid* 33, 64.
36. *ibid*; cf Pliny, *op. cit.* 25, 75.
37. Marcellus, *op. cit.* 33, 26.
38. Artemisia, dittany, opopanax, pepper, saffron, giant fennel, myrrh, and colocynth; see Riddle, *Contraception and Abortion from the Ancient World to the Renaissance*, 90.
39. Riddle, *op. cit.* 91, Marcellus 'does not appear expertly knowledgeable about...women and fertility'.
40. The *Paignia* of Democritus, PGM 7, 167–186, as cited by Davidson, *Don't Try This at Home: Pliny's Salpe, Salpe's* Paignia *and Magic*, 591.
41. Pliny, *op. cit.* 28, 262, crediting Salpe the obstetrician.

5 Buggery, Beasts and Brothels: the Need for *Virtus*

1. *Popular Culture*, 77. DSM in *The Diagnostic and Statistical Manual of Mental Disorders*. After protests by the gay rights movement the references to homosexuality were replaced with a category labelled 'sexual orientation disturbance' for the 1974 edition. Pliny, *Natural History* 28, 4, 7. Seneca, *Controversiae*, 4, 10. Polybius, *Histories* 32, 2. Lucretius, *De Rerum Natura* 4, 1052–1056; Catullus 24, 48, 81, 99; Tibullus, 1, 4, 8, 9; Propertius 4.2. For *virtus* see *CIL*. 1, 6–7 and the stele commemorating Lucius Cornelius Scipio Barbatus (cos. 298 BC) and his *virtus*.
2. *Tribas*: Liddle & Scott: *A Greek-English Lexicon, ad loc*; Lewis & Short: *A Latin Dictionary, ad loc*.
3. Ovid, *Metamorphoses* 9, 727; 733–734. Martial 7, 67; 1, 90. See also 7, 70.
4. Catullus, 97.
5. Pliny, *NH* 28, 99. *CIL* 4,5296; translation is by Richlin, *Sexuality in the Roman Empire*, 347. Cicero *Oratio de Domo Sua* 10, 25.
6. Lucian, *Dialogues of the Courtesans*, 5.
7. Seneca *Ep.* 122. Seneca the Elder, *Controversiae* 1,2,23. Juvenal, 6, 306ff. Ovid, *Ars Amatoria* 2, 683–684. Lucretius, *De Rerum Natura* 4, 1052–1056. Ovid, *Metamorphoses* 9, 727, 733–4. See Braund, *A Woman's Voice?* Sappho: Lucian, *Affairs of the Heart* 28.
8. Strato, *Greek Anthology* 12,7. Martial, 11, 43. Juvenal 6 314–326;

Lucilius, *Satires* 7; Petronius, *Satyricon* 140; Lucretius, *De Rerum Natura* 4, 1263–1273. Horace, *Satires* 2, 7, 46–56; Martial 11, 104. *Hectoreus equus;* Ovid, *op. cit.* 3, 777–778. Petronius, *Satyricon* 24,4; see also CIL 4, 1825; Juvenal 6, 311.

9. Ovid, *Ars Amatoria* 3, 771 ff. See also *Tristia* 2, 1, 523 for his description of wall paintings.
10. Suetonius, *Tiberius* 44, 2.
11. Firmicus Maternus, 5,2,4, 5,3,11 and 17, 5,6,8, 6,30,15; Vettius Valens, a Hellenistic astrologer, 1,1, 2,16, 2,36 and 38.
12. Ovid, *Ars Amatoria* 2, 725–8.
13. Masturbation CIL 10, 4483. Martial, 2, 28, 4; 9, 27, 14; 4, 84, 1–4; 4, 71, 5–6. Cf Clarke, *Looking at Lovemaking* 220 who says that no Roman of the elite class would ask his wife to perform fellatio. Suetonius, *Ad Gramm.* 23. See Arena, *Roman Oratorical Invective* 156 and Woman, *Abusive Mouths in Classical Athens* 322. Catullus, 39, 78b, 97, 99.
14. Martial 11, 61. See Younger, *Sex, ad loc.* Catullus, 99,10; Martial, 7, 94;3, 17. The graffito, CIL 4, 1383, was found decorating a doorway to a shop in Pompeii; see Varone, *Erotica Pompeiana* 81. *Irrumatio*: Catullus 16; Martial 2, 47, 4.
15. Voyeurism: see Horace, *Odes* 3, 6; Seneca, *Natural Questions* 1, 16. *Greek Anthology* 5, 49; 11, 328. Tiberius: Suetonius, *Tiberius* 43. Ausonius, 43.
16. Ovid, *Ars Amatoria* 3, 769ff.
17. 7, 681ff. For bestiality, see Johns, 1982, 110–11.
18. *Eclogue* 6.
19. Ovid, *Met.* 6, 109. Martial *De Spectaculis* 6 (5) Pliny, *NH* 8, 64. Apuleius, *Metamorphoses* 16; 17; 10, 29, 34. Dio 76, 8, 2. Juvenal 6, 60ff.
20. Juvenal 11, 162ff; Martial 3, 82, 13. Tacitus, *Annals* 2, 85. Propertius 2, 23, 5–6; 21.
21. Horace, *Satires*, 1, 2. Seneca, *Controv.* 1, 2; Petronius, *Satyricon* 7; Juvenal, 6, 121ff; aediles: Tacitus, *op.cit.* 2, 85, 1–2; Suetonius, *Caligula* 40. Vistilia, Tacitus, *op. cit.* 2, 85, 1–4.
22. Horace, *Satires* 1, 2, 28–36.
23. Cicero, *Pro Caelio*, 48–50.
24. Suetonius, *Life of Horace*. Seneca, *Natural Questions* 1, 16.
25. Martial, 9, 32; 10, 75.
26. Juvenal, 9, 24; Strabo 6,2, 6; 8, 6, 20. CIL 9, 2689. *Codex Theodos.* 60, tit. 7, ed. Ritter; Ulpian 54, 23, *De Ritu Nupt.*
27. CIL 4, 794; 9847; 1391; 2273; 4185; 10004; 1751. Nude bathing: Plutarch, *Cato* 20, 5; see Fagan, *Bathing in Public in the Roman World* 26–27.
28. See Beard, *Pompeii* 233. Artemidorus, *Oneirocritica* 5–12. Roger Pack, *Artemidori Daldiani Onirocriticon Libri V* 88. Plutarch, *Cato* 21, 2. See Joshel, *Women and Slaves in Greco-Roman Culture*, 11.
29. 6, 114ff.
30. 11, 162–174.
31. Candida CIL 4, 1512–4. Ovid, *Remedia Amoris* 327. Petronius *Satyricon* 7.
32. Martial 4, 28; 6, 93.
33. *idem* 1, 34, 8.
34. Petronius, *Satyricon* 126.
35. Juvenal, 6, 103–112.
36. Lucilius, *Fragment* 1182W.

Notes

37. Horace, *Epodes* 12, 1, 1–20.
38. Martial, 3, 93. See also, 3, 75; 8, 31; 9, 66; 10, 91, 11, 25; 11, 46; 11,71; 12, 86.
39. Ovid, *Amores* 3,7,1; 3,3. Tibullus, 1, 5; 1, 39. Petronius, *Satyricon* 132.
40. *Greek Anthology* 5, 76.
41. *Priapea, Virgilian Appendix* 83, 26–37.
42. *CIL*, 4, 1516; 4, 10004: Marin 1959.
43. Pliny, *Ep.* 4,19.
44. Martial, 4,13.
45. *CIL* 8, 12613.
46. *CIL* 2, 5464.
47. Ovid, *Tristia*, 2, 431; Propertius 2, 6, 27–34; Ovid, *op. cit.* 2, 521–28. *Milesiaca: op. cit.* 2, 413 and 443–444. Carrhae: Plutarch, *Crassus* 32. Suetonius, *Tiberius* 44, 2.
48. See Brock, *Introduction to Holy Women of the Syrian Orient* 24–25; Harvey, *Women in Early Byzantine Hagiography*.
49. Lucretius, 4, 1153ff; 1278 –1287. Ovid, *Ars Amatoria* 2, 657–666.
50. *Priapea* 4. Martial 12, 43; 10, 35; Martial, 12, 95.
51. Propertius, 1, 2, 1–8.
52. Ovid, *Ars Amatoria* 3, 255–286.
53. See Clarke, *op. cit.* 275ff. For female sexual dominance see, for example, Apodyterium 7, Scene 1 Pompeii Suburban Baths; Pompeii House of the Centenary Ix, 8, 6 room 43.
54. Plutarch, *Gaius Gracchus* 4, 3–4; Tacitus, *Annals* 59, 3; Dio 58, 11, 5.
55. Eg: Rufinus 5, 60, 62.
56. Martial, 1, 100, 2,52, 14, 66, 14, 134, 14, 149.
57. See Marshall, *The Stagecraft and Performance of Roman Comedy* 65. Plautus, *Poenulus* 1416. Ugly cheeks: see Minerva in Ovid's *Fasti* 6.693–710). Plautus, *Casina*, 848.
58. Ovid, *Amores* 1, 5,20. See also Philodemus, 12 (*Palatine Anthology* 5, 132); Dalby, *Empires of Pleasures*, 24, 64–65, 263.
59. Achilles Tatius's *Leucippe and Clitophon* 37, 7.
60. *Necdum inclinatae prohibent te ludere mammae*, Propertius, 2,15, 21; Tibullus, 1, 6, 18.
61. Manetho, *Aegyptica* 4, 312.
62. See for example, Seneca, *Phaedra* 247, *Hercules Oetaeus* 926. 'One of the commonest literary motifs for mourning in ancient texts is women baring and beating their breasts,' notes Alan Cameron, *The Last Pagans of Rome* (Oxford, 2011), 725.
63. Servius, ad *Aeneid* 5,78.
64. Caesar, *Bellum Gallicum* 7, 47,5; Tacitus, *Germania* 8,1.
65. Valerius Maximus, 9, 1, 8.
66. Cicero, *In Verrem* 2,3,6, 2,4,83, 2,5, 81–82, 137; *Post Reditum in Senatu* 11, 14; *Philippicae* 2, 15, 62–63, 69.
67. See Kuttner, *Culture and History at Pompey's Museum* 348–349.
68. Pliny, *NH* 7,34.
69. *Isaiah* 3:8, 25–26.
70. See Lopez, *Before Your Very Eyes* 122, 145.

6 Sex in the Afternoon: the *domina* and Her Love Slave

1. Cf Chalmers, 24–25; 30ff.
2. *Poenulus* 32–35, 28–31.
3. *Women's Roles.*
4. See Arnott, *Menander* 33–34: 'it was obvious...that Plautus...had larded in a whole host of purely Roman features'.
5. All originally by Cicero: *Orator* 161; *Att.* 7, 2, 21; *Tusculanae Disputationes* 3, 45. See Chrystal, *Investigation* 15ff; Ross, *Backgrounds*; Tuplin, Cantores Euphorionis; *idem*, Cantores Euphorionis, *Again*; Luck, *Latin Love Elegy* 49ff; Crowther, *Valerius Cato*; see Lyne *Latin Love Poets* 169–174. For *otium* see André, *L'Otium*. 14.
6. Plutarch, 8, 1; 18; Polybius 31.
7. Plutarch, *loc cit*; Livy 24, 2–4; Aulus Gellius 7, 6–8. Cf Arkins, *Aspects of Sexuality* 8ff.
8. See G. Colin, *Rome et la Grèce*; J. Griffin *Augustan Poetry* 88ff and the Appendix, *Some Imperial Servants*. Various suggestions for the start and or cause of the decline have been made: Polybius, 31, 25 ascribes it to the victory over Macedonia; L. Calpurnius Piso (Pliny, *NH* 17, 38, 244) goes with 154 BC; Appian, *Bellum Civile* 1, 7 for the end of the war in Italy; Livy, 39, 6, 7 prefers 186 BC; Valleius Paterculus, *Historiae Romanae*, and Sallust, *Catilina* 10 opt for the end of the Third Punic War. See also Putnam, *The Roman Lady*; Reinhold, *The Generation Gap* 52ff.
9. See Pomeroy, *Relationship* 222ff; del Castillo, *Position* 171; and Villers, *Statut* 184f.
10. Kiefer, *Sexual Life* 24.
11. See Horace, *Odes* 3, 6; Kajanto, *On Divorce*; Hamilton, *Society Women*. Pomeroy, *op. cit.*, argues that in Catullus' day women were enjoying a kind of *de facto* freedom on account of the disinterest shown by many *propinqui*. Decline in *patria potestas* is covered by Reinhold, *op. cit.* 49; see also Fau 30 and del Castillo, *op. cit.* 167–170; Richlin, *Approaches*.
12. On educated women generally, see Best, *Cicero*; Griffin, *op. cit.* 103, and Fau, *op. cit.* 12. Eucharis: *CIL* 1, 1214; Cytheris: Cicero, *Ad Fam* 9, 26; *Phil* 2, 69. See also Hallet, *The Role of Women,* and Lyne, *op. cit.* 7.
13. Catullus, 10, 4, 17; 33–34; 6, 1–2; 32, 1–2.
14. *ibid* 86, 3–4; 43, 4; 35, 16–17.
15. Cicero, *Pro Caelio* 13, 32. On the identification issue see Dixon, *Reading Roman* 137ff.
16. So Rankin, *Clodia II* 505, 'it would be possible to claim Clodia (Lesbia) as an intellectual on the grounds of poem 36 alone'. Gallus' wife (78,2) is *lepidissima coniunx*; Laodamia, in Lesbia, is *docta* (68, 80).
17. Propertius, 4, 11.
18. Tibullus, 1,5, 25–28; 1, 3, 85–88.
19. Horace, *Odes* 1, 36, 13–13, 17–20; 2, 11, 22–24; 3, 14, 21–22.
20. *ibid* 2, 12, 17–20; 3, 9, 10; 2, 11, 22; 3, 28, 11; 4, 11, 35–37; 3, 14, 21; 1, 17, 10f.
21. Horace, *Odes* 3, 6, 21–25. The quotation is from Balsdon, *Roman Women* 275.
22. Scipio: Macrobius *Sat*, 3,14. Cornelius Nepos, *Epam* 1f.
23. Ovid, *Amores* 2, 4, 9–10; 47–48. See also 2, 10, 5–6. *Ars Amatoria* 3, 311–28; 3, 349–52.

24. Ovid, *Ars Amatoria* 1, 97–98; *ibid* 1, 462; *Amores* 2, 4, 22; *ibid* 3, 8, 5–7; *Ars* 2, 107–112.
25. Ovid, *op. cit.* 281ff.
26. *ibid* 3, 771ff.
27. Propertius, 4, 5.
28. For Sulpicia, see Pearcy, *op. cit.*; Santirocco, *Sulpicia Reconsidered*; Keith, – *Critical Trends*; Hubbard, *The Invention of Sulpicia*; Holzberg, *Four Poets*; Hallett, *The Eleven Elegies*; Churchill, *Women Writing Latin*.
29. Martial, 10, 35; see also 10, 38.
30. Virgil, *Aeneid* 4, 192–4.
31. *op. cit.* 8, 388ff.
32. Caesar, *De Bello Gallico* 5, 14; 6, 21.
33. Diodorus Siculus, 3, 15, 1–2; 17, 1–5.
34. Strabo 4, 5, 4.
35. *ibid* 164, 25.
36. Strabo, 7, 3, 4; Frr 577–578.
37. Diodorus Siculus, 5, 32, 7–8.
38. Juvenal, 3, 109–114.
39. Ammianus Marcellinus, 14, 4, 4; 31, 9, 6; 23, 6, 76. Wagons: 3,2,10.
40. Strabo, 15, 1, 59–60.
41. Arrian, *Indica* 17; cf Strabo 15, 1, 54.
42. Valerius Maximus, 4, 5.
43. Polybius, 21, 38; Livy 38, 24, 2–9; Plutarch *Mulierum Virtutes* 38c; Valerius Maximus, 6, 1 ext 2. Other non-Roman chaste women are at Valerius Maximus, 6,1; Plutarch, *op. cit.* 257f–8c.
44. Martial, 11, 53.
45. Dio, 62, 6, 4.
46. Tacitus, *Germania* 17–19; cf Horace, *Odes* 3, 24, 17–24 for Scythian women.
47. Cicero, *In Verrem* 3, 2, 33; Lucan, *Pharsalia* 8, 422–447; Justin 41, 3.
48. Strabo, 15, 3, 17; 15, 1, 59.
49. Diodorus Siculus, 1, 80, 3.
50. Ammianus Marcellinus, 23, 6, 76.
51. Athenaeus, 12, 522d–e.

7 Cross-Dressing, Transsexualism & Same-Sex Marriage

1. 'Transsexualism' has been replaced in *DSM-IV* by 'gender identity disorder in adolescents and adults'. Cicero, *De Haruspicium Responso* 2, 44. Ulpian, *Digest* 34, 2, 23; 34, 2, 33. Seneca the Elder, *Controversiae* 5, 6.
2. Tacitus, *Annals* 15. Suetonius, *Nero* 29.
3. See Vermaseren, *Cybele and Attis*, 96.
4. Catullus 63; trans. Sir Richard Francis Burton, 1894.
5. Dio, 67, 2, 3
6. Statius, *Silvae* 3, 4; Martial, 9, 5; translations by J. T. Quinn.
7. Martial 12, 42. Trans. D. R. Shackleton Bailey.
8. Juvenal, 2, 117–142.
9. *Theodosian Code* 9, 7, 3.
10. Eusebius, *Historia Ecclesiastica* 6,8.
11. *Matthew* 19, 12: 'For there are some eunuchs, which were so born from

their mother's womb: and there are some eunuchs, which were made eunuchs of men: and there be eunuchs, which have made themselves eunuchs for the kingdom of heaven's sake. He that is able to receive it, let him receive it'. King James Version.
12. Celsus, *Concerning Medicine* 7, 25.
13. Martial, 2, 45; 7, 30; 7, 35; 7, 82.

8 Bacchanalian Orgies and Vestal Virginity

1. Cicero, *De Officiis* 1, 17, 54. Translation adapted from Walter Miller, Loeb 1913. Cicero, *De Deorum Natura* 2, 70–72; Virgil, *Georgics* 4, 221ff.
2. Cf, however, Beard, *Rome* 25ff who argues against this view. For Caesar see Suetonius, *Julius Caesar* 7. For Julia Domna see Herodian, 4, 9, 3; *Historia Augusta, Caracella* 10, 1–4; *Severus* 21, 6–8; Etropius, 8, 20.
3. Ovid, *Fasti* 3, 269–72; see also Propertius 2, 32, 9–10.
4. Lactantius, 1, 20, 36. Arnobius, *Adversus Nationes* 4, 7 and 4, 11. Compare Tertullian, *Ad Nationes* 2, 11 and *Apologeticus* 25, 3. Augustine of Hippo, *De Civitate Dei* 4, 11 and 6, 9.
5. Augustine, *op. cit.*
6. The ancients believed that women too ejaculated during intercourse.
7. Dionysius, 4. 1, 2; Ovid *Fasti*. vi. 625, etc.; Pliny, *NH*. 36. 27. s. 70; Festus, *s.v. Nothum;* Plutarch. *de Fort. Rom.* 10.
8. *Fasti* 6, 473–568.
9. Juvenal, 6, 306–310.
10. *Caesar* 9.
11. Juvenal, 6, 314–334.
12. Cicero, *De Domo Sua*, 53, 136.
13. See Brouwer, *Bona Dea*.
14. *De Haruspicum Responsis* 17, 37–18, 38.
15. *Roman Questions* 104; *Moralia* 288–289; trans. F.C. Babbitt, 1936 Vol 4.
16. Livy, 39, 15, 6; 39, 8.
17. *De Legibus* 2, 9, 21.
18. Livy, 39, 17.
19. *Fabulae* 277.
20. Ovid, *Fasti* 1, 461–542; Servius, *In Aeneida* 8, 51; Solinus, *Collectanea Rerum Memorabilium* 1, 10, 13
21. Plutarch, *Numa* 10.
22. Livy, 22, 57, 2.
23. Dionysius 2, 68; *RE* vii A 768–770; Valerius Maximus 8, 1, 5; see also Richlin, *Carrying Water*.
24. Suetonius, *Domitian* 8, 3–5; Pliny, *Ep* 4, 11,6.
25. Valerius Maximus, 3,7,9; 6,8, 1.
26. Cicero, *Cat* 3, 9.
27. Dio, 777, 16, 1–3; 79, 9.
28. Pliny, *NH*.28, 13; Macrobius, *Saturnalia* 3, 13, 11.
29. Ovid, *op. cit.* 2, 303–358.
30. See Fantham, *Sexual Comedy in Ovid's* Fasti: *Sources and Motivation*, 185–216.
31. Ovid *op. cit.* 2, 441. See Holleman, *Ovid and the Lupercalia*, 260–268; Wiseman, *The God of the Lupercal*.

32. Livy, 1,5.
33. Servius, *ad. Aen.* 1,273.
34. Plutarch, Romulus 21; Servius *op. cit.* 8, 343.
35. Cicero, *Phil.* 2, 34, 43; 3, 5; 13,15. Plutarch, *Caesar* 61.
36. Suetonius, *Augustus* 31. Horace, *Odes* 3, 18 describes the Lupercalia. Shakespeare's *Julius Caesar* begins during the Lupercalia; Mark Antony is ordered by Caesar to strike his wife Calpurnia, in the hope that she will conceive: *'the barren touched in this holy chase shake off their sterile curse'*.

9 Raping the Romans

1. Ovid, *Ars Amatoria* 1, 663–668.
2. See Gordon, *Some Unseen Monster* 105.
3. Lucretius, *De Rerum Natura* 5, 964: *Violenta viri vis atque impensa libido.*
4. Under the *Lex Aquilia*: see McGinn, *Prostitution, Sexuality and the Law in Ancient Rome* 314; Gardner, *Women in Roman Law and Society* 119.
5. Gardner, *Women in Roman Law and Society*; see McGinn, *op. cit.* 326.
6. Richlin, *Not Before Homosexuality,* 558–559, quoting the jurist Pomponius: 'whatever man has been raped by the force of robbers or the enemy in wartime (*vi praedonum vel hostium*)' ought to bear no stigma (*Digest* 3,1, 1, 6).
7. Quintilian, *Institutio Oratoria* 4, 2, 69–71; Richlin, *op. cit.* 565. Diocletian: *Digest*, 9, 9, 20. Cicero, *Pro Planco* 30.
8. Gardner, *op. cit.* 118; Richlin, *op. cit.* 562–563.
9. See Brundage, *Law, Sex, and Christian Society in Medieval Europe,* 107.
10. Gardner, *op. cit.* 120.
11. *Theodosian Code* 9, 24, 1, 2–3; *Cod.* 9, 13, 1; Brundage, *Law, Sex, and Christian Society* 107. Brundage, *op. cit.* 107. Odahl, *Constantine and the Christian Empire* 179; Clark, *Women in Late Antiquity* 36–37.
12. Staples, *From Good Goddess to Vestal Virgins,* 164, citing Bryson, *Two Narratives of Rape in the Visual Arts: Lucretia and the Sabine Women*, in *Rape* (Blackwell, 1986), 199.
13. Ovid, *Metamorphoses* 6, 412–67. Cf. Homer, *Odyssey* 19, 518–29 and Sappho fr. 136.
14. In a fragment of the speech *De Re Floria* by Cato the Elder (frg. 57 Jordan in Aulus Gellius 9, 1, 7). See Richlin, *Not Before Homosexuality* 561.
15. *Digest* 48, 6, 3, 4 and 48, 6, 5, 2.
16. *ibid*, 47, 11, 1, 2. See *Digest* 48, 5, 35 for legal definitions of rape that involved boys.
17. Valerius Maximus 6,1.
18. Seneca, *Controversia* 5, 6.
19. Martial, 2, 60, 2.
20. Translation by Micaela Wakil Janan in *When the Lamp Is Shattered* 4. 5 See Winter, Catullus Purified: A Brief History of *Carmen* 16, *Arethusa* 6 (1973): 257–265; Beard, Pedicabo ego vos et irrumabo: *what was Catullus on about?*
21. To Persius, *Satire* 5, 30–31, the *praetexta* is the guardian (*custos*) of childhood.
22. Festus, 282–283.

23. Plutarch, *Cato* 20, 5.
24. Plutarch, *Moralia* 288a; see Habinek, 'The Invention of Sexuality in the World-City of Rome,' in *The Roman Cultural Revolution* 39.
25. Paulus, *Digest* 47, 11, 1, 2.
26. Cicero, *Verrine* 3, 23.
27. Quintilian, *Institutio Oratoria* 1, 2, 7–8.
28. For details, see Chrystal, *Roman Women*.

10 The Power of Sex: In Bed with a Soldier

1. *Life of Lucullus* 6 and Cicero, *Parad.* v. 3.
2. Cicero, *Phillipics* 3, 16.
3. Velleius Paterculus, *Histories* 2, 74, 3.
4. See Hallet, *Perusinae Glandes*.
5. 11, 20.
6. Herodian, 3, 8, 5.
7. *Periochae* to Livy 57; Valerius Maximus, 2, 7, 1.
8. Bowman and Thomas No 5, 1987.
9. Phaedrus, *Appendix* 10, 2–3 Perotti; Suetonius, *Domitian* 10; cf Dio, 67, 11, 4.
10. Dionysius, *Roman Antiquities* 16, 4; Valerius Maximus 6, 1, 12; Suetonius, *Galba* 22.
11. Valerius Maximus, 6, 1, 11; cf Dionysius, *op. cit.*
12. Juvenal, 14, 194–195.

11 Gladiator Adulator

1. Petronius, *Satyricon* 126; Juvenal 6, 103–112.
2. Ovid, *Ars Amatoria* 1, 663–668.
3. CIL 4.434 and 4353.
4. Tertullian *De Spectaculus* 22-23. Calpurnius Flaccus, *Declamatians*. 52.
5. Juvenal 6, 82–103.
6. Pliny, *NH* 28, 256. *Historia Augusta*: Marcus Aurelius 19.
7. Dio 61, 17, 3.
8. Tacitus, *Annals*, 15, 32.
9. Dio, 63, 3, 1.
10. Petronius, *Satyricon*, 45.
11. Dio, 66, 25, 1.
12. Martial, *De Spectaculis* 6; 8.
13. Suetonius, *Domitian* 6, 1. Dio, 67, 8, 4.
14. Statius, *Silvae*, 1, 6, 53.
15. Juvenal 1, 22-23; 6, 252ff.
16. Nicolaus of Damascus, *Athletica* 4, 153.
17. Dio, 66, 26, 7.
18. Dio, 76, 16.
19. CIL, 9, 2237.
20. Ovid, *Ars Amatoria*, 1, 156.

12 Bad Language – Roman Sexual Vocabulary

1. But not always; for example, in the mid-third century BC, Naevius uses *stuprum* in his *Bellum Punicum* to denote the military disgrace of desertion or cowardice. See Fantham, *Stuprum*, 118 and Moses, *Livy's Lucretia and the Validity of Coerced Consent in Roman Law*, 50. See Adams, *Latin Sexual Vocabulary* for a comprehensive dicussion of the subject, and Lewis & Short for uses of these words.
2. Martial, 11, 15, 8ff.
3. Cicero, *Ad Familiares* 9, 22.
4. Catullus, 28, 12; 47. Martial 11, 46, 2; *Priapea* 34, 5. See also Catullus 105.
5. Varro, *On Agriculture* 2.4.9; see Hersch, *The Roman Wedding: Ritual and Meaning in Antiquity* 122, 276; Spaeth, *The Roman Goddess Ceres* 17.
6. Martial, 11, 21, 1, 10: *tam laxa... quam turpe guttur onocrotali.*
7. Juvenal, 6, 422. *Priapea* 79.
8. Martial, 1, 90. Lucilius, fr. 61 Warmington: *in bulgam penetrare pilosam.*
9. CIL 4, 1830: *futuitur cunnus pilossus multo melliur quam glaber; eadem continet vaporem et eadem vellit mentulam.*
10. Catullus, 40, 12, 61, 101, 64, 65, 66, 81. Ovid, *Amores* 1, 4, 37; see also 1, 5, 20 and 2, 15, 11; Propertius, 3, 14,20.
11. Plautus, frg. 68 (Lindsay). Martial, 11, 21.
12. Martial, 11, 20, 7. Octavian would rather be sodomised than have sex with Fulvia, after Antony, is the implication.
13. See Richlin, *The Meaning of* irrumare *in Catullus and Martial.*
14. Horace, *Sermones* 1, 2, 68. See also Lucilius, 307 and 959.
15. Martial, 3, 73, 1 and 11, 63, 2; *Corpus Priapeorum* 52, 10. The *Corpus Priapeorum*, or *Priapeia*, is a collection of ninety-five poems about the phallic god Priapus and found on various statues of the god in the shape of large phalluses. As can be seen, it is a fertile souce of Latin profanities.

13 Augustus's Women: Flawless, Faithful and Fornicating

1. Tacitus, *Dialogus de Oratoribus* 28-9. Suetonius, *Augustus* 3.
2. Pliny, *NH* 10, 154; Suetonius, *Tiberius* 14, 2.
3. Dio, 48, 34, 3.
4. Suetonius, *Galba* 1. Pliny, *op. cit.* 15, 136–7; Dio, 48, 52, 3–4; 63, 29, 3.
5. Dio, 41, 39, 2; 43, 43, 1.
6. Velleius Paterculus, 2, 75, 3; Tacitus, *op. cit.* 5, 1, 2.
7. Suetonius, *Augustus* 69, 1; Tacitus, *op. cit.* Seneca, *Consolatio ad Marciam* 3,
8. Suetonius, *op. cit.* 70–71.
9. Dio, 48, 44, 3; Seneca, *Cons. Sap.* 11, 3; Statius, *Silvae* 2, 1, 72; 5, 5, 66; Quintilian, *Inst. Or.* 1, 2, 7.
10. For more, see Chrystal, *Women in Ancient Rome*.
11. Mark Antony made Antyllus (the Archer) his official heir; Octavian had him executed in 30 BC when he was seventeen.
12. Suetonius, *op. cit.* 63. Dio discredits the Dacian connection.
13. Dio, 53, 30; Velleius Paterculus 2, 93.
14. Suetonius, *Tiberius* 7; *Augustus*, 65.
15. Dio, 54, 31.

16. Macrobius, *Saturnalia* 2, 5; based on Domitius Marsus' contemporary *De Urbanitate*.
17. Suetonius, *Augustus*, 64–5.
18. Velleius Paterculus, *op. cit.* 2, 100.
19. Seneca, *De Beneficiis* 6.32. Pliny, *NH* 21, 8–9.

14 Capricious Depravity with Tiberius

1. Suetonius, *Tiberius* 43–45; Tacitus, *Annals* 6, 1.
2. *Suetonius, Vitellius* 3, 2.
3. *idem, Tiberius* 7; Tacitus, *op. cit.* 1, 53.
4. Tacitus, *op. cit.* 1, 3.

15 'The Whore Augusta', Incest with Caligula and Claudius, and Nero's Necrophilia

1. Juvenal, 6, 117. Propertius, 3, 11. Dio, 60, 31; translation is by Cary, *History of Rome*.
2. Dio, 60, 27, 2–4; 29, 4–6, 6a; Suetonius, *op. cit.* 29, 2.
3. Seneca, *Dialogus* 11, 5, 2. Dio 60,31,2.
4. Suetonius, *Vitellius.* 2, 5. For Lucius Vitellius' career under Claudius, see Suetonius *Vitellius* 2, 4. For Messalina's importance in the court see Seneca, *Octavia* 947.
5. Tacitus, *Annals* 11, 26, 1.
6. Tacitus, *op. cit,* 11, 26, 3.
7. *ibidem.*
8. Tacitus, *op. cit.* 11, 26–38; Dio, 60, 31; Suetonius, *Claudius* 36–37; 39.
9. Juvenal, 6, 115 –132.
10. Juvenal, 10, 329–345.
11. Pliny, *NH.* 10, 172.
12. Tacitus, *op. cit.* 11, 12–13; Dio, 60, 18.
13. Pliny, *op. cit.* 8, 145.
14. Dio, 63.
15. Suetonius, *op. cit.* 6. The first use of forensic dental identification for which there is record. Luntz, L. L. (1977) History of Forensic Dentistry. *Dent Clin North Am* 21: 7–17.
16. Pliny, *op. cit.* 7, 46.
17. Suetonius, *ibid.*
18. Suetonius, *Galba* 5.
19. Tacitus, *op. cit.* 14, 2, 4.
20. Tacitus, *op. cit.* 12, 1. Seneca, Octavia, 141–3.
21. *Idem, op. cit.* 12, 22.
22. Pliny, *op. cit.* 9, 117; Suetonius, *Claudius* 27.
23. For Cleopatra, see Chrystal, *Roman Military Disasters*.
24. Tacitus, *op. cit.* 12, 5–7.
25. Tacitus, *op. cit.* 12, 5.
26. Suetonius, *op. cit.* 29.
27. Phlegon, *Miracles* 7.

28. Tacitus, *op. cit.* 12, 64. Suetonius, *op.cit.* 43, 46.
29. Tacitus, *op. cit.* 12, 66–69.
30. Tacitus, *op. cit.* 13, 11.
31. Tacitus, *op. cit.* 13, 12–14.
32. Tacitus, *op. cit.* 13, 20–22.
33. Tacitus, *op. cit.* 13, 45.
34. Tacitus, *op. cit.* 12, 28; Dio 62, 28.
35. Tacitus, *op. cit.* 13, 36.
36. Tacitus, *op. cit.* 13, 20–22.
37. Dio, 61, 12.
38. Tacitus, *op. cit.* 14, 12.
39. Tacitus, *op. cit.* 14, 3, 1. Dio Cassius, 63, 12 and 13, says that Acerronia drowned and mentions nothing about Agrippina being rescued, and instead claims she swam all the way to shore unaided. Dio prefers a vessel where the bottom opened up while at sea; Agrippina duly fell into the water when exactly that happened.
40. Suetonius, *op. cit.* 34. Dio, 61, 12; 13. Translation, Cary *op. cit.*
41. Tacitus, *op. cit.* 14, 7–8. Suetonius, *op. cit.* Dio, 61, 13; translation, Cary *op. cit.*
42. Suetonius, *op. cit.* Dio, 61, 14; translation, Cary *op. cit.*
43. Dio, 62, 134.
44. Tacitus, *op. cit.* 16, 6; 15, 38. Dio, 63, 13.
45. Suetonius, *Nero* 35, 3.
46. *idem*, *Titus* 10.
47. *idem*, *Domitian* 1; 3.
48. *ibid*, 8.
49. *ibid*, 22.
50. Eusebius, *Church History* 425.
51. *ibid*, 10.

16 Hadrian and Antinous: A Man Worth Dying For

1. Historia Augusta (*c.* 395) *Hadrian*, 14, 5–7; attrib. to Aelius Spartianus. Antinous' dates are *c.* 111 – before 30 October 130, making him eighteen or so when he died.
2. See Lambert, *Beloved and God*, 97.
3. Dawson, *Cities of the Gods*, 193.
4. Boys-Stones, *Eros in Government* 168–174. Tibullus, 1, 4; 1, 8; and 1, 9, 53. Pliny, *Panegyricus* 83, 2–3; Dio 68, 7, 4. Julian, *The Caesars* 311.
5. Dio, *Epitome Book* 69.
6. Vout, *Antinous, Archaeology, History* 82.
7. Lambert, *op. cit.* 80; 209.
8. Historia Augusta, *ibid* 11, 3.
9. Historia Augusta, *ibid*; *Epitome De Caesaribus* 24.
10. Historia Augusta, *Aelius*, 5, 11.

17 Faustina and the Gladiator's Blood Bath; the Vile Corruption of Commodus

1. Historia Augusta, *Marcus Aurelius* 26, 4–9.
2. *ibid, Aurelius Victor* 16.
3. Historia Augusta, *Marcus Aurelius* 29, 1–3.
4. Philostratus, *Lives of the Sophists* 549; 558.
5. *ibid*, 554–556.
6. *ibid*, 560.
7. *ibid*.
8. Marcus Aurelius, *Meditations* 1, 17, 7.
9. Historia Augusta, *Commodus* 1.
10. Dio Cassius, 72, 4.
11. Historia Augusta, *Commodus,* 5.
12. *op. cit.* 10.
13. See also Herodian, *History of the Roman Empire since the Death of Marcus Aurelius* 1, 15.
14. Nero: Tacitus *Annals* 13, 25; Suetonius *Nero*, 26; Dio, 61,8, The same thing is also told about Otho in Suetonius, *Otho* 2,1 and Commodus, *Commodus* 3,7.
15. Historia Augusta, *Lucius* Verus 5.
16. Historia Augusta, *Antoninus Caracella* 10.

18 Elagabalus: 'An Unspeakably Disgusting Life'

1. Niebuhr, *History of Rome* 144. Elagabalus' vices were 'too disgusting even to allude to them.' So also Gibbon: *Decline and Fall of the Roman Empire*, Chapter 6: Elagabalus 'abandoned himself to the grossest pleasures and ungoverned fury'.
2. First by Aurelius Victor, *Liber de Caesaribus*, 23, 1.
3. Dio, 80, 15; 16.
4. *Historia Augusta*, Elagabalus 4.
5. Dio, 80, 9.
6. Plutarch, *Numa* 10.
7. Dio, 80, 11. See also Herodian, *Roman History* 5–6.
8. *Historia Augusta*, Elagabalus 3.
9. Herodian, *op. cit.*
10. Dio, 80, 15.
11. *Historia Augusta*, Elagabalus 10.
12. Dio, 80, 14.
13. Dio, 80, 13.
14. Herodian, *op. cit.*
15. Trans. by Anthony Birley, *Lives of the Later Caesars.*
16. Historia Augusta, *Life of Elagabalus* 5.
17. Dio, 80, 16. For Elagabalus' probable transgender tendencies and transsexuality see Godbout, *Elagabalus. GLBTQ: An Encyclopedia of Gay, Lesbian, Bisexual, Transgender, and Queer Culture.*
18. Dio, 80, 20.
19. Gibbon, *op.cit.* Chapter 40.
20. Historia Augusta, *Life of Severus Alexander*, 23.

21. *op. cit.* 24.
22. *op. cit.* 33.
23. *op. cit.* 41.
24. *op. cit.* 49; P. Herennius Dexippus of Athens. His *Chronicle*, frequently cited in the later biographies of the *Historia Augusta* began with the mythical period and extended down to AD 268. He held important municipal offices in Athens, and about 267 A.D., with the aid of a hastily collected army, he repelled an invasion of the Goths (the Heruli).
25. *op. cit.* 52.
26. *Historia Augusta*, The Three Gordians 19, 3–4.

19 Theodora: Slut or Saint?

1. Procopius, *De Aedificiis* 1, 8, 5.
2. *idem*, *Secret History* 10, 11.
3. *ibid* 9. John of Ephesus *PO* 17, 1, 188–89.
4. *idem*, *Buildings of Justinian* 1, 9, 3ff.
5. *idem, Secret History* 12, 29–32.
6. A monophysite, in Christianity, believed that Jesus Christ's nature remains altogether divine and not human even though he has taken on an earthly and human body with its cycle of birth, life, and death.
7. *Codex Justinianus* 5, 4, 23.
8. A celibate priest, one below a bishop. A famous Greek Orthodox monastery is named after Mar Saba, east of Bethlehem. Women have never been allowed in, even to this day, so female visitors have to make do with a glimpse from a nearby two-storey tower, the Women's Tower.
9. Procopius, *Wars* 1, 24, 33–37.
10. Procopius, *Secret History* 30, 23–6.
11. *The History of the Decline and Fall of the Roman Empire*, ed. David Womersley, (Harmondsworth 1994) II, 567–8.
12. Procopius *De Aedificiis*, 1,9, 1–10. *Secret History* 17,5–6.
13. *ibid*, 1, 11.
14. Translations are by G.A. Williamson in *Procopius: The Secret History* (London 1966).

Abbreviations

AC	*L'Antiquite Classique*
ACD	*Acta Classica Debrecen*
Ad Att.	*Epistulae Ad Atticum (Cicero)*
Ad Fam.	*Epistulae Ad Familiares (Cicero)*
AE	*L'Année Epigraphique*
AJAH	*Americal Journal of Ancient History*
AJP	*American Jnl of Philology*
BGU	*Berliner Griechische Urkunden*
Anc Soc	*Ancient Society (Louvain)*
APA	*American Psychiatric Association*
BHM	*Bulletin of the History of Medicine*
BICS	*Bulletin of the Institute of Classical Studies*
C&M	*Classica et Mediaevalia*
CB	*Classical Bulletin*
CEG	*P. A. Hansen, Carmina Epigraphica Graeca, Berlin 1983*
CJ	*Classical Journal*
CIL	*Corpus Inscriptionum Latinarum, Berlin 1863*
Cl. Ant	*Classical Antiquity*
CP	*Classical Philology*
CW	*Classical World*
Dent Clin North Am	*Dental Clinics of North America*
DSM	*The Diagnostic and Statistical Manual of Mental Disorders*
EMC	*Echos du Monde Classique*
G&R	*Greece and Rome*
GRBS	*Greek, Roman and Byzantine Studies*
HN	*Historia Naturalis, (Pliny the Elder)*
HSCP	*Harvard Studies in Classical Philology*
JRS	*Journal of Roman Studies*
LCM	*Liverpool Classical Monthly*
P. Bour	*Les Papyrus Bouriant*
PCPS	*Proceedings of the Cambridge Philosophical Society*
PGM	*K. Preisendanz, Papyri Graecae Magicae, Leipzig 1928.*

Abbreviations

P. Lond	*London papyrus*
P. Oxy	*The Oxyrhynchus Papyrus*
PSI	*Papyri Greci e latini: Societa italiana per la Ricerca dei Papiri Greci e Latini Egitto*
REL	*Revue des Etudes Latines*
RhM	*Rheinisches Museum für Philologie*
SO	*Symbolae Osloensis*
SHPBBS	*Studies in the History & Philosophy of Biological & Biomedical Sciences*
TAPA	*Transactions of the Proceedings of the American Philological Asscn*
WS	*Wiener Studien*

Bibliography

Abusch, R. Circumcision and Castration under Roman Law in the Early Empire, in *The Covenant of Circumcision: New Perspectives on an Ancient Jewish Rite* (Brandeis University Press, 2003), 77–78.

Adams, J. N. Latin Words for Woman and Wife, *Glotta* 50 (1972), 234–255

Adams, J. N. *The Latin Sexual Vocabulary* (London 1982)

Adams, J. N. Words for Prostitute in Latin, *RhM* 126 (1983), 321–358

Allason-Jones, L. *Women in Roman Britain* (London 1989)

Allason-Jones, L. Women in Roman Britain in James, *Companion* (2012), 467–477

Allison, P. 'Soldiers' Families in the Early Roman Empire' in Rawson, *A Companion to Families in the Greek and Roman Worlds* (Chichester 2011), 161–182

American Psychiatric Association, *Diagnostic and Statistical Manual of Mental Disorders IV* (Arlington 1994)

Amunsden, D. W. 'The Age of Menarche in Classical Greece and Rome', *Human Biology* 42, (1970), 79–86

Andre, J. M. *L'Otium dans la Vie Morale et Intellectuelle Romaine des Origins a la Epoque Augusteenne* (Paris 1966)

Androutsos, G. 'Hermaphroditism in Greek and Roman Antiquity', *Hormones* (2006), 214–217

Ankerloo, B. *Witchcraft and Magic in Europe Vol 2: Ancient Greece and Rome* (London 1998)

Archer, L. J. (ed.) *Women in Ancient Societies* (London 1994)

Arieti, J. A. 'Rape and Livy's View of Roman History' in Deacy, *Rape in Antiquity*, (1997) 209–22

Arieti, J. A. 'Empedocles in Rome: Rape and the Roman Ethos', *Clio* 10 (1980), 5–20

Arkins, B. A. *Aspects of Sexuality in Catullus*, diss NUI (1974)

Arnott, W. G. *Menander, Plautus and Terence* (Oxford 1975)

Ash, R. *Women in Imperial Roman Literature* in James, *Companion* (2012), 442–452

Auanger, L. 'Glimpses through a Window: An Approach to Roman Female Homoeroticism through Art Historical and Literary Evidence' in Rabinowitz (2002), 211–255

Augoustakis, A. *Motherhood and the Other: Fashioning Female Power in Flavian Epic* (Oxford 2010)
Aune, D. E. 'Magic in Early Christianity: Glossolalia and *Voces Magicae*', reprinted in *Apocalypticism, Prophecy and Magic in Early Christianity: Collected Essays* (2006)
Baader, G. 'Spezialarzte in der Spatantike', *Medizinhistorisches Journal* 2 (1967), 231–238
Babcock, C. 'The Early Career of Fulvia', *AJP* 86, (1965), 1–32
Baird, J. *Ancient Graffiti in Context* (London 2010)
Baldwin, B. 'Horace on Sex', *AJP* 91 (1970), 460–465
Baldwin, B. 'Women in Tacitus', *Prudentia* 4 (1972), 83–101
Balsdon, J. P. V. D. *Roman Women* (London 1962)
Balsdon, J. P. V. D. *Life and Leisure in Ancient Rome* (London 1969)
Barnard, S. 'Cornelia and the Women of her Family', *Latomus* 49 (1990), 383–392
Barras, V. *Galen's Psychiatry* in Hamanaka, 3–8
Bartman, E. Eros' Flame: Images of Sexy Boys in Roman Ideal Sculpture, in Gazda E. K. (ed.) *The Ancient Art of Emulation*, (Ann Arbor 2002), 249–271
Barton, C. A. *The Sorrows of the Ancient Romans: The Gladiator and the Monster* (Princeton, 1993).
Bauman, R. A. 'The Rape of Lucretia, *quod metus causa* and the Criminal Law', *Latomus* 52 (1993): 550–566
Bauman, R. A. *Women and Politics in Ancient Rome* (London 1992)
Beard, M. (25 November 2009). 'Pedicabo ego vos et irrumabo: what was Catullus on about?' *The Times Literary Supplement*.
Beard, M. *Pompeii: The Life of a Roman Town* (London 2008)
Beard, M. *Religions of Rome: A Sourcebook* (Cambridge 1998)
Beard, M. 'The Erotics of Rape. Livy, Ovid and the Sabine Women' in Setäl *Female Networks and the Public Sphere in Roman Society* (1999), 1–10
Beard, M. Re-Reading (*Vestal*) *Virginity* in Hawley (1995), 166–177
Beard, M. '"With this body I thee worship": Sacred Prostitution in Antiquity' in Wyke, M. *Gender and the Body in the Ancient Mediterranean*, 56–79 (Oxford)
Beard, M. 'The Sexual Status of the Vestal Virgins', *JRS* 70 (1980), 12–27
Bernstein, F. 'Pompeian Women' in Dobbins, *The World of Pompeii* (2007)
Bertman, S. *The Conflict of Generations in Ancient Greece and Rome* (Amsterdam 1976)
Best, E. E. 'Cicero, Livy and Educated Roman Women', *CJ* 65 (1970), 199–204
Betz, H. D. *Greek Magical Papyri in Translation 2/e* (Chicago 1997)
Blanshard, A. J. L. 'Roman Vice', in *Sex: Vice and Love from Antiquity to Modernity* (Oxford 2010), 1–88.
Blayney, J. 'Theories of Conception in the Ancient Roman World' in Rawson, *Family* 230–236
Blok, J. (ed.) *Sexual Asymmetry: Studies in Ancient Society* (Amsterdam 1987)
Blondel. R. *Ancient Sex: New Essays* (Columbus OH forthcoming),
Boatwright, M. T. 'Imperial Womenof the Early Second Century AD', *AJP* 112 (1991), 513–40
Boatwright, M. T. Women and Gender in the *Forum Romanum*, *TAPA* 141 (2011), 107–143
Bodel, J. *Epigraphic Evidence: Ancient History from Inscriptions* (London 2001)
Boehringer, S. *L'Homosexualite Feminine dans l'Antiquite Greque et Romain* (Paris 2007)

Boehringer, S. *Homosexualite: Aimer en Grece et Rome* (Paris 2010)
Boehringer, S. 'Sex, Lies and (Video) Trap: The Illusion of Sexual Identity in Lucian's Dialogues of the Courtesans 5' in Blondel, *Ancient*
Boehringer, S. 'Female Homoeroticism', in Hubbard, T. K. *A Companion to Greek and Roman Sexualities* (Chichester 2014), 150–163.
Bosman, P. (ed.) *Mania: Madness in the Greco-Roman World* (Pretoria 2009)
Boswell, J. *The Kindness of Strangers: The Abandonment of Children in Western Europe from Antiquity to the Renaissance*, (New York 1998)
Bouvrie, S. 'des Augustus' Legislation on Morals', SO 59 (1984), 93–113
Bowman, A. K. *Life and Letters on the Roman Frontier: Vindolandia and its People* (London 1994)
Boys-Stones, G. *The Oxford Handbook of Hellenic Studies* (Oxford 2009)
Bradley, K. R. 'Wet Nursing in Rome' in Rawson, *The Family* (1986)
Bradley, K. R. *Discovering the Roman Family: Studies in Roman Social History* (New York 1991)
Bradley, K. R. 'The Roman Child in Sickness and in Health' in George, *The Roman Family* (2005), 68–92
Brashear, W. M, 'The Greek Magical Papyri: "Voces Magicae"', *Aufstieg und Niedergang der Römischen Welt* II, 18, 5 (1995), 34–35
Braund, S. 'Juvenal: Misogynist or Misogamist?' *JRS* 82 (1992), 61–76
Braund, S. 'A Woman's Voice? Laronia's Role in Juvenal 2', in Hawley *Women* (1995), 207–219
Bridge, A. *Theodora. Portrait in a Byzantine Landscape* (London, 1978)
Briquel, D. 'Les Femmes Gladiateurs: Examen du Dossier'. *Ktema* 17 (1992), 47–53
Brennan, T. C. 'Perception of Women's Power in the Late Republic: Terentia, Fulvia and the Generation of 63 BC' in James, *Companion* (2012), 354–366
Brisson, C. *Sexual Ambivalence: Androgyny and Hermaphroditism in Graeco-Roman Antiquity* (Berkeley 2002)
Brooten, B. J. *Love between Women: Early Christian Responses to Female Homoeroticism* (Chicago, 1996)
Brooten, B. J. 'Lesbian Historiography before the Name?' *GLQ: A Jnl of Lesbian and Gay Studies* 4 (1998), 606–630
Brouwer, H. H. J. *Bona Dea: The Sources and a Description of the Cult* (Leiden 1989)
Brown, R. 'Livy's Sabine Women and the Ideal of *concordia*', *TAPA* 125, (1995), 291–319
Brown, R.D. *Lucretius on Love and Sex* (Leiden, 1987)
Browning, R, *Justinian and Theodora* (second ed., London, 1987)
Brumfeld, A. 'Aporetta: Verbal and Ritual Obscenity in the Cults of Ancient Women', in Hagg, R. (ed.), *The Role of Religion in the Early Greek* polis, 67–74 (Stockholm 1996)
Bryson, N. 'Two narratives of Rape in the Visual Art: Lucretia and the Sabine Women' in Tomaselli (ed.), *Rape: an Historical and Social Enquiry* (Oxford 1986), 152–173
Brunet, S. 'Female and Dwarf Gladiators', *Mouseion*, 4 (2004), 145–151.
Brunt, P. A. *Roman Manpower 225 BC- AD 14* (Oxford 1971)
Budin, S. *The Myth of Sacred Prostitution in Antiquity* (Cambridge 2008)
Buis, E. J. Mythology in *Encyclopedia of Rape*. Ed. Merril D. Smith. (Westport 2004), 132–134

Bullock, A. Rape of Lucretia in *Encyclopedia of Rape*. Ed. Merril D. Smith. (Westport 2004), 193–197
Burns, J. *Great Women of Imperial Rome* (London 2007)
Butrica, J. L. 'Some Myths and Anomalies in the Study of Roman Sexuality', in *Same-Sex Desire and Love in Greco-Roman Antiquity*, 218, 224
Bryk, F. *Circumcision in Man and Woman: Its History, Psychology and Ethnology* (Honolulu 2001)
Butterworth, A. *Pompeii: The Living City* (London 2005)
Cairns, F. (ed.) *Papers of the Liverpool Latin Seminar V 1985* (1986)
Caldwell, J. M. *Religion and Sexual Violence in Late Greco-Roman Antiquity*. (PhD thesis, Syracuse University, 2003)
Cameron, A. (ed.) *Images of Women in Antiquity* (London 1983)
Cameron, A. 'Love (and Marriage) Between Women', *GRBS* 39 (1998), 137–156
Campbell, J. B. The Marriage of Soldiers under the Empire, *JRS* 68, 153–166
Cantarella, E. *Bisexuality in the Ancient World* (London 2002)
Cantarella, E. 'Marriage and Sexuality in Republican Rome' in Nussbaum (2002), 269–282
Cantarella, E. *Pandora's Daughters: The Role and Status of Women in Greek and Roman Antiquity* (London 1987)
Carlon, J. M. *Pliny's Women: Constructing Virtue and Creating Identity in the Roman World* (Cambridge 2009)
Carp, T. 'Two Matrons of the Late Republic', *Women's Studies* 8 (1981), 189–200 in Foley, *Reflections*, 343–353
Catelli, G. *Behind Lesbia's Door: Her Slave-Girls' Shocking Revelations* (New York 2012)
Chalmers, W. A. *Plautus and His Audience* in Dorey, *Roman Drama*, 1965
Challet, C.-E. C *Like Man, Like Woman: Roman Women, Gender Qualities and Conjugal Relationships at the Turn of the first Century* (Frankfurt 2013)
Champlin, E. 'Sex on Capri', *TAPA* 141 (2011), 315–332
Chandezon, C. Dream Interpretation, Physiognomy, Body Divination, in Hubbard (2014), 297–313
Chrystal, P. *Roman Military Disasters* (Barnsley 2015)
Chrystal, P. *Roman Women: The Women who Infuenced the History of Rome* (Stroud 2015)
Chrystal, P. *Women in Ancient Rome* (Stroud 2014)
Chrystal, P. *Differences in Attitude to Women as Reflected in the Work of Catullus, Propertius, the Corpus Tibullianum, Horace and Ovid* (MPhil thesis, University of Southampton, 1982)
Cilliers, L. *Mental Illness in the Greco-Roman Era* in Bosman (2009), 130–140
Claasen, J. 'Documents of a Crumbling Marriage: The Case of Cicero and Terentia', *Phoenix* 50 (1996), 208–232
Clark, A. J. *Divine Qualities: Cult and Community in Republican Rome* (Oxford 2007)
Clark, G. *Women in the Ancient World* (Oxford 1989)
Clark, G. *Women in Late Antiquity: Pagan and Christian Lifestyles* (Oxford, 1993)
Clarke, J. R. *Looking at Lovemaking: Constructions of Sexuality in Roman Art 100 BC – AD 250* (Berkeley 1998)
Clarke, J. R. *Roman Sex 100 BC to AD 250* (London 2003)
Clarke, J. R. 'Sexuality and Visual Representation', in Hubbard (2014), 509–533

Clayton, B. 'Lucretius' Erotic Mother: Maternity as a Poetic Construct' in *DRN*, *Helios* 26 (1999), 69–84

Cohen, D. 'Seclusion, Separation and the Status of Women' in McAuslan, I. *Women in Antiquity* 134–145

Cohen, E. E. 'Sexual Abuse and Sexual Rights: Slaves' Erotic Experience at Athens and Rome' in Hubbard (2014), 184–198

Colin, G. *Rome et la Grèce de 200 à 146 BC avant JC* (Paris 1905)

Colin, G. 'Luxe Oriental et Parfums Masculins dans la Rome Alexandrine', *RBPH* 33 (1935), 5–19

Collins, D. (ed.) *Magic in the Ancient Greek World* (Oxford 2008)

Collins, J. H. 'Tullia's Engagement and Marriage to Dolabella', *CJ* 1952, 164–168

Colton, R. E. 'Juvenal and Martial on Women who Ape Greek Ways', *CB* 50 (1973), 42–44

Cooper, K. 'The Virgin and the Bride: Idealized Womanhood in Late Antiquity' (Cambridge MA 1996)

Copley, F.O. Exclusus amator: *A Study in Latin Love Poetry*, (Madison 1956)

Corbeil, A. Sexing the World: Grammatical Gender and Biological Sex in Ancient Rome (Princeton 2015)

Corbier, M. Divorce and Adoption as Roman Familial Strategies, in Rawson, B. (1991), 47–78

Corbier, M. Male Power and Legitimacy through Women, in Hawley, (1995), 178–93

Corbier, M. Child Exposure and Abandonment, in Dixon (2001), 52–73

Corte, M. D. *Loves and Lovers in Ancient Pompeii* (Salerno 1976)

Crook, J. A. *Patria Potestas, CQ* 17 (1967), 113

Crook, J. A. Titus and Berenice. *The American Journal of Philology* 72 (1951), 162–175

Croom, A. *Roman Clothing and Fashion* (Stroud 2010)

Cruse, A. *Roman Medicine* (Stroud 2004)

Curran, L. C. 'The Mythology of Rape', *CW* 72 (1978), 97–98

Curran, L. C. 'Rape and Rape victims in the *Metamorphoses*', *Arethusa* 11 (1978), 213–241

Currie, H. Mac 'The Poems of Sulpicia', ANRW II, 30.3, 1751–1764

Cyrino, M. S. *Screening Love and Sex in the Ancient World* (London 2013)

Daehner, J. (ed) *The Herculaneum Women: History, Context, Identities* (Los Angeles 2007)

Daehner, J. (ed.) *The Herculaneum Women and the Origins of Archaeology* (New York 2008)

Dalby, A. *Empires of Pleasures: Luxury and Indulgence in the Roman* (London 2000)

D'Ambra, E. 'The Cult of Virtues and the Funerary Relief of Ulpia Epigone' *Latomus* 48 (1989), 392–400

D'Ambra, E.The Calculus of Venus: Nude Portraits of Roman Matrons, in Kampen, N. *Sexuality in Ancient Art,* (1996), 219–232

D'Ambra, E. 'Nudity and Adornment in Female Portrait Sculpure of the second Century AD', in Kleiner, D. *I Claudia II*, (2000), 101–114

D'Ambra, E. *Roman Women* (Cambridge, 2007)

D'Ambra, E. *Women in the Bay of Naples* in James, *Companion* (2012), 400–413

D'Ambrosio, A. *Women and Beauty in Pompeii* (New York 2002)

De Arrizabalaga y Prado, L. *The Emperor Elagabulus: Fact or Fiction?* (Cambridge 2010)

De Arrizabalaga y Prado, L. 'Pseudo-Eunuchs in the Court of Elagabalus: The Riddle of Gannys, Eutychianus, and Comazon', in *Collected Papers in Honour of the Ninety-Fifth Anniversary of Ueno Gakuen* (Tokyo, 1999), 117–41

Dasen, V. Multiple Births in Graeco-Roman Antiquity, *Oxford Journal of Archaeology* 16, 1 (1997), 61

Dauphin, C.M. Brothels, Baths and Babes: Prostitution in the Byzantine Holy Land, *Classics Ireland* 3 (1996), 47–72

Davidson, J.N. Don't Try This at Home: Pliny's Salpe, Salpe's *Paignia* and Magic, *CQ* 45, 2 (1995), 591

D'Avino, M. *The Women of Pompeii* (Naples 1967)

Dayton, L. 'The Fat, Hairy Women of Pompeii', *New Scientist* 1944 (24 September 1994)

Deacy, S. (ed.) *Rape in Antiquity* (London 1997)

Dean-Jones, L. *The Politics of Pleasure: Female Sexual Appetite in the Hippocratic Corpus* in Stanton 1992, *Discourses* 48–77

Dean-Jones, L. *Medicine: The 'Proof' of Anatomy*, in Fantham, *Women in the Classical World* 183–215: 1994

del Castillo, A. The Position of Women in the Augustan Age, *LCM* 2 (1977), 167–173

Delia, D. *Fulvia Reconsidered* in Pomeroy, (1991), 197–217

Demand, N. *Women and Slaves as Hippocratic Patients* in Joshel, *Women* (1998), 69–84

Deslauriers, M. *Women, Education and Philosophy* in James, *Companion* (2012), 343–353

Deutsch, M. 'The Women of Caesar's Family', *CJ* 13 (1918), 502–514

Dickie, M.W. 'Who Practised Love-magic in Classical Antiquity and in the Late Roman World?' *CQ* 50 (2000), 563–583

Dickie, M.W. *Magic and Magicians in the Graeco-Roman World* (London 2001)

Dickison, S. 'Abortion in Antiquity', *Arethusa* 6 (1973), 158–166

Dixon, S. 'Women and Rape in Roman Law', in Christensen, E. (ed.) Roman Law in *Kønsroller, parforhold og samlivsformer. Rapport fra en seminarræk* (Copenhagen 1982)

Dixon, S. 'The Family Business: Women and Politics in the Late Republic', *C&M* 34 (1983), 91–112

Dixon, S. 'Family Finances: Tullia and Terentia', *Antichthon* 18 (1984), 78–101

Dixon, S. Polybius on Roman Women and Property, *AJP* 106 (1985), 147–170

Dixon, S. *The Roman Mother* (London 1988)

Dixon, S. *The Roman Family* (Baltimore 1992)

Dixon, S. *Reading Roman Women* (London, 2001)

Dixon, S. *Exemplary Housewife or Luxurious Slut: Cultural Representations of Women in the Roman Economy* in McHardy, *Women's Influence* (2004)

Dixon, S. *Cornelia: Mother of the Gracchi* (London 2007)

Dixon, S. 'From Ceremonial to Sexualities: A Survey of Scholarship on Roman Marriage' in Rawson, *A Companion* (2011), 245–261

Dobbins, J. J. (ed.) *The World of Pompeii* (London 2007)

Dobbins, J. J. 'A Roman Funerary Relief of a Potter and His Wife', *Arts in Virginia* 25 (1985), 24–33

Dover, K. J. *Greek Homosexuality* (London 1978)

Dover, K. J. 'Greek Homosexuality and Initiation' in *Que(e)rying Religion: A Critical Anthology* (London 1997), 19–38

Du Bois, P. Sowing the Body: Psychoanalysis and Ancient Representations of Women (Chicago 1988)

Dudley, D. (ed.) *Neronians and Flavians: Silver Latin I* (London 1972)

Duff, T. *Plutarch's Lives: Exploring Virtue and Vice* (Oxford 1999)

Dugan, G. Preventing Ciceronianism: C. Licinius Calvus' Regimen for Sexual and Oratorical Self-Mastery, *CP* 96 (2001)

Duke, T. T. Women and Pygmies in the Roman Arena, *CJ* 50 (1955), 223–224

Dupont, F. *Daily Life in Ancient Rome* (Oxford 1992)

Dupont, F. *L'erotisme Masculin dans la Rome Antique* (Paris 2001)

Durry, M. 'Le Mariage des Filles Impuberes dans la Rome Antique', *REL* 47 (1970), 17–25

Easterling, P. (ed.) *Greek and Roman Actors* (Cambridge 2002)

Edmonds, R. G. 'Bewitched, Bothered, Bewildered: Erotic Magic in the Greco-Roman World', in Hubbard T.K. (ed) *A Companion to Greek and Roman Sexualities* (Chichester 2014), 282–296

Edwards, C. *The Politics of Immorality in Ancient Rome* (Cambridge 1993)

Edwards, C. *Unspeakable Professions: Public Performance and Prostitution in Ancient Rome* in Hallett, *Roman Sexualities* (1998), 66–95

Edwards, C. *Death in Ancient Rome* (London 2007)

Edwards, C. 'Putting Agrippina in her Place: Tacitus and Imperial Women', *Omnibus* 63 (2012), 22–24

Elia J. P. 'History, Etymology, and Fallacy: Attitudes Toward Male Masturbation in the Ancient Western World', *Journal of Homosexuality* (1987) 14 (3–4), 1–19

Elia, O. *Pitture Murali e Mosaici nel Musea Nazionale di Napoli* (Rome 1932)

Ellis, H. *Studies in the Psychology of Sex*, vol. 2: Sexual Inversion. Project Gutenberg text

Elsom, H. E. Callirhoe: Displaying the Phallic Woman, in Richlin, *Pornography* (1992)

Engel, D. M. Women's Role in the Home and the State, *History of Political Thought* 101 (2003), 267–288

Engels, D. The Problem of Female Infanticide in the Greco-Roman World, *CP* 75 (1980), 112–120

Evans, J. A. S. *The Age of Justinian: The Circumstances of Imperial Power*, (London, 1996)

Evans, J. A. S. *The Empress Theodora: Partner of Justinian*, (Ann Arbor, 2003)

Evans, J. K. *War, Women and Children in Ancient Rome* (London 1991)

Evans-Grubbs, J. 'Abduction Marriage in Antiquity: A Law of Constantine (*CTh* IX.24.I) and its Social Context', *JRS* 79 (1989), 59–83

Evans-Grubbs, J. *Women and the Law in the Roman Empire: A Sourcebook on Marriage, Divorce and Widowhood* (New York 2002)

Ewigleben, C. '"What these Women Love is the Sword": The Performers and their Audiences' in Kohne, *Gladiators and Caesars: The Power of Spectacle in Ancient Rome*, 125–139. (Berkeley 2000)

Eyben, E. 'Antiquity's View of Puberty', *Latomus* 31 (1972), 677–697

Eyben, E. 'Family Planning in Graeco-Roman Antiquity', *Anc.Soc* 11–12 (1980), 5–82

Fagan, G. G. *Bathing in Public in the Roman World* (Chicago, 2002)

Famin, S. M. C. *Musée Royal de Naples; Peintures, Bronzes et Statues Erotiques du Cabinet Secret, avec leur Explication* (Paris, 1861)

Fantham, E. Sexual Comedy in Ovid's Fasti: Sources and Motivation, *Harvard Studies in Classical Philology* 87, (1983), 185–216

Fantham, E. '*Stuprum*: Public Attitudes and Penalties for Sexual Offences in Republican Rome', *EMC 35 (1991)*, 267–291

Fantham, E. *Women in the Classical World: Image and Text* (New York, 1994)

Fantham, E. *Amelia Pudentilla or the Wealthy Widow's Choice* in Hawley R.

Fantham, E. *Women in Antiquity* (1995), 220–232

Fantham, E. The Ambiguity of *Virtus* in Lucan's Civil War and Statius, *Arachnion* 3

Faraone, C. 'Magical and Medical Approaches to the Wandering Womb in the Ancient Greek World', *Cl Ant* 30 (2011), 1–31

Faraone, C. *Prostitutes and Courtesans in the Ancient World* (Madison WI, 2006)

Faraone, C. *Ancient Greek Love Magic* (Harvard 2001)

Faraone, C. 'Agents and Victims: Constructions of Gender and Desire in Ancient Greek Love Magic', in *The Sleep of Reason*, p. 410

Fau, G. *L'Emancipation Feminine a Rome* (Paris 1978)

Fenton, T. 'The Late Roman Infant Cemetery Near Lugnano', *Journal of Paleopathology* (1995), 13–42

Ferrill, A. Augustus and his Daughter: A Modern Myth, *Latomus* 168 (1980), 332–346

Ferris, I. *The Mirror of Venus: Woman in Roman Art* (Stroud 2015)

Filbee, M. *A Woman's Place* (London 1980)

Fildes, V. *Breasts, Bottles and Babies: A History of Infant Feeding* (Edinburgh 1987)

Fildes, V. *Wet Nursing: A History from Antiquity to the Present* (Oxford 1998)

Finley, M. I. *Aspects of Antiquity* (Harmondsworth 1972)

Finley, M. I. *The Etruscans and Early Rome* in Finley, *Aspects*, 110–123

Finley, M. I. *The Silent Women of Rome* in Finley, *Aspects*, 124–137

Finley, M. I. *Studies in Ancient Society* (London 1974)

Fisher, E. A. 'Theodora and Antonina in the *Historia Arcana*: History and/or Fiction?' in Peradotto, J. (ed.) *Women in the Ancient World: The Arethusa Papers* (1984), 287–314

Fisher, N. Athletics and Sexuality, in Hubbard (2014), 244–264

Fitton, J. W. 'That was No Lady, That Was', *CQ* 64 (1970), 56–66

Fitzgerald, W. *Catullan Provocations* (Berkeley 1995)

Flemming, R. '*Quae corpora quaestum facit*: The Sexual Economy of Female Prostitution in the Roman Empire', *JRS* 89 (1999), 38–61

Flemming, R. *Medicine and the Making of Roman Women* (Oxford 2000)

Flemming, R. 'Women, Writing and Medicine in the Classical World', *CQ* 57 (2007), 257–279

Florence, M. 'The Body Politic: Sexuality in Greek and Roman Comedy and Mime', in Hubbard (2014), 366–380

Fogen, T. *Bodies and Boundaries in Graeco- Roman Antiquity* (Amsterdam 2009)

Foley, H. (ed.) *Reflections of Women in Antiquity* (London 1981)

Women in Ancient Epic in Foley, J. M. (ed.) *A Companion to Ancient Epic*, 105–118 (Chichester 2008)

Forberg, F. K. (1824). *De figuris Veneris* (trans. into English as *Manual of Classical*

Erotology by Viscount Julian Smithson, and printed privately in 1884 in Manchester; repr. in 1966 ed.)

Foucault, M. *The History of Sexuality: The Care of the Self* (New York, 1988)

Foxhall, L. (ed.) *Thinking Men: Masculinity and Self-presentation in the Classical Tradition* (London 1998)

Frank, R. I. Augustus' Legislation on Marriage and Children, CSCA 8 (1975), 41–52

Fraschetti, A. (ed.) *Roman Women* (Chicago 2001)

Frazel, T. D. 'Priapus's Two Rapes in Ovid's *Fasti*', *Arethusa* 36 (2003), 61–97

Frederic, D. (ed.) *The Roman Gaze: Vision, Power, and the Body* (Baltimore 2002)

Frederick, D. C. 'Beyond the Atrium to Ariadne: Erotic Painting and Visual Pleasure in the Roman House', *Cl. Ant* 14 (1995), 266–287

Frederick, D. C. *Reading Broken Skin: Violence in Roman Elegy* in Hallett, *Roman Sexualities* (1998), 172–193

Freisenbruch. A. *The First Ladies of Rome* (London 2010)

French, R. (ed.) *Science in the Early Roman Empire* (London 1986)

French, V. *Midwives and Maternity Care in the Roman World* in M. Skinner, *Rescuing Creusa* (1987), 69–84

Friedlander, L. *Roman Life and Manners under the Early Empire Vols 1–4* (London) 1965

Frier, B. W. 'Natural Fertility and Family Limitation in Roman Marriage', *CP* 89 (1994), 318–33

Frier, B. W. 'Roman Same-Sex Weddings from the Legal Perspective', *Classical Studies Newsletter* X. (2004, University of Michigan)

Furst, L.R. (ed.) *Women Physicians and Healers* (Lexington 1997)

Gaca, K. L. *The Making of Fornication: Eros, Ethics and Political Reform in Greek Philosophy and Early Christianity*. (Berkeley 2003)

Gaca, K. L. 'Girls, Women, and the Significance of Sexual Violence in Ancient Warfare' in Heineman, E. D. *Sexual Violence in Conflict Zones: From the Ancient World to the Era of Human Rights* (Philadelphia 2011), 73–88.

Gaca, K. L. 'Ancient Warfare and the Ravaging Martial Rape of Girls and Women: Evidence from Homeric Epic and Greek Drama' in Masterson, M. *Sex in Antiquity: Exploring Gender and Sexuality in the Ancient World* (New York 2015)

Gage, J. 'Matronalia', *Latomus* 60, 1963

Gager, J. *Curse Tablets and Binding Spells from the Ancient World* (New York 1992)

Gaimster, D. 'Sex and Sensibility at the Art Museum', *History Today*, 50 (9), September, 2000, 10–15

Galinsky, K. Augustus' Legislation on Morals and Marriage, *Philologus* 125 (1981), 126–144

Gardner, J. F. *The Roman Household: A Sourcebook* (London 1991)

Gardner, J. F. *Women in Roman Law and Society* (Bloomington 1995)

Gardner, J. F. *Family and Familia in Roman Law and Life* (Oxford 1998)

Garland, L. *Byzantine Empresses: Women and Power in Byzantium, AD 527–1204* (London, 1999)

Garland, R. *The Eye of the Beholder: Deformity and Disability in the Graeco-Roman World* (Bristol 2010)

Garlick, B. (ed.) *Stereotypes of Women in Power* (New York 1992)

George, M. (ed.) *The Roman Family in the Empire: Rome, Italy, and Beyond* (Oxford 2005)

George, M. (ed.) *Family Imagery and Family Values in Roman Italy* in George, *The Roman Family* 37–66

Giacosa, G. *Women of the Caesars* (Milan 1980)

Gilhuly, K. 'The Phallic Lesbian: Philosophy, Comedy and Social Inversion in Lucian's *Dialogues of the Courtesans*' in Faraone (2006), 274–291

Gill, C. (ed.), *Galen and the World of Knowledge* (Cambridge 2009)

Gillis, D. *Eros and Death in the* Aeneid (Rome, 1983)

Gilman, S. *Hysteria Beyond Freud* (Berkeley 1993)

Glazebrook, A. Greek and Roman Marriage in Hubbard (2014), 69–82

Glazebrook, A. Sexual Rhetoric from Athens to Rome in Hubbard (2014), 431–445

Glendinning, E. 'Reinventing Lucretia: Rape, Suicide and Redemption from Classical Antiquity to the Medieval Era', *International Journal of the Classical Tradition* (2013)

Gloyn, E. 'Reading Rape in Ovid's *Metamorphoses*: A Test-Case Lesson', CW 106 (2013), 675–681

Godbout, L. 'Elagabalus', *GLBTQ: An Encyclopedia of Gay, Lesbian, Bisexual, Transgender, and Queer Culture.* (Chicago 2004)

Gold, B.K. 'The House I Live In Is Not My Own: Women's Bodies in Juvenal's *Satires*', *Arethusa* 31 (1998), 368–386

Golden, M. 'Did the Ancients Care When their Children Died?' G&R 35, 1988, 152–163

Golden, M. *Sex and Difference in Ancient Greece and Rome* (Edinburgh 2008)

Goldhill, S. *Foucault's Virginity: Ancient Erotic Fiction and the History of Sexuality* (Cambridge 1995)

Gordon, P. 'Some Unseen Monster: Rereading Lucretius on Sex', in Frederick, D. *The Roman Gaze* (Baltimore, 2002)

Gordon, R. L. 'Aelian's Peony: The Location of Magic in Graeco-Roman Tradition', *Comparative Criticism* 9 (1987)

Gordon, R. L. 'Imagining Greek and Roman Magic', in Ankerloo, B. (ed.) *Magic and Witchcraft in Europe: Greece and Rome* (Philadelphia PA 1999)

Gordon, R. L. 'Innovation and Authority in Graeco-Egyptian Magic', in *Kykeon Studies in Honour of H. S. Versnel* (Leiden 2002)

Gosselin, C. A. *Rape, Seduction and Love in Ovid's Metamorphoses.* (M.A. Thesis, Concordia University, 1990)

Gourevitch, D. Women Who Suffer from a Man's Disease in Hawley, *Women* (1995), 149–165

Graf, F. *Magic in the Ancient World* (Cambridge MA 1999)

Grant, M. 'Eros in Pompeii: The Erotic Art Collection of the Museum of Naples', (New York 1997)

Green, M. H. *Making Women's Medicine Masculine: The Rise of Male Authority in Pre-Modern Gynaecology* (Oxford 2008)

Greene, E. *The Erotics of Domination: Male Desire and the Mistress in Latin Love Poetry* (Baltimore 1998)

Griffin, J. 'Augustan Poetry and the Life of Luxury', *JRS* 66 (1976), 87–105

Griffin, M.T. *Nero: The End of a Dynasty* (London 2000)

Grimal, P. *Love in Ancient Rome* (Norman, OK 1986)

Grmek, M. *Les Maladies a l'Aube de la Civilisation Occidentale* (Paris 1983)

Grmek, M. *Diseases in the Ancient Greek World* (Baltimore 1989)
Grubbs, J. E. *Women and the Law in the Roman Empire: A Sourcebook on Marriage, Divorce and Widowhood* (London 2002)
Grubbs, J. E. *Parent-Child Conflict in the Roman Family* in George, *The Roman Family* (2005) 93–128
Gruen, E. S. M. 'Antonius and the Trial of the Vestal Virgins', *RhM* 111 (1968), 59–63
Gunderson, E. Catullus, Pliny and Love Letters, *TAPA* 127 (1997), 201–231
Gunderson, E. 'The Libidinal Rhetoric of Satire', in *The Cambridge Companion to Roman Satire* (Cambridge, 2005)
Gusman, P. *Pompeii: The City, It's Life and Art* (London 1910)
Haas, N. 'Hairstyles in the Art of Greek and Roman Antiquity', *Jnl of Investigative Dermatology Proceedings* 10 (2005), 298–300
Habinek, T. 'The Invention of Sexuality in the World-City of Rome', in Habinek, T. *The Roman Cultural Revolution,* (Cambridge 2004)
Hallet, J. P. 'The Role of Women in Roman Elegy: Cross-Cultural Feminism', *Arethusa* 6 (1973), 103–124
Hallet, J. P. *Masturbator, mascarpio,* Glotta 54 (1976) 292–308
Hallet, J. P. '*Perusinae Glandes* and the Changing Image of Augustus', *AJAH* 2 (1977), 151–171
Hallet, J. P. *Fathers and Daughters in Roman Society: Women and the Elite Family* (Princeton 1984)
Hallet, J. P. 'Female Homoeroticism and the Denial of Roman Reality in Latin Literature, *Yale Journal of Criticism* 3 (1989), 209–227
Hallet, J. P. 'Martial's Sulpicia and Propertius' Cynthia', *CW* 86 (1992), 99–123
Hallet, J. P. (ed.) *Roman Sexualities* (Princeton 1997)
Hallet, J. P. *The Eleven Elegies of the Augustan Poet Sulpicia* in Churchill, *Women Writing* (2002), 45–65
Hallet, J. P. 'Feminae Furentes: *The Frenzy of Noble Women in Virgil's* Aeneid *and the Letter of Cornelia*' in Anderson (2002), 159–167
Hallet, J. P. *Matriot Games? Cornelia and the the Forging of Family-oriented Political Values* in McHardy, Women's *Influence* (2004) 26–39
Hallet, J. P. *Women in Augustan Rome* in James, *Companion* (2012), 372–384
Hamilton, G. Society Women Before Christ, *North American Review* 151 (1896)
Hanson, A. E. The Restructuring of Female Physiology at Rome, in *Les Ecoles Médicales à Rome* (Nantes, 1991) 267ff.
Hallet, J. P. 'The Medical Writers' Woman', in Halperin, *Before Sexuality* (1990), 309–338
Hallet, J. P. 'The Eight Months' Child and the Etiquette of Birth: *obsit omen!*', *BHM* 61 (1987), 589–602
Harkness, A. G. Age at Marriage and at Death in the Roman Empire, *TAPA* 27 (1896), 35–72
Harlow, M. *Galla Placida: Conduit of Culture?* in McHardy, *Women's Influence* (2004), 138–150
Harris, W. V. 'The Theoretical Possibility of Extensive Female Infanticide in the Graeco-Roman World', *CQ* 32 (1982), 114–116
Harris, W. V. *Ancient Literacy* (Cambridge Mass 1989)
Harris, W. V. 'Child Exposure in the Roman Empire', *JRS* 84 (1994), 1–22
Hart, G. D. *Asclepius: the God of Medicine* (London 2001)

Harvey, S. A. (1990) *Ascetism and Society in Crisis: John of Ephesus and the Lives of the Eastern Saints* (Berkeley)

Harvey, S. A. *Women in Early Byzantine Hagiography: Reversing the Story*, in *That Gentle Strength: Historical Perspectives on Women in Christianity* (University Press of Virginia, 1990)

Hawley R. (ed.) *Women in Antiquity: New Assessments* (London 1995)

Hawley R. 'Ancient Collections of Women's Sayings', *BICS* 50 (2007), 161–169

Hawley R. '"Give Me a Thousand Kisses": The Kiss, Identity, and Power in Greek and Roman Antiquity', *Leeds International Classical Studies* 6 (2007)

Hejduk, J. D. *Clodia: A Sourcebook* (Norman OK 2008)

Helzle, M. 'Mr and Mrs Ovid', *G&R* 36, (1989), 183–193

Hemelrijk, E. *Women's Demonstrations in Republican Rome* in Blok, *Sexual Asymmetry*, 217–240

Hemelrijk, E. 'Public Roles for Women in the Cities of the Latin West' in James, *Companion* (2012), 478–490

Hemker, J. 'Rape and the Founding of Rome', *Helios* 12 (1985), 1–47

Henriksén, C. 'Earinus: An Imperial Eunuch in the Light of the Poems of Martial and Statius' *Mnemosyne* 50 (1997), 281–294

Hermann, C. 'Le Role Judicaire et Politique des Femmes sous la Republique Romain', *Latomus* 67 (1964)

Hersch, K. K. *The Roman Wedding: Ritual and Meaning in Antiquity* (Cambridge 2010)

Heyob, S. K. *The Cult of Isis Among Women of the Graeco-Roman World* (Leiden 1975)

Hill, T. B. Ambitiosa Mors: *Suicide and the Self in Roman Thought and Literature* (London 1997)

Hillard, T. 'Republican Politics, Women and the Other Evidence', *Helios* 16 (1989), 165–182

Hodges, F. M. 'The Ideal Prepuce in Ancient Greece and Rome: Male Genital Aesthetics and their Relationship to Lipodermos, Circumcision, Foreskin Restoration, and the *Kynodesme*', *BHM* 75 (2001), 375–405

Hodkinson, O. 'Epistolography', in Hubbard, T. K. (ed.) *Companion to Greek and Roman Sexualities*, Chichester 2014), 463–478

Hoffsten R, *Roman Women of Rank in the Early Empire As Portrayed by Dio, Paterculus, Suetonius and Tacitus* (Philadelphia 1939)

Holland, L. L. *Women and Roman Religion* in *Companion to Women* (2012), 204–214

Holmberg, I. E. Sex in Ancient Greek and Roman Epic, in Hubbard, (2014), 314–334

Holmes, W. G. *The Age of Justinian and Theodora*, 2 vols (London, 1912)

Hong, Y. 'Talking About Rape in the Classics Classroom', *CW* 106 (2013), 669–675

Hopkins, K. 'The Age of Roman Girls at Marriage', *Population Studies* 18 (1965), 309–327

Hopkins, K. 'Contraception in the Roman Empire', *Comparative Studies in Society & History* 8 (1965), 124–151

Hopkins, K. *Conquerors and Slaves* (Cambridge 1978)

Horsfall, N. Allia Potestas and Murdia: Two Roman Women, *Ancient Society* 12 (1982), 27–33

Hosack, K. A. 'Can One Believe the Ancient Sources that Describe Messalina?' *Constructing the Past* 12 (2011), article 7

Hubbard, T. K. (ed.) *Companion to Greek and Roman Sexualities* (Chichester 2014)
Hubbard, T. K. (ed.) *Homosexuality in Greece and Rome: A Sourcebook of Basic Documents* (Berkeley 2003)
Hubbard, T. K. 'The Invention of Sulpicia', *CJ* 100 (2004), 177–194
Hubbard, T. K. 'Peer Homosexuality' in Hubbard (2014), 128–149
Hyde, H. M. *A History of Pornography* (London 1969)
ICD: *International Classification of Diseases* (10 version, Geneva 2010) see WHO
Icks, M. *The Crimes of Elagabalus: The Life and Legacy of Rome's Decadent Boy Emperor* (Cambridge MA 2012)
Icks, M. 'Heliogabalus, a Monster on the Roman Throne: The Literary Construction of a "Bad" Emperor', in Ineke Sluiter (ed.), *Kakos: Badness and Anti-value in Classical Antiquity*, Mnemosyne 307
Ireland, S. *Terence: The Mother-in-Law* (Oxford 1990)
Jackson, R. *Doctors and Diseases in the Roman Empire* (London 1988)
James, S. L. 'Gender and Sexuality in Terence', in A. Augoustakis, *A Companion to Terence* (Oxford 2013, 175–194)
James, S.L. *Companion to Women in the Ancient World* (Chichester 2012)
James, S.L. *Virgil's Dido* in James, *Companion* (2012), 369–371
James, S.L. 'Teaching Rape in Roman Love Elegy, Part II' in Gold, B.K, *A Companion to Roman Love Elegy* (Oxford 2012), 549–557
James, S.L. 'From Boys to Men: Rape and Developing Masculinity in Terence's *Hecyra* and *Eunuchus*', *Helios* 25 (1998), 31–48
James, S.L. 'Slave-Rape and Female Silence in Ovid's Love Poetry', *Helios* 24 (1997), 60–76
James, S.L. *Learned Girls and Male Persuasion: Gender and Reading in Roman Love Elegy* (Berkeley 2003)
Janowitz, N. *Magic in the Roman World* (London 2001)
Jenkins, T. E. 'Livia the *Princeps*: Gender and Ideology in the *Consolatio ad Liviam*', *Helios* 36 (2009), 1–25
Johansson, L. 'The Roman Wedding and the Household Gods' in Loven, L. L. (ed.) *Ancient Marriage in Myth and Reality* (Newcastle 2010), 136–149
Johns, C. *Sex or Symbol: Erotic Images of Greece and Rome* (London 1982)
Johnson, M. *Sexuality in Greek and Roman Society and Literature: A Sourcebook* (London 2005)
Johnson W.H. 'The Sister-in-law of Cicero', *CJ* 1913, 160–165
Jones, B. W. *The Emperor Domitian.* (London 1992)
Jones, C. P. Stigma: Tattooing and Branding in Graeco-Roman Antiquity, *JRS* 77 (1987), 139–155
Jope, J. 'Stoic and Epicurean Sexual Ethics', in Hubbard, (2014), 417–430
Joplin, P. K. 'The Voice of the Shuttle Is Ours' in Higgins, L.A. *Rape and Representation* (New York 1991), 35–64
Joshel, S. R. 'Female Desire and the Discourse of Empire: Tacitus' Messalina', in Hallett, *Roman Sexualities* (1997), 221–254
Joshel, S. R. *The Body Female and the Body Politic: Livy's Lucretia and Verginia* in Richlin, *Pornography* (1992), 112–130
Joshel, S. R. *Women and Slaves in Graeco-Roman Culture* (London 1998)
Joyce, R. A. *Ancient Bodies, Ancient Lives: Sex, Gender and Archaeology* (London 2008)

Kahn, M. *Why Are We Reading Ovid's Handbook on Rape? Teaching and Learning at a Women's College* (Boulder 2005)
Kajanto, I. 'On Divorce among the Common People of Rome', *REL* 47 (1969), 97-113
Kampen, N. (ed.) *Sexuality in Ancient Art: Near East, Egypt, Greece, and Italy*, (Cambridge 1996)
Kampen, N. *Family Fictions in Roman Art* (Cambridge 2009)
Kapparis, K. A. *Abortion in Antiquity* (London 2002)
Karras, R. M. 'Active/Passive, Acts/Passions: Greek and Roman Sexualities', *American Historical Review* 105 (2000), 1250-1265
Katz, K. T. '*Testimonia Ritus Italici*: Male Genitalia, Solemn Declarations, and a New Latin Sound Law', *HSCP* 98 (1998), 210-213
Keith, A. '*Corpus Eroticum*: Elegiac Poets and Elegiac *Puellae* in Ovid's *Amores*', *CW* 88 (1994), 27-40
Keith, A. 'Tandem Venit Amor: *A Roman Woman Speaks of Love*' in Hallet, *Sexualities* (1997), 295-310
Keith, A. *Engendering Rome: Women in Latin Epic* (Cambridge 1999)
Keith, A. 'Critical Trends in Interpreting Sulpicia', *CW* 100 (2006), 3-10
Keith, A. *Women in Augustan Literature* in James, *Companion* (2012), 385-399
Kellum, K. 'The Phallus as Signifier: The Forum of Augustus and Rituals of Masculinity', in *Sexuality in Ancient Art* (Cambridge,1996), 170-173
Kellum, K. 'Concealing/Revealing: Gender and the Play of Meaning in the Monuments of Ancient Rome', in *The Roman Cultural Revolution* (Cambridge 2000)
Keuls, E.C. *The Reign of the Phallus: Sexual Politics in Ancient Athens* (Berkeley 1993)
Kiefer, O. *Sexual Life in Ancient Rome* (London 1934)
King, H. 'Sowing the Field: Greek and Roman Sexology', in *Sexual Knowledge, Sexual Science: The History of Attitudes to Sexuality* (Cambridge, 1994), 38ff
King, H. Producing Woman: Hippocratic Gynecology, in Archer, *Women in Ancient Societies* (1994), 102-114
King, H. 'Once upon a Text: Hysteria from Hippocrates' in Gilman, S. *Hysteri Beyond Freud* (California 1993), 3-90
King, H. 'Self-help, Self-knowledge: in Search of the Patient in Hippocratic Gynaecology' in Hawley, (1995), 135-148
King, H. *Women and Goddess Traditions*, (Minneapolis 1997)
King, H. *Hippocrates' Woman: Reading the Female Body in Ancient Greece* (London 1998)
King, H. *Greek and Roman Medicine* (London 2003)
King, H. *The Disease of Virgins: Green Sickness, Chlorosis and the Problems of Puberty* (New York 2004)
King, H. 'Healthy, Wealthy and – Dead?' *Ad Familiares* 33 (2007), 3-4
King, J. E. 'Sophistication versus Chastity in Propertius' Latin Love Elegy', *Helios* 4 (1976), 69-76
Kleiner, D. *I Claudia: Women in Ancient Rome* (New Haven, 1996)
Kleiner, D. *I Claudia II: Women in Roman Art and Society* (Austin, 2000)
Knapp, R. K. *Invisible Romans: Prostitutes, Outlaws, Slaves, Gladiators, Ordinary Men and Women... the Romans that History Forgot* (London 2013)
Knight, R. P. *A Discourse on the Worship of Priapus* (London 1786)
Kokkinos, N. *Antonia Augusta: Portrait of a Great Roman Lady* (London 1992)

Koortbojian, M. 'In Commemorationem Mortuorum: *Text and Image Along the Street of Tombs* in Elsner, 210–233

Kraemer, R. S. *Maenads, Martyrs, Matrons, Monastics* (Philadelphia 1988)

Kraemer, R. S. *Women's Religions in the Greco-Roman World: A Sourcebook* (New York, 2004)

Krenkel, W. A. '*Fellatio* and *Irrumatio*', *W.Z. Rostock* 29 (1980), 77–88

Krenkel, W. A. 'Tonguing', *W. Z. Rostock* 30 (1981), 37–54

Kudlien, F. 'Medical Education in Classical Antiquity' in O'Malley, *The History of Medical Education* (1970), 3–37

Kuttner, A. L. 'Culture and History at Pompey's Museum', *TAPA* 129 (1999), 343

Laes, C. *Children in the Roman Empire: Outsiders Within* (Cambridge 2009)

La Follette, L. *The Costume of the Roman Bride* in Sebesta, 54–64

Laidlaw, W. A. *Otium*, *G&R* 15 (1968), 42–52

Laiou, A. E. *Consent and Coercion to Sex and Marriage in Ancient and Medieval Societies* (Washington DC 1993)

Lambert, R. *Beloved and God: The Story of Hadrian and Antinous* (London 1984)

Langlands, R. 'A Woman's Influence on a Roman Text' in McHardy, *Women's Influence* (2004), 115–126

Langlands, R. *Sexual Morality in Ancient Rome* (Cambridge 2006)

Larson, J. *Greek and Roman Sexualities: A Sourcebook* (London 2012)

Larson, J. 'Sexuality in Greek and Roman Religion' in Hubbard (2014), 214–229

Larsson, L. L. (ed.) *Aspects of Women in Antiquity* (1997)

Larsson, L. L. (ed.)*Lanam fecit: Woolmaking and Female Virtue* in Larsson, *Aspects* (1997), 85–95

Laurence, R. (ed.) *Families in the Greco-Roman World* (London 2011)

Laurence, R. (ed.) *Roman Passions* (London 2009)

Lauriola, R. 'Teaching About the Rape of Lucretia', *CW* 106 (2013), 682–687

Lavery, H. *The Impotency Poem from Ancient Latin to Restoration English Literature* (London 2014)

Lear, A. 'Ancient Pederasty: An Introduction' in Hubbard (2014), 102–127

Leen, A. '*Clodia Oppugnatrix*: The *Domus* Motif in Cicero's *Pro Caelio*'. *CJ* 96 (2000), 142–160

Lefkowitz, M. R. *Heroines and Hysterics* (London 1981)

Lefkowitz, M. R. *Women's Life in Greece & Rome* third Ed. (London 2005)

Leigh, M. Funny Clones: 'Greek' Comedies on the Roman Stage, *Omnibus* 54 (2007), 26–28

Leisner-Jensen, M. '*Vis comic*. Consummated Rape in Greek and Roman New Comedy', *C&M* 53 (2002), 173–196

Leitao, D. D. Sexuality in Greek and Roman Military Contexts in Hubbard (2014), 230–243

Leunissen, M. Physiognomy in Ancient Science and Medicine, *https://mleunissen.files.wordpress.com/.../leunissen-physiognomy* (2012), accessed 11.05.2015

Levick, B. 'Corbulo's Daughter', *G&R* 49 (2002), 199–211

LiDonnici, L. 'Burning for It: Erotic Spells for Fever and Compulsion in the Ancient Mediterranean World', *GRBS* 39 (1998), 63–98

Lightman, M. *A to Z of Ancient Greek and Roman Women* (New York 2008)

Lilja, S. *Homosexuality in Republican and Augustan Rome* (Helsinki 1983)

Lilja, S. *The Roman Elegists' Attitude to Women* (Helsinki, 1965)

Lindsay, H. *Adoption in the Roman World* (Cambridge 2009)

Liveley, G. 'Who's that Girl? The Case of Ovid's Corinna', *Omnibus* 54 (2007), 1–3
Lloyd, G. E. R. (ed.) *Hippocratic Writings* (Harmondsworth 1978)
Lloyd, G. E. R. (ed.) *Magic, Reason and Experience* (Cambridge 1979)
Longrigg, J. *Greek Rational Medicine* (London 1993)
Longrigg, J. *Greek Medicine: From the Heroic to the Hellenistic Age A Source Book* (London 1998)
Loven, L. L. (ed.) *The Family in the Imperial and Late Antique Roman World* (New York 2011)
Lowe, J. E. *Magic in Greek and Latin Literature* (Oxford 1929)
Luck, G. Arcana Mundi: *Magic and the Occult in the Greek and Roman Worlds* (Baltimore 1985)
Luck, G. *Latin Love Elegy* 2/e (London 1969)
Luntz L. L. (1977) 'History of Forensic Dentistry', *Dent Clin. North Am.* 21: 7–17.
Lyne, R.O.A.M. *The Latin Love Poets from Catullus to Ovid* (Oxford 1980)
Macmullen, R. 'Women in Public in the Roman Empire', *Historia* 29 (1980), 208–218
Macmullen, R. 'Women's Power in the Principate', *Klio* 68 (1986), 434–443
Macurdy, G. H. 'Julia Berenice', *AJP* 56 (1935), 246–253
Maines, R. P. *The Technology of Orgasm: "Hysteria", the Vibrator, and Women's Sexual Satisfaction* (Baltimore 1998)
Maiuri, A. *Pompeii* (Rome 1934)
Manas, A. 'New Evidence of Female Gladiators: The Bronze Statuette at the Museum für Kunst und Gewerbe of Hamburg', *The International Journal of the History of Sport*, 28(18), (2011) 2726–2752
Mander, J. *Portraits of Children on Roman Funerary Monuments* (Cambridge 2012)
Manning, C. E. 'Canidia in the *Epodes* of Horace', *Mnemosyne* 23 (1970), 393–401
Mantle, I. *Violentissimae et Singulares Mortes*, *CA News* 39 (2008), 1–2
Mantle, I. Women of the Bardo, *Omnibus* 65, January 2013, 4–6
Mantos, K. 'Women and Athletics in the Roman East', *Nikephoros* 8 (1995), 125–144
Marshall, A. J. 'Roman Women and the Provinces', *Anc Soc* 6 (1975), 109–129
Marshall, A. J. 'Tacitus and the Governor's Lady, A Note on *Annals* 3, 33–34', *G&R* 22 (1975), 11–18
Marshall, A. J. 'Roman Ladies on Trial: The Case of Maesia of Sentinum', *Phoenix* 44(1990), 46–59
Marshall, C. W. *The Stagecraft and Performance of Roman Comedy* (Cambridge 2006)
Martin, M. *Magie et Magiciens dans le Monde Gréco-romain* (Paris 2005)
Martin, M. *Sois maudit!: Malédictions et Envoûtements dans l'Antiquité* (Paris 2010)
Martin, M. *La Magie dans l'Antiquité* (Paris 2012)
Martindale, C. (ed) *Cambridge Companion to Virgil* (Cambridge 2007)
Massey, M. *Women in Ancient Greece and Rome* (Cambridge 1988)
Masterson, M. *Sex in Antiquity Exploring Gender and Sexuality in the Ancient World* (London 2015)
Masterson, M. 'Studies in Ancient Masculinity in Hubbard' (2014), 17–30 *Exploring Gender and Sexuality in the Ancient World* (2014)

Matthews, V. J. 'Some Puns on Roman *Cognomina*', *G&R* 20 (1973), 20–23

Matz, D. *Voices of Ancient Greece and Rome: Contemporary Accounts of Daily Life* (New York 2012)

McAuslan, I.(ed.) *Women in Antiquity* (Oxford 1996)

McCarthy, K. 'Servitium Amoris: Amor Servitii' in Joshel, *Women* (1998), 174–192

McClure, L. K. *Sexuality and Gender in the Classical World* (Chichester 2002)

McCullough, A. 'Female Gladiators in Imperial Rome: Literary Context and Historical Fact' *CW*, 101(2), (2008) 197–209

McDermott, W. C. The Sisters of P. Clodius, *Phoenix* 24 (1970), 39–47

McDonald, G. *Mapping Madness: Two Medical Responses to Insanity in Later Antiquity* in Bosman (2009), 106–129

McDonnell, M. *Roman Manliness: "Virtus" and the Roman Republic* (Cambridge 2009)

McGinn, T. A. 'Concubinage and the *Lex Iulia* on Adultery', *TAPA* 121 (1991), 342

McGinn, T. A. The Legal Definition of Prostitute in Late Antiquity, *Memoirs of the American Academy in Rome 42* (1997), 73–116

McGinn, T. A. *Prostitution, Sexuality and the Law in Ancient Rome* (New York 1998)

McGinn, T. A. *The Economy of Prostitution in the Roman World* (Ann Arbor 2004)

McGinn, T. A. 'Prostitution: Controversies and New Approaches' in Hubbard (2014) 83–101

McHardy, F. (ed.) *Women's Influence on Classical Civilisation* (London 2004)

McManus, B. *Classics and Feminism: Gendering the* Classics (New York 1997)

Miles, G. B. 'The First Roman Marriage and the The Theft of the Sabine Women' in Hexter (1992), 161–196

Miller, P. A. *Latin Erotic Elegy: An Anthology and Reader* (London 2002)

Miller, S. *Rape and Metamorphosis: Reading Embodied Experience in Ovid's* Metamorphosis *and Richardson's* Clarissa. (MA Thesis, University of North Carolina, Chapel Hill, 2003).

Milnor, K. 'No Place for a Woman: Critical Narratives and Erotic Graffiti from Pompeii', *Institute for Research and Gender Working Paper 14* (Ann Arbor 1998) Sulpicia's (Corpo) Reality, *CA* 21 (2002), 259–82

Minaud, G., *Les Vies de 12 Femmes D'empereur Romain – Devoirs, Intrigues & Voluptés* (Paris, 2012) ch. 5, *La Vie de Domitia Longina, Femme de Domitien*, 121–146

Mohler, S. L. Feminism in the *CIL. CW* 25 (1932), 113–116

Montserrat, D. *Sex and Society in Graeco-Roman Egypt* (London 1996)

Montserrat, D. 'Reading Gender in the Roman World', in *Experiencing Rome: Culture, Identity, and Power in the Roman Empire* (London 2000), 168–170

Moog, F. P. 'Between Horror and Hope: Gladiator's Blood as a Cure for Epileptics in Ancient Medicine', *Journal of the History of the Neurosciences* 12, 2 (2003), 137–43

Moore, T. J. 'Morality, History and Livy's Wronged Women', *Eranos* 91 (1993), 38–46

Moore, T. J. *The Theater of Plautus: Playing to the Audience* (Austin 1998)

Moreau, P. Incestus et prohibitae nuptiae: *L'inceste à Rome* (Paris 2002)

Moses, D. 'Livy's Lucretia and the Validity of Coerced Consent in Roman Law', in *Consent and Coercion to Sex and Marriage in Ancient and Medieval Societies* (Dunbarton Oaks, 1993)

Motto, A. L. 'Seneca on Women's Liberation', *CW* 65 (1972), 155–157

Murgatroyd, P. 'Plotting in Ovidian Rape Narratives', *Eranos* 98 (2000), 75–92

Murgatroyd, P. 'The Rape Attempts on Lotis and Vesta', *CQ* 52 (2002), 622–624

Murison, C. L. 'Tiberius, Vitellius and the *spintriae*', *AHB* 1 (1987), 97–99

Murray, S. 'Female Gladiators of the Ancient Roman World', *Journal of Combative Sport* (July 2003)

Mustakallio, K. *Hoping for Continuity: Childhood Education and Death in Antiquity* (Helsinki 2005)

Myers, S. 'The Poet and the Procuress: the *lena* in Latin Love Elegy', *JRS* 86 (1996), 1–21

Nagel, B. N. The Tyrant as Artist: Legal Fiction and Sexual Violence under Tiberius, *Law & Literature* 25 (2013), 286–310

Neils, J. *Women in the Ancient World* (London 2011)

Nikolaidis, A. G. 'Plutarch on Women and Marriage', *WS* 110 (1997), 27–88

Nikoloutsos, K.P. *Beyond Sex: The Poetics and Politics of Pederasty in Tibullus 1.4*, Phoenix 61 (2007), 55–82

Noonan, J. D. 'Livy 1.9.6. The Rape at the Consualia', *CW* 83 (1990), 493–501

North, J. A. 'Caesar at the Lupercalia', *JRS*, 98 (2008), 144–160

Noy, D. 'Wicked Stepmothers in Roman Society and Imagination', *Jnl of Family History* 16 (1991), 345–361

Nussbaum, M. C. 'The Incomplete Feminism of Musonius Rufus, Platonist, Stoic,and Roman' in Nussbaum *The Sleep of Reason: Erotic Experience and Sexual Ethics in Ancient Greece and Rome* (2002), 305

Nussbaum, M. C. *Same-Sex Desire and Love in Greco-Roman Antiquity and in the Classical Tradition of the West* (Binghamton 2005)

Nutton, V. 'Galen and Medical Autobiograph'y, *PCPS* 18 (1972), 50f.

Nussbaum, M. C. 'The Drug Trade in Antiquity', *Jnl of the Royal Society of Medicine* 78 (1985), 138–145

Nussbaum, M. C. *Murders and Miracles: Lay Attitudes to Medicine in Antiquity* (1985) in Porter: *Patients and Practitioners*, 25–53

Nussbaum, M. C. *Ancient Medicine 2/e* (London 2013)

Ogden, D. *Magic, Witchcraft and Ghosts in the Greek and Roman Worlds* (Oxford 2002)

Ogden, D. *Greek and Roman Necromancy* (Princeton 2004)

Ogden, D. *Night's Black Agents: Witches Wizards and the Dead in the Ancient World* (London 2008)

Ogden, D. *Polygamy, Prostitutes and Death: The Hellenistic Dynasties* (Swansea 2010)

Ogilvie, R. M. *The Romans and their Gods in the Age of Augustus* (London 1974)

Ogilvie, R. M. *Early Rome and the Etruscans* (Glasgow 1976)

Ogilvie, R. M. *Roman Literature and Society* (Harmondsworth 1980)

Oliensis, E. Canidia, Canicula and the Decorum of Horace's *Epodes*, *Arethusa* 24 (1991), 107–138

Ogilvie, R. M. 'The Erotics of *Amicitia*: Readings in Propertius, Tibullus and Horace', in Hallett (1997), 151–171

Ogilvie, R. M. *Sons and Lovers: Sexuality and Gender in Virgil's Poetry,* in Martindale (2007)

Olson, K. '*Matrona* and Whore: The Clothing of Women in Roman Antiquity', *Fashion Theory* 6 (2002), 387–420

Olson, K. *Dress and the Roman Woman: Self-Presentation and Society* (London 2008)

Olson, K. 'The Appearance of the Young Roman Girl', in *Roman Dress and the Fabrics of Roman Culture* (Toronto 2008)

O'Malley, C.D. (ed.) *The History of Medical Education* (Berkeley 1970)

Ormand, K. 'Impossible Lesbians in Ovid's *Metamorphoses*' in Ancona, R. *Gendered Dynamics in Latin Love Poetry* (Baltimore MD 2005), 79–110

Ormand, K. *Controlling Desires: Sexuality in Ancient Greece and Rome* (New York 2008)

Packman, Z. M. 'Call it Rape. A Motif in Roman Comedy and its Suppression in English-Speaking Publications', *Helios* 20 (1993), 42–55

Packman, Z. M. 'Rape and Consequences in the Latin Declamations', *Scholia* 8 (1999), 17–36

Pantel, P. S. *A History of Women from Ancient Goddesses to Christian Saints* (Cambridge MA 1992)

Paoli, U. E. *Rome: Its People, Life and Customs* (Bristol 1990)

Papadopoulos I. 'Priapus and Priapism: From Mythology to Medicine'. *Urology* (1988); 32(4), 385–386

Parca, M. Finding Persephone: Women's Rituals in the Ancient Mediterranean (Urbana-Champaign 2007)

Parke, H. W. *Sibylls and Sibylline Prophecy in Classical Antiquity* (London 1998)

Parker, H. N. 'Love's Body Anatomized: The Ancient Erotic Handbooks and the Rhetoric of Sexuality', in Richlin, *Pornography* (1992)

Parker, H. N. 'The Myth of the Heterosexual: Anthropology and Sexuality for Classicists', *Arethusa* 34 (2001), 313–362

Parker, H. N. 'Women Physicians in Greece, Rome and the Byzantine Empire', in Furst (2004), 134–150

Parker, H. N. 'Why Were the Vestal Virgins?' *AJP* 125 (2004), 563–601

Parker, H. N. 'Women and Medicine in James', *Companion* (2012), 107–124

Parkin, T. G. *Old Age in the Roman World* (Baltimore 2003)

Parry, H. 'Ovid's *Metamorphoses*: Violence in a Pastoral Landscape', *TAPA* 95(1964), 268–282

Paul, G. M. *Sallust's Sempronia: the Portrait of a Lady* in Cairns, *Papers* (1986), 9–22

Pearcy, L. T. 'Erasing Cerinthus; Sulpicia and Her Audience', *CW* 100 (2006), 31–36

Pellauer, M., 'Augustine on Rape' in Adams, C.J. *Violence Against Women and Children: A Christian Theological Sourcebook* (New York 1998), 207–241

Pellison, N. *Women and Marriage During Roman Times* (New York 2008)

Peradotto, J. (ed.) *Women in the Ancient World: The Arethusa Papers* (Albany 1984)

Petersen, L. H. *Mothering and Motherhood in Ancient Greece and Rome* (Austin 2013)

Petrocelli, C. *Cornelia the Matron* in Fraschetti, *Roman Women* (1993), 34–65

Phang, S. E. *Soldiers, Cities and Civilians in Roman Syria* (Ann Arbor 2000)

Phang, S. E. *The Marriage of Roman Soldiers (13 B.C.-A.D. 235): Law and Family in the Imperial Army* (Leiden 2001)

Phillipides, S. N. 'Narrative Strategies and Ideology in Livy's "Rape of Lucretia"', *Helios* 10 (1983),113–119

Phillipides, S. N. 'Terence's *Euchunus*. Elements of the Marriage Ritual in the Rape Scene', *Mnemosyne* 48 (1995), 272–284

Phillips, E. 'D. Doctor and Patient in Classical Greece', *G&R* (1953), 70–81

Phillips, J. E. 'Roman Mothers and the Lives of their Adult Daughters', *Helios* 6 (1978), 69–80

Pierce, K. F. 'The Portrayal of Rape in New Comedy' in Deacy, S. *Rape in Antiquity*. (London 1997), 163–184

Pinault, J. R. 'The Medical Case for Virginity in the Early Second Century CE: Soranus', *Helios* 19, 123–39

Pintabone, D. T. 'Ovid's Iphis and Ianthe: When Girls Won't Be Girls', in Rabinowitz (2002), 256–287

Pintabone, D. T. *Women and the Unspeakable: Rape in Ovid's Metamorphoses* (Ann Arbor 1998)

Pitcher, R. A. *Martial and Roman Sexuality* in Hillard, *Ancient History* (1998), 309–315

Pollard, E. A. 'Witch-Crafting in Roman Literature and Art: New Thoughts on an Old Image', *Magic, Ritual, and Witchcraft* 3 (2008)

Pollini, J. 'Slave-Boys for Sexual and Religious Service: Images of Pleasure and Devotion' in Boyle, A. J. *Flavian Rome: Culture, Image, Text* (Leiden 2003), 149–166

Pomeroy, S. B. 'Selected Bibliography on Women in Antiquity', *Arethusa* 6 (1973) 125–157

Pomeroy, S. B. 'The Relationship of the Married Woman to Her Blood Relatives in Rome', *Ant. Soc.* 7 (1976), 215–227

Pomeroy, S. B. *Women in Roman Egypt: A Preliminary Study Based on Papyri* in Foley pp. 301–322

Pomeroy, S. B. (ed.) *Women's History and Ancient History* (Chapel Hill, 1991),

Pomeroy, S. B. *Goddesses, Whores, Wives and Slaves* (New York 1995)

Pomeroy, S. B. *Spartan Women* (Oxford 2002)

Pomeroy, S. B. *The Murder of Regilla: A Case of Domestic Violence in Antiquity* (Cambridge 2007)

Porter, R. (ed.) *Patients and Practitioners* (Cambridge 1985)

Potter, D. S. *Prophecy and History in the Crisis of the Roman Empire: A Historical Commentary on the Thirteenth Sibylline Oracle* (Oxford 1990)

Powell, A. (ed.) *Roman Poetry and Propaganda in the Age of Augustus* (Bristol 1992)

Prince, M. 'Medea and the Inefficacy of Love Magic', *CB* 79 (20030, 205–218

Pringle, H. 'Gladiatrix'. *Discover*, 22 (12) (2001), 48–55

Purcell, N. 'Livia and the Motherhood at Rome', *PCPS* 212 (1986), 78–105

Puschmann, T. (ed.) *Alexander of Tralles, Twelve Books on Medicine* (1878)

Putnam, E. J. 'The Roman Lady', *Atlantic Monthly* 105 (1910)

Rabinowitz, N. S. *Among Women: From the Homosocial to the Homoerotic in the Ancient World* (Austin TX 2002)

Raia, A. *Women's Roles in Plautine Comedy* (paper delivered October 1983) www.vroma.org/~araia/plautinewomen

Raia, A. (ed.) *Marriage, Divorce and Children in Ancient Rome* (Oxford 1986)

Raia, A. *Villains, Wives and Slaves in the Comedies of Plautus* in Joshel, *Women* (1998), 92–108

Raia, A. *The Worlds of Roman Women: A Latin Reader* (Newburyport, MA 2001)
Randall, J. G. 'Mistress' Pseudonyms in Latin Elegy, *LCM* 4 (1979), 27–35.
Rankin, H. D. 'Catullus and the Beauty of Lesbia', *Latomus* 35, 1 (1976)
Rankin, H. D. 'Catullus and Incest', *Eranos* 74, (1976), 113–121
Rankin, H. D. 'Catullus and the Privacy of Love', *WS* 9, 1975
Rankin, H. D. 'Clodia II', *AC* 38 (1969), 501–506
Rapsaet-Charlier, M. –Th. 'Ordre Senatorial et Divorce sous le Haut Empire', *ACD* (1981) 17–18, 161–173
Rawson, B. 'Family Life Among the Lower Classes at Rome in the First Two Centuries of the Empire', *CP* 61 (1966), 71–83
Rawson, B. 'Roman Concubinage and Other de facto Marriages', *TAPA* 104 (1974), 279–305
Rawson, B. *Marriage, Divorce and Children in Ancient Rome* (Oxford 1991)
Rawson, B. *Children and Childhood in Roman Italy* (Oxford 2005)
Rawson, B. *A Companion to Families in the Greek and Roman Worlds* (Chichester 2011)
Rawles, R. 'Erotic Lyric', in Hubbard, (2014), 335–351
Reckford, K. 'Only a Wet Dream? Hope and Scepticism in Horace, Satire 1,5', *AJP* 120 (1999), 525–524
Reinhold, M. 'The Generation Gap in Antiquity', in Bertman, 15–54
Reiss, W. Rari Exempla Femina: *Female Virtues on Roman Funerary Inscriptions* in James, *Companion* (2012), 491–501
Ricci, J. V, *The Development of Gynaecological Surgery and Instruments* (Philadelphia 1949)
Richlin, A. *Sexuality in the Roman Empire* in Potter (2006)
Richlin, A. Not before Homosexuality: The Materiality of the *Cinaedus* and the Roman Law against Love between Men, *Journal of the History of Sexuality* 3 (1993), 523–73
Richlin, A. *Approaches to the Sources on Adultery at Rome* in Foley, *Reflections* (1981), 379–404
Richlin, A. 'Invective Against Women in Roman Satire', *Arethusa* 17 (1984), 67–80
Richlin, A. *Carrying Water in a Sieve: Class and the Body in Roman Women's Religion* in King, *Women and Goddess Traditions* (1997), 330–374
Richlin, A. 'Sulpicia the Satirist', *CW* 86 (1992), 125–140
Richlin, A. *Julia's Jokes, Galla Placidia and the Romans Use of Women as Political Icons* in Garlick, *Stereotypes* (1992), 65–91
Richlin, A. (ed.) *Pornography and Representation in Greece and Rome* (Oxford 1992)
Richlin, A. *The Garden of Priapus: Sexuality and Aggression in Roman Humour* second Ed (Oxford 1992)
Richlin, A. 'Reading Ovid's Rapes', in Richlin, *Pornography*, 158–179
Richlin, A. 'The Meaning of *irrumare* in Catullus and Martial', *CP* 76 (1981), 40–46
Richlin, A. 'Sexuality in the Roman Empire', in Potter, (2011), 327– 353
Richlin, A. 'Reading Boy-love and Child-love in the Greco-Roman World' in Masterson, M. *Sex in Antiquity* (New York 2015)
Riddle, J. M. *Contraception and Abortion from the Ancient World to the Renaissance* (Cambridge MA, 1992)

Rinaldo, M. 'Women, Culture and Society', in Blok, J. *Sexual Assymetry* (Amsterdam 1987), 17–42
Rist, J. M. 'Hypatia', *Phoenix* 19 (1965), 214–225
Roisman, H .M. 'Women in Seneca: Phadra and Medea', *Scholia* 14 (2005), 72–88
Roisman, H. M. 'Sexuality in the Extant Greek and Roman Tragedies', in Hubbard, (2014), 352–365
Roisman, H. M. 'Greek and Roman Ethnosexuality', in Hubbard (2014), 398–416
Rose, M. 'Ashkelon's Dead Babies', *Archaeology* 50 (1997) www.archaeology.org/9703/newsbriefs/ashkelon
Rosen, R. M. 'Greco-roman Satirical Poetry', in Hubbard (2014), 381–397
Rosivach, V. J. *When a Young Man Falls in Love: The Sexual Exploitation of Women in New Comedy* (London 1998)
Ross, D. O. *Style and Tradition in Catullus* (Cambridge, MA, 1969)
Ross, D. O. *Backgrounds to Augustan Poetry: Gallus, Elegy and Rome* (Cambridge 1975)
Rouselle, A. *Body Politics in Ancient Rome* in Pantel (1992), 296–336
Rouselle, A. Porneia: *On Desire and the Body In Antiquity* (Oxford 1993)
Rowlandson, J. *Women and Society in Greek and Roman Egypt: A Sourcebook* (Cambridge 1998)
Rudd, N. 'Romantic Love in Classical Times?' *Ramus* 10 (1981), 140–158
Salisbury, J. *Perpetua's Passion: The Death and Passion of a Young Roman Woman* (London 1997)
Saller, R. P. '*Familia, Domus* and the Roman Conception of the Family', *Phoenix* 38 (1984), 336–355
Saller, R. P. 'Roman Dowry and the Devolution of Property in the Principate', *CQ* 34 (1984), 195–205
Saller, R. P. '*Patria Potestas* and the Stereotype of the Roman Family', *Continuity & Change* 1 (1986), 7–22
Saller, R. P. 'Men's Age at Marriage and Its Consequences in the Roman Family', *CP* 82 (1987), 21–34
Saller, R. P. *Patriarchy, Property and Death in the Roman Family* (Cambridge 1994)
Saller, R. P. *Symbols of Gender and Status Hierarchies in the Roman Household* in Joshel, *Women* (1998), 85–91
Salway, B.' What's in A Name?' *JRS* 84 (1994), 124–145
Santirocco, M.S. 'Sulpicia Reconsidered', *CJ* 74 (1979), 229–239
Santoro L'Hoir, F.S. 'Tacitus and Women's Usurpation of Power', *CW* 88 (1994), 5–25
Savunem, *Women and Elections in Pompeii* in Hawley, *Women* (1995), 194–206
Scafuro, A. (ed.) *Studies on Roman Women Part 2, Helios* 16 (1989)
Scafuro, A.*Livy's Comic Narrative of the Bacchanalia* in Scafuro (1989), 119–142
Scarborough, J. *Roman Medicine* (London 1969)
Scarborough, J. *Pharmacy in Pliny's Natural History: Some Observations on Substances and Sources* in French, *Science in the Early Roman Empire* (1986), 59–85
Scheid, J. *The Religious Roles of Roman Women* in Pantel (1992), 377–408
Scheid, J. *Claudia the Vestal Virgin* in Fraschetti, (1993), 23–33
Scheidel, W. 'The Most Silent Women of Greece and Rome: Rural Labour and Women's Life', *G&R* 42 and 43 (1995–1996), 202–17, 1–10

Scheidel, W. 'Libitina's Bitter Gains: Seasonal Mortality and Endemic Disease', *Ancient Society* 25 (1994), 151–175

Scheidel, W. *The Cambridge Economic History of the Greco-Roman World* (Cambridge 2007)

Schmitt, J-Cl. 'Prostituées, Lépreux, Hérétiques: les Rayures de l'infamie', *L'Histoire* 148 (1991), 89

Schulz, C. E. *Women's Religious Activity in the Roman Republic* (Chapel Hill NC 2006)

Scobie, A. 'Slums, Sanitation and Mortality in the Roman World', *Klio* 68 (1986), 399–343

Scurlock, J. A. 'Baby-snatching Demons, Restless Souls and the Dangers of Childbirth', *Incognita* 2 (1991), 135–183

Sebesta, J. L. 'Women's Costume and Feminine Civic Morality in Augustan Rome', *Gender & History* 9, 3 (1997), 532

Seller, R. *The Family and Society* in Bodel (2001), 95–117

Sharrock, A.R. 'Womanufacture', *JRS* 81 (1991), 36–49

Shaw, B.D. 'Age of Roman Girls at Marriage: Some Reconsiderations', *JRS* 77 (1987), 30–46

Shelton, J-A. 'Pliny the Younger and the Ideal Wife', *C&M* 61 (1990), 163–186

Shepherd, G. *Women in Magna Graecia* in James, *Companion* (2012), 215–228

Sissa, J. *Sex and Sensuality in the Ancient World* (London 2008)

Skinner, M. B. (ed.) 'Rescuing Creusa', *Helios* 13 (1987)

Skinner, M. B. '*Ego Mulier*: The Construction of Male Sexuality in Catullus', *Helios* 20 (1993), 107–130

Skinner, M. B. (ed.) *Sexuality in Graeco-Roman Culture* second ed (Oxford 2005)

Skinner, M. B. *Clodia Metelli: The Tribune's Sister* (New York 2011)

Smith, L. P. 'Audience Response to Rape: Chaerea in Terence *Eunuchus*', *Helios* 21 (1994), 21–38

Smith, P. 'Identification of Infanticide in Archaeological Sites', *Jnl of Archaeological Science* 19 (1992), 667–675

Smith, P. 'Bones of a Hundred Infants Found in Ashkelon Sewer', *Biblical Archaeology Review* 17, 4 (1991), 51

Smith, W. S. (ed.) *Satiric Advice on Women and Marriage: From Plautus to Chaucer* (Ann Arbor 2005)

Snyder, J. M. 'Lucretius and the Status of Women' *CB* 53, (1976), 17–20

Soren, D. 'What Killed the Babies of Lugnano?' *Archaeology* 48/5 (1995), 43–48

Soren, D. *Excavations of a Roman Villa and a Late Roman Infant Cemetery Near Lugnano* (Rome 1999)

Staden, H. von 'Women, Dirt and Exotica in the *Hippocratic Corpus*', *Helios* 19 (1992), 7–30

Stannard, J. 'Marcellus of Bordeaux and the Beginnings of the Medieval Materia Medica', *Pharmacy in History* 15 (1973), 48

Stanton, D.C. (ed.) *Discourses of Sexuality: From Aristotle to Aids* (Ann Arbor 1992)

Staples, A. *From Good Goddess to Vestal Virgins: Sex and Category in Roman Religion* (London 1998)

Stavrakakis, Y. 'Thessaloniki Brothel', *Archaeology Archive* (51, 3, 1998) archive. archaeology.org/9805/newsbriefs/brothel.html

Stehle, E. 'Venus, Cybele and the Sabine Women: The Roman Construction of Female Sexuality', *Helios* 16 (1989), 143–164

Stirrup, B. E. 'Techniques of Rape: Variety and Art in Ovid's *Metamorphoses*', *G&R* 24 (1977), 170–184

Stratton, K. B. *Naming the Witch: Magic, Ideology and Stereotype in the Ancient World* (Columbus OH 2007)

Stromberg, A. *The Family in the Graeco-Roman World* (New York 2011)

Strunk, T. E. 'Rape and Revolution: Livia and Augustus in Tacitus' *Annales*', *Latomus* 73 (2014), 26–148

Sullivan, J. P. 'Martial's Sexual Attitudes', *Philologus* 123 (1979), 288–302

Summerton, N. *Medicine and Healthcare in Roman Britain* (Princes Risborough 2007)

Swain, S. (ed.) *Seeing the Face, Seeing the Soul: Polemon's Physiognomy from Classical Antiquity to Medieval Islam* (Oxford 2007)

Swancutt, D. M. '*Still* before Sexuality: 'Greek' Androgyny, the Roman Imperial Politics of Masculinity and the Roman Invention of the *tribas*', in *Mapping Gender in Ancient Religious Discourses*, 22ff

Syme, R. 'Princesses and Others in Tacitus', *G&R* 28 (1981), 40–52

Tacaks, S. *Vestal Virgins, Sibyls, and Matrons* (Austin 2008)

Taylor, R. 'Two Pathic Subcultures in Ancient Rome', *Jnl of the History of Sexuality* 7 (1997), 319–371

Temkin, O. *Soranus'* Gynecology (Baltimore 1956)

Theodorakopoulos, T. 'Catullus 63, A Song of Attis for the Megalesia', *Omnibus* 61 (2011), 21–23

Thomas, Y. *The Division of the Sexes in Roman Law* in Pantel (1992), 83–138

Thomsen, O. 'An Introduction to the Study of Catullus' Wedding Poems', *C&M* 53 (2002), 255–288

Thonemann, P. 'The Women of Akmoneia', *JRS* 100 (2010) 163–178

Thorndike, L. *The Place of Magic in the Intellectual History of Europe* (New York 1905)

Thorndike, L. *History of Magic and Experimental Science* (Columbia OH 1923)

Toner, J. *Popular Culture in Ancient Rome* (Cambridge 2009

Toner, J. *The Day Commodus Killed a Rhino: Understanding the Roman Games* (Baltimore 2015)

Totelin, L. 'Sex and Vegetables in the Hippocratic Gynecological Treatises', *SHPBBS* 38 (2007), 531–540

Townend, G. *The Augustan Poets and the Permissive Society* (Abingdon 1972)

Tracy, V. A. 'The Poet-Lover in Augustan Elegy', *Latomus* 35 (1976), 571–581

Treggiari, S. 'Libertine Ladies', *CW* 64 (1971), 196–198

Treggiari, S. 'Domestic Staff at Rome During the Julio-Claudian Period', *Histoire Sociale* 6 (1973), 241–255

Treggiari, S. *Concubinae*, Papers of the British School at Rome 49 (1981), 59–81

Treggiari, S. *Roman Marriage* (Oxford 1991)

Treggiari, S. *Putting the Family Across: Cicero on Natural Affection* in George, *The Roman Family* (2005) 9–36

Treggiari, S. *Roman Social History* (London 2002)

Treggiari, S. *Terentia, Tullia and Publilia: The Women of Cicero's Family* (New York 2007)

Trimble, J. *Women and Visual Replication in Roman Imperial Art and Culture* (Cambridge 2011)

Tuplin, C. 'Cantores Euphorionis' in Cairns, *Papers*, 1–23.

Tuplin, C. 'Cantores Euphorionis Again'. *CQ* 72 (1979), 358–360

Varone, A. Erotica Pompeiana: *Love Inscriptions on the Walls of Pompeii* (Rome, 2002)

Vendries, C. 'Abstinence Sexuelle et Infibulations des Chanteurs dans la Rome Imperiale', in Prost, F. *Penser et Representer le Corps* (Rennes, 2006), 247–261

Vermaseren, M. J. *Cybele and Attis* (London, 1977)

Versnal, H. S. *The Festival for* Bona Dea *and the* Thesmophoria in McAuslan, *Women in Antiquity* (1996), 182–204

Verstraete, B. C. 'Roman Pederasty in Relation to Roman Slavery: The Portrayal of *Pueri Delicati* in the Love-Poetry of Catullus, Tibullus, and Horace', *Uluslarara Sosyal Araştırmala Dergisi* 5 (2012), 157–167

Verstraete, B. C. *Same-Sex Desire and Love in Greco-Roman Antiquity and in the Classical Tradition* (2005 London)

Verstraete, B. C. 'Slavery and Social Dynamics of Male Homosexual Relations in Ancient Rome', *Jnl of Homosexuality* 499, (1980). 299–313

Vesley, M. 'Gladiatorial Training for Girls in the Collegia Iuvenum of the Roman Empire'. *ECM* 62, 17 (1998), 88–90.

Veyne, P. 'Homosexuality in Ancient Rome', in Aries, P. (ed.) *Western Sexuality* (Oxford 1985), 26–35

Veyne, P. (ed.) *A History of Private Life Vol I* (Cambridge, Mass 1987)

Villers, R. 'Le Statut de la Femme a Rome jusqu'a la Fin de la Republique. *Recueils de la Societe Jean Bodin II* (1958), 177–189

Virlouvet, C. *Fulvia the Woman of Passion* in Fraschetti, (1993), 66–81

Vout, C. *Sex on Show: Seeing the Erotic in Greece and Rome.* (London 2013)

Vout, C. *Power and Eroticism in Imperial Rome* (Cambridge 2007)

Vout, C. *Antinous: the Face of the Antique* (Leeds, 2006)

Vout, C. 'Antinous, Archaeology and History', *JRS* 95 (2005), 80–96

Vout, C. Biography, in Hubbard (Chichester 2014), 446–462

Walcot, P. 'Plutarch on Sex', *G&R* 45 (1998), 166–187

Walker, J. Before the Name: Ovid's Deformulated Lesbianism, *Comparative Literature* 58 (2006), 205–222

Walker, L.C. *The Women Who Influenced The Lives of Cicero, Caesar, and Vergil* (MA diss. University of South Carolina, 1935)

Walter, K. *The Secret Museum: Pornography in Modern Culture* (Berkeley, 1996)

Walters, J. 'Invading the Roman Body: Manliness and Impenetrability in Roman Thought', in Hallet, *Roman Sexualities* (1997), 30–31

Walters, J. 'Soldiers and Whores in a Pseudo-Quintilian Declamation' in T.J. Cornell, *Gender and Ethnicity in Ancient italy*, (London), 109–14

Waters, S. 'The Most Famous Fairy in History: Antinous and Homosexual Fantasy' *Journal of the History of Sexuality* 6 (2), 194–230.

Watson, L.C. Catullus and the Poetics of Incest, *Antichthon* 40 (2006), 35–48

Watson, P.A. Ancient Stepmothers, *Mnemosyne* (1995), 143

Watts, W.J. Ovid, the Law and Roman Society on Abortion, *AC* 16 (1973), 89–101

Wells, C. 'Daughters of the Regiment: Sisters and Wives in the Roman Army' in Groen, W. *Roman Frontier Studies* 1995, (1997), 571–574

Westerhold, J. *Silence and Power: The Metamorphosis of Rape Myths in Ovid.* (Ann Arbor MI 2006)

Wheeler, A. L. 'Erotic Teaching in Roman Elegy and the Greek Sources Part II', *CP* 6 (1911), 56–77

Wheeler, A. L. 'Erotic Teaching Part I', *CP* 5 (1910), 440–450

Wheeler, A. L. 'Propertius as *Praeceptor Amoris*', *CP* 5 (1910), 28–40
Whittaker, T. 'Sex and the Sack of the City', *G&R* 56 (2009), 234–242
WHO *ICD: International Classification of Diseases (10 version*, Geneva 2010)
Wildfang, R. I. *Divination and Portents in the Roman World* (Odense 2000)
Wildfang, R. I. *Rome's Vestal Virgins* (London 2006)
Wilkinson, B. M. 'Family Life among the Lower Classes in Rome in the First Two Centuries of the Empire', *CP* 61 (1966), 71–83
Wilkinson L. P. 'Classical Approaches: I. Population and Family Planning', *Encounter* (1978) 50 (4), 22–32
Will, E. L. 'Women in Pompeii', *Archaeology* 32 (1979), 34–43
Williams, C. 'Greek Love at Rome', *CQ* 45 (1995), 517–38
Williams, C. Sexual Themes in Greek and Latin Graffiti, in Hubbard (2014), 493–508
Williams, C. A. *Roman Homosexuality: Ideologies of Masculinity in Classical Antiquity*, (Oxford 1999)
Williams, G. 'Some Aspects of Roman Marriage Ceremonies and Ideals', *JRS* 48 (1958), 16–29
Winter, T. N. 'Catullus Purified: A Brief History of *Carmen* 16'. *Arethusa* 6 (1973), 257–265.
Wiseman, T. P. *Cinna the Poet* (Leicester 1974)
Wiseman, T. P. *Catullus and His World* (Cambridge 1985)
Wiseman, T. P. 'The God of the Lupercal', *JRS*, 85, (1995)
Wiseman, T. P. *Summoning Jupiter: Magic in the Roman Republic* in Wiseman, *Unwritten Rome*
Wiseman, T. P. *Unwritten Rome* (Exeter 2008)
Woman, N. *Abusive Mouths in Classical Athens* (Cambridge, 2008)
Woodhull, M. L. *Matronly Patrons in the Early Roman Empire: the Case of Salvia Postuma* in McHardy, *Women's Influence* (2004), 75–91
Woods, D. 'Nero and Sporus', *Latomus* 68 (2009), 73–82
Worsfold, T. C. *The History of the Vestal Virgins of Rome* (London 1934)
Wray, D. *Catullus and the Poetics of Roman Manhood* (Cambridge 2001)
Wyke, M. 'Written Women: Propertius' *scripta puella*', *JRS* 77, (1987), 47–61
Wyke, M. 'The Elegiac Woman at Rome', *PCPS* 213 (ns 330) (1987), 153–178
Wyke, M. 'Mistress and Metaphor in Augustan Elegy', *Helios* 16 (1989), 25–47
Wyke, M. 'Augustan Cleopatras: Female Power and Poetic Authority' in Powell, *Roman Poetry* (1992), 98–140
Wyke, M. *Women in the Mirror: The Rhetoric of Adornment in the Roman World* in Archer, *Women in Ancient Societies* (1994), 134–151
Wyke, M. 'Taking the Woman's Part: Engendering Roman Love Elegy', *Ramus* 23 (1994), 110–128
Wyke, M. *Projecting the Past: Ancient Rome, Cinema and History* (London 1997)
Wyke, M. *The Roman Mistress* (Oxford 2002)
Yardley, J. H. *The Symposium in Roman Elegy* in Slater, *Dining in a Classical Context*, 149–155
Younger, J. G. *Sex in the Ancient World from A-Z* (London 2005)
Zajko, V. '"Listening with" Ovid: Intersexuality, Queer Theory, and the Myth of Hermaphrodites and Salmacis', *Helios* 36 (2009), 175–202
Zissos, A. 'The Rape of Proserpina in Ovid *Met.* 5.341–661: Internal Audience and Narrative Distortion', *Phoenix* 53 (1999), 97–113.